Fodor's 96

San Francisco

"When it comes to information on regional history, what to see and do, and shopping, these guides are exhaustive."

—*USAir Magazine*

"Usable, sophisticated restaurant coverage, with an emphasis on good value."

—Andy Birsh, *Gourmet Magazine* columnist

"Valuable because of their comprehensiveness."

—*Minneapolis Star-Tribune*

"Fodor's always delivers high quality...thoughtfully presented...thorough."

—*Houston Post*

"An excellent choice for those who want everything under one cover."

—*Washington Post*

Fodor's Travel Publications, Inc.
New York • Toronto • London • Sydney • Auckland

Fodor's San Francisco

Editor: Amy McConnell

Contributors: Dianne Aaronson, Steven K. Amsterdam, Robert Andrews, John Burks, Toni Chapman, Karen Croft, Janet Foley, Sheila Gadsden, Claudia Gioseffi, Dennis Harvey, Patrick Hoctel, Jacqueline Killeen, Daniel Mangin, Catherine McEver, Mary Ellen Schultz, M. T. Schwartzman, Sharon Silva, Dinah Spritzer, Craig Sullivan, Robert Taylor, Casey Tefertiller

Creative Director: Fabrizio La Rocca

Cartographer: David Lindroth

Cover Photograph: Catherine Karnow/Woodfin Camp

Text Design: Between the Covers

Copyright

ISBN 0-679-03066-2

Special Sales

Fodor's Travel Publications are available at special discounts for bulk purchases for sales promotions or premiums. Special editions, including personalized covers, excerpts of existing guides, and corporate imprints, can be created in large quantities for special needs. For more information, contact your local bookseller or write to Special Markets, Fodor's Travel Publications, 201 East 50th Street, New York, NY 10022. Inquiries from Canada should be directed to your local Canadian bookseller or sent to Random House of Canada, Ltd., Marketing Department, 1265 Aerowood Drive, Mississauga, Ontario L4W 1B9. Inquiries from the United Kingdom should be sent to Fodor's Travel Publications, 20 Vauxhall Bridge Road, London SW1V 2SA, England.

MANUFACTURED IN THE UNITED STATES OF AMERICA

10 9 8 7 6 5 4 3 2 1

CONTENTS

ON THE ROAD WITH FODOR'S

A GOOD TRAVEL GUIDE IS LIKE A wonderful traveling companion. It's charming, it's brimming with sound recommendations and solid ideas, it pulls no punches in describing lodging and dining establishments, and it's consistently full of fascinating facts that make you view what you've traveled to see in a rich new light. In the creation of *San Francisco '96,* we at Fodor's have gone to great lengths to provide you with the very best of all possible traveling companions—and to make your trip the best of all possible vacations.

About Our Writers

The information in these pages is a collaboration of a number of extraordinary writers.

Sports, fitness, and beaches updater **Dianne Aaronson** has been writing a health and fitness column for the *Bay Area Reporter* for five years and is currently writing a book about weight training for women.

Shopping updater **Alan Frutkin,** a San Francisco–based writer who was born in New York, discovered the pleasures of shopping at a tender age. He misses Bloomingdale's but has found plenty of alternatives in the City by the Bay.

Claudia Gioseffi, who updated the Wine Country chapter, is an editor of *Epicurean Rendez-Vous,* which covers all the restaurants and wineries in the Napa Valley. A San Francisco writer and artist of Italian descent, she loves the Napa Valley because it's so much like Tuscany.

Even in the midst of March floods, **Dennis Harvey** could be spotted updating exploring sights by day and nightlife spots by night. A longtime San Francisco resident, Harvey writes about music, theater, culture, and history for *Variety,* the *Bay Guardian,* and the *San Francisco Chronicle.*

Thanks to his training as a fiction writer, **Patrick Hoctel** brings a meticulous eye for detail to every lodging review. Mr. Hoctel is also an assistant editor at the *Bay Area Reporter.* His favorite pastime is being pampered at hotels and bed-and-breakfasts.

Jacqueline Killeen, whose expert opinion on San Francisco restaurants has been a star asset to Fodor's for years, recently passed away. She had been writing about San Francisco restaurants for more than 20 years, most recently as a critic for *San Francisco Focus* magazine. In collaboration with Ms. Killeen, longtime San Francisco food critic **Sharon Silva** updated this year's dining chapter.

Robert Taylor, who updated the Arts and Excursions chapters, has been exploring and writing about the Bay Area since 1975, covering mostly local entertainment. Now a features editor at the *Oakland Tribune,* he has lived on the South Peninsula and the East Bay as well as the city.

San Francisco '96 editor **Amy McConnell** was born and raised in Marin County and graduated from Stanford. She says nothing but wild horses—and Fodor's—could have dragged her from her favorite city.

We'd also like to thank **Daniel Mangin,** a longtime Fodor's contributor who recommended many of the writers for *San Francisco '96.*

What's New

A New Design

If this is not the first Fodor's guide you've purchased, you'll immediately notice our new look. More readable and easier to use than ever? We think so—and we hope you do, too.

New Takes On Exploring, Shopping, the Wine Country, and More

Because the Mission District has become an increasingly popular tourist destination, Dennis Harvey has created a new, improved tour itinerary for the Mission, along with a map—and reorganized the Exploring chapter accordingly. Because new stores are always opening in San Francisco, Alan Frutkin has expanded and reorganized the Shopping chapter to make it more comprehensive and user-friendly. Amy McConnell has restructured the Wine Country tour, focusing on differences among regions and emphasizing alternatives to wine-tasting.

Let Us Do Your Booking

Our writers have scoured San Francisco to come up with an extensive and well-balanced list of the best B&Bs, inns, resorts, and hotels, both small and large, new and old. But you don't have to beat the bushes to come up with a reservation. Now we've teamed up with an established hotel-booking service to make it easy for you to secure a room at the property of your choice. It's fast, it's free, and confirmation is guaranteed. If your first choice is booked, the operators can line up your second right away. Just call 800/FODORS–1 or 800/363–6771 (0800/89–1030 when in Great Britain; 0014/800–12–8271 when in Australia; 1800/55–9101 when in Ireland).

Travel Updates

In addition, just before your trip, you may want to order a Fodor's Worldview Travel Update. From local publications all over San Francisco, the lively, cosmopolitan editors at Worldview gather information on concerts, plays, opera, dance performances, gallery and museum shows, sports competitions, and other special events that coincide with your visit. See the order blank in the back of this book, call 800/799–9609, or fax 800/799–9619.

And in San Francisco

The recent opening of the $62 million **San Francisco Museum of Modern Art** (SFMOMA) across 3rd Street from the **Center for the Arts at Yerba Buena Gardens** has catapulted San Francisco into the cultural big leagues. The new building, designed by internationally celebrated Mario Botta, gives the city's collection of 20th-century art a world-class setting for the first time, attracting hundreds of residents and visitors who never found their way to the museum's cramped quarters in the Civic Center. The new Yerba Buena Gardens complex, with its inviting grass esplanade, its growing number of art galleries and museums, and its performance spaces which host events ranging from computer-assisted jazz improvisations to re-created settings from the *Star Wars* movies, has transformed a tired South of Market neighborhood of residential hotels and marginal industries into a new civic center for the arts. The newest additions to the neighborhood are the **Cartoon Art Museum,** with exhibits ranging from 19th century political satire to the latest in underground comic books, and the California Historical Society's library and gallery (slated to open in January 1996), with rotating exhibitions of paintings and artifacts covering the gold rush and other events in the state's history.

Another main event was **Union Square**'s transformation from a shopping district serving San Francisco's old guard to a livelier neighborhood for international visitors—dramatized by the closing of the I. Magnin department store early in 1995. Across the square, the newest arrival is a three-level **"Nike Town"** (expected to open in April 1996), a virtual retail theater of athletic wear and video entertainment. Facing another corner of the square, a **Borders Books and Music** store and a **Disney Store** have taken over a former airline ticketing office at Powell and Stockton streets. The landmark **Gump's,** which has specialized in Asian art goods since the 1860s, moved a block east on Post Street into retail space that resembles a lantern-filled Oriental courtyard; the store's venerable, gilded, 18th-century Buddha statue, newly refurbished, made the move, too.

Performing-arts organizations are changing locations this year, primarily because civic buildings are being seismically upgraded. The **War Memorial Opera House** closes in January 1996 for an expected 18 months. The **San Francisco Opera** will perform its 1996 season nearby in the Civic Auditorium and the Orpheum Theatre. The **San Francisco Ballet,** which normally performs a winter season at the Opera House, will be performing at three temporary locations until 1997. Meanwhile, the **American Conservatory Theater,** the city's leading nonprofit theater company, hopes to return to its rebuilt Geary Theater—damaged by the Loma Prieta earthquake—by the end of 1996. On the northwestern edge of the city, the California **Palace of the Legion of Honor,** which specializes in European painting, drawings and sculpture, was scheduled to open in the fall of 1995.

The long-delayed **Underwater World** at **Pier 39,** slated to open in the spring of 1996, will offer visitors views, from a transparent tunnel, of some 2,000 marine species in a 700,000-gallon aquarium. Another new attraction at Pier 39 is *San Francisco: The Movie,* a 35-minute, 70-millimeter travelogue projected onto an oversize screen.

How to Use This Book

Organization

Up front is the **Gold Guide,** comprising two sections on gold paper that are chockfull of information about traveling within your destination and traveling in general. Both are in alphabetical order by topic. **Important Contacts A to Z** gives addresses and telephone numbers of organizations and companies that offer destination-related services and detailed information or publications. Here's where you'll find information about how to get to San Francisco from wherever you are. **Smart Travel Tips A to Z,** the Gold Guide's second section, gives specific tips on how to get the most out of your travels, as well as information on how to accomplish what you need to in San Francisco.

At the end of the book you'll find a Portrait chapter, with a wonderful essay about earthquakes in San Francisco, followed by suggestions for pretrip reading, both fiction and nonfiction. Here we also recommend movies you can rent on videotape to get you in the mood for your travels.

Stars

Stars in the margin are used to denote highly recommended sights, attractions, hotels, and restaurants.

Hotel Facilities

Note that in general you incur charges when you use many hotel facilities. We wanted to let you know what facilities a hotel has to offer, but we don't always specify whether or not there's a charge, so when planning a vacation that entails a stay of several days, it's wise to ask what's included in the rate.

Credit Cards

The following abbreviations are used: **AE,** American Express; **D,** Discover; **DC,** Diners Club; **MC,** MasterCard; and **V,** Visa.

Please Write to Us

Everyone who has contributed to *San Francisco '96* has worked hard to make the text accurate. All prices and opening times are based on information supplied to us at press time, and the publisher cannot accept responsibility for any errors that may have occurred. The passage of time will bring changes, so it's always a good idea to call ahead and confirm information when it matters—particularly if you're making a detour to visit specific sights or attractions. When making reservations at a hotel or inn, be sure to mention if you have a disability or are traveling with children, if you prefer a private bath or a certain type of bed, or if you have specific dietary needs or any other concerns.

Were the restaurants we recommended as described? Did our hotel picks exceed your expectations? Did you find a museum we recommended a waste of time? We would love your feedback, positive and negative. If you have complaints, we'll look into them and revise our entries when the facts warrant it. If you've happened upon a special place that we haven't included, we'll pass the information along to the writers so they can check it out. So please send us a letter or postcard (we're at 201 East 50th Street, New York, NY 10022). We'll look forward to hearing from you. And in the meantime, have a wonderful trip!

Karen Cure
Editorial Director

San Francisco

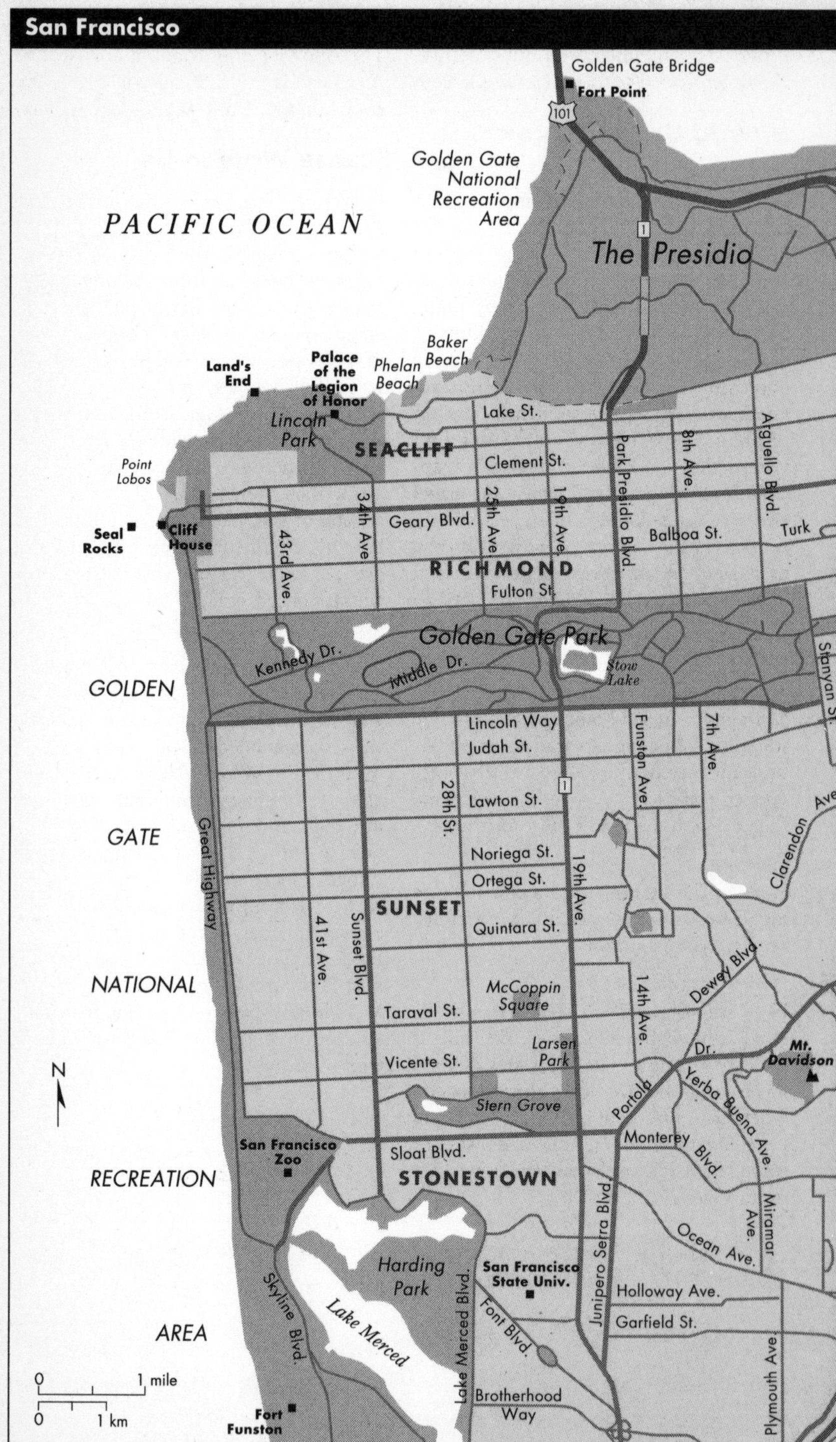

Golden Gate Bridge
Fort Point
101
Golden Gate National Recreation Area
PACIFIC OCEAN
The Presidio
1
Baker Beach
Phelan Beach
Palace of the Legion of Honor
Land's End
Lincoln Park
SEACLIFF
Lake St.
Clement St.
Park Presidio Blvd.
8th Ave.
Arguello Blvd.
Point Lobos
Seal Rocks
Cliff House
43rd Ave.
34th Ave.
Geary Blvd.
25th Ave.
19th Ave.
Balboa St.
Turk
RICHMOND
Fulton St.
Golden Gate Park
Kennedy Dr.
Middle Dr.
Stow Lake
Stanyan St.
GOLDEN
GATE
NATIONAL
RECREATION
AREA
Lincoln Way
Judah St.
Funston Ave.
7th Ave.
28th St.
Lawton St.
Clarendon Ave
Great Highway
Noriega St.
Ortega St.
19th Ave.
SUNSET
41st Ave.
Sunset Blvd.
Quintara St.
Dewey Blvd.
McCoppin Square
14th Ave.
Taraval St.
Larsen Park
Dr.
Mt. Davidson
Vicente St.
N
Stern Grove
Portola
Yerba Buena Ave.
San Francisco Zoo
Sloat Blvd.
Monterey Blvd.
STONESTOWN
Junipero Serra Blvd
Ocean Ave.
Miramar Ave.
Harding Park
San Francisco State Univ.
Skyline Blvd.
Lake Merced
Lake Merced Blvd.
Font Blvd.
Holloway Ave.
Garfield St.
Plymouth Ave.
0 1 mile
0 1 km
Brotherhood Way
Fort Funston

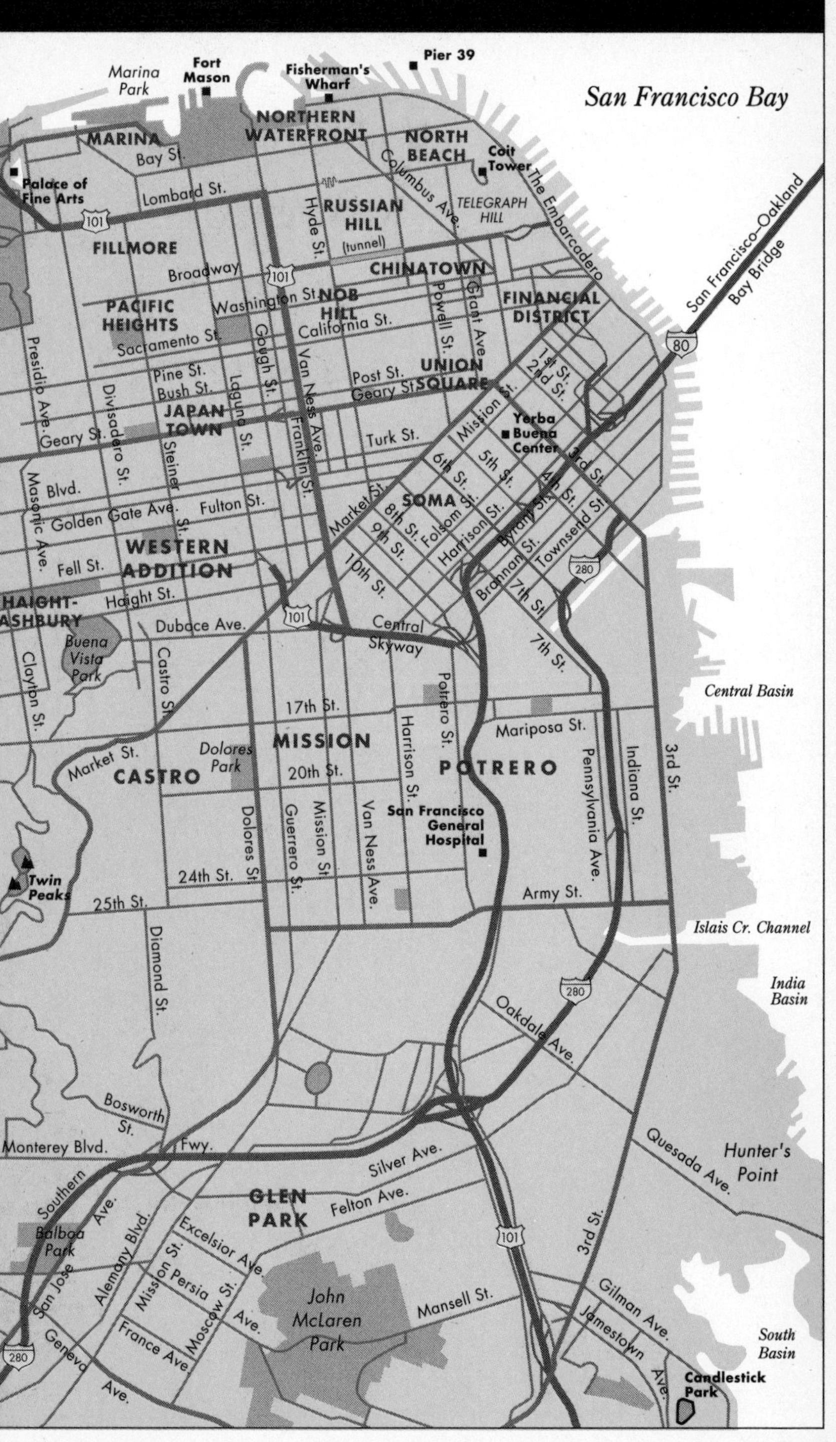

San Francisco Bay
Marina Park
Fort Mason
Fisherman's Wharf
Pier 39
NORTHERN WATERFRONT
MARINA
NORTH BEACH
Coit Tower
Bay St.
Palace of Fine Arts
Lombard St.
Columbus Ave.
The Embarcadero
RUSSIAN HILL
TELEGRAPH HILL
Hyde St.
(tunnel)
FILLMORE
Broadway
CHINATOWN
San Francisco–Oakland Bay Bridge
PACIFIC HEIGHTS
Washington St.
NOB HILL
California St.
FINANCIAL DISTRICT
Sacramento St.
Powell St.
Grant Ave.
Gough St.
Van Ness Ave.
UNION SQUARE
Presidio Ave.
Pine St.
Bush St.
Laguna St.
Post St.
Geary St.
1st St.
2nd St.
Divisadero St.
JAPAN TOWN
Mission St.
Yerba Buena Center
Geary St.
Steiner St.
Franklin St.
Turk St.
6th St.
5th St.
3rd St.
Masonic Ave.
Blvd.
Fulton St.
Market St.
SOMA
4th St.
Golden Gate Ave.
8th St.
Folsom St.
Harrison St.
Bryant St.
Townsend St.
WESTERN ADDITION
9th St.
Fell St.
10th St.
Brannan St.
HAIGHT-ASHBURY
Haight St.
7th St.
Duboce Ave.
Central Skyway
Buena Vista Park
Clayton St.
Castro St.
7th St.
Central Basin
Potrero St.
17th St.
Harrison St.
Mariposa St.
MISSION
Market St.
Dolores Park
CASTRO
20th St.
POTRERO
Indiana St.
3rd St.
Pennsylvania Ave.
Dolores St.
Guerrero St.
Mission St.
Van Ness Ave.
San Francisco General Hospital
Twin Peaks
24th St.
25th St.
Army St.
Islais Cr. Channel
Diamond St.
India Basin
Oakdale Ave.
Bosworth St.
Monterey Blvd.
Fwy.
Quesada Ave.
Hunter's Point
Silver Ave.
Southern
GLEN PARK
Felton Ave.
Ave.
Balboa Park
Alemany Blvd.
Excelsior Ave.
3rd St.
San Jose
Mission St.
Persia Ave.
John McLaren Park
Mansell St.
Gilman Ave.
Moscow St.
Jamestown Ave.
South Basin
France Ave.
Geneva Ave.
Candlestick Park
101
80
280

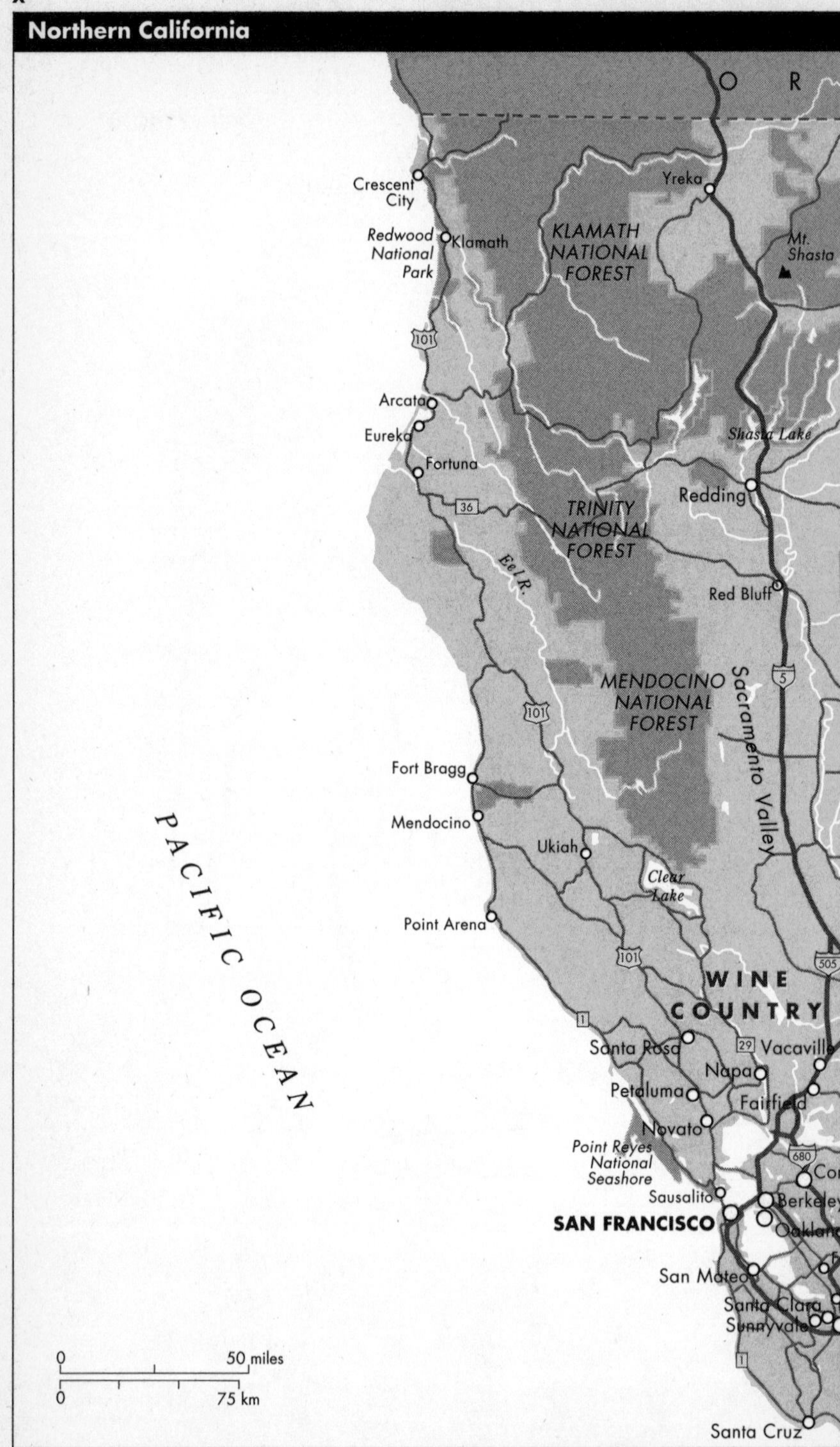
Northern California
O R
Crescent City
Yreka
Redwood National Park
Klamath
KLAMATH NATIONAL FOREST
Mt. Shasta
101
Arcata
Eureka
Shasta Lake
Fortuna
Redding
36
TRINITY NATIONAL FOREST
Eel R.
Red Bluff
5
MENDOCINO NATIONAL FOREST
Sacramento Valley
101
Fort Bragg
Mendocino
PACIFIC OCEAN
Ukiah
Clear Lake
Point Arena
101
505
WINE COUNTRY
1
Santa Rosa
29
Vacaville
Napa
Petaluma
Fairfield
Novato
680
Point Reyes National Seashore
Sausalito
Berkeley
SAN FRANCISCO
Oakland
San Mateo
Santa Clara
Sunnyvale
1
Santa Cruz
0
50 miles
0
75 km

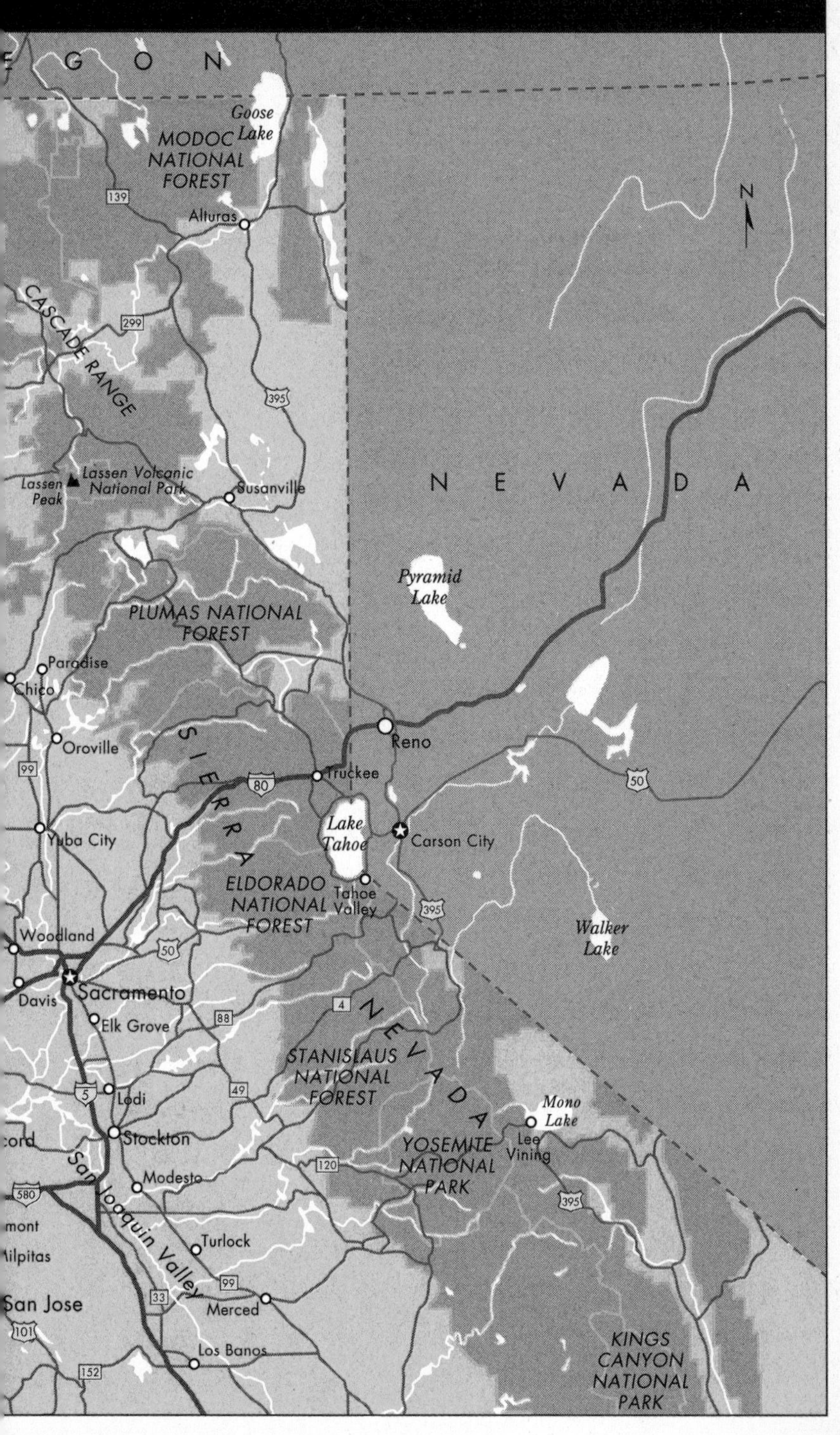

EGON
Goose Lake
MODOC NATIONAL FOREST
139
Alturas
CASCADE RANGE
299
395
Lassen Volcanic National Park
Lassen Peak
Susanville
NEVADA
Pyramid Lake
PLUMAS NATIONAL FOREST
Paradise
Chico
Oroville
SIERRA
99
80
Truckee
Reno
50
Yuba City
Lake Tahoe
Carson City
ELDORADO NATIONAL FOREST
Tahoe Valley
395
Walker Lake
Woodland
50
Sacramento
Davis
4
NEVADA
Elk Grove
88
STANISLAUS NATIONAL FOREST
5
Lodi
49
Mono Lake
Stockton
Lee Vining
YOSEMITE NATIONAL PARK
San Joaquin Valley
Modesto
120
580
395
Turlock
99
33
Merced
San Jose
101
Los Banos
152
KINGS CANYON NATIONAL PARK

World Time Zones

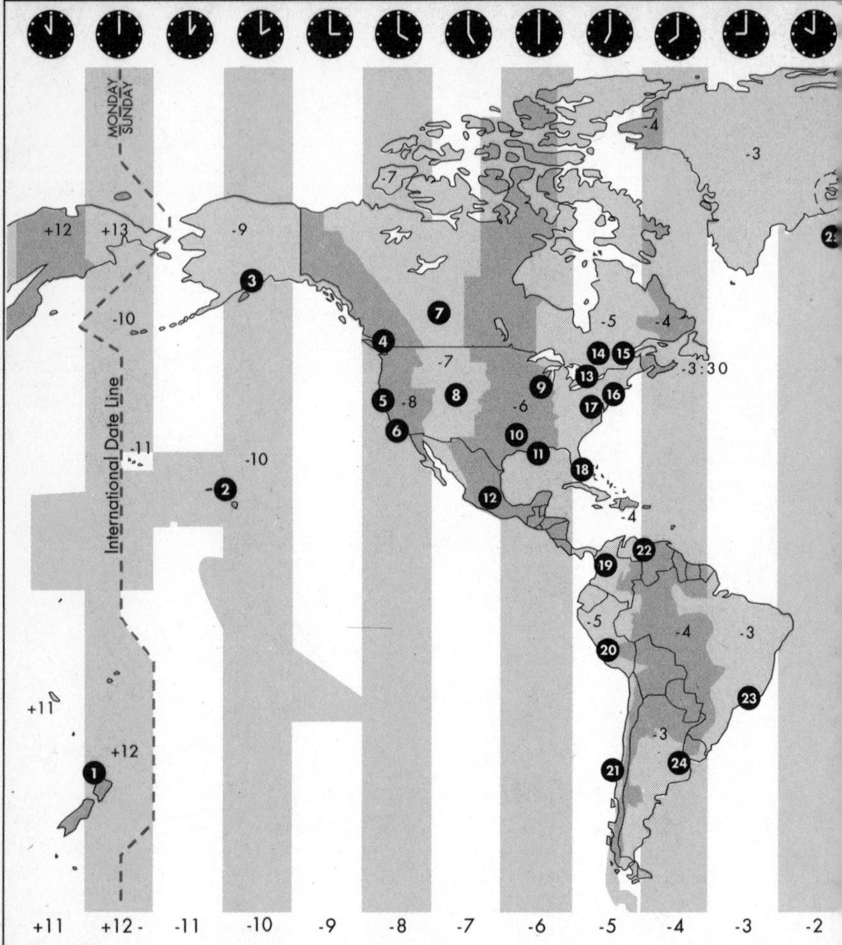

+11 +12 - -11 -10 -9 -8 -7 -6 -5 -4 -3 -2

Numbers below vertical bands relate each zone to Greenwich Mean Time (0 hrs.). Local times frequently differ from these general indications, as indicated by light-face numbers on map.

Algiers, **29**
Anchorage, **3**
Athens, **41**
Auckland, **1**
Baghdad, **46**
Bangkok, **50**
Beijing, **54**
Berlin, **34**
Bogotá, **19**
Budapest, **37**
Buenos Aires, **24**
Caracas, **22**
Chicago, **9**
Copenhagen, **33**
Dallas, **10**
Delhi, **48**
Denver, **8**
Djakarta, **53**
Dublin, **26**
Edmonton, **7**
Hong Kong, **56**
Honolulu, **2**
Istanbul, **40**
Jerusalem, **42**
Johannesburg, **44**
Lima, **20**
Lisbon, **28**
London (Greenwich), **27**
Los Angeles, **6**
Madrid, **38**
Manila, **57**

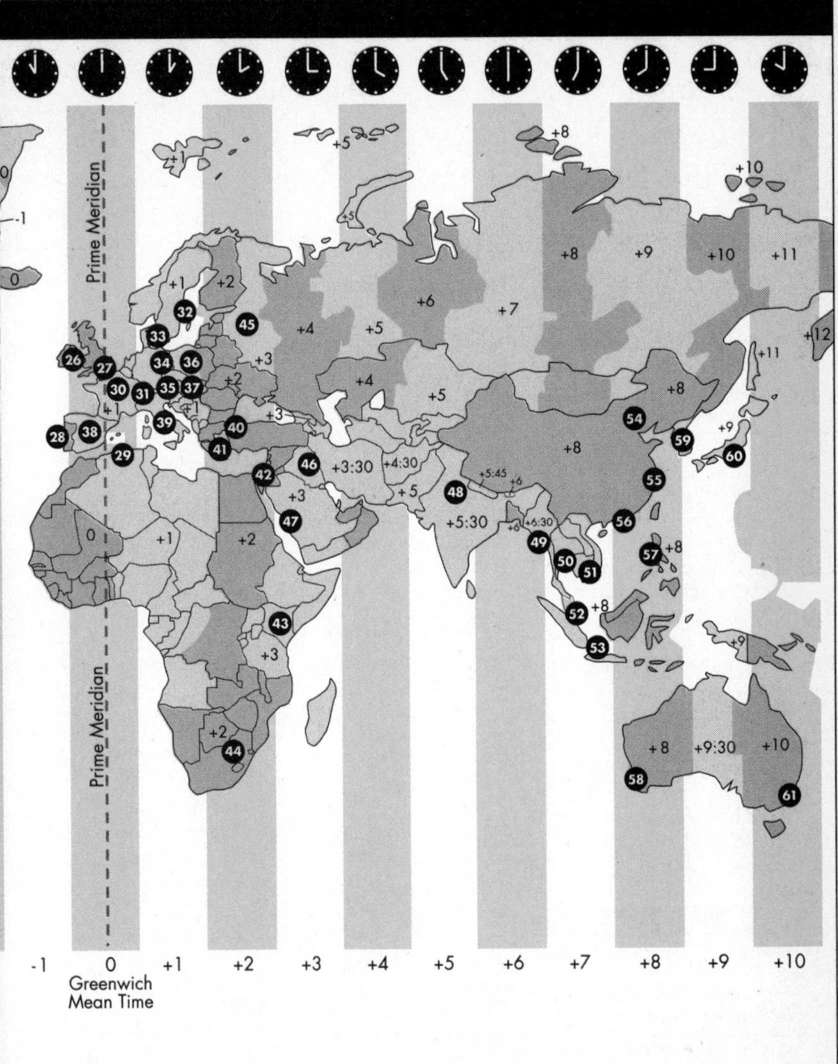

Prime Meridian
-1
0
+1
+2
+3
+4
+5
+6
+7
+8
+9
+10
Greenwich
Mean Time

IMPORTANT CONTACTS A TO Z

An Alphabetical Listing of Publications, Organizations, and Companies That Will Help You Before, During, and After Your Trip

No single travel resource can give you every detail about every topic that might interest or concern you at the various stages of your journey—when you're planning your trip, while you're on the road, and after you get back home. The following organizations, books, and brochures will supplement the information in Fodor's *San Francisco '96*. For related information, including both basic tips on visiting San Francisco and background information on many of the topics below, study Smart Travel Tips A to Z, the section that follows Important Contacts A to Z.

A

AIR TRAVEL

The major gateway to San Francisco is the San Francisco International Airport (☎ 415/761-0800), just south of the city, off U.S. 101. Several domestic airlines serve the Oakland Airport (☎ 510/577-4000), which is across the bay but not much farther away from downtown San Francisco (via I-880 and I-80), although traffic on the Bay Bridge may at times make travel time longer. Flying time is six hours from New York, four hours from Chicago, and one hour from Los Angeles.

AIRPORT TRANSFERS

SFO Airporter (☎ 415/495-8404) provides bus service between downtown and the airport, making the round of downtown hotels. Buses run every 20 minutes from 5 AM to 11 PM, from the lower level outside the baggage claim area. The fare is $8 one-way, $14 round-trip.

For $11, **Supershuttle** will take you from the airport to anywhere within the city limits of San Francisco. At the airport, after picking up your luggage, call 415/871-7800 and a van will pick you up within five minutes. To go to the airport, make reservations (☎ 415/558-8500) 24 hours in advance. The Supershuttle stops at the upper level of the terminal, along with several other bus and van transport services.

Taxis to or from downtown take 20-30 minutes and average $30.

CARRIERS

Carriers serving San Francisco include **Alaska Air** (☎ 800/426-0333), **American** (☎ 800/433-7300), **Continental** (☎ 800/525-0280), **Delta** (☎ 800/221-1212), **Southwest** (☎ 800/435-9792), **TWA** (☎ 800/221-2000), **United** (☎ 800/241-6522), and **USAir** (☎ 800/428-4322).

LOW-COST CARRIERS

For inexpensive, no-frills flights, contact **Midwest Express** (☎ 800/452-2022), based in Milwaukee, which serves 45 U.S. cities in the Midwest and on both coasts, including San Francisco; and **Private Jet** (☎ 404/231-7571, 800/546-7571, or 800/949-9400), based in Atlanta, serving San Francisco.

FROM THE U.K.➢ Some travel agencies that offer cheap fares to San Francisco include **Trailfinders** (42-50 Earl's Court Rd., London W8 6FT, ☎ 0171/937-5400), specialists in round-the-world fares and independent travel; **Travel Cuts** (295a Regent St., London W1R 7YA, ☎ 0171/637-3161), the Canadian Students' travel service; and **Flightfile** (49 Tottenham Court Rd., London W1P 9RE, ☎ 0171/700-2722), a flight-only agency.

COMPLAINTS

To register complaints about charter and scheduled airlines, contact the U.S. Department of Transportation's **Office of Consumer Affairs** (400 7th St. NW, Washington, DC 20590, ☎ 202/366-2220 or 800/322-7873).

CONSOLIDATOR

An established consolidator selling to the public is **TFI Tours International** (34 W. 32nd St., New York, NY 10001, ☎ 212/736–1140 or 800/745–8000).

PUBLICATIONS

For general information about charter carriers, ask for the Office of Consumer Affairs' brochure **"Plane Talk: Public Charter Flights."** The Department of Transportation also publishes a 58-page booklet, **"Fly Rights"** ($1.75; Consumer Information Center, Dept. 133B, Pueblo, CO 81009).

For other tips and hints, consult the Consumers Union's monthly **"Consumer Reports Travel Letter"** ($39 a year; Box 53629, Boulder, CO 80322, ☎ 800/234–1970) and the newsletter **"Travel Smart"** ($37 a year; 40 Beechdale Rd., Dobbs Ferry, NY 10522, ☎ 800/327–3633); ***The Official Frequent Flyer Guidebook,*** by Randy Petersen ($14.99 plus $3 shipping; 4715-C Town Center Dr., Colorado Springs, CO 80916, ☎ 719/597–8899 or 800/487–8893); ***Airfare Secrets Exposed,*** by Sharon Tyler and Matthew Wonder (Universal Information Publishing; $16.95 plus $3.75 shipping from Sandcastle Publishing, Box 3070-A, South Pasadena, CA 91031, ☎ 213/255–3616 or 800/655–0053); and ***202 Tips Even the Best Business Travelers May Not Know,*** by Christopher McGinnis ($10 plus $3.00 shipping; Irwin Professional Publishing, Box 52927, Atlanta, GA 30355, ☎ 708/789–4000 or 800/634–3966).

B

BETTER BUSINESS BUREAU

Contact San Francisco's **Better Business Bureau** (114 Sansome St., Suite 1103, 94104, ☎ 415/243–9999). For other local contacts, consult the **Council of Better Business Bureaus** (4200 Wilson Blvd., Arlington, VA 22203, ☎ 703/276–0100).

BUS TRAVEL

WITHIN SAN FRANCISCO

San Francisco Municipal Railway System, or **Muni** (☎ 415/673–6864).

C

CAR RENTAL

Major car-rental companies represented in San Francisco include **Alamo** (☎ 800/327–9633, 0800/272–2000 in the U.K.), **Avis** (☎ 800/331–1212, 800/879–2847 in Canada), **Budget** (☎ 800/527–0700, 0800/181–181 in the U.K.), **Dollar** (known as Eurodollar outside North America, ☎ 800/800–4000 in the U.S. and Canada, 0181/952–6565 in the U.K.), **Hertz** (☎ 800/654–3131, 800/263–0600 in Canada, 0181/679–1799 in the U.K.), and **National** (☎ 800/227–7368, 0181/950–5050 in the U.K., where it is known as Europcar). Rates in San Francisco begin at $30 a day and $175 a week for an economy car with unlimited mileage. This does not include tax, which in San Francisco is 8¼% on car rentals.

San Francisco has many good budget rental-car companies: **American International** (☎ 415/692–4100), **Enterprise** (☎ 800/325–8007), and **Reliable** (☎ 415/928–4414) are a few. At the other end of the price spectrum, **Sunbelt** (☎ 415/771–9191) specializes in BMWs, and Corvette and Miata convertibles.

CHILDREN AND TRAVEL

FLYING

Look into **"Flying With Baby"** ($5.95 plus $1 shipping; Third Street Press, Box 261250, Littleton, CO 80126, ☎ 303/595–5959), cowritten by a flight attendant. **"Kids and Teens in Flight,"** free from the U.S. Department of Transportation's Office of Consumer Affairs, offers tips for children flying alone. Every two years the February issue of ***Family Travel Times*** (*see* Know-How, *below*) details children's services on three dozen airlines.

KNOW-HOW

Family Travel Times, published 10 times a year by Travel With Your Children (TWYCH, 45 W. 18th St., New York, NY 10011, ☎ 212/206–0688; annual subscription $55), covers destinations, types of

City Transport

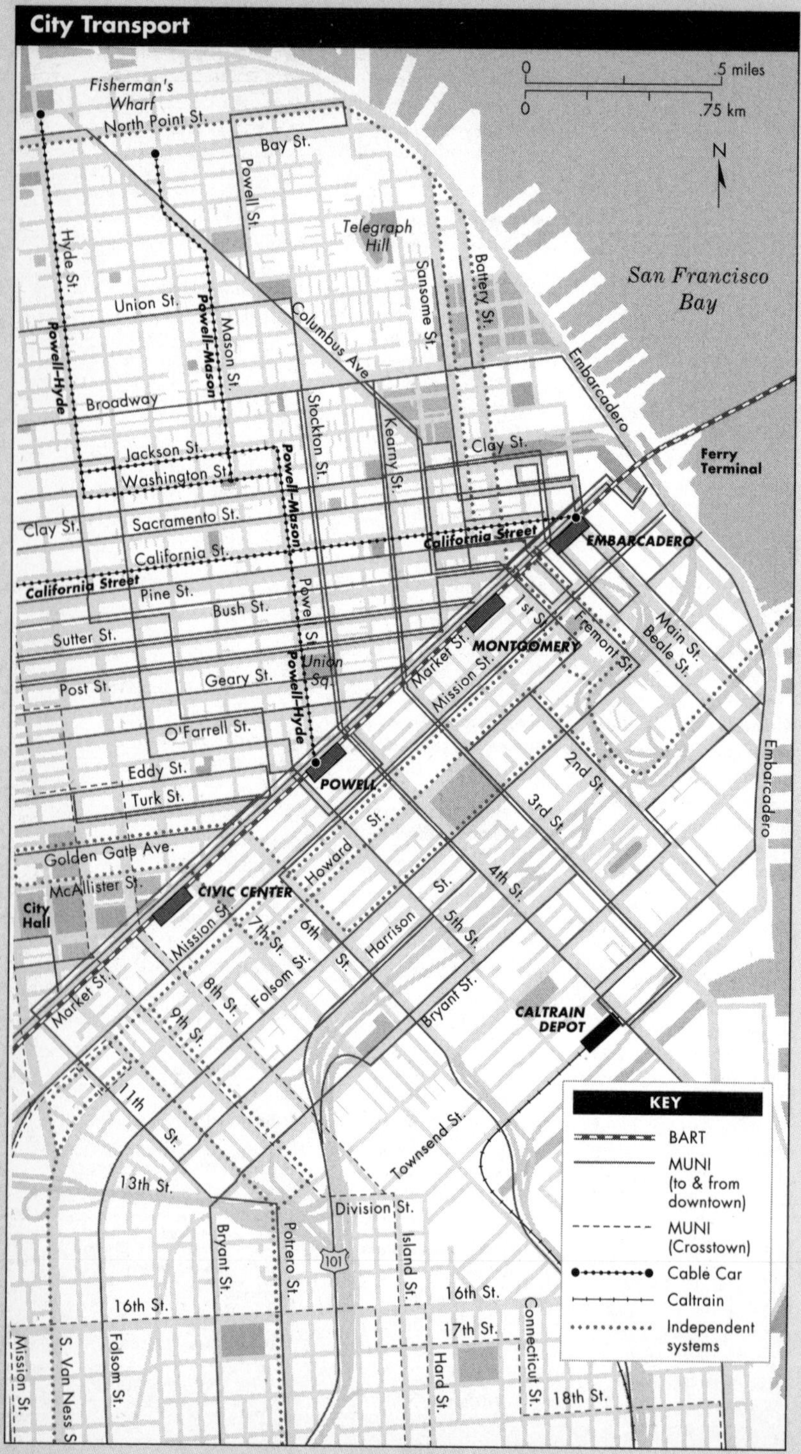

Fisherman's Wharf
North Point St.
Bay St.
Powell St.
Telegraph Hill
Hyde St.
Union St.
Powell–Mason
Mason St.
Columbus Ave
Sansome St.
Battery St.
San Francisco Bay
Embarcadero
Powell–Hyde
Broadway
Stockton St.
Kearny St.
Clay St.
Ferry Terminal
Jackson St.
Washington St.
Sacramento St.
California Street
EMBARCADERO
California St.
Pine St.
Bush St.
1st St.
Fremont St.
Main St.
Beale St.
Sutter St.
Market St.
MONTGOMERY
Mission St.
Union Sq.
Post St.
Geary St.
O'Farrell St.
2nd St.
Eddy St.
POWELL
Turk St.
3rd St.
Golden Gate Ave.
Howard St.
McAllister St.
CIVIC CENTER
4th St.
City Hall
7th St.
6th St.
Harrison St.
5th St.
Folsom St.
8th St.
9th St.
Bryant St.
CALTRAIN DEPOT
11th St.
Townsend St.
13th St.
Division St.
Island St.
Potrero St.
101
16th St.
17th St.
Connecticut St.
Hard St.
18th St.
Mission St.
S. Van Ness
Folsom St.
0 .5 miles
0 .75 km
N
KEY
BART
MUNI (to & from downtown)
MUNI (Crosstown)
Cable Car
Caltrain
Independent systems

vacations, and modes of travel.

The ***Family Travel Guides*** catalog ($1 postage; ☎ 510/527–5849) lists about 200 books and articles on family travel. Also check ***Take Your Baby and Go! A Guide for Traveling with Babies, Toddlers and Young Children,*** by Sheri Andrews, Judy Bordeaux, and Vivian Vasquez ($5.95 plus $1.50 shipping; Bear Creek Publications, 2507 Minor Ave., Seattle, WA 98102, ☎ 206/322–7604 or 800/326–6566). ***The 100 Best Family Resorts in North America,*** by Jane Wilford with Janet Tice ($12.95), and the two-volume ***50 Great Family Vacations in North America*** ($18.95 per volume), both from Globe Pequot Press (plus $3 shipping; Box 833, 6 Business Park Rd., Old Saybrook, CT 06475, ☎ 203/395–0440 or 800/243–0495, 800/962–0973 in CT) help plan your trip with children, from toddlers to teens.

LOCAL INFORMATION

Consult the lively by-parents, for-parents ***Where Should We Take the Kids? California*** ($17.00; Fodor's Travel Publications, ☎ 800/533–6478 and in bookstores).

CUSTOMS

CANADIANS

Contact **Revenue Canada** (2265 St. Laurent Blvd. S, Ottawa, Ontario, K1G 4K3, ☎ 613/993–0534) for a copy of the free brochure **"I Declare/Je Déclare"** and for details on duties that exceed the standard duty-free limit.

U.K. CITIZENS

HM Customs and Excise (Dorset House, Stamford St., London SE1 9NG, ☎ 0171/202–4227) can answer questions about U.K. customs regulations and publishes **"A Guide for Travellers,"** detailing standard procedures and import rules.

D

FOR TRAVELERS WITH DISABILITIES

COMPLAINTS

To register complaints under the provisions of the Americans With Disabilities Act, contact the U.S. Department of Justice's **Public Access Section** (Box 66738, Washington, DC 20035, ☎ 202/514–0301, TTY 202/514–0383, FAX 202/307–1198).

ORGANIZATIONS

FOR TRAVELERS WITH HEARING IMPAIRMENTS➢ Contact the **American Academy of Otolaryngology** (1 Prince St., Alexandria, VA 22314, ☎ 703/836–4444, FAX 703/683–5100, TTY 703/519–1585).

FOR TRAVELERS WITH MOBILITY PROBLEMS➢ Contact the **Information Center for Individuals with Disabilities** (Fort Point Pl., 27–43 Wormwood St., Boston, MA 02210, ☎ 617/727–5540, 800/462–5015 in MA, TTY 617/345–9743); **Mobility International USA** (Box 10767, Eugene, OR 97440, ☎ and TTY 503/343–1284, FAX 503/343–6812), the U.S. branch of an international organization headquartered in Belgium (*see below*) that has affiliates in 30 countries; **MossRehab Hospital Travel Information Service** (1200 W. Tabor Rd., Philadelphia, PA 19141, ☎ 215/456–9603, TTY 215/456–9602); the **Society for the Advancement of Travel for the Handicapped** (347 5th Ave., Suite 610, New York, NY 10016, ☎ 212/447–7284, FAX 212/725–8253); the **Travel Industry and Disabled Exchange** (TIDE, 5435 Donna Ave., Tarzana, CA 91356, ☎ 818/344–3640, FAX 818/344–0078); and **Travelin' Talk** (Box 3534, Clarksville, TN 37043, ☎ 615/552–6670, FAX 615/552–1182).

FOR TRAVELERS WITH VISION IMPAIRMENTS➢ Contact the **American Council of the Blind** (1155 15th St. NW, Suite 720, Washington, DC 20005, ☎ 202/467–5081, FAX 202/467–5085) or the **American Foundation for the Blind** (15 W. 16th St., New York, NY 10011, ☎ 212/620–2000, TTY 212/620–2158).

IN THE U.K.

Contact the **Royal Association for Disability and Rehabilitation** (RADAR, 12 City Forum, 250 City Rd., London EC1V 8AF, ☎ 0171/250–3222) or **Mobility International** (Rue de Manchester 25, B1070 Brussels, Belgium, ☎ 00–322–410–

6297), an international clearinghouse of travel information for people with disabilities.

NATIONAL PARKS

For a Golden Access Passport to national parks, contact the **National Park Service** (Box 37127, Washington, DC 20013-7127).

PUBLICATIONS

Several free publications are available from the U.S. Information Center (Box 100, Pueblo, CO 81009, ☎ 719/948–3334): **"New Horizons for the Air Traveler with a Disability"** (address to Dept. 355A), describing legally mandated changes; the pocket-size **"Fly Smart"** (Dept. 575B), good on flight safety; and the Airport Operators Council's worldwide **"Access Travel: Airports"** (Dept. 575A).

Fodor's ***Great American Vacations for Travelers with Disabilities*** ($18; available in bookstores, or call 800/533–6478) details accessible attractions, restaurants, and hotels in U.S. destinations. The 500-page ***Travelin' Talk Directory*** ($35; Box 3534, Clarksville, TN 37043, ☎ 615/552–6670) lists people and organizations who help travelers with disabilities. For specialist travel agents worldwide, consult the ***Directory of Travel Agencies for the Disabled*** ($19.95 plus $2 shipping; Twin Peaks Press, Box 129, Vancouver, WA 98666, ☎ 206/694–2462 or 800/637–2256). The Sierra Club publishes ***Easy Access to National Parks*** ($16 plus $3 shipping; 730 Polk St., San Francisco, CA 94109, ☎ 415/776–2211 or 800/935–1056).

San Francisco Convention and Visitors Bureau (Box 429097, San Francisco 94142-9097, ☎ 415/974–6900, TTY 415/392–0328) has free pamphlets with information about public transportation and the accessibility of various attractions. These include the dated but still helpful **"Guide to San Francisco for the Person Who Is Disabled,"** published in 1987.

The California State Coastal Conservancy (Publications Dept., 1330 Broadway, Suite 1100, Oakland 94612, ☎ 510/286–1015) publishes the free booklet **"Wheelchair Riders Guide to San Francisco Bay and Nearby Shorelines."**

SUBWAYS

All stations in **Bay Area Rapid Transit** (BART) are equipped with elevators. Call the station agent on the white courtesy telephone. Stations also have wheelchair-accessible rest rooms, phones, and drinking fountains. For information on a Bay Region Transit Discount Card, call BART (☎ 415/922–2278).

TRAVEL AGENCIES AND TOUR OPERATORS

The Americans with Disabilities Act requires that travel firms serve the needs of all travelers. However, some agencies and operators specialize in making group and individual arrangements for travelers with disabilities, among them **Access Adventures** (206 Chestnut Ridge Rd., Rochester, NY 14624, ☎ 716/889–9096), run by a former physical-rehab counselor; and **Tailored Tours** (Box 797687, Dallas, TX 75379, ☎ 214/612–1168 or 800/628–8542). In addition, many general-interest operators and agencies (*see* Tour Operators, *below*) can also arrange vacations for travelers with disabilities.

FOR TRAVELERS WITH MOBILITY IMPAIRMENTS➢ A number of operators specialize in working with travelers with mobility impairments: **Hinsdale Travel Service** (201 E. Ogden Ave., Suite 100, Hinsdale, IL 60521, ☎ 708/325–1335 or 800/303–5521), a travel agency that will give you access to the services of wheelchair traveler Janice Perkins; and **Wheelchair Journeys** (16979 Redmond Way, Redmond, WA 98052, ☎ 206/885–2210), which can handle arrangements worldwide.

FOR TRAVELERS WITH DEVELOPMENTAL DISABILITIES➢ Contact the nonprofit **New Directions** (5276 Hollister Ave., Suite 207, Santa Barbara, CA 93111, ☎ 805/967–2841) as well as the general-interest operations above.

DISCOUNTS

Options include **Entertainment Travel Editions** (fee $28–$53, depending on destination; Box

1068, Trumbull, CT 06611, ☎ 800/445–4137), **Great American Traveler** ($49.95 annually; Box 27965, Salt Lake City, UT 84127, ☎ 800/548–2812), **Moment's Notice Discount Travel Club** ($25 annually, single or family; 163 Amsterdam Ave., Suite 137, New York, NY 10023, ☎ 212/486–0500), **Privilege Card** ($74.95 annually; 3391 Peachtree Rd. NE, Suite 110, Atlanta, GA 30326, ☎ 404/262–0222 or 800/236—9732), **Travelers Advantage** ($49 annually, single or family; CUC Travel Service, 49 Music Sq. W, Nashville, TN 37203, ☎ 800/548–1116 or 800/648–4037), and **Worldwide Discount Travel Club** ($50 annually for family, $40 single; 1674 Meridian Ave., Miami Beach, FL 33139, ☎ 305/534–2082).

E

EMERGENCIES

For **police** or **ambulance,** telephone 911.

DOCTORS

Two hospitals with 24-hour emergency rooms are **San Francisco General Hospital** (1001 Potrero Ave., ☎ 415/206–8000) and the **Medical Center at the University of California, San Francisco** (500 Parnassus Ave. at 3rd Ave., near Golden Gate Park, ☎ 415/476–1000).

Physician Access Medical Center (26 California St., ☎ 415/397–2881) is a drop-in clinic in the Financial District, open weekdays 7:30 AM–5:30 PM. **Access Health Care** (☎ 415/565–6600) provides drop-in medical care at Davies Medical Center, Castro Street at Duboce Avenue, daily 8 AM–8 PM.

24-HOUR PHARMACIES

Several **Walgreen Drug Stores** have 24-hour pharmacies, including stores at 500 Geary Street near Union Square (☎ 415/673–8413) and 3201 Divisadero Street at Lombard Street (☎ 415/931–6417). Also try the Walgreen pharmacy at 135 Powell Street near Market Street (☎ 415/391–7222), which is open Monday–Saturday 8 AM–midnight, Sunday 9 AM–9 PM.

G

GAY AND LESBIAN TRAVEL

ORGANIZATION

The **International Gay Travel Association** (Box 4974, Key West, FL 33041, ☎ 800/448–8550), a consortium of 800 businesses, can supply names of travel agents and tour operators.

PUBLICATIONS

The premier international travel magazine for gays and lesbians is ***Our World*** ($35 for 10 issues; 1104 N. Nova Rd., Suite 251, Daytona Beach, FL 32117, ☎ 904/441–5367). The 16-page monthly **"Out & About"** ($49 for 10 issues; ☎ 212/645–6922 or 800/929–2268) covers gay-friendly resorts, hotels, cruise lines, and airlines.

In San Francisco, the biweekly *San Francisco Bay Times* and weekly *Bay Area Reporter* are free newspapers with extensive community and entertainment listings.

TOUR OPERATORS

Cruises and resort vacations are handled by **R.S.V.P. Travel Productions** (2800 University Ave. SE, Minneapolis, MN 55414, ☎ 800/328–7786) for gays, **Olivia** (4400 Market St., Oakland, CA 94608, ☎ 800/631–6277) for lesbian travelers. For mixed gay and lesbian travel, contact **Toto Tours** (1326 W. Albion, Suite 3W, Chicago, IL 60626, ☎ 312/274–8686 or 800/565–1241).

TRAVEL AGENCIES

The largest agencies serving gay travelers are **Advance Travel** (10700 Northwest Freeway, Suite 160, Houston, TX 77092, ☎ 713/682–2002 or 800/695–0880), **Islanders/Kennedy Travel** (183 W. 10th St., New York, NY 10014, ☎ 212/242–3222 or 800/988–1181), **Now Voyager** (4406 18th St., San Francisco, CA 94114, ☎ 415/626–1169 or 800/255–6951), and **Yellowbrick Road** (1500 W. Balmoral Ave., Chicago, IL 60640, ☎ 312/561–1800 or 800/642–2488). **Skylink Women's Travel** (746 Ashland Ave., Santa Monica, CA 90405, ☎ 310/452–0506 or 800/225-5759) works with lesbians.

I

INSURANCE

Travel insurance covering baggage, health, and trip cancellation or interruptions available from **Access America** (Box 90315, Richmond, VA 23286, ☎ 804/285-3300 or 800/284-8300), **Carefree Travel Insurance** (Box 9366, 100 Garden City Plaza, Garden City, NY 11530, ☎ 516/294-0220 or 800/323-3149), **Near Travel Service** (Box 1339, Calumet City, IL 60409, ☎ 708/868-6700 or 800/654-6700), **Tele-Trip** (Mutual of Omaha Plaza, Box 31716, Omaha, NE 68131, ☎ 800/228-9792), **Travel Insured International** (Box 280568, East Hartford, CT 06128-0568, ☎ 203/528-7663 or 800/243-3174), **Travel Guard International** (1145 Clark St., Stevens Point, WI 54481, ☎ 715/345-0505 or 800/826-1300), and **Wallach & Company** (107 W. Federal St., Box 480, Middleburg, VA 22117, ☎ 703/687-3166 or 800/237-6615).

IN THE U.K.

The **Association of British Insurers** (51 Gresham St., London EC2V 7HQ, ☎ 0171/600-3333; 30 Gordon St., Glasgow G1 3PU, ☎ 0141/226-3905; Scottish Provident Bldg., Donegall Sq. W, Belfast BT1 6JE, ☎ 01232/249176; and other locations) gives advice by phone and publishes the free **"Holiday Insurance,"** which sets out typical policy provisions and costs.

L

LODGING

APARTMENT AND VILLA RENTAL

Among the companies to contact are **Hometours International** (Box 11503, Knoxville, TN 37939, ☎ 615/588-8722 or 800/367-4668), **Rent-a-Home International** (7200 34th Ave. NW, Seattle, WA 98117, ☎ 206/789-9377 or 800/488-7368), **Vacation Home Rentals Worldwide** (235 Kensington Ave., Norwood, NJ 07648, ☎ 201/767-9393 or 800/633-3284), and **Villas and Apartments Abroad** (420 Madison Ave., Suite 1105, New York, NY 10017, ☎ 212/759-1025 or 800/433-3020). Members of the travel club **Hideaways International** ($99 annually; 767 Islington St., Portsmouth, NH 03801, ☎ 603/430-4433 or 800/843-4433) receive two annual guides plus quarterly newsletters, and arrange rentals among themselves.

HOME EXCHANGE

Principal clearinghouses include **HomeLink International/Vacation Exchange Club** ($60 annually; Box 650, Key West, FL 33041, ☎ 305/294-1448 or 800/638-3841), which gives members four annual directories, with a listing in one, plus updates; **Intervac International** ($65 annually; Box 590504, San Francisco, CA 94159, ☎ 415/435-3497), which has three annual directories; and **Loan-a-Home** ($35–$45 annually; 2 Park La., Apt. 6E, Mount Vernon, NY 10552-3443, ☎ 914/664-7640), which specializes in long-term exchanges.

M

MONEY MATTERS

ATMS

For specific **Cirrus** locations in the United States and Canada, call 800/424-7787. For U.S. **Plus** locations, call 800/843-7587 and enter the area code and first three digits of the number you're calling from (or of the calling area where you want an ATM).

WIRING FUNDS

Funds can be wired from the United States and Canada via **American Express MoneyGram** (☎ 800/926-9400 for locations and information) or **Western Union** (☎ 800/325-6000 for agent locations or to send using MasterCard or Visa, 800/321-2923 in Canada).

P

PASSPORTS AND VISAS

U.K. CITIZENS

For fees, documentation requirements, and to get an emergency passport, call the **London passport office** (☎ 0171/271-3000). For visa information, call the **U.S. Embassy Visa Information Line** (☎ 0891/200-290; calls cost 48p per minute or 36p per minute cheap rate) or write the **U.S. Embassy Visa Branch** (5 Upper Grosvenor St., London

W1A 2JB). If you live in Northern Ireland, write the **U.S. Consulate General** (Queen's House, Queen St., Belfast BTI 6EO).

PHOTO HELP

The **Kodak Information Center** (☎ 800/242–2424) answers consumer questions about film and photography.

R

RAIL TRAVEL

Amtrak (☎ 800/872–7245) trains (the *Zephyr,* from Chicago via Denver, and the *Coast Starlight,* traveling between Los Angeles and Seattle) stop in Emeryville (5885 Landregan St.) and Oakland (245 2nd St. in Jack London Sq.). Shuttle buses connect the Emeryville station and San Francisco's Ferry Building (30 Embarcadero at the foot of Market St.).

WITHIN SAN FRANCISCO

Contact the **Bay Area Rapid Transit (BART)** (☎ 415/992–2278).

S

SENIOR CITIZENS

EDUCATIONAL TRAVEL

The nonprofit **Elderhostel** (75 Federal St., 3rd Floor, Boston, MA 02110, ☎ 617/426–7788), for people 60 and older, has offered inexpensive study programs since 1975. The nearly 2,000 courses cover everything from marine science to Greek myths and cowboy poetry. Fees for programs in the United States and Canada, which usually last one week, run about $300, not including transportation.

ORGANIZATIONS

Contact the **American Association of Retired Persons** (AARP, 601 E St. NW, Washington, DC 20049, ☎ 202/434–2277; $8 per person or couple annually). Its Purchase Privilege Program gets members discounts on lodging, car rentals, and sightseeing, and the AARP Motoring Plan furnishes domestic trip-routing information and emergency road-service aid for an annual fee of $39.95 per person or couple ($59.95 for a premium version).

For other discounts on lodgings, car rentals, and other travel products, along with magazines and newsletters, contact the **National Council of Senior Citizens** (membership $12 annually; 1331 F St. NW, Washington, DC 20004, ☎ 202/347–8800) and **Mature Outlook** (subscription $9.95 annually; 6001 N. Clark St., Chicago, IL 60660, ☎ 312/465–6466 or 800/336–6330).

PUBLICATIONS

The 50+ Traveler's Guidebook: Where to Go, Where to Stay, What to Do, by Anita Williams and Merrimac Dillon ($12.95; St. Martin's Press, 175 5th Ave., New York, NY 10010, ☎ 212/674–5151 or 800/288–2131), offers many useful tips. **"The Mature Traveler"** ($29.95; Box 50400, Reno, NV 89513, ☎ 702/786–7419), a monthly newsletter, covers travel deals.

STUDENTS

GROUPS

Contiki Holidays (300 Plaza Alicante, Suite 900, Garden Grove, CA 92640, ☎ 714/740–0808 or 800/466–0610) is a major tour operator.

HOSTELING

Contact **Hostelling International–American Youth Hostels** (733 15th St. NW, Suite 840, Washington, DC 20005, ☎ 202/783–6161) in the United States, **Hostelling International–Canada** (205 Catherine St., Suite 400, Ottawa, Ontario K2P 1C3, ☎ 613/237–7884) in Canada, and the **Youth Hostel Association of England and Wales** (Trevelyan House, 8 St. Stephen's Hill, St. Albans, Hertfordshire AL1 2DY, ☎ 01727/855215 or 01727/845047) in the United Kingdom. Membership ($25 in the U.S., C$26.75 in Canada, and £9 in the U.K.) gets you access to 5,000 hostels worldwide that charge $7–$20 nightly per person.

I.D. CARDS

To get discounts on transportation and admissions, get the **International Student Identity Card** (ISIC) if you're a bona fide student or the **International Youth Card** (IYC) if you're under 26. In the United States, the ISIC and IYC cards cost $16 each and include basic travel accident and illness coverage, plus a toll-free travel hot line. Apply through the Council on International Educational Exchange (*see* Organizations, *below*). Cards are available for $15 each in Canada from Travel Cuts (187 College St., Toronto, Ontario M5T 1P7, ☎ 416/979–2406 or 800/667–2887) and in the United Kingdom for £5 each at student unions and student travel companies.

ORGANIZATIONS

A major contact is the **Council on International Educational Exchange** (CIEE, 205 E. 42nd St., 16th Floor, New York, NY 10017, ☎ 212/661–1450) with locations in Boston (729 Boylston St., Boston, MA 02116, ☎ 617/266–1926), Miami (9100 S. Dadeland Blvd., Miami, FL 33156, ☎ 305/670–9261), Los Angeles (1093 Broxton Ave., Los Angeles, CA 90024, ☎ 310/208–3551), 43 college towns nationwide, and the United Kingdom (28A Poland St., London W1V 3DB, ☎ 0171/437–7767). Twice a year, it publishes *Student Travels* magazine. The CIEE's Council Travel Service offers domestic air passes for bargain travel within the United States and is the exclusive U.S. agent for several student-discount cards.

Campus Connections (325 Chestnut St., Suite 1101, Philadelphia, PA 19106, ☎ 215/625–8585 or 800/428–3235) specializes in discounted accommodations and airfares for students. The **Educational Travel Centre** (438 N. Frances St., Madison, WI 53703, ☎ 608/256–5551) offers rail passes and low-cost airline tickets, mostly for flights departing from Chicago.

In Canada, also contact **Travel Cuts** (*see above*).

PUBLICATIONS

See the *Berkeley Guide to California* ($17.50; Fodor's Travel Publications, ☎ 800/533–6478 or from bookstores).

T

TOUR OPERATORS

Among the companies selling tours and packages to San Francisco, the following have a proven reputation, are nationally known, and have plenty of options to choose from.

GROUP TOURS

For deluxe escorted tours of San Francisco, contact **Maupintour** (Box 807, Lawrence, KS 66044, ☎ 913/843–1211 or 800/255–4266) and **Tauck Tours** (11 Wilton Rd., Westport, CT 06880, ☎ 203/226–6911 or 800/468–2825). Another operator falling between deluxe and first-class is **Globus** (5301 South Federal Circle, Littleton, CO 80123, ☎ 303/797–2800 or 800/221–0090). In the first-class and tourist range, try **Collette Tours** (162 Middle St., Pawtucket, RI 02860, ☎ 401/728–3805 or 800/832–4656), **Domenico Tours** (750 Broadway, Bayonne, NJ 07002, ☎ 201/823–8687 or 800/554–8687), and **Mayflower Tours** (1225 Warren Ave., Downers Grove, IL 60515, ☎ 708/960–3430 or 800/323–7604). For budget and tourist class programs, contact **Cosmos** (*see* Globus, *above*).

PACKAGES

Independent vacation packages are available from major tour operators and airlines. Contact **American Airlines Fly AAway Vacations** (☎ 800/321–2121), **SuperCities** (139 Main St., Cambridge, MA 02142, ☎ 617/621–0099 or 800/333–1234), **Continental Airlines' Grand Destinations** (☎ 800/634–5555), **Delta Dream Vacations** (☎ 800/872–7786), **Certified Vacations** (Box 1525, Fort Lauderdale, FL 33302, ☎ 305/522–1414 or 800/233–7260), **United Vacations** (☎ 800/328–6877), **Kingdom Tours** (300 Market St., Kingston, PA 18704, ☎ 717/283–4241 or 800/872–8857), and **USAir Vacations** (☎ 800/455–0123). **Funjet Vacations,** based in Milwaukee, Wisconsin, and **Gogo Tours,** based in Ramsey, New Jersey, sell tours to San Francisco only through travel agents. For rail packages, try **Amtrak** (☎ 800/872–7245).

FROM THE U.K.➢ Tour operators offering packages to San Francisco include **British Airways Holidays** (Astral Towers, Betts Way, London Rd., Crawley, West Sussex RH10 2XA, ☎ 01293/518–0222), **Jetsave** (Sussex House, London Rd., East Grinstead,

West Sussex RH19 1LD, ☎ 01342/312033), **Key to America** (1–3 Station Rd., Ashford, Middlesex TW15 2UW, ☎ 01784/248–777), **Kuoni Travel Ltd.** (Kuoni House, Dorking, Surrey RH5 4AZ, ☎ 01306/742–222), **Premier Holidays** (Premier Travel Center, Westbrook, Milton Rd., Cambridge CB4 1YG, ☎ 01223/516–688), and **Trailfinders** (42–50 Earl's Court Rd., London W8 6FT, ☎ 0171/937–5400; 58 Deansgate, Manchester, M3 2FF, ☎ 0161/839–6969).

THEME TRIPS

ADVENTURE➢ All Adventure Travel (5589 Arapahoe #208, Boulder, CO 80303, ☎ 800/537–4025), with 80 member operators, can book camping, canoe, sailing, and hiking trips in California. Trek America (Box 470, Blairstown, NJ 07825, ☎ 908/362–9198 or 800/221–0596) includes hiking, camping, and hotels on inland and Pacific coast tours.

BALLOONING➢ Champagne balloon trips out of San Francisco and the Napa Valley area are run by **Above the West Hot Air Ballooning** (Box 2290, Yountville, CA 94599, ☎ 707/944–8638 or 800/6272–759) and **Bonaventura Balloon Company** (133 Wall Rd., Napa, CA 94558, ☎ 707/944–2822 or 800/359–6272).

BICYCLING➢ For bike trips that use inns or campsites for overnight stays, contact **Backroads** (1516 5th St., Suite A550, Berkeley, CA 94710, ☎ 510/527–1555 or 800/462–2848).

LEARNING VACATIONS➢ **Earthwatch** (680 Mount Auburn St., Box 403SI, Watertown, MA 02272, ☎ 617/926–8200 or 800/776–0188) operates natural-history programs led by specialists in a variety of scientific fields. **Oceanic Society Expeditions** (Fort Mason Center, Bldg. E, San Francisco, CA 94123, ☎ 415/441–1106 or 800/326–7491) runs natural-history, whale-watching, and dolphin-research expeditions.

MUSIC➢ **Dailey-Thorp Travel** (330 W. 58th St., New York, NY 10019, ☎ 212/307–1555; book through travel agents) has San Francisco opera packages that include dining at fine restaurants and sightseeing.

SAILING➢ Whale watching and yachting in northern California are the specialties of **Adventure Sailing International** (3020 Bridgeway, Suite 271, Sausalito, CA 94965, ☎ 415/381–9503 or 800/762–6287).

ORGANIZATIONS

The **National Tour Association** (546 E. Main St., Lexington, KY 40508, ☎ 606/226–4444 or 800/682–8886) and **United States Tour Operators Association** (USTOA, 211 E. 51st St., Suite 12B, New York, NY 10022, ☎ 212/750–7371) can provide lists of member operators and information on booking tours.

PUBLICATIONS

Consult the brochure **"Worldwide Tour & Vacation Package Finder"** from the National Tour Association (*see above*) and the Better Business Bureau's **"Tips on Travel Packages"** (publication No. 24-195, $2; 4200 Wilson Blvd., Arlington, VA 22203).

TRAVEL AGENCIES

For names of reputable agencies in your area, contact the **American Society of Travel Agents** (1101 King St., Suite 200, Alexandria, VA 22314, ☎ 703/739–2782).

V

VISITOR INFORMATION

Contact the **San Francisco Convention and Visitors Bureau** (201 3rd St., Suite 900, 94103, ☎ 415/974–6900). The attractive 80-page *San Francisco Book* ($2; from the SFCVB at Box 6977, 94101) includes up-to-date information on theater offerings, art exhibits, sporting events, and other special events.

The **Redwood Empire Association Visitor Information Center** (The Cannery, 2801 Leavenworth St., 2nd Floor, 94133, ☎ 415/543–8334) covers San Francisco and surrounding areas, including the Wine Country, the redwood groves, and northwestern California. For $3 they will send *The Redwood Empire Visitor's Guide*; or pick it up at their office for free. For the

Silicon Valley area, contact the visitor information center in **Santa Clara** (1515 El Camino Real, Box 387, Santa Clara 95050, ☏ 408/283–8833).

In addition, there are chambers of commerce in dozens of San Francisco Bay Area towns, including **Berkeley** (1834 University Ave., Box 210, Berkeley 94703, ☏ 510/549–7040), and convention and visitors bureaus in **Oakland** (1000 Broadway, Suite 200, Oakland 94607, ☏ 510/839–9000 or 800/262–5526), **San Jose** (333 W. San Carlos St., Suite 1000, San Jose 95110, ☏ 408/295–9600 or 800/726–5673), and **Santa Clara** (2200 Laurelwood Rd., Santa Clara 95054, ☏ 408/970–9825).

The **California Division of Tourism** (801 K St., Suite 1600, Sacramento 95814, ☏ 916/322–1397) can answer many questions about travel in the state. You can also order a travel package including the magazine-size *Golden California* guidebook, accommodations guide, and state map (free; ☏ 800/862–2543).

IN THE U.K.

In the United Kingdom, also contact the **United States Travel and Tourism Administration** (Box 1EN, London W1A 1EN, ☏ 0171/495–4466). For a free USA pack, write the USTTA at Box 170, Ashford, Kent TN24 0ZX). Enclose stamps worth £1.50.

W

WEATHER

For current conditions and forecasts, plus the local time and helpful travel tips, call the **Weather Channel Connection** (☏ 900/932–8437; 95¢ per minute) from a touch-tone phone.

SMART TRAVEL TIPS A TO Z

Basic Information on Traveling in San Francisco and Savvy Tips to Make Your Trip a Breeze

The more you travel, the more you know about how to make trips run like clockwork. To help make your travels hassle-free, Fodor's editors have rounded up dozens of tips from our contributors and travel experts all over the world, as well as basic information on visiting San Francisco. For names of organizations to contact and publications that can give you more information, *see* Important Contacts A to Z, *above.*

A

AIR TRAVEL

If time is an issue, **always look for nonstop flights,** which require no change of plane and make no stops. If possible, **avoid connecting flights,** which stop at least once and can involve a change of plane, although the flight number remains the same; if the first leg is late, the second waits.

CUTTING COSTS

The Sunday travel section of most newspapers is a good source of deals.

MAJOR AIRLINES➢ The least-expensive airfares from the major airlines are priced for round-trip travel and are subject to restrictions. You must usually **book in advance and buy the ticket within 24 hours** to get cheaper fares, and you may have to **stay over a Saturday night.** The lowest fare is subject to availability, and only a small percentage of the plane's total seats are sold at that price. It's good to **call a number of airlines—and when you are quoted a good price, book it on the spot**—the same fare on the same flight may not be available the next day. Airlines generally allow you to change your return date for a $25 to $50 fee, but most low-fare tickets are nonrefundable. However, if you don't use it, you can apply the cost toward the purchase price of a new ticket, again for a small charge.

CONSOLIDATORS➢ Consolidators, who buy tickets at reduced rates from scheduled airlines, sell them at prices below the lowest available from the airlines directly—usually without advance restrictions. Sometimes you can even get your money back if you need to return the ticket. Carefully read the fine print detailing penalties for changes and cancellations. If you doubt the reliability of a consolidator, **confirm your reservation with the airline.**

ALOFT

AIRLINE FOOD➢ If you hate airline food, **ask for special meals when booking.** These can be vegetarian, low cholesterol, or kosher, for example; commonly prepared to order in smaller quantities than standard catered fare, they can be tastier.

JET LAG➢ To avoid this syndrome, which occurs when travel disrupts your body's natural cycles, try to maintain a normal routine. At night, **get some sleep.** By day, move about the cabin to **stretch your legs, eat light meals, and drink water—not alcohol.**

SMOKING➢ Smoking is banned on all flights within the United States of less than six hours' duration and on all Canadian flights; the ban also applies to domestic segments of international flights aboard U.S. and foreign carriers. Delta has banned smoking system-wide.

B

BUS TRAVEL

WITHIN SAN FRANCISCO

The San Francisco Municipal Railway System, or Muni, includes buses and trolleys, surface streetcars, and the new below-surface streetcars, as well as cable cars. There is 24-hour service, and the fare is $1 for adults, 35¢ for senior citizens and children 5–17. The exact fare is always required; dollar bills or change are accepted. Eighty-cent tokens can be purchased (in rolls of 10, 20, or 40) to reduce the cost of transferring; otherwise you must pay $1 each time you board a bus or light-rail vehicle.

A $6 pass good for unlimited travel all day on all routes can be purchased from ticket machines at cable-car terminals and at the Visitor Information Center in Hallidie Plaza (Powell and Market Sts.).

C

CABLE CARS

Cable cars are popular, crowded, and an experience to ride: Move toward one quickly as it pauses, wedge yourself into any available space, and hold on! The sensation of moving up and down some of San Francisco's steepest hills in a small, open-air, clanging conveyance is not to be missed.

The fare (for one direction) is $2 for adults and children. Exact change is preferred, but operators will make change. There are self-service ticket machines (which do make change) at a few major stops and at all the terminals. The one exception is the busy cable car terminal at Powell and Market streets; purchase tickets at the kiosk there. Be wary of street people attempting to "help" you buy a ticket.

The Powell-Mason line (No. 59) and the Powell-Hyde line (No. 60) begin at Powell and Market streets near Union Square and terminate at Fisherman's Wharf. The California Street line (No. 61) runs east and west from Market Street near the Embarcadero to Van Ness Avenue.

CAMERAS, CAMCORDERS, AND COMPUTERS

LAPTOPS

Before you depart, **check your portable computer's battery** because you may be asked at security to turn on the computer to prove that it is what it appears to be. At the airport, you may prefer to **request a manual inspection,** although security X-rays do not harm hard-disk or floppy-disk storage.

PHOTOGRAPHY

If your camera is new or if you haven't used it for a while, **shoot and develop a few rolls of film** before you leave. Always **store film in a cool, dry place**—never in the car's glove compartment or on the shelf under the rear window.

Every pass through an X-ray machine increases film's chance of clouding. To protect it, carry it in a clear plastic bag and **ask for hand inspection at security.** Such requests are virtually always honored at U.S. airports. Don't depend on a lead-lined bag to protect film in checked luggage—the airline may increase the radiation to see what's inside.

VIDEO

Before your trip, **test your camcorder, invest in a skylight filter to protect the lens, and charge the batteries.** (Airport security personnel may ask you to turn on the camcorder to prove that it's what it appears to be.)

Videotape is not damaged by X-rays, but it may be harmed by the magnetic field of a walk-through metal detector, so **ask that videotapes be hand-checked.**

CHILDREN AND TRAVEL

BABY-SITTING

For recommended local sitters, **check with your hotel desk.**

DRIVING

If you are renting a car, **arrange for a car seat when you reserve.** Sometimes they're free.

FLYING

On domestic flights, children under two not occupying a seat travel free, and older children currently travel on the "lowest applicable" adult fare.

BAGGAGE➢ In general, the adult baggage allowance applies for children paying half or more of the adult fare.

SAFETY SEATS➢ According to the FAA, it's a good idea to **use safety seats aloft.** Airline policy varies. U.S. carriers allow FAA-approved models, but airlines usually require that you buy a ticket, even if your child would otherwise ride free, because the seats must be strapped into regular passenger seats.

FACILITIES➢ When making your reservation, **ask for children's meals or a freestanding bassinets** if you need them; the latter are available only to those with seats at the bulkhead, where there's enough legroom. If you don't need the bassinet, **think twice before requesting bulkhead seats**—the only storage for in-flight necessities is in the inconveniently distant overhead bins.

LODGING

Most hotels allow children under a certain age to stay in their parents' room at no extra charge, while others charge them as extra adults; be sure to **ask about the cut-off age.**

CUSTOMS AND DUTIES

IN SAN FRANCISCO

Visitors aged 21 or over may import the following into the United States: 200 cigarettes or 50 cigars or 2 kilograms of tobacco; 1 U.S. liter of alcohol; gifts to the value of $100. Restricted items include meat products, seeds, plants, and fruits. Never carry illegal drugs.

BACK HOME

IN CANADA➢ Once per calendar year, when you've been out of Canada for at least seven days, you may bring in C$300 worth of goods duty-free. If you've been away less than seven days but more than 48 hours, the duty-free exemption drops to C$100 but can be claimed any number of times (as can a C$20 duty-free exemption for absences of 24 hours or more). You cannot combine the yearly and 48-hour exemptions, use the C$300 exemption only partially (to save the balance for a later trip), or pool exemptions with family members. Goods claimed under the C$300 exemption may follow you by mail; those claimed under the lesser exemptions must accompany you.

Alcohol and tobacco products may be included in the yearly and 48-hour exemptions but not in the 24-hour exemption. If you meet the age requirements of the province through which you reenter Canada, you may bring in, duty-free, 1.14 liters (40 imperial ounces) of wine or liquor *or* 24 12-ounce cans or bottles of beer or ale. If you are 16 or older, you may bring in, duty-free, 200 cigarettes, 50 cigars or cigarillos, and 400 tobacco sticks or 400 grams of manufactured tobacco. Alcohol and tobacco must accompany you on your return.

An unlimited number of gifts valued up to C$60 each may be mailed to Canada duty-free. These do not count as part of your exemption. Label the package "Unsolicited Gift—Value under $60." Alcohol and tobacco are excluded.

IN THE U.K.➢ From countries outside the EU, including the United States, you may import duty-free 200 cigarettes, 100 cigarillos, 50 cigars or 250 grams of tobacco; 1 liter of spirits or 2 liters of fortified or sparkling wine; 2 liters of still table wine; 60 milliliters of perfume; 250 milliliters of toilet water; plus £136 worth of other goods, including gifts and souvenirs.

D

FOR TRAVELERS WITH DISABILITIES

California is a national leader in making attractions and facilities accessible to travelers with disabilities. Since 1982, the state building code has required that all construction for public use include access for people with disabilities. State laws more than a decade old provide special privileges, such as license plates allowing special parking spaces, unlimited parking in time-limited spaces, and free parking in metered spaces. Identification from states other than California is honored.

When discussing accessibility with an operator or reservationist, **ask hard questions.** Are there any stairs, inside *or* out? Are there grab bars next to the toilet *and* in the shower/tub? How wide is the doorway to the room? To the bathroom? For the most extensive facilities, meeting the latest legal specifications, **opt for newer facilities,** which more often have been designed with access in mind. Older properties or ships must usually be retrofitted and may offer more limited facilities as a result. Be sure to **discuss your needs before booking.**

PARKS

The National Park Service provides a Golden Access Passport for all national parks free of charge to those who are medically blind or have a permanent disability; the passport covers the entry fee for the holder and anyone accompanying the holder in the same private vehicle as well as a 50% discount on camping and various other user fees. Apply for the passport in person at a national recreation facility that charges an entrance fee; proof of disability is required.

DISCOUNT CLUBS

Travel clubs offer members unsold space on airplanes, cruise ships, and package tours at as much as 50% below regular prices. Membership may include a regular bulletin or access to a toll-free hot line giving details of available trips departing from three or four days to several months in the future. Most also offer 50% discounts off hotel rack rates. Before booking with a club, **make sure the hotel or other supplier isn't offering a better deal.**

DRIVING

Route I–80 finishes its westward journey from New York's George Washington Bridge at the Bay Bridge, which links Oakland and San Francisco. U.S. 101, running north–south through the entire state, enters the city across the Golden Gate Bridge and continues south down the peninsula, along the west side of the bay.

WITHIN SAN FRANCISCO

Driving in San Francisco can be a challenge because of the hills, the one-way streets, and the traffic. Take it easy, remember to curb your wheels when parking on hills, and use public transportation whenever possible. This is a great city for walking and a terrible city for parking. On certain streets, parking is forbidden during rush hours. Look for the warning signs; illegally parked cars are towed. Downtown parking lots are often full and always expensive. Finding a spot in North Beach at night, for instance, may be impossible.

I

INSURANCE

Travel insurance can protect your investment, replace your luggage and its contents, or provide for medical coverage should you fall ill during your trip. Most tour operators, travel agents, and insurance agents sell specialized health-and-accident, flight, trip-cancellation, and luggage insurance as well as comprehensive policies with some or all of these features. Before you make any purchase, **review your existing health and homeowner policies** to find out whether they cover expenses incurred while traveling.

BAGGAGE

Airline liability for your baggage is limited to $1,250 per person on domestic flights. On international flights, the airlines' liability is $9.07 per pound or $20 per kilogram for checked baggage (roughly $640 per 70-pound bag) and $400 per passenger for unchecked baggage. However, this excludes valuable items such as jewelry and cameras that are listed in your ticket's fine print. You can buy additional insurance from the airline at check-in, but first **see if your homeowner's policy covers lost luggage.**

FLIGHT

You should **think twice before buying flight insurance.** Often purchased as a last-minute impulse at the airport, it pays a lump sum when a plane crashes, either to a beneficiary if the insured dies or sometimes to a surviving passenger who loses eyesight or a limb. Supplementing the airlines' coverage described in the limits-of-liability paragraphs on your ticket, it's expensive and basically unnecessary. Charging an airline ticket to a major credit card often automatically entitles you to coverage and may also embrace travel by bus, train, and ship.

FOR U.K. TRAVELERS➢ According to the Association of British Insurers, a trade association representing 450 insurance companies, it's wise to **buy extra medical coverage when you visit the United States.**

You can buy an annual travel-insurance policy valid for most vacations during the year in which it's purchased. If you go this route, make sure it covers you if you have a preexisting medical condition or are pregnant.

TRIP

Without insurance, you will lose all or most of your money if you must cancel your trip due to illness or any other reason. Especially if your airline ticket, cruise, or package tour is nonrefundable and cannot be changed, it's essential that you **buy trip-cancellation-and-interruption insurance.** When considering how much coverage you need, look for a policy that will cover the cost of your trip plus the nondiscounted price of a one-way airline ticket should you need to return home early. Read the fine print carefully, especially sections defining "family member" and "preexisting medical conditions." Also **consider default or bankruptcy insurance,** which protects you against a supplier's failure to deliver. However, such policies often do not cover default by a travel agency, tour operator, airline, or cruise line if you bought your tour and the coverage directly from the firm in question.

L

LODGING

APARTMENT AND VILLA RENTALS

If you want a home base that's roomy enough for a family and comes with cooking facilities, **consider a furnished rental.** It's generally cost-wise, too, although not always—some rentals are luxury properties (economical only when your party is large). Home-exchange directories do list rentals—often second homes owned by prospective house swappers—and some services search for a house or apartment for you (even a castle if that's your fancy) and handle the paperwork. Some send an illustrated catalogue and others send photographs of specific properties, sometimes at a charge; up-front registration fees may apply.

HOME EXCHANGE

If you would like to find a house, an apartment, or other vacation property to exchange for your own while on vacation, **become a member of a home-exchange organization,** which will send you its annual directories listing available exchanges and will include your own listing in at least one of them. Arrangements for the actual exchange are made by the two parties to it, not by the organization.

M

MONEY MATTERS

ATMS

Chances are that you can **use your bank card at ATMs** to withdraw money from an account and get cash advances on a credit-card account if your card has been programmed with a personal identification number, or PIN. Before leaving home, **check in on frequency limits** for withdrawals and cash advances. Also **ask whether your card's PIN must be reprogrammed** for use in San Francisco.

On cash advances you are charged interest from the day you receive the money from ATMs as well as from tellers. Transaction fees for ATM withdrawals outside your home turf may be higher than for withdrawals at home.

TRAVELER'S CHECKS

Whether or not to buy traveler's checks depends on where you are headed; **take cash to rural areas and small towns, traveler's checks to cities.** The most widely recognized are American Express, Citicorp, Thomas Cook, and Visa, which are sold by major commercial banks for 1% to 3% of the checks' face value—it pays to **shop around.** Both American Express and Thomas Cook issue checks that can be countersigned and used by you or your traveling companion. Record the numbers of the checks, cross them off as you spend them, and keep this information separate from your checks.

WIRING MONEY

You don't have to be a cardholder to send or receive funds through MoneyGram[SM] from American Express. Just go to a MoneyGram agent, located in retail and convenience stores and in American Express Travel Offices. Pay up to $1,000 with cash or a credit card, anything over that in cash. The money can be picked up within 10 minutes in cash or check at the nearest MoneyGram agent. There's no limit, and the recipient need only present photo identification. The cost, which includes a free long-distance phone call, runs from 3% to 10%, depending on the amount sent, the destination, and how you pay.

You can also send money using Western Union. Money sent from the United States or Canada will be available for pickup at agent locations in 100 countries within 15 minutes. Once the money is in the system, it can be picked up at any one of 25,000 locations. Fees range from 4% to 10%, depending on the amount you send.

P

PACKAGES AND TOURS

A package or tour to San Francisco can make your vacation less expensive and more convenient. Firms that sell tours and packages purchase airline seats, hotel rooms, and rental cars in bulk and pass some of the savings on to you. In addition, the best operators have local representatives to help you out at your destination.

A GOOD DEAL?

The more your package or tour includes, the better you can predict the ultimate cost of your vacation. Make sure you know exactly what is included, and **beware of hidden costs.** Are taxes, tips, and service charges included? Transfers and baggage handling? Entertainment and excursions? These can add up.

Most packages and tours are rated deluxe, first-class superior, first class, tourist, and budget. The key difference is usually accommodations. If the package or tour you are considering is priced lower than in your wildest dreams, **be skeptical.** Also, **make sure your travel agent knows the hotels** and other services. Ask about location, room size, beds, and whether it has a pool, room service, or programs for children, if you care about these. Has your agent been there or sent others you can contact?

BUYER BEWARE

Each year consumers are stranded or lose their money when operators go out of business—even very large ones with excellent reputations. If you can't afford a loss, take the time to **check out the operator**—find out how long the company has been in business, and ask several agents about its reputation. Next, **don't book unless the firm has a consumer-protection program.** Members of the United States Tour Operators Association and the National Tour Association are required to set aside funds exclusively to cover your payments and travel arrangements in case of default. Nonmember operators may instead carry insurance; look for the details in the operator's brochure—and the name of an underwriter with a solid reputation. Note: When it comes to tour operators, **don't trust escrow accounts.** Although there are laws governing those of charter-flight operators, no governmental body prevents tour operators from raiding the till.

Next, **contact your local Better Business Bureau and the attorney general's office** in both your own state and the operator's; have any complaints been filed? Last, **pay with a major credit card.** Then you can cancel payment, provided that you can document your complaint. Always **consider trip-cancellation insurance** (*see* Insurance, *above*).

BIG VS. SMALL➢ An operator that handles several hundred thousand travelers annually can use its purchasing power to give you a good price. Its high volume may also indicate financial stability. But some small companies provide more personalized service; because they tend to specialize, they may also be experts on an area.

USING AN AGENT

Travel agents are an excellent resource. In fact, large operators accept bookings only through travel agents. But it's good to **collect brochures from several agencies,** because some agents' suggestions may be skewed by promotional relationships with tour and package firms that reward them for volume sales. If you have a special interest, **find an agent with expertise in that area;** the American Society of Travel Agents can give you leads in the United States. (Don't rely solely on your agent, though; agents may be unaware of small niche operators, and some special-interest travel companies only sell direct.)

SINGLE TRAVELERS

Prices are usually quoted per person, based on two sharing a room. If traveling solo, you may be required to pay the full double occupancy rate. Some operators eliminate this surcharge if you agree to be matched up with a roommate of the same sex, even if one is not found by departure time.

PACKING FOR SAN FRANCISCO

When packing for a vacation in the San Francisco Bay Area, prepare for temperature variations. An hour's drive can take you up or down many degrees, and the variation from daytime to nighttime in a single location is often marked. Take along sweaters, jackets, and clothes for layering as your best insurance for coping with variations in temperature. Include shorts or cool cottons for summer, and always tuck in a bathing suit, since most lodgings include a pool. Bear in mind, though, that the city can be chilly at any time of the year, especially in summer, when the fog is apt to descend and stay.

Although casual dressing is a hallmark of the California lifestyle, men will need a jacket and tie for many good restaurants in the evening, and women will be more comfortable in something dressier than regulation sightseeing garb.

Bring an extra pair of eyeglasses or contact lenses in your carry-on luggage, and if you have a health problem, **pack enough medication** to last the trip. In case your bags go astray, **don't put prescription drugs or valuables in luggage to be checked.**

LUGGAGE

Free airline baggage allowances depend on the airline, the route, and the class of your ticket; ask in advance. In general, on domestic flights you are entitled to check two bags—neither exceeding 62 inches, or 158 centimeters (length + width + height), or weighing more than 70 pounds (32 kilograms). A third piece may be brought aboard; its total dimensions are generally limited to less than 45 inches (114 centimeters), so it will fit easily under the seat in front of you or in the overhead compartment. In the United States, the Federal Aviation Administration gives airlines broad latitude to limit carry-on allowances and tailor them to different aircraft and operational conditions. Charges for excess, oversize, or overweight pieces vary.

SAFEGUARDING YOUR LUGGAGE➢ Before leaving home, **itemize your bags' contents** and their worth, and label them with your name, address, and phone number. (If you use your home address, cover it so that potential thieves can't see it.) Inside your bag, **pack a copy of your itinerary.** At check-in, **make sure that your bag is correctly tagged** with the airport's three-letter destination code. If your bags arrive damaged or not at all, file a written report with the airline before leaving the airport.

PASSPORTS AND VISAS

CANADIANS

No passport is necessary to enter the United States.

U.K. CITIZENS

British citizens need a valid passport. If you are staying fewer than 90 days and traveling on a vacation, with a return or onward ticket, you will probably not need a visa. However, you will need to fill out the Visa Waiver Form, 1-94W, supplied by the airline.

While traveling, **keep one photocopy of the data page** separate from your wallet and leave another copy with someone at home. If you lose your passport, promptly call the nearest embassy or consulate, and the local police; having the data page can speed replacement.

R

RAIL TRAVEL

The Bay Area Rapid Transit sends air-conditioned aluminum trains at speeds of up to 80 miles an hour under the bay to Oakland, Berkeley, Concord, Richmond, and Fremont, with extensions expected to open this year southeast to Castro Valley and Dublin. Trains also travel south from San Francisco as far as Daly City. Wall maps in the stations list destinations and fares (90¢–$3.45). Trains run Monday–Saturday 6 AM–midnight, Sunday 9 AM–midnight.

A $3 excursion ticket buys a three-county tour. You can visit any of the 34 stations for up to four hours as long as you exit and enter at the same station.

RENTING A CAR

The best approach to renting a car in San Francisco is not to, at least for a day or two. First see how well suited the cable cars are to this city of hills, how well the Muni buses and streetcars get you around every neighborhood, how efficiently BART delivers you practically anywhere on the bay. Chances are that you won't want a car, unless you're preparing to take excursions into Marin County, the Wine Country, or Silicon Valley.

CUTTING COSTS

To get the best deal, **book through a travel agent and shop around.** When pricing cars, **ask where the rental lot is located.** Some off-airport locations offer lower rates—even though their lots are only minutes away from the terminal via complimentary shuttle. You may also want to **price local car-rental companies,** whose rates may be lower still, although service and maintenance standards may not be up to those of a national firm. Also **ask your travel agent about a company's customer-service record.** How has it responded to late plane arrivals and vehicle mishaps? Are there often lines at the rental counter, and, if you're traveling during a holiday period, does a confirmed reservation guarantee you a car?

INSURANCE

When you drive a rented car, you are generally responsible for any damage or personal injury that you cause as well as damage to the vehicle. Before you rent, **see what coverage you already have** by means of your personal auto-insurance policy and credit cards. For about $14 a day, rental companies sell insurance, known as a collision damage waiver (CDW), that eliminates your liability for damage to the car; it's always optional and should never be automatically added to your bill. California, New York, and Illinois have outlawed the sale of CDW altogether.

SURCHARGES

Before picking up the car in one city and leaving it in another, **ask about drop-off charges or one-way service fees,** which can be substantial. Note, too, that some rental agencies charge extra if you return the car before the time specified on your contract. To avoid a hefty refueling fee, **fill the tank just before you turn in the car.**

FOR U.K. CITIZENS

In the United States you must be 21 to rent a car; rates may be higher for those under 25. Extra costs cover child seats, compulsory for children under five (about $3 per day), and additional drivers (about $1.50 per day). To pick up your reserved car you will need the reservation voucher, a passport, a U.K. driver's license, and a travel policy covering each driver.

S

SENIOR-CITIZEN DISCOUNTS

To qualify for age-related discounts, **mention your senior-citizen status up front** when booking hotel reservations, not when checking out, and before you're seated in restaurants, not when paying your bill. Note that discounts may be limited to certain menus, days, or hours. When renting a car, **ask about promotional car-rental discounts**—they can net lower costs than your senior-citizen discount.

SIGHTSEEING

Golden Gate Tours (☎ 415/788–5775) uses both vans and buses for its 3½-hour city tour, offered mornings and afternoons. You can combine the tour with a bay cruise. Customers are picked up at hotels and motels. Senior-citizen and group rates are available. Cost: $25 adults, $20.50 senior citizens, $12 children under 12. Tours daily. Make reservations the day before. Cruise combo: $30 adults, $28 senior citizens, $15 children under 12.

Gray Line (☎ 415/558–9400) offers a variety of tours of the city, the Bay Area, and northern California. The city tour, on buses or double-decker buses, lasts 3½ hours and departs from the Transbay Terminal at 1st and Mission streets five to six times daily. Gray Line also picks up at centrally located hotels. Cost: $26 adults, $13 children. Tours daily. Make reservations the day before.

Gray Line-Cable Car Tours sends motorized cable cars on a one-hour loop from Union Square to Fisherman's Wharf and two-hour tours including the Presidio, Japantown, and the Golden Gate Bridge. Cost: $15 and $22 adults, $7.50 and $11 children. No reservations necessary.

The **Great Pacific Tour** (☎ 415/626–4499) uses 13-passenger vans for its daily 3½-hour city tour. Bilingual guides may be requested. They pick up at major San Francisco hotels. Tours are available to Monterey, the Wine Country, and Muir Woods. Cost: $27 adults, $25 senior citizens, $20 children 5–11. Tours daily. Make reservations the day before, or, possibly, the same day.

Tower Tours (☎ 415/434–8687) uses 20-passenger vans for city tours and 25-passenger buses for trips outside San Francisco to Muir Woods and Sausalito, the Wine Country, Monterey and Carmel, and Yosemite. The city tour runs 3½ hours. The Wine Country tour includes the historic Sonoma town square. Cost: $25 adults, $12 children. Tours daily. Make reservations the day before.

SPECIAL-INTEREST TOURS

Near Escapes (Box 193005-K, San Francisco 94119, ☎ 415/386–8687) plans unusual activities in the city and around the Bay Area. Recent tours and activities included tours of a Hindu temple in the East Bay, the Lawrence Berkeley Laboratory, the aircraft maintenance facility at the San Francisco Airport, and the quicksilver mines south of San Jose. Send $1 and a self-addressed, stamped envelope for a schedule for the month you plan to visit San Francisco.

WALKING TOURS

Castro District. Trevor Hailey (☎ 415/550–8110) leads a 3½-hour tour focusing on the history and development of the city's gay and lesbian community, including restored Victorian homes, shops and cafés, and the NAMES Project, home of the AIDS memorial quilt. Tours depart at 10 AM Tuesday–Saturday from Castro and Market streets. Cost: $30, including brunch.

Chinatown with the "Wok Wiz." Cookbook author Shirley Fong-Torres leads a 3½-hour tour of Chinese markets, other businesses, and a fortune-cookie factory (☎ 415/355–9657). Cost: $35, including lunch; $25 without lunch. Shorter tours start at $15.

Chinese Cultural Heritage Foundation (☎ 415/986–1822) offers two walking tours of Chinatown. The Heritage Walk leaves Saturday at 2 PM and lasts about two hours. The Culinary Walk, a three-hour stroll through the markets and food shops, plus a dim sum lunch, is held every Wednesday at 10:30 AM. Heritage Walk: $12 adults, $2 children under 12. Culinary Walk: $25 adults, $10 children under 12.

City Guides (☎ 415/557–4266), a free service sponsored by Friends of the Library, offers the greatest variety of walks, seven days a week. They include Chinatown, North Beach, Coit Tower, Pacific Heights mansions, Japantown, the Haight-Ashbury, historic Market Street, the Palace Hotel, and downtown roof gardens and atriums. Schedules are available at the San Francisco Visitors Center at Powell and

Market streets and at library branches.

SMOKING

The trend in California is toward more NO SMOKING signs. Expect to see them in many places.

Most hotels and motels have no-smoking rooms; in larger establishments entire floors are reserved for nonsmokers. Most bed-and-breakfast inns do not allow smoking on the premises.

Most San Francisco restaurants do not permit smoking at all, except in adjacent bar or lounge areas. Many cities and towns in California have ordinances requiring areas for nonsmokers in restaurants and many other public places.

STUDENTS ON THE ROAD

To save money, **look into deals available through student-oriented travel agencies.** To qualify, you'll need to have a bona fide student I.D. card. Members of international student groups also are eligible. *See* Students *in* Important Contacts A to Z, *above.*

T

TAXIS

Rates are high in the city, although most rides are relatively short. It is almost impossible to hail a passing cab, especially on weekends. Either phone or use the nearest hotel taxi stand to grab a cab.

TELEPHONES

LONG-DISTANCE

The long-distance services of AT&T, MCI, and Sprint make calling home relatively convenient and let you avoid hotel surcharges; typically, you dial an 800 number.

W

WHEN TO GO

Any time is the right time to go to San Francisco, where the year-round climate feels Mediterranean and moderate—albeit with a foggy, sometimes chilly twist. As Mark Twain said, "The coldest winter I ever spent was a summer in San Francisco." It is true that summers can be damp and foggy. Still, the temperature rarely drops lower than 40° at any time of the year, and anything warmer than 80° is considered a heat wave.

North, east, and south of the city, summers are warmer. Shirtsleeves and thin cottons are usually fine for the Wine Country.

Be prepared for rain in winter, especially December and January. Winds off the ocean can add to the chill factor, so pack warm clothing.

What follows are the average daily maximum and minimum temperatures for San Francisco.

Climate in San Francisco

Jan.	55F	13C	May	66F	19C	Sept.	73F	23C
	41	-5		48	-9		51	11
Feb.	59F	15C	June	69F	21C	Oct.	69F	21C
	42	-6		51	11		50	10
Mar.	60F	16C	July	69F	21C	Nov.	64F	18C
	44	-7		51	11		44	-7
Apr.	62F	17C	Aug.	69F	21C	Dec.	57F	14C
	46	-8		53	12		42	-6

1 Destination: San Francisco

SPLENDOR IN THE FOG

THAT VISITORS WILL ENVY San Franciscans is a given—so say Bay Area residents, who tend to pity anyone who did not have the fortune to settle here. (There's probably never been a time when the majority of the population was native born.) Their self-satisfaction may surprise some, considering how the city has been battered by fires and earthquakes from the 1840s onward, most notably in the 1906 conflagration and in 1989, when the Loma Prieta earthquake rocked its foundations once more. Since its earliest days, San Francisco has been a phoenix, the mythical bird that periodically dies in flame to be reborn in greater grandeur.

Its latest rebirth has occurred in SoMa, the neighborhood south of Market Street, where the Yerba Buena Gardens development has been introduced with the world-class SFMOMA (Museum of Modern Art) at its heart—transforming a formerly seedy neighborhood into a magnet of culture. As a peninsula city, surrounded on three sides by water, San Francisco grows from the inside out; its dysfunctional areas are improved, not abandoned. The museum development's instant success—measured by a huge influx of residents, suburban commuters, and international visitors—perfectly exemplifies a long tradition of starting from scratch to rebuild and improve.

In its first life, San Francisco was little more than a small, well-situated settlement. Founded by Spaniards in 1776, it was prized for its natural harbor, so commodious that "all the navies of the world might fit inside it," as one visitor wrote. Around 1849, the discovery of gold at John Sutter's sawmill in the nearby Sierra foothills transformed the sleepy little settlement into a city of 30,000. Millions of dollars' worth of gold was panned and blasted out of the hills as a "western Wall Street" sprang up. Fueled by the 1859 discovery of a fabulously rich vein of silver in Virginia City, Nevada, the population soared to 342,000. In 1869 the transcontinental railway was completed, linking the once-isolated western capital to the east; San Francisco had become a major city of the United States.

The boom was not without its prices; the hardships of immigrant railroad workers led to a strong tradition of feisty labor unions. Contentiousness is still part of the price San Francisco pays for variety. Consider, as an indicator, the makeup of the city's chief administrative body, the 11-member Board of Supervisors: Past boards have included a healthy mix of Chinese, Hispanics, gays, blacks, and women. The city is a bastion of what it likes to refer to as "progressive" politics. The Sierra Club, founded here in 1892 by its first president, John Muir, has its national headquarters on Polk Street. The turn-of-the-century "yellow journalism" of William Randolph Hearst's *San Francisco Examiner* gave way to leftish publications such as *Mother Jones* magazine and today's daily newspapers. Political bitterness has sometimes led to violence, most spectacularly with the "Bloody Thursday" face-off between striking longshoremen and scab labor in 1934, and in the 1978 assassinations of the city's liberal mayor, George Moscone, and its first gay supervisor, Harvey Milk, by a vindictive right-wing ex-supervisor. (On a more eccentric note, San Francisco is also the city where, in 1974, the Symbionese Liberation Army and its most famous victim/inductee, Patty Hearst, held up the Sunset District branch of the Hibernia Bank.) But, despite a boomtown tendency toward raucousness, and a sad history of anti-Asian discrimination, the city today prides itself on its tolerance. The mix, everybody knows, is what makes San Francisco. On any given night at the Opera House—a major civic crossroads—you can see costumes ranging from torn denim and full leather to business suits, dinner jackets, and sequined, feathered gowns—expensive originals gracing society dowagers and the occasional goodwill-store find on a well-dressed drag queen.

Loose, tolerant, and even licentious are words that are used to describe San Francisco; bohemian communities thrive here. As early as the 1860s, the "Barbary Coast"—a collection of taverns, whorehouses, and gambling joints along Pacific Avenue close to the waterfront—was famous, or infamous. North Beach, the city's Little Italy, became the home of the Beat Movement in the 1950s. (Herb Caen, the city's best-known columnist, coined the term "beatnik.") Lawrence Ferlinghetti's City Lights, a bookstore and publishing house, which still stands on Columbus Avenue, brought out, among other titles, Allen Ginsberg's *Howl* and *Kaddish*. Across Broadway, a plaque identifies the Condor as the site of the nation's first topless and bottomless performances, a monument to a slightly later era. In the '60s, the Free Speech Movement began at the University of California in Berkeley, and Stanford's David Harris, who went to prison for defying the draft, numbered among the nation's most famous student leaders. In October 1965, Allen Ginsberg introduced the term "flower power," and the Haight-Ashbury district became synonymous with hippiedom, giving rise to such legendary bands as the Jefferson Airplane, Big Brother and the Holding Company (fronted by Janis Joplin), and the Grateful Dead. Thirty years later, the Haight's history and its name still draw neo-hippies, as well as New Wavers with black lips and blue hair, and some rather menacing skinheads. Transients who now sleep in nearby Golden Gate Park make panhandling one of Haight Street's major business activities, and the potential for crime and violence after dark has turned many of the liberal residents into unlikely law-and-order advocates, organizing neighborhood patrols to watch for trouble. Still, most remain committed to keeping the Haight the Haight.

SOUTHWEST OF THE HAIGHT is the onetime Irish neighborhood known as the Castro, which during the 1970s became identified with gay and lesbian liberation. Castro Street is dominated by the elaborate Castro Theatre, a 1922 vision in Spanish Baroque, which presents first-run art and independent films with occasional revivals of Hollywood film classics. (The grand old pipe organ still plays during intermissions, breaking into "San Francisco" just before the feature begins.) There's been much talk, most of it exaggerated, about how AIDS has chastened and "matured" the Castro. One thing it has done is to spawn the creation of AIDS education, treatment, and caregiving networks, such as Shanti and Open Hand, that are models for the rest of the nation. The Castro is still an effervescent neighborhood, and—as housing everywhere has become more and more scarce—an increasingly mixed one. At the same time, gays, like Asians, are moving out of the ghetto and into neighborhoods all around the city.

In terms of both geography and culture, San Francisco is about as close as you can get to Asia in the continental United States. (The city prides itself on its role as a Pacific Rim capital, and overseas investment has become a vital part of its financial life.) The first great wave of Chinese immigrants came as railroad laborers. Chinese workers quickly became the target of race hatred and discriminatory laws; Chinatown—which began when the Chinese moved into old buildings that white businesses seeking more fashionable locations had abandoned—developed, as much as anything else, as a refuge. Chinatown is still a fascinating place to wander, and it's a good bet for late-night food, but it's not the whole story by any means. The Asian community, which now accounts for a fifth of San Francisco's population, reaches into every San Francisco neighborhood, and particularly into the Sunset and Richmond districts, west toward the ocean. Clement Street, which runs through the center of the Richmond District, has become the main thoroughfare of a second Chinatown. Southeast Asian immigrants, many of them ethnic Chinese, are transforming the seedy Tenderloin into a thriving Little Indochina. There was heavy Japanese immigration earlier in this century, but most of it went to southern California, where organized labor had less of a foothold and where there were greater opportunities for Asian workers. Still, San Francisco has its Japantown, with the Japan Center complex including a handful of shops and restaurants. In the past, Asians tended toward a backseat—or at least an offstage—role in the city's politics; but like so much else on the city's cultural/political landscape, that, too, has changed. Asian Americans are now at the highest levels of the city's elected and appointed government.

Geographically, San Francisco is the thumbnail on a 40-mile thumb of land, the San Francisco Peninsula, which stretches northward between the Pacific Ocean and San Francisco Bay. Hemmed in on three sides by water, the land area (less than 50 square miles) is relatively small; the population, at about three-quarters of a million, is small, too. Technically speaking, it's only California's fourth-largest city, behind Los Angeles, San Diego, and nearby San Jose. But that statistic is misleading: The Bay Area, which stretches from the bedroom communities north of Oakland and Berkeley south through Silicon Valley (the cluster of Peninsula cities that have become the center of America's computer industry) and San Jose, is really one continuous megacity, with San Francisco as its heart—its hub.

NOT SO MANY CENTURIES ago the area that was to become San Francisco was a windswept, virtually treeless, and, above all, sandy wasteland. Sand even covered the hills. The sand is still there, but—except along the ocean—it's well hidden. City Hall is built on 80 feet of it. The westerly section of the city—the Sunset and Richmond districts and Golden Gate Park—seems flat only because sand has filled in the contours of the hills.

But the hills that remain are spectacular. They provide vistas all over the city—nothing is more common than to find yourself staring out toward Angel Island or Alcatraz, or across the bay at Berkeley and Oakland. They also explain why the cable cars became a necessity early on. The city's two bridges, which are almost as majestic as their surroundings, had their 50th birthdays in 1986 and 1987. The Golden Gate Bridge, which crosses to Marin County, got a bigger party, but the San Francisco–Oakland Bay Bridge got a better present: a necklace of lights along its spans. They were supposed to be temporary, but the locals were so taken with the glimmer that bridge boosters started a drive to make them permanent; radio DJs and newspaper columnists put out daily appeals, drivers gave extra quarters to the toll takers, various corporations put up shares, and—close to a million dollars later—the lights on the Bay Bridge now shine nightly.

First-time visitors to San Francisco sometimes arrive with ideas about its weather gleaned from movie images of sunny California or from a misinformed 1967 song that celebrated "a warm San Franciscan night." Sunny, perhaps; warm—not likely. That's *southern* California. (A perennially popular T-shirt quotes Mark Twain's alleged remark: "The coldest winter I ever spent was a summer in San Francisco.") Still, it almost never freezes here, and heat waves are equally rare. Most San Franciscans come to love the climate, which is genuinely temperate—sufficiently welcoming for the imposing row of palms down the median of Dolores Street but seldom warm enough for just a T-shirt at night. The coastal stretch of ocean may look inviting, but the surfers you sometimes see along Ocean Beach are wearing wet suits. (The beach, though, can be fine for sunning.) And, of course, there's the famous fog—something that tourists tend to find more delightful than do the residents. It's largely a summer phenomenon; San Francisco's real summer begins in September, when the fog lifts and the air warms up for a while. November brings on the rains.

Victorian architecture is as integral to the city as fog and the cable cars. Bay-windowed, ornately decorated Victorian houses—the multicolor, ahistorical paint jobs that have become popular make them seem even more ornate—are the city's most distinguishing architectural feature. They date mainly from the latter part of Queen Victoria's reign, 1870 to the turn of the century. In those three decades, San Francisco more than doubled in population (from 150,000 to 342,000); the transcontinental railway, linking the once-isolated western capital to the east, had been completed in 1869. That may explain the exuberant confidence of the architecture.

Over the years, plenty of the Victorians have gone under the wrecker's ball to make way for such commercial projects as shopping complexes, or for the low-income housing projects that went under the rubric of "urban renewal" but quickly degenerated into slums. The decrepit old houses were out of favor for a while, but once the era of gentrification arrived, those that were left standing were snatched up, fixed up, and sold at exorbitant prices. Parts of the city that not so long ago were considered ghettos are becoming expensive places to live.

But higher prices in no way deter the hordes from flocking to the City by the Bay. In addition to a skyrocketing population, visitors keep coming for events throughout the year. The Gay and Lesbian Freedom Day Parade, each June, vies with the Chinese New Year Parade, in February, as the city's most elaborate. They both get competition from Japantown's Cherry Blossom Festival, in April; the Columbus Day and St. Patrick's Day parades; Carnaval in the Hispanic Mission District, in May; and the May Day march, a labor celebration in a labor town. The mix of ethnic, economic, social, and sexual groups can be bewildering, but the city's residents—whatever their origin—face it with aplomb and even gratitude. Everybody in San Francisco has an opinion about where to get the best burrito or the hottest Szechuan eggplant or the strongest cappuccino, and even the most staid citizens have learned how to appreciate good camp. Nearly everyone smiles on the fortunate day they arrived on, or were born on, this windy, foggy patch of peninsula.

WHAT'S WHERE

The Neighborhoods

THE CASTRO/NOE VALLEY➢ The vintage Castro Theater is the main draw in the gay-friendly Castro, where a mixed crowd lives among Victorian houses, alternative shops, and a handful of cafés. South of the Castro, the heart of Noe Valley is 24th Street, which teems with ethnic restaurants, bakeries, and sidewalk activity.

CHINATOWN➢ Buddhist temples, Chinese restaurants, ginseng and root stores, and throngs of people coexist in this crowded, ever-expanding miniature city. With Grant Avenue as the heart of the gastronomical and retail activity, the neighborhood stretches from Bush Street to Broadway.

CIVIC CENTER➢ Once the center of San Francisco's cultural life, the Civic Center is still home to the War Memorial Opera House, the Louise M. Davies Symphony Hall, a brand new public library, and the City Hall (closed until 1998 for earthquake repairs). Dignified and imposing, this area is relatively quiet by day.

THE FINANCIAL DISTRICT AND JACKSON SQUARE➢ The Wall Street of San Francisco, dominated by the towering Bank of America and Transamerica buildings, is within walking distance of Chinatown, the Embarcadero, Nob Hill, and Union Square. Its closest neighbor is Jackson Square, a tiny, tony district of antiques stores housed in former town houses.

GOLDEN GATE PARK➢ Here, 1,000 acres of grassy fields, trees, lakes, and ponds surround such attractions as the De Young Memorial Museum, the California Academy of Sciences, Strybing Arboretum, and a Japanese tea garden. Springtime brings a brilliant profusion of cherry blossoms and rhododendrons.

HAIGHT-ASHBURY➢ Twenty years after its era of flower power, the Haight has become a peculiar mix. Haight Street itself is a shopping strip known for its vintage clothing and record stores, while the once-funky Victorians that housed the communes have been purchased and restored by wealthy yuppies.

JAPANTOWN➢ Centered around the 5-acre Japan Center complex, Japantown consists mainly of stores and restaurants. The other attraction is its modern, multiscreen Kabuki Cinema.

LINCOLN PARK AND THE WESTERN SHORELINE➢ This wild, windswept stretch of shoreline is dotted with landmarks: the Cliff House (originally built in 1863), the ruins of the Sutro Baths, and the San Francisco Zoo. The elegant Palace of the Legion of Honor stands as the pinnacle of Lincoln Park, surrounded by cypress-lined walking trails and an 18-hole golf course.

THE MARINA AND THE PRESIDIO➢ Known for its waterfront homes with views of the Golden Gate Bridge, and for its circa-1915 Palace of Fine Arts, the Marina comprises the northernmost part of San Francisco. The Presidio, with its 1,500 acres of hills, woods, and former army barracks, was recently declared national park land, after having been used as a military base for more than 100 years.

THE MISSION DISTRICT➢ Though people call it San Francisco's Latino neighborhood, the Mission is actually a mix of ethnic cultures and alternative movements. The main attractions are the Mission Dolores, the outdoor murals (explained at the Precita Eyes Mural Arts Center), the Galeria de la Raza (a gallery of Hispanic art), and a slew of inexpensive eateries.

NOB HILL AND RUSSIAN HILL➢ On Nob Hill, the very exclusive Pacific Union Club, the Gothic Grace Cathedral, and the landmark Fairmont Hotel stand as beacons of old San Francisco. Adjacent Russian Hill is full of small parks, historic houses, quiet lanes, and stairways with spectacular views of the bay.

NORTH BEACH AND TELEGRAPH HILL➢ With its mix of Italian cafés and beatnik landmarks, North Beach evokes a mood of distant places and long-ago eras. The smell of garlic wafts in the streets, which are lined with pint-size antiquarian shops; and Coit Tower rises, beaconlike, from the top of Telegraph Hill.

THE NORTHERN WATERFRONT➢ Fisherman's Wharf and Pier 39 aren't the only draws along this stretch of piers, whose bay-side views draw masses of tourists. Here you'll also find Ghirardelli Square, the Cannery, and Fort Mason, which is known for its ethnic museums, Greens restaurant, and the Magic Theater.

SOUTH OF MARKET AND THE EMBARCADERO➢ The San Francisco Museum of Modern Art and the Center for the Arts at Yerba Buena Gardens have transformed the once-seedy area called SoMa into one of San Francisco's most important and highly-visited areas. Nearby attractions are the Center for the Arts, Moscone Center, and several noteworthy art galleries. Along the waterfront boulevard known as the Embarcadero are Embarcadero Center—a huge complex of offices, shops, and a Hyatt Hotel—and the Ferry Building, with its landmark clock tower.

UNION SQUARE➢ In many ways the heart of San Francisco, classy Union Square attracts countless visitors with its fine department stores, its hotels, and its proximity to the theater district. It's also the headquarters of the San Francisco Convention and Visitor Bureau and the starting point of two of the city's three cable-car lines.

Excursions

THE EAST BAY➢ Across the Bay Bridge, Berkeley is a university town whose liberal, bohemian spirit persists from its glory days as the center of the magical, mythical '60s. Next door is Oakland, a largely industrial city with scattered attractions such as Lake Merritt and Jack London Square, with its harbor-side shops and restaurants.

MARIN COUNTY➢ North of the Golden Gate Bridge lies some of the most desirable real estate in all of California. Beyond Sausalito and Tiburon—both villagelike towns famous for their bay views, the outdoors attractions abound: The Marin Headlands, Muir Woods, Mt. Tamalpais, and Point Reyes offer a virtually limitless choice of hiking trails and outstanding natural beauty.

THE SOUTH BAY➢ With its yellow hills and adobe architecture, the San Francisco Peninsula—now home to Stanford University—recalls the days of the Spanish missions. Nearby, the sprawling community of Silicon Valley, best known as the birthplace of computer microchips, is home to Paramount's Great America amusement park, as well as a surprising number of museums, missions, and wineries.

THE WINE COUNTRY➢ Its hilly landscapes redolent of the ripe smells and rich colors of vines, the Napa Valley is the undisputed capital of wine production in the United States. First-class wineries, outstanding restaurants, spas, and elegant lodgings make the valley and surrounding towns a top tourist destination.

PLEASURES & PASTIMES

The Bay and Its Bridges

The sight of a suit-clad stockbroker unloading a windsurfer from his Jeep Cherokee is not uncommon in San Francisco, where the Bay perpetually beckons to pleasure seekers of every stripe. On sunny weekends the Bay teems with sailboats, and when the surf's up, daredevils in wetsuits line the beaches. For those not inclined to get wet, the Bay offers ferries, tour boats, and dinner cruises that give participants a fish's-eye view of all three bridges—the Golden Gate, the Richmond, and the Bay; as well as Angel Island, Treasure Island, and the legendary Alcatraz.

The Fog

If you've never seen fog before, you might wonder about the white shroud of mist that rolls down from the Marin Headlands each summer morning, often obliterating all but the tops of the towers of the Golden Gate Bridge, and evaporating by noon. To native San Franciscans, summer fog is a part of life, as dependable as the sunrise. It's part of what makes San Francisco feel like a living, breathing city exposed to the whims of nature.

Hidden Lanes and Stairways

Though it does have its share of major boulevards, San Francisco is a city of small side streets—many one-way only; hidden lanes; and out-of-the-way stairways. Whether you're in Chinatown, Nob Hill, North Beach, Pacific Heights, Potrero Hill, or Russian Hill, there's always a quiet lane or stairway nearby, where a stray cat might join you for some quiet contemplation. A few of the most scenic hidden corners are in Nob Hill, Russian Hill, and North Beach—but if you look carefully, you'll find them where they're least expected.

The Hills

Anyone who's afraid of heights would do well to stay away from San Francisco, where almost everything worth getting to lies at the top of or just beyond a steep hill. Driving the city streets often feels like riding a roller coaster, where your stomach catches up to the rest of you at the base of each extreme dip. But for all the challenges they present to drivers and walkers alike, the hills are what give San Francisco its distinctly European look and its dazzling bay views, as well as its beloved cable cars and its landmark hilltop hotels and monuments. It's a city of hills: Nob Hill, Russian Hill, Telegraph Hill, Potrero Hill, the smaller hills within neighborhoods, and the larger hills across the bay.

Patches of Green

With its hills and fresh air, its myriad parks and waterfront promenades, San Francisco is a mecca for physical-fitness enthusiasts who can't stand to sweat indoors. Golden Gate Park, with its 1,000 acres of trails and fields, is deservedly popular, but the choices don't end there. The Presidio, a former military base, offers 2,500 acres of hilly, wooded trails interspersed with old army barracks. The Marina, which stretches from the Presidio to the Northern Waterfront, is the turf of choice for a stylishly outfitted crowd of runners and rollerbladers. Along the western shore, there's the 275-acre Lincoln Park; the 6-mile loop around Lake Merced; and the Great Highway, a 3-mile ocean-side stretch with a paved jogging path. Across the bay, Muir Woods and the Marin Headlands beckon to nature lovers from around the world.

Wining and Dining

Europhiles who bemoan the lack of a sophisticated food and wine culture in America will feel at home in San Francisco, where the coupling of fresh, seasonal food and locally produced wine is a way of life. As the birthplace of nouvelle cuisine—cooking that combines fresh, locally grown ingredients in visually stunning ways; and as the next-door neighbor of Napa Valley, the city has been attracting notable chefs—Alice Waters, Bradley Ogden, Jeremiah Towers, to name just a few—for years.

FODOR'S CHOICE

No two people will agree on what makes a perfect vacation, but it's fun and helpful to know what others think. We hope you'll have a chance to experience some of Fodor's Choices yourself while visiting San Francisco. For more information about each entry, refer to the appropriate chapters within this guidebook.

Special Moments

★ From the **Crown Room,** atop the Fairmont Hotel, you can drink in a panoramic view of the city and its surroundings along with your martini.

★ A walk across the **Golden Gate Bridge** will give you an unforgettable view of all that the city offers: the bay, Alcatraz, Angel and Treasure islands, the Pacific Ocean crashing against the rocks, the city skyline—and to the north, the majestic Marin Headlands.

★ A ride on a **cable car** is the best way to appreciate the steepness of the city's hills and the quaintness of its past.

★ On the shores of the lagoon at the **Palace of Fine Arts,** you can feed the ducks and enjoy one of San Francisco's most historic landmarks.

★ Crossing the sky bridge in the atrium of the **Museum of Modern Art,** you'll appreciate the cutting-edge designs of architect Mario Botta.

★ A classic double feature at the **Castro Theater,** the grandest of San Francisco's few remaining movie palaces, is a good old-fashioned treat.

★ **City Lights** bookstore in North Beach is a treasure trove of books from San Francisco's beatnik era.

★ For a dose of team spirit, watch the Giants beat the Dodgers at **Candlestick Park,** where the wind howls and the crowd roars.

Memorable Sights

★ From a nighttime **ferry on the bay,** the city's lit bridges look like celestial creations.

★ Called "the crookedest street in the world," **Lombard Street**—with its winding brick paths and its well-tended flower beds—is worth the queue.

★ The **fog** rolling into the city over Twin Peaks is a mystical sight.

★ Crates of vegetables spilling out of **Chinatown**'s bustling markets make the neighborhood one of the city's most colorful.

★ Sea lions howling in the surf at the **Cliff House and at Pier 39** are fun to hear as well as to see.

Restaurants

★ The food is as inventive as the decor at Wolfgang Puck's three-level, palm-tree-lined **Postrio,** whose magical open kitchen keeps fans coming back for more. *$$$–$$$$*

★ Quietly elegant and ultrafashionable, **Aqua** is the place for the best and most-original seafood in town. *$$$*

★ With its magnificent landmark setting and its exciting, ever-changing menu, **Le Boulevard** is about the hottest ticket in town. *$$–$$$*

★ **Greens,** San Francisco's best-known vegetarian restaurant, delights the senses with its bay-side setting and its truly gourmet food. *$$*

★ Legions of regulars can't resist the northern Italian food and friendly atmosphere of **Pane e Vino,** the city's best neighborhood trattoria. *$$*

★ **Stars Cafe,** the new offshoot of Stars, has Stars's exciting location—next to the Opera Plaza, and its otherworldly cuisine—thanks to superchef Jeremiah Towers, at down-to-earth prices. *$–$$*

Hotels

★ **Sherman House,** a landmark mansion in Pacific Heights, is San Francisco's most luxurious small hotel. *$$$$*

★ Known for attentive service and its exceptional restaurant, the **Campton Place Hotel** is as tasteful as they come. *$$$*

★ One of San Francisco's original grand hotels, the gingerbread-style **Hotel Majestic** is romantic in an old-fashioned way. *$$$*

★ The ivy-covered, redbrick **Huntington Hotel** has a traditional British mood and a winningly understated style. *$$$*

★ The opulent lobby and elegant rooms at the **Ritz-Carlton, San Francisco** have earned it its rating as one of the top three hotels in the world. *$$$*

★ **The Phoenix Inn,** with its turquoise-and-coral decor and its Caribbean theme, has been called the city's "hippest hotel" by *People* magazine. *$$*

FESTIVALS AND SEASONAL EVENTS

WINTER

JAN.➢ The **Shrine East-West All-Star Football Classic** (1651 19th Ave., 94122, ☎ 415/661–0291), America's oldest all-star sports event, is played every year in the Stanford University Stadium in Palo Alto, some 25 miles south of San Francisco.

JAN.–APR.➢ Whale watching can be enjoyed throughout the winter, when hundreds of gray whales migrate along the Pacific coast. For information about viewing sites and special excursions, contact the California Office of Tourism (801 K St., Suite 1600, Sacramento 95814, ☎ 916/322–1397).

FEB.➢ The **Chinese New Year** celebration in San Francisco's Chinese community, North America's largest, lasts for two weeks, culminating with the justly famous Golden Dragon Parade and fireworks, "to scare away the evil spirits." For a complete schedule of events, send a stamped, self-addressed envelope to the Chinese Chamber of Commerce (730 Sacramento St., 94108, ☎ 415/982–3000).

SPRING

MAR.➢ On the Sunday closest to March 17, San Francisco's **St. Patrick's Day** celebration is marked by a long parade through the downtown area and by snake races.

APR.➢ The **Cherry Blossom Festival,** an elaborate presentation of Japanese culture and customs, winds up with a colorful parade through San Francisco's Japantown. A detailed schedule is available after mid-March; send a stamped, self-addressed envelope to Japan Center (1520 Webster St., 94115, ☎ 415/922–6776).

MAY➢ **Carnaval,** held in the city's Mission District in May or June, is a Mardi Gras–like revel that includes a parade, a street festival, and a costume contest in which participants indulge their fantasies through masquerade, music, and dance.

MAY–JUNE➢ May's ***San Francisco Examiner* Bay to Breakers Race** (Examiner Bay to Breakers, Box 7260, 94120, ☎ 415/777–7770) is a hallowed tradition for runners and nonrunners alike. Thousands sign up to run the 7½-mile route from bay side to ocean-side, many in costume, and crowds line the race course to cheer.

SUMMER

JUNE➢ **The Lesbian, Gay, Bisexual, and Transgendered Freedom Day Parade and Celebration**(☎ 415/864–3733), on the third or fourth Sunday in June, draws hundreds of thousands of participants and spectators.

JULY➢ The city's **Fourth of July** celebration, at Crissy Field in the Presidio, features family festivities beginning in mid-afternoon and a fireworks display at 9 PM.

JULY➢ The **Cable Car Bell-Ringing Championship** (☎ 415/923–6202) is held on the third Thursday of July at noon in Union Square.

AUTUMN

SEPT.➢ **Opera in the Park** (☎ 415/864–3330), an annual free event, takes place in Golden Gate Park on the Sunday after Labor Day.

SEPT.➢ The **San Francisco Blues Festival** (☎ 415/826–6837), on the Great Meadow at Fort Mason, is held on the third weekend of September.

OCT.➢ Beginning the second weekend of October, **Fleet Week** celebrates the Navy's first day with a Blue Angels air show over Pier 39 and the Bay.

OCT.➢ On the Sunday closest to Columbus Day, a weekend festival of Italian food and music kicks off the **Columbus Day** celebration (678 Green St., 94133, ☎ 415/434–1492), which also includes a parade through North Beach.

OCT.➢ The **Grand National Livestock Exposition, Rodeo, and Horse Show,** is held at an immense San Francisco facility appropriately named the Cow Palace (Box 34206, 94134, ☏ 415/469–6065); it's a world-class annual competition, with thousands of top livestock and horses.

DEC.➢ As the first American city to perform the full-length ***Nutcracker*** (☏ 415/703–9400), San Francisco remains one of the best places to see the well-known Christmas ballet.

DEC.➢ The annual **Sing-It-Yourself Messiah** (☏ 415/759–3401), another local tradition, takes place at Davies Symphony Hall on two nights during the first week of December.

DEC.➢ The **New Pickle Circus** (☏ 415/544–9344), a particularly joyous group that started out as a band of street performers during the early 1970s, performs annually during the holiday season at the Palace of Fine Arts Theater in the Marina District or at nearby Fort Mason.

2 Exploring San Francisco

By Toni Chapman

Updated by Dennis Harvey

"YOU COULD LIVE IN SAN FRANCISCO a month and ask no greater entertainment than walking through it," waxed Inez Hayes Irwin, the author of *The Californiacs,* an effusive 1921 homage to the state of California and the City by the Bay. Her claim remains as true as ever today: As in the '20s, touring on foot is the best way to experience this diverse metropolis.

San Francisco is a relatively small city, with just over 750,000 residents nested on a 46.6-square-mile tip of land between San Francisco Bay and the Pacific Ocean. San Franciscans cherish the city's colorful past, and many older buildings have been spared from demolition and nostalgically converted into modern offices and shops. Longtime locals rue the sites that got away—spectacular railroad and mining-boom-era residences lost in the '06 quake, the elegant Fox Theater, Playland at the Beach. But despite acts of God, the indifference of developers, and the mixed record of the city's Planning Commission, much of architectural and historical interest remains. Bernard Maybeck, Julia Morgan, Willis Polk, and Arthur Brown, Jr., are among the noted architects whose designs still grace the city's downtown and neighborhoods.

San Francisco's charms are great and small. First-time visitors won't want to miss Golden Gate Park, the Palace of Fine Arts, the Golden Gate Bridge, or a cable-car ride on Nob Hill. A walk down the Filbert Steps or through Macondray Lane, though, or a peaceful hour gazing east from Ina Coolbrith Park, can be equally inspiring.

It's no accident that the San Francisco Bay Area has been a center for the environmental movement. An awareness of geographical setting permeates life in San Francisco, where views of the surrounding mountains, ocean, and bay are ubiquitous. Much of the city's neighborhood vitality comes from the distinct borders provided by its hills and valleys, and many areas are so named: Nob Hill, Twin Peaks, Eureka Valley, the East Bay. San Francisco neighborhoods are self-aware, and they retain strong cultural, political, and ethnic identities. Locals know this pluralism is the real life of the city. Experiencing San Francisco means visiting the neighborhoods: the colorful Mission District, gay Castro, countercultural Haight Street, serene Pacific Heights, bustling Chinatown, and still-exotic North Beach.

Exploring involves navigating a maze of one-way streets and restricted parking zones. Public parking garages or lots tend to be expensive, as are hotel parking spaces. The famed 40-plus hills can be a problem for drivers who are new to the terrain. Cable cars, buses, and trolleys can take you to or near many of the area's attractions. Many of the following exploring tours include information on public transportation.

TOUR 1: UNION SQUARE

Numbers in the margin correspond to points of interest on the Downtown San Francisco: Tours 1–9 map.

★ Since 1850 **Union Square** has been the heart of San Francisco's downtown. Its name derives from a series of violent pro-Union demonstrations staged in this hilly area just prior to the Civil War. Union Square is where you will find the city's finest department stores and its most elegant boutiques. There are 40 hotels within a three-block walk of the square, and the downtown theater district is nearby.

The square itself is a 2.6-acre oasis planted with palms, boxwood, and seasonal flowers, and peopled with a kaleidoscope of characters: office workers sunning and brown-bagging, street musicians, several very vocal preachers, and the ever-increasing parade of panhandlers. Throughout the year, the square hosts numerous public events: fashion shows, free noontime concerts, ethnic celebrations, and noisy demonstrations. Auto and bus traffic is often gridlocked on the four streets bordering the square. Post, Stockton, and Geary are one-way, while Powell runs in both directions until it crosses Geary, where it then becomes one-way to Market Street. Union Square covers a convenient but costly four-story underground garage. Close to 3,000 cars use it on busy holiday shopping and strolling days.

1 Any visitor's first stop should be the **San Francisco Visitors Information Center** (☎ 415/391–2000) on the lower level of Hallidie Plaza at Powell and Market streets. It is open daily (except holidays), and the multilingual staff will answer specific questions as well as provide maps, brochures, and information on daily events. Visitors can pick up coupons for substantial savings on tourist attractions, as well as pamphlets (and, depending on the season, discount vouchers) for most of the downtown hotels. The office provides 24-hour recorded information (☎ 415/391–2001).

2 The **cable-car terminus** at Powell and Market streets is the starting point for two of the three operating lines. The Powell-Mason line climbs up Nob Hill, then winds through North Beach to Fisherman's Wharf. The Powell-Hyde car also crosses Nob Hill, but then continues up Russian Hill and down Hyde Street to Victorian Park across from the Buena Vista Cafe and near Ghirardelli Square.

The cable-car system dates from 1873, when Andrew Hallidie demonstrated his first car on Clay Street; in 1964 the tramlike vehicles were designated national historic landmarks. Before 1900, 600 cable cars spanned a network of 100 miles. Today there are 39 cars in the three lines, and the network covers just 12 miles. Most of the cars date from the last century, although the cars and lines had a complete $58 million overhaul during the early 1980s. There are seats for about 30 passengers, with usually that number standing or straphanging. If possible, plan your cable-car ride for mid-morning or mid-afternoon during the week to avoid crowds. In summertime there are often long lines to board any of the three systems. Buy your ticket ($2, good in one direction) at nearby hotels or at the police/information booth near the turnaround. (*See* Getting Around *in* The Gold Guide.)

Note that the array of panhandlers, street preachers, and other regulars at this terminus can be daunting. A pleasant alternative is to stand in line instead at the Hyde Street end of the Powell-Hyde line, which affords views of the bay and Golden Gate Bridge. (*See* Tour 10, *below.*) Better yet, if it's just the experience of riding a cable car you're after (rather than a trip to the wharf or Nob Hill), try boarding the less-busy California line at Van Ness Avenue and ride it down to the Hyatt Regency. (*See* Tour 7, *below.*)

A two-block stroll, heading north of the cable-car terminus along
3 bustling Powell Street, leads to **Union Square** itself. At center stage, the Victory Monument by Robert Ingersoll Aitken commemorates Commodore George Dewey's victory over the Spanish fleet at Manila in 1898. The 97-foot Corinthian column, topped by a bronze figure symbolizing naval conquest, was dedicated by Theodore Roosevelt in 1903 and withstood the 1906 earthquake.

Exploring San Francisco *(Boxes Refer To Detail Maps)*

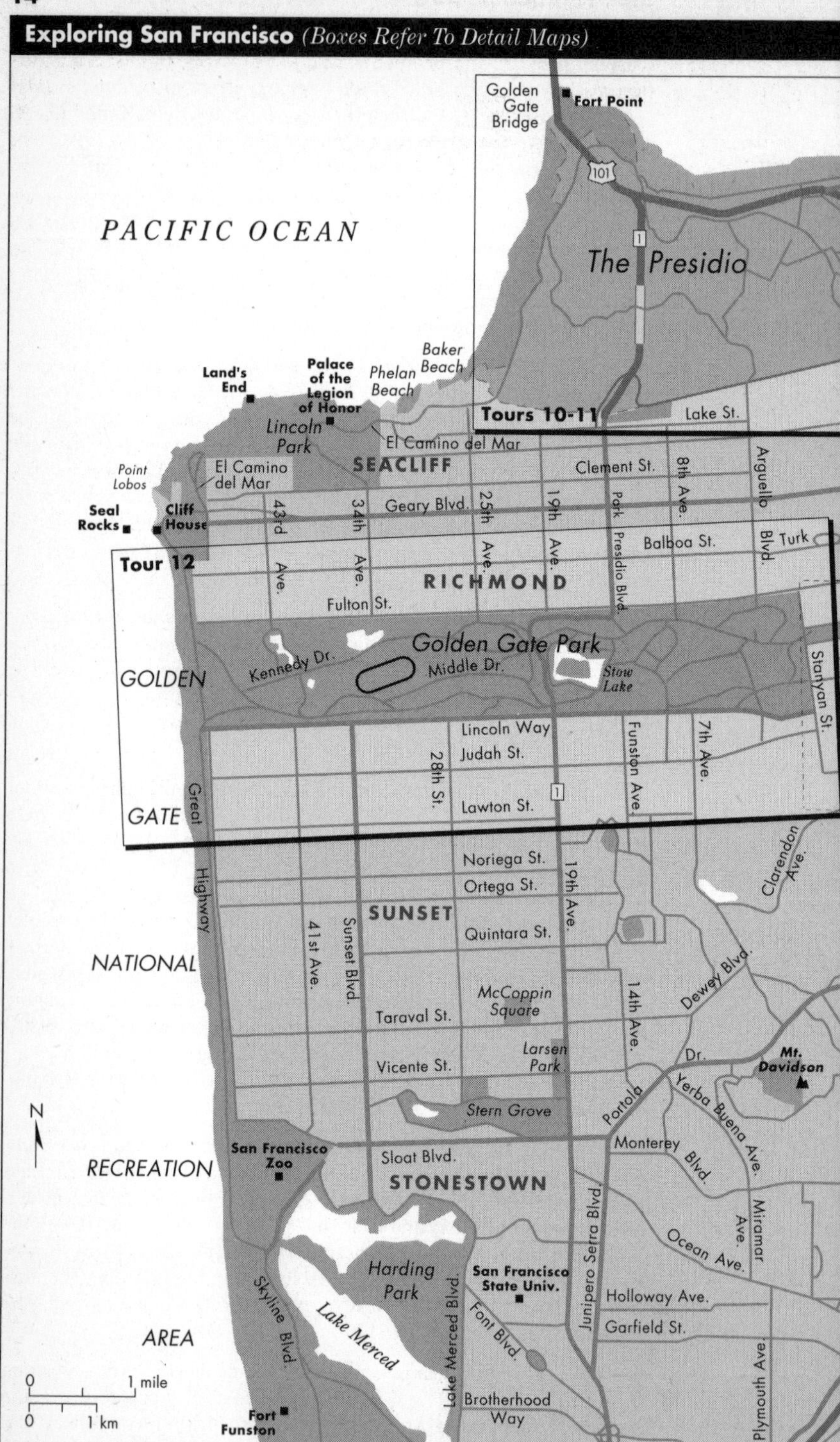

PACIFIC OCEAN
Golden Gate Bridge
Fort Point
101
The Presidio
Tours 10-11
Lake St.
Land's End
Palace of the Legion of Honor
Phelan Beach
Baker Beach
Lincoln Park
El Camino del Mar
SEACLIFF
Point Lobos
Seal Rocks
Cliff House
Clement St.
Geary Blvd.
Balboa St.
Turk
43rd Ave.
34th Ave.
25th Ave.
19th Ave.
Park Presidio Blvd.
8th Ave.
Arguello Blvd.
Tour 12
RICHMOND
Fulton St.
Golden Gate Park
Kennedy Dr.
Middle Dr.
Stow Lake
Stanyan St.
GOLDEN GATE
Lincoln Way
Judah St.
Lawton St.
28th St.
Funston Ave.
7th Ave.
Great Highway
Noriega St.
Ortega St.
Quintara St.
19th Ave.
Clarendon Ave.
SUNSET
41st Ave.
Sunset Blvd.
McCoppin Square
Taraval St.
Vicente St.
Larsen Park
14th Ave.
Dewey Blvd.
Mt. Davidson
Portola Dr.
Yerba Buena Ave.
Stern Grove
NATIONAL RECREATION AREA
San Francisco Zoo
Sloat Blvd.
STONESTOWN
Monterey Blvd.
Junipero Serra Blvd.
Miramar Ave.
Ocean Ave.
Harding Park
Lake Merced
Skyline Blvd.
Lake Merced Blvd.
Font Blvd.
San Francisco State Univ.
Holloway Ave.
Garfield St.
Brotherhood Way
Plymouth Ave.
Fort Funston
0 1 mile
0 1 km
N

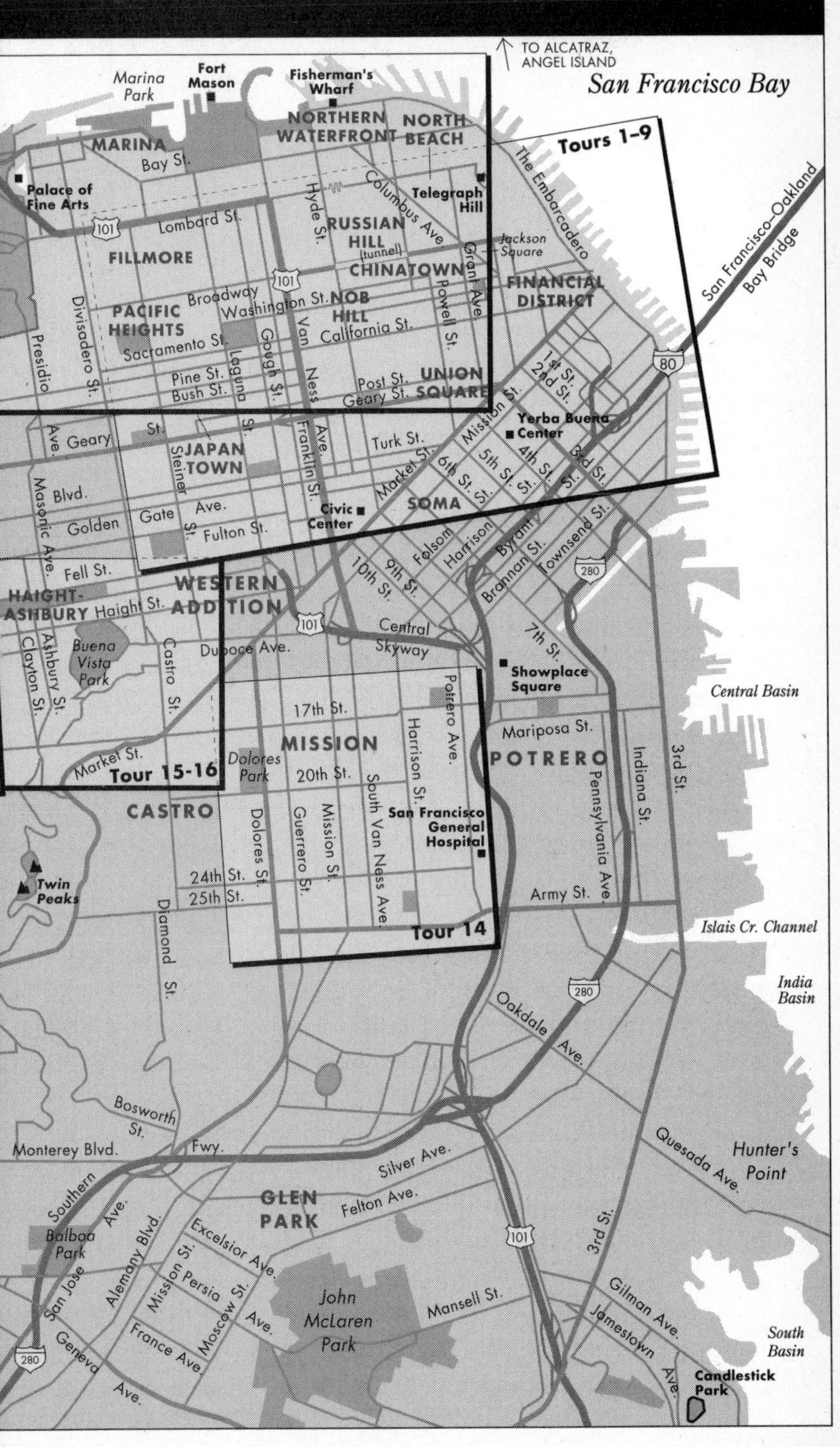
TO ALCATRAZ, ANGEL ISLAND
San Francisco Bay
Marina Park
Fort Mason
Fisherman's Wharf
NORTHERN WATERFRONT
NORTH BEACH
Tours 1–9
MARINA
Bay St.
Palace of Fine Arts
Telegraph Hill
The Embarcadero
Lombard St.
RUSSIAN HILL
(tunnel)
Hyde St.
Columbus Ave.
Jackson Square
FILLMORE
CHINATOWN
San Francisco–Oakland Bay Bridge
FINANCIAL DISTRICT
PACIFIC HEIGHTS
Broadway
Washington St.
NOB HILL
California St.
Sacramento St.
Divisadero St.
Presidio
Laguna
Gough St.
Van Ness Ave.
Powell St.
Grant Ave.
Pine St.
Bush St.
Post St.
Geary St.
UNION SQUARE
1st St.
2nd St.
Mission St.
Yerba Buena Center
Geary Blvd.
JAPAN TOWN
Steiner St.
Franklin St.
Turk St.
Market St.
6th St.
5th St.
4th St.
3rd St.
Masonic Ave.
Golden Gate Ave.
Fulton St.
Civic Center
SOMA
Folsom
Harrison
Bryant St.
Townsend St.
Brannan St.
Fell St.
10th St.
9th St.
WESTERN ADDITION
HAIGHT-ASHBURY
Haight St.
Central Skyway
Duboce Ave.
Buena Vista Park
Clayton St.
Ashbury St.
Castro St.
7th St.
Showplace Square
Potrero Ave.
17th St.
Central Basin
Mariposa St.
MISSION
Harrison St.
POTRERO
Indiana St.
3rd St.
Dolores Park
20th St.
Market St.
Tour 15-16
CASTRO
South Van Ness Ave.
San Francisco General Hospital
Pennsylvania Ave.
Dolores St.
Guerrero St.
Mission St.
Twin Peaks
24th St.
25th St.
Army St.
Diamond St.
Tour 14
Islais Cr. Channel
India Basin
Oakdale Ave.
Bosworth St.
Monterey Blvd.
Fwy.
Quesada Ave.
Hunter's Point
Silver Ave.
Southern
GLEN PARK
Felton Ave.
Balboa Park
Ave.
Alemany Blvd.
Excelsior Ave.
3rd St.
San Jose Ave.
Mission St.
Persia Ave.
Moscow St.
John McLaren Park
Mansell St.
Gilman Ave.
Jamestown Ave.
South Basin
Geneva Ave.
France Ave.
Candlestick Park
101
80
280

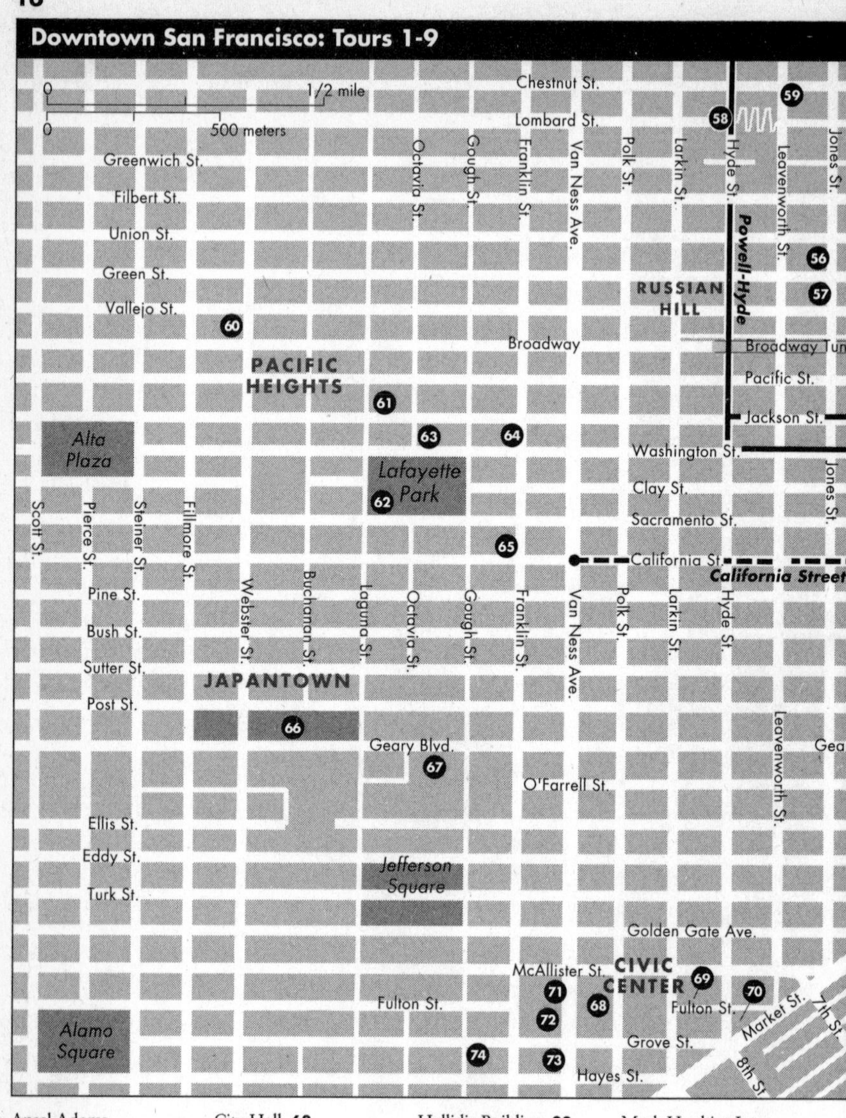

Ansel Adams Center, **17**
Bank of America, **27**
Buddha's Universal Church, **38**
Cable Car Museum, **54**
Cable-car terminus, **2**
Center for the Arts, **15**
Chinatown Gate, **31**
Chinese Cultural Center, **35**
Chinese Historical Society, **36**
Chinese Six Companies, **40**
City Hall, **68**
City Lights Bookstore, **45**
Coit Tower, **47**
Coleman House, **65**
Curran Theatre, **6**
Embarcadero Center, **19**
Fairmont Hotel, **51**
Ferry Building, **21**
Feusier House, **56**
450 Sutter Street, **11**
Geary Theatre, **5**
Grace Cathedral, **49**
Haas-Lilienthal House, **64**
Hallidie Building, **23**
Hammersmith Building, **10**
Hyatt Regency Hotel, **19**
Ina Coolbrith Park, **55**
Jackson Square, **30**
Japan Center, **66**
Justin Herman Plaza, **20**
Lafayette Park, **62**
Lombard Street, **58**
Louise M. Davies Symphony Hall, **73**
Macondray Lane, **57**
Maiden Lane, **9**
Mark Hopkins Inter-Continental Hotel, **52**
Masonic Auditorium, **50**
Mills Building and Tower, **24**
Moscone Convention Center, **13**
Old Chinese Telephone Exchange, **37**
Old St. Mary's Church, **32**
Pacific Stock Exchange, **26**
Pacific Union Club, **48**
Portsmouth Square, **34**

Rincon Center, **22**
Russ Building, **25**
Ruth Asawa's Fantasy Fountain, **8**
St. Francis of Assisi Church, **44**
St. Mary's Cathedral, **67**
St. Mary's Park, **33**
Sts. Peter and Paul, **43**
San Francisco Art Institute, **59**
San Francisco Marriott at Moscone Center, **16**
San Francisco Museum of Modern Art, **12**
San Francisco Performing Arts Library and Museum, **74**
San Francisco Public Library, **69**
San Francisco Visitors Information Center, **1**
Sheraton Palace Hotel, **18**
Spreckels Mansion, **63**
Stockton Street Tunnel, **41**
Stouffer Renaissance Stanford Court Hotel, **53**
Telegraph Hill, **46**
Tien Hou Temple, **39**
TIX Bay Area, **7**
Transamerica Pyramid, **29**
2222 Broadway, **60**
Union Square, **3**
United Nations Plaza, **70**
Veterans Building, **71**
War Memorial Opera House, **72**
Washington Square, **42**
Wells Fargo Bank History Museum, **28**
The Westin St. Francis Hotel, **4**
Whittier Mansion, **61**
Yerba Buena Gardens, **14**

After the earthquake and fire in 1906, the square was dubbed "Little St. Francis" because of the temporary shelter erected for residents of the St. Francis Hotel. Actor John Barrymore was among the guests pressed into volunteering to stack bricks in the square. His uncle, thespian John Drew, remarked, "It took an act of God to get John out of bed and the United States government to get him to work."

4 The **Westin St. Francis Hotel,** on the southwest corner of Post and Powell, was built in 1904 and was gutted by the 1906 disaster. The second-oldest hotel in the city was conceived by Charles Crocker and his associates as an elegant hostelry for their millionaire friends. Swift service and sumptuous surroundings were hallmarks of the property. A sybarite's dream, the hotel's Turkish baths had ocean water piped in. A new, larger, more luxurious residence was opened in 1907 to attract loyal clients from among the world's rich and powerful. The hotel has known its share of notoriety as well. Silent comedian Fatty Arbuckle's career plummeted faster than one of the St. Francis's glass-walled elevators after a wild 1921 party in one of the hotel's suites went awry. In 1975 Sara Jane Moore, standing among a crowd outside the hotel, attempted to shoot then-president Gerald Ford. As might be imagined, no plaques commemorate these events in the establishment's lobby. The ever-helpful staff will, however, gladly direct you to the traditional teatime ritual—or, if you prefer, to champagne and caviar—in the dramatic art deco Compass Rose lounge. Elaborate Chinese screens, secluded seating alcoves, and soothing background music make it an ideal time-out after frantic shopping or sightseeing.

Both the Geary and Curran theaters are a few blocks west on Geary
5 Street. The 1,038-seat **Geary** (415 Geary St., ☎ 415/749–2228), built in 1910, is home of the American Conservatory Theatre, one of North America's leading repertory companies (*see* Chapter 7, The Arts and Nightlife). The building's serious neoclassical design is lightened by the colorful, carved terra-cotta columns depicting a cornucopia of fruits. The theater was closed as a result of the October 1989 earthquake and, though the main box office remains open, current productions are being run at the Stage Door theater (420 Mason St.) and elsewhere until repairs are complete (at press time, the theater was expected to reopen
6 in January '96). The **Curran** (445 Geary St., ☎ 415/474–3800) is noted for showcasing traveling companies of Broadway shows. Farther up the street, and a must for film buffs, is the **Cinema Shop** (606 Geary St., ☎ 415/885–6785), a tiny storefront jammed with posters, stills, lobby cards, and rare videotapes of Hollywood classics and schlock films alike.

7 **TIX Bay Area** has a booth on the Stockton Street side of Union Square, opposite Maiden Lane. It provides half-price day-of-performance tickets (cash or traveler's checks only) to all types of performing-arts events, as well as regular full-price box-office services. Telephone reservations are not accepted for half-price tickets. Also available are $10 Golden Gate Park Cultural Passes, which provide admission to all of the park's museums at a discount rate. MUNI Passports (short-term tourist passes for all city buses and cable cars) are sold here as well. ☎ *415/433–7827.* ⏲ *Tues.–Thurs. 11–6, Fri. and Sat. 11–7.*

Just a dash up from TIX Bay Area, in front of the Grand Hyatt San
8 Francisco (345 Stockton St.), is sculptor **Ruth Asawa's fantasy fountain** honoring the city's hills, bridges, and unusual architecture, plus a wonder world of real and mythical creatures. Children and friends helped the artist shape the hundreds of tiny figures from baker's clay; these were assembled on 41 large panels from which molds were made

for the bronze casting. Asawa's distinctive designs decorate many public areas in the city. Her famous mermaid fountain is in Ghirardelli Square.

9 Directly across Stockton Street from TIX Bay Area is **Maiden Lane,** which runs from Stockton to Kearny streets. Known as Morton Street in the raffish Barbary Coast era, this red-light district reported at least one murder a week. The 1906 fire destroyed the brothels and the street emerged as Maiden Lane, now a chic and costly mall. As the two blocks are closed to vehicles from 11 AM until 5 PM, take-out snacks can be enjoyed under umbrella-shaded tables. During the annual spring festival, masses of daffodils, bright blossoms, and balloons bedeck the lane, and throngs of zany street musicians, arts-and-crafts vendors, and spectators give the street a carnival mood.

Note **140 Maiden Lane**: This handsome brick structure is the only Frank Lloyd Wright building in San Francisco. With its circular interior ramp and skylights, it is said to have been a model for the Guggenheim Museum in New York. It now houses the Circle Gallery, a showcase of contemporary artists. Be sure to examine the unique limited-edition art jewelry designed by internationally acclaimed Erté. ☎ *415/989–2100.* ⏲ *Mon.–Sat. 10–6, Sun. noon–5.*

Many of San Francisco's leading fine-arts galleries are around Union Square. Among them are **John Berggruen** (one of several establishments at 228 Grant Ave., ☎ 415/781–4629; open weekdays 9:30–5:30, Sat. 10:30–5) and **Meyerovich** (251 Post St., 4th Floor, ☎ 415/421–9997; open weekdays 10–5:30, Sat. 11–5). At 49 Geary Street are **Fraenkel** (☎ 415/981–2661; open Tues.–Fri. 10:30–5:30, Sat. 11–5) and **Robert Koch** (☎ 415/421–0122; open Tues.–Sat. 11–5:30), both of which showcase contemporary and historic photographs.

10 At 301 Sutter Street, on the corner of Grant Avenue, is the colorful **Hammersmith Building.** The small beaux arts structure, built in 1907, is noteworthy for its extensive use of glass and its playful design. Sutter Street is lined with prestigious art galleries, antiques dealers, smart hotels, and noted designer boutiques. Art deco aficionados will want to head one block up Sutter Street for a peek at the striking medical/dental of-
11 fice building at **450 Sutter Street.** Handsome Mayan-inspired designs cover both the exterior and interior surfaces of the 1930 terra-cotta skyscraper.

TOUR 2: SOUTH OF MARKET (SOMA) AND THE EMBARCADERO

The vast tract of downtown land **South of Market** Street along the waterfront and west to the Mission District is also known by the acronym SoMa (inspired by New York City's south-of-Houston SoHo). Formerly known as South of the Slot because of the cable-car slot that ran up Market Street, the area has a history of housing recent immigrants to the city—beginning with tents set up in 1848 by the gold-rush miners and continuing for decades. Except for a brief flowering of English-inspired elegance during the mid-19th century in the pockets of South Park and Rincon Hill, the area was reserved for newcomers who couldn't yet afford to move to another neighborhood. Industry took over most of the area when the big earthquake collapsed most of the homes into their quicksand bases.

For years the industrial South of Market area west of 4th Street was a stomping ground for alternative artists and the gay leather set. A dozen bars frequented by the latter group existed alongside warehouses, small factories, and art studios. In the wake of the AIDS crisis, most of the area's gay bars have given way to trendy straight bars. Although many artists moved away when urban renewal started in earnest, they still hang out in SoMa and show their work in several galleries on the cutting edge of San Francisco's art scene. Among them is **Capp Street Project** (525 2nd St., ☎ 415/495–7107).

12 The **San Francisco Museum of Modern Art** (SFMOMA) took center stage in the SoMa arts scene in January 1995, winning immediate international acclaim for its adventuresome programming, which includes traveling exhibits and film/video series. The strong permanent collection—including works by Matisse, Picasso, O'Keeffe, Frida Kahlo, Jackson Pollock, and Warhol—is now seen to much greater advantage than the old Civic Center building allowed. The striking Modernist structure, designed by Swiss architect Mario Botta, features a stepped-back, burnt-sienna brick facade and a central tower constructed of alternating bands of black and white stone. Inside, natural light from the tower floods the central atrium and some of the museum's galleries. A grand staircase leads from the atrium up to four floors of galleries. Accessible from the street, SFMOMA's café provides a comfortable, reasonably priced refuge for drinks and light meals. *151 3rd St., ☎ 415/357–4000. ☛ $7 adults, $3.50 senior citizens and students over 12; free 1st Tues. of each month. ⏲ Tues.–Sun. 11–6, Thurs. until 9 (1/2-price ☛ 5–9); closed major holidays.*

In the mid-1960s, the San Francisco Redevelopment Agency grabbed 87 acres of rundown downtown land, leveled anything that stood on them, and planned the largest building program in the city's history: **Yerba Buena Center.** The $1.5 billion project turned into something of a quagmire, proceeding in fits and starts throughout the 1970s and '80s. After more than two decades, it has finally taken shape, although parts of it are still under construction and still other portions aren't past the blueprint stage.

13 **Moscone Convention Center,** on Howard Street between 3rd and 4th streets, was the first major Yerba Buena Center building to be completed. The site of the 1984 Democratic convention, it is distinguished by a contemporary glass-and-girder lobby at street level (all exhibit space is underground) and a monolithic, column-free interior. In 1992 the center finished a $150 million expansion project that doubled its size and incorporated a new building with underground exhibit space, across Howard Street.

14 Above the new exhibit space is the **Yerba Buena Gardens** complex (in the block surrounded by 3rd, Mission, Howard, and 4th streets). A large expanse of green is surrounded by a circular walkway lined with benches and sculptures. A waterfall memorial to Martin Luther King, Jr., is the focal point of the gardens; above it are two restaurants and an overhead walkway that traverses Howard Street to Moscone Center's main entrance. Retail shopping spaces and a multiplex cinema on the western side of the block are scheduled for completion in 1996.
15 On the eastern side of the block is the **Center for the Arts** (701 Mission St., ☎ 415/978–2787), which showcases dance, music, performance, theater, visual arts, film, video, and installations—from the community-based to the international. The center includes two theaters, three visual-arts galleries, a film and video screening room, a gift shop, and an outdoor performance stage.

Diagonally across Mission Street from the Center for the Arts, you can't
16 miss the main entrance to the **San Francisco Marriott at Moscone Center** (4th and Mission Sts.). Its 40-story ziggurat construction topped with reflecting glass pinwheels elicited gasps from newspaper columnists and passersby alike, earning it comparisons with a jukebox, a high-rise parking meter, and a giant rectal thermometer. In contrast, a bit of history has been preserved next door: The brick, Gothic Revival **St. Patrick's Church** (756 Mission St.) was completed in 1872 and rebuilt after the 1906 earthquake and fire destroyed its interior.

17 Just across 4th Street from the Moscone Center is the **Ansel Adams Center,** which showcases historical and contemporary photography, as well as an extensive permanent collection of Adams's work. *250 4th St., ☎ 415/495–7000. ☛ $4 adults, $3 students, $2 ages 12–17 and senior citizens, free for children under 12. ⏲ Tues.–Sun. 11–5, 1st Thurs. of the month 11–8.*

One block north of SFMOMA on 3rd Street, at the traffic island where 3rd, Market, Kearny, and Geary streets come together, is **Lotta's Fountain.** This quirky monument, now largely unnoticed by local passersby, was a gift to the city from singer Lotta Crabtree, a Madonna prototype. Her "brash music-hall exploits" so enthralled San Francisco's early population of miners that they were known to shower her with gold nuggets and silver dollars after her performances. The buxom Ms. Crabtree is depicted in one of the Anton Refregier murals in Rincon Center (*see below*).

Heading east on Market Street toward the waterfront, the venerable
18 **Sheraton Palace Hotel** (at the corner of New Montgomery St., ☎ 415/392–8600) has resumed its place among San Francisco's grandest. Opened in 1875, the hotel has a storied past, some of which is recounted in small cases off the main lobby; President Warren Harding died here while still in office in 1923. The original Palace was destroyed by fire following the 1906 earthquake, despite a 28,000-gallon reservoir fed by four artesian wells. The current building dates from 1909; late-1980s renovations included the restoration of the glass-domed Garden Court restaurant and the installation of original mosaic-tile floors in Oriental-rug designs. Maxfield Parrish's wall-size painting, *The Pied Piper,* graces the hotel's Pied Piper Bar. The hotel offers interesting guided tours (☎ 415/546–5026; call a day or two in advance) Tuesday, Wednesday, and Saturday at 10:30 AM and Thursday at 2 PM.

Market Street, which bisects the city at an angle, has consistently challenged San Francisco's architects. One of the most intriguing responses sits diagonally across Market Street from the Palace. The tower of the **Hobart Building** (582 Market St.) combines a flat facade and oval sides, and is considered one of architect Willis Polk's best works in the city; walk south down 2nd Street (which runs right into the building) to get a full view of the tower. Farther east on Market Street between Sutter and Post is another classic solution, Charles Havens's triangular **Flatiron Building** (540–548 Market St.). Farther on, at **388 Market,** a sleek, modern building by Skidmore, Owings, and Merrill is another must-see.

Continue down Market Street's north side to Battery Street. Holding its own against the skyscrapers that tower over this intersection is the **Donahue Monument.** This homage to waterfront mechanics was designed by Douglas Tilden, a noted California sculptor who was deaf-mute. The plaque below it marks the spot as the location of the San Francisco Bay shoreline in 1848.

19 Dominating the Embarcadero is the **Hyatt Regency Hotel** (Embarcadero 5), part of the huge **Embarcadero Center** complex. The Hyatt, designed by John Portman, is noted for its spectacular lobby and 20-story hang-
20 ing garden. On the waterfront side of the hotel is **Justin Herman Plaza,** where arts-and-crafts shows, street musicians, and mimes perform on weekends year-round; it's also a popular place to fly kites. A huge concrete sculpture, the **Vaillancourt Fountain,** has had legions of critics since its installation in 1971: The fountain rarely works, and many feel it is an eyesore.

A three-tier pedestrian mall connects the eight buildings that comprise Embarcadero Center. Frequently called "Rockefeller Center West," the complex includes more than 100 shops, 40 restaurants, and two hotels, as well as office and residential space (*see* Chapter 3, Shopping). Louise Nevelson's dramatic 54-foot-high black-steel sculpture, *Sky Tree,* stands guard over Building 3. The Center has recently added two "virtual reality centers," an ice-skating rink, and a volleyball sandlot (both in season only) to its roster of diversions. Guided tours are given, and a five-screen cinema opened in mid-1995. For information on events, call 800/733–6318.

TIME OUT On sunny days, Justin Herman Plaza is a nice place to enjoy a snack from one of Embarcadero Center's dozen or so take-out shops. For something more substantial, **Splendido** (*see* Chapter 5, Dining) is a comfortable Mediterranean restaurant among the high-rises.

Due to the 1989 Loma Prieta earthquake, the Embarcadero freeway was torn down, making the foot of Market Street clearly visible for
21 the first time in 30 years. The trademark of the port is the quaint **Ferry Building** that stands at the Embarcadero. The clock tower is 230 feet high and was modeled by Arthur Page Brown after the campanile of Seville's cathedral. The four great clock faces on the tower, powered by the swinging of a 14-foot pendulum, stopped at 5:17 on the morning of April 18, 1906, and stayed that way for 12 months. The 1896 building survived the quake and is now the headquarters of the Port Commission and the World Trade Center. A waterfront promenade that extends from this point to the San Francisco–Oakland Bay Bridge is great for jogging, in-line skating, watching sailboats on the bay, or enjoying a picnic. Check out the beautiful pedestrian pier adjacent to Pier 1, with its old-fashioned lamps, wrought-iron benches, and awe-inspiring views of the bay. Ferries from behind the Ferry Building sail to Sausalito, Larkspur, and Tiburon.

South of the Ferry Building is the initial section of the 5-foot-wide, 2½-mile-long glass-and-concrete Promenade Ribbon, construction of which began in 1994. Billed by the city as the "longest art form in the nation," upon its completion in 1997 the artwork will span the waterfront from the base of Telegraph Hill to South Beach—a burgeoning complex of upscale town houses and restaurants.

Continuing down the promenade, notice the curiously styled Audiffred Building at the corner of Mission Street and the Embarcadero. It was built by a homesick gentleman as a reminder of his native France. A few doors down, an old brick YMCA building is now the Harbor Court Hotel. Cross the Embarcadero at Howard Street, and turn right on Steuart Street.

Across Steuart Street from the main entrance to the hotel is the new—
22 and old—**Rincon Center.** Two modern office/apartment towers overlook a small shopping and restaurant mall behind an old post office

built in the Streamline Moderne Style. A stunning five-story rain column draws immediate attention in the mall. In the "Historic Lobby" (which formerly housed the post office's walk-up windows) is a mural by Anton Refregier. One of the largest WPA-era art projects, its 27 panels depict California life, from the days when Indians were the state's sole inhabitants through World War I. Completion of this significant work was interrupted by World War II and political infighting; the latter led to some alteration in Refregier's "radical" historical interpretations. A permanent exhibit below the mural contains interesting photographs and artifacts of life in the Rincon area in the 1800s. Back in the mall, several new murals reflect San Francisco in the '90s—office workers at computers, sporting events, and the like.

Rincon Center represents the best aspects of the sometimes uneasy tension between preservationist forces and developers (and, in this case, the U.S. government). It took a fight to preserve the murals and the architecturally important post office, which now enhance what might otherwise be just another modern office space. The exhibit and the murals form a fascinating minimuseum, a 15-minute cultural and historical interlude for residents and tourists alike. The Historic Lobby is a modest example of something the city pioneered years ago: bringing art and history "to the people." The most visible of these programs are the large-scale permanent and temporary exhibits at the airport, among the first of their kind in the nation.

Two blocks farther south on Steuart Street is the former **Hills Brothers Coffee** factory, now a retail and office complex. Nearby, the **Gordon Biersch Brewing Co.** (2 Harrison St.), a restaurant and microbrewery, is in the forefront of San Francisco's brew-pub craze. It's open for lunch and dinner.

TOUR 3: THE FINANCIAL DISTRICT AND JACKSON SQUARE

The heart of San Francisco's Financial District is Montgomery Street. It was here in 1848 that Sam Brannan proclaimed the historic gold discovery on the American River. At that time, all the streets below Montgomery between California and Broadway were wharves. At least 100 ships were abandoned by frantic crews and passengers all caught up in the '49 gold fever. Many of the wrecks served as warehouses or were used as foundations for new constructions.

The Financial District is roughly bordered by Kearny Street on the west, Washington Street on the north, and Market Street on the southeast. On workdays it is a congested canyon of soaring skyscrapers, gridlock traffic, and bustling pedestrians. Evenings and weekends are peaceful times to admire the distinctive architecture. Unfortunately, the museums in corporate headquarters are closed at those times.

23 Head down Sutter Street toward the Financial District to see the **Hallidie Building** (130 Sutter St., between Kearny and Montgomery Sts.), named for cable-car inventor Andrew Hallidie. The building, best viewed from across the street, is believed to be the world's first all-glass curtain-wall structure. Willis Polk's revolutionary design hangs a foot beyond the reinforced concrete of the frame. With its reflecting glass, decorative exterior fire escapes that appear to be metal balconies, and Venetian Gothic cornice, the unusual building dominates the block. Also notice the horizontal ornamental bands of birds at feeders.

24 The **Mills Building and Tower** (220 Montgomery St.) was the outstanding prefire building in the Financial District, erected in 1891. The original Burnham and Root design was white marble and brick, but it was actually built as a 10-story all-steel construction with its own electric plant in the basement. Damage from the 1906 fire was slight; its walls were somewhat scorched but were easily refurbished. Two compatible additions east on Bush Street were added in 1914 and 1918 by Willis Polk, and in 1931 a 22-story tower completed the design.

25 The **Russ Building** (235 Montgomery St.) was called "the skyscraper" when it was built in 1927. The Gothic design was modeled after the Chicago Tribune Tower, and until the 1960s was San Francisco's tallest—at just 31 stories. Prior to the 1906 earthquake and fire, the site was occupied by the Russ House, considered one of the finest hostelries in the city.

Ralph Stackpole's monumental 1930 granite sculptural groups, *Earth's Fruitfulness* and *Man's Inventive Genius*, flank another imposing
26 structure, the 301 Pine Street **Pacific Stock Exchange** (which dates from 1915), on the south side of Pine Street at Sansome Street. The Stock Exchange Tower around the corner at 155 Sansome Street, a 1930 modern classic by architects Miller and Pfleuger, features an art deco gold ceiling and black marble-walled entry.

27 The granite-and-marble **Bank of America** building dominates the territory bounded by California, Pine, Montgomery, and Kearny streets. The 52-story, polished red granite complex is crowned by a chic cocktail lounge and restaurant. Inside, impressive original art is displayed, while outdoor plazas showcase avant-garde sculptures. In the mall, a massive abstract black granite sculpture designed by the Japanese artist Masayuki has been dubbed the "Banker's Heart" by local wags.

Soaring 52 stories above the Financial District, the Bank of America's **Carnelian Room** (☎ 415/433–7500) offers elegant and pricey dining with a nighttime view of the city lights. This is an excellent spot for a drink at sunset. By day, the room is the exclusive Banker's Club, open to members or by invitation.

TIME OUT At lunchtime on weekdays you can rub elbows with power brokers and politicians in **Jack's Restaurant** (615 Sacramento St., ☎ 415/986-9854). This venerable eatery opened in 1864 and survived the 1906 quake.

28 A quick but interesting stop is the **Wells Fargo Bank History Museum.** There were no formal banks in San Francisco during the early years of the gold rush, and miners often entrusted their gold dust to saloon keepers. In 1852 Wells Fargo opened its first bank in the city, and the company established banking offices in the Mother Lode camps, using stagecoaches and pony express riders to service the burgeoning state. (California's population boomed from 15,000 to 200,000 between 1848 and 1852.) The museum displays samples of nuggets and gold dust from major mines, a mural-size map of the Mother Lode, original art by Western artists Charlie Russell and Maynard Dixon, mementos of the poet bandit Black Bart, and letters of credit and old bank drafts. The showpiece is the red, century-old Concord stagecoach that in the mid-1850s carried 18 passengers from St. Joseph, Missouri, to San Francisco in three weeks. *420 Montgomery St.,* ☎ *415/396–2619.* ☛ *Free.* ⏲ *Banking days 9–5.*

29 The city's most-photographed high-rise is the 853-foot **Transamerica Pyramid** at 600 Montgomery Street, between Clay and Washington streets at the end of Columbus Avenue. Designed by William Pereira and Associates in 1972, the controversial $34 million symbol has become more acceptable to local purists over time. There is a public viewing area on the 27th floor, but call building management (☎ 415/983–4100) first—recent elevator-system renovations have closed the floor for an undetermined period. A redwood grove along the east side of the building is a nice place to unwind.

In the Gay '90s San Francisco earned the title of "the Wickedest City
in the World." The saloons, dance halls, cheap hotels, and brothels of
its Barbary Coast attracted sailors and gold rushers. Most of this red-
light district was destroyed in the 1906 fire; what remains is now part
30 of **Jackson Square.** A stroll through this district recalls some of the ro-
mance and rowdiness of early San Francisco.

Some of the city's earliest business buildings still stand in the blocks of Jackson Square between Montgomery and Sansome streets. By the end of World War II, most of the 1850 brick structures had fallen on hard times. In 1951, however, things changed. A group of talented, preservation-minded designers and furniture wholesale dealers selected the centrally located, depressed area for their showrooms. By the 1970s, the reclaimed two- and three-story renovated brick buildings were acclaimed nationwide. In 1972 the city officially designated the area—bordered by Columbus Avenue on the west, a line between Broadway and Pacific Avenue on the north, Washington on the south, and Sansome Street on the east—San Francisco's first historic district. Seventeen buildings were given landmark status.

Jackson Square became the interior-design center of the West. When property values soared, many of the fabric and furniture outlets were forced to move to the developing Potrero Hill section. Advertising agencies, attorneys, and antiques dealers now occupy the charming renovations.

Directly across Washington Street from the Transamerica redwood grove is Hotaling Place, a tiny alley east of and parallel to Montgomery Street. The alley is named for the head of the **A. P. Hotaling and Company whiskey distillery,** which was located at 451 Jackson. This handsome brick building retains the iron shutters installed in 1866 to "fireproof" the house. A plaque on the side of the building repeats a famous query about its surviving the quake: "If, as they say, God spanked the town/for being over-frisky,/Why did He burn the churches down/and spare Hotaling's Whisky?"

The **Ghirardelli Chocolate Factory** was once housed at 415 Jackson. As it was quite common for the upper floors of these buildings to be used as flats by owners and tenants, Domenico Ghirardelli moved both his growing business and his family into this property in 1857. By 1894 the enterprise had become large enough to necessitate the creation of Ghirardelli Square.

Head back up Jackson and turn left on Montgomery Street to see the much-photographed compound at **722–28 Montgomery Street.** For years this was the headquarters of Melvin Belli, the "King of Torts," one of the nation's most flamboyant attorneys. The site was originally a warehouse and later the **Melodeon Theater,** where the immortal Lotta Crabtree (*see* Lotta's Fountain *in* Tour 2, *above*) performed.

The **Golden Era Building** at 732 Montgomery Street was the home of the most substantial literary periodical published locally during the 1850s and 1860s. Mark Twain and Bret Harte were two of its celebrated contributors.

Return to Union Square via Montgomery Street (turn right when you get to Post Street) or, if you're in the mood for more sightseeing, head up Columbus Avenue to North Beach. (*See* Tour 5, *below.*)

TOUR 4: CHINATOWN

San Francisco is home to one of the largest Chinese communities out-
★ side Asia. While Chinese culture is visible throughout the city, **Chinatown,**
bordered roughly by Bush, Kearny, Powell and Broadway, remains the community's spiritual and political center. Recent immigrants from Southeast Asia have added new character and life to the neighborhood.

Visitors usually enter Chinatown through the green-tiled dragon-
31 crowned **Chinatown Gate** at Bush Street and Grant Avenue. To best
savor this district, explore it on foot (it's not far from Union Square), even though you may find the bustling, noisy, colorful stretches of Grant and Stockton streets north of Bush difficult to navigate. Parking is extremely hard to find, and traffic is impossible. As in Hong Kong, most families shop daily for fresh meats, vegetables, and bakery products. The street shines with good-luck crimson and gold; giant beribboned floral wreaths mark the opening of new bakeries, bazaars, and banks. Note the dragon-entwined lampposts, the pagoda roofs, and street signs with Chinese calligraphy.

Merely strolling through Chinatown and its many bazaars, restaurants, and curio shops yields endless pleasures, but you also have an opportunity here to experience a bit of one of the world's oldest cultures. You needn't be shy about stepping into a temple or an herb shop. Chinatown has been a tourist stop for more than 100 years now and most of its residents welcome "foreign" guests.

Dragon House Oriental Fine Arts and Antiques (455 Grant Ave.), several doors up from the Chinatown gate, is an excellent place to start your Chinatown visit. Its collection of ivory carvings, ceramics, and jewelry dates back 2,000 years and beyond. The shop's display window is a history lesson in itself.

San Francisco pioneered the resurrection of Chinese regional cooking for American palates. Cantonese cuisine, with its familiar staples of chow mein and chop suey (said to be invented in San Francisco by gold rush–era Chinese cooks) now exists alongside spicier Szechuan, Hunan, and Mandarin specialties. With almost 100 restaurants squeezed into a 14-block area, Chinatown offers plenty of food. In the windows of markets on Stockton Street and Grant Avenue you can see roast ducks hanging, fresh fish and shellfish swimming in tanks, and strips of Chinese-style barbecued pork shining in pink glaze.

32 The handsome brick **Old St. Mary's Church** at Grant and California streets
served as the city's Catholic cathedral until 1891. Granite quarried in
China was used in the structure, which was dedicated in 1854. Diago-
33 nally across the intersection from the church is **St. Mary's Park,** a tran-
quil setting for local sculptor Beniamino (Benny) Bufano's heroic stainless-steel and rose-colored granite *Sun Yat-sen.* The 12-foot statue of the founder of the Republic of China was installed in 1937 on the site of the Chinese leader's favorite reading spot during his years of exile in San Francisco. Bufano was born in Rome on October 14, 1898, and died

in San Francisco on August 16, 1970. His stainless-steel and mosaic statue of St. Francis welcomes guests at San Francisco International Airport.

The city's first house was built in 1836 at the corner of Grant Avenue
and Clay Street; it was later destroyed in the 1906 earthquake. Turn
right on Clay Street, continue one block to Kearny Street, and turn left
34 to reach **Portsmouth Square,** the potato patch that became the plaza
for Yerba Buena. This is where Montgomery raised the American flag
in 1846. Note the bronze galleon atop a 9-foot granite shaft. Designed
by Bruce Porter, the sculpture was erected in 1919 in memory of
Robert Louis Stevenson, who often visited the site during his 1879–
80 residence. In the morning, the park is crowded with people performing
solemn t'ai chi exercises. By noontime, dozens of men huddle around
mah jongg tables, engaged in not-always-legal competition. Occasionally, undercover police rush in to break things up, but this ritual,
solemn as the t'ai chi, is an established way of life.

35 From here you can walk to the **Chinese Cultural Center,** which frequently
displays the work of Chinese-American artists as well as traveling exhibits of Chinese culture. The center also offers $15 Saturday-after-
noon (2 PM) walking tours of historic points in Chinatown. *In the Holiday
Inn, 750 Kearny St., ☎ 415/986–1822. ☛ Free. ⏲ Tues.–Sat. 10–4.*

In an alley parallel to and a half block south of the side of the Holi-
36 day Inn, the **Chinese Historical Society** traces the history of Chinese immigrants and their contributions to the state's rail, mining, and fishing
industries. *650 Commercial St., parallel to Clay St. off Kearny, ☎
415/391–1188. ☛ Free. ⏲ Tues.–Sat. noon–4.*

The original Chinatown burned down after the 1906 earthquake; the
first building to set the style for the new Chinatown is near Portsmouth
37 Square, at 743 Washington Street. The three-tier pagoda, called the **Old
Chinese Telephone Exchange** (now the Bank of Canton), was built in
1909. The exchange's operators were renowned for their "tenacious mem-
ories," about which the San Francisco Chamber of Commerce boasted
in 1914: "These girls respond all day with hardly a mistake to calls that
are given (in English or one of five Chinese dialects) by the name of the
subscriber instead of by his number—a mental feat that would be practically impossible to most high-schooled American misses."

38 **Buddha's Universal Church** is a five-story, hand-built temple decorated
with murals and tile mosaics. The church is open the second and
fourth Sunday of the month, except from January to March, when it
presents a bilingual costume play Saturdays and Sundays to celebrate
the Chinese New Year. *720 Washington St., ☎ 415/982–6116. Play
tickets: $8–$10, reservations accepted.*

TIME OUT Chinatown is the place to get dim sum, a variety of pastries filled with meat, fish, and vegetables—the Chinese version of a smorgasbord. In most dim sum restaurants, stacked food-service carts patrol the premises; customers select from the varied offerings, and the final bill is tabulated by the number of different saucers on the table. A favorite on Pacific Avenue, two blocks north of Washington Street, is **New Asia.** *772 Pacific Ave., ☎ 415/391-6666. ⏲ For dim sum 8:30 am–3 pm.*

Waverly Place is noted for ornate painted balconies and Chinese tem-
39 ples. **Tien Hou Temple** was dedicated to the Queen of the Heavens and
the Goddess of the Seven Seas by Day Ju, one of the first three Chinese to arrive in San Francisco in 1852. Climb three flights of stairs—
past two mah jongg parlors whose patrons hope the spirits above will
favor them. In the entryway, elderly ladies can often be seen prepar-

ing "money" to be burned as offerings to various Buddhist gods. A (real) dollar placed in the donation box on their table will bring a smile. Notice the wood carving suspended from the ceiling, depicting a number of gods at play. *125 Waverly Pl. ⏲ Daily 10–4.*

Throughout Chinatown you will notice herb shops that sell an array of Chinese medicines. The **Great China Herb Co.** (857 Washington St.), around the corner from the Tien Hou Temple, is one of the largest. All day, sellers fill prescriptions from local doctors, measuring exact amounts of tree roots, bark, flowers, and other ingredients with their hand scales, and adding up the bill on an abacus (an ancient calculator). The shops also sell "over-the-counter" treatments for the common cold, heartburn, hangovers, and even impotence.

The other main thoroughfare in Chinatown, where locals shop for everyday needs, is Stockton Street, which parallels Grant Avenue. This is the real heart of Chinatown. Housewives jostle one another as they pick apart the sidewalk displays of Chinese vegetables. Double-parked trucks unloading crates of chickens or ducks add to the all-day traffic jams. Excellent examples of Chinese architecture line this street. Most
40 noteworthy is the elaborate **Chinese Six Companies** (843 Stockton St.), with its curved roof tiles and elaborate cornices. At 855 Stockton is **Kong Chow Temple,** established in 1851 and moved to this new building in 1977. Take the elevator up to the fourth floor. Again, a dollar bill is an appropriate gift from you or your group. The air at Kong Chow Temple is often thick with incense, a bit ironic what with the Chinese Community Smoke-Free Project but two floors below.

Around the corner at 965 Clay Street is the handsome, redbrick **Chinatown YWCA,** originally set up as a meeting place and residence for Chinese women in need of social services. It was designed by architect Julia Morgan, who was also responsible for the famous Hearst Castle at San Simeon, California. It's an easy 15-minute walk back downtown
41 to Union Square via the **Stockton Street Tunnel,** which runs from Sacramento Street to Sutter Street. Completed in 1914, this was the city's first tunnel to accommodate vehicular and pedestrian traffic.

TOUR 5: NORTH BEACH AND TELEGRAPH HILL

Like neighboring Chinatown, North Beach, centered on Columbus Avenue north of Broadway, is best explored on foot. In the early days it was truly a beach. At the time of the gold rush, the bay extended into the hollow between Telegraph and Russian hills. North Beach, less than a square mile, is the most densely populated district in the city, and among the most cosmopolitan. Though residents worry about the increasing encroachment of Chinatown—the ever-increasing Pacific Rim influx has resulted in a blurring of the borders between the two neighborhoods—North Beach still retains its Old World ambience and offbeat mood. Novelist Herbert Gold, a North Beach resident, calls the area "the longest-running, most glorious American bohemian operetta outside Greenwich Village."

Like Chinatown, this is a section of the city where eating is unavoidable: Restaurants, cafés, delis, and bakeries abound. Many Italian restaurants specialize in family-style full-course meals at reasonable prices. A local North Beach delicacy is focaccia—spongy pizzalike bread slathered with olive oil and chives or tomato sauce—sold fresh from the oven at quaint old **Liguria Bakery** at the corner of Stockton and Filbert streets. Eaten warm or cold, it is the perfect walking food.

Among the first immigrants to Yerba Buena during the early 1840s were young men from the northern provinces of Italy. The Genoese started the still-active fishing industry in the newly renamed boomtown of San Francisco, as well as a much-needed produce business. Later the Sicilians emerged as leaders of the fishing fleets and eventually as proprietors of the seafood restaurants lining Fisherman's Wharf. Meanwhile, their Genoese cousins established banking and manufacturing empires.

42 **Washington Square** may well be the daytime social heart of what was
once considered "Little Italy"—though in the early morning, the dominating sight is a hundred or more older Asian neighbors engaged in
t'ai chi. Nevertheless, by mid-morning groups of conservatively dressed
elderly Italian men arrive to sun and sigh at the state of their immediate world. Nearby, laughing playmates of a half-dozen cultures race
through the grass with Frisbees or colorful kites. Denim-clad mothers
exchange shopping tips and ethnic recipes. Elderly Chinese matrons
stare impassively at the passing parade. Camera-toting tourists focus
43 their lenses on the adjacent Romanesque splendor of **Sts. Peter and Paul,**
often called the Italian Cathedral: Completed in 1924, its twin-turreted
terra-cotta towers are local landmarks. On the first Sunday of October, the annual Blessing of the Fleet is celebrated with a mass followed
by a parade to Fisherman's Wharf. Another popular annual event is
the Columbus Day pageant.

The 1906 earthquake and fire devastated North Beach, and the park provided shelter for hundreds of the homeless. **Fior d'Italia,** facing the cathedral, is San Francisco's oldest Italian restaurant. The original opened in 1886 and continued to operate in a tent after the 1906 earthquake until new quarters were ready. Surrounding streets are packed with savory Italian delicatessens, bakeries, Chinese markets, coffeehouses, and ethnic restaurants. Wonderful aromas fill the air; coffee beans roasted at **Graffeo** at 735 Columbus Avenue are shipped to customers all over the United States. Stop by the **Panelli Brothers deli** (1419 Stockton St.) for a memorable, reasonably priced meat-and-cheese sandwich to go. **Florence Ravioli Factory** (1412 Stockton St.) features garlic sausages, prosciutto, and mortadella, as well as 75 tasty cheeses and sandwiches to go. **Victoria** (1362 Stockton St.) has heavenly cream puffs and eclairs. Around the corner on Columbus Avenue is **Molinari's,** noted for the best salami in town and a mouthwatering array of salads: be prepared for a wait.

44 South of Washington Square and just off Columbus Avenue is the **St. Francis of Assisi Church** (610 Vallejo St.). This 1860 Victorian Gothic building stands on the site of the frame parish church that served the gold-rush Catholic community.

Over the years, North Beach has attracted creative individualists. The
Beat Renaissance of the 1950s was born, grew up, flourished, then fal-
tered in this then-predominantly Italian enclave. Though most Beat gathering places are gone and few of the original leaders remain, poet
45 Lawrence Ferlinghetti still holds court at his **City Lights Bookstore**
(261 Columbus Ave.). Today's bohemian community has migrated up
Grant Avenue above Columbus Avenue. Originally called Calle de la
Fundacion, Grant Avenue is the oldest street in the city. Each June a
street fair is held on the upper part of the avenue, where a cluster of
cafés, boutiques, and galleries attract crowds.

The view from Columbus and Broadway characterizes the crossroads at which the area finds itself. Chinatown encroaches on Broadway west of Columbus; on the east side of the street the self-proclaimed "birthplace of topless dancing," the Condor, is now a coffee shop. Up Columbus, farther from the Financial District, the traditional North Beach mix of Italian restaurants and cafés remains. To the south, skyscrapers loom overhead, although one of the earliest and shortest examples, the triangular Sentinel Building (916 Kearny St.), owned by moviemaker Francis Ford Coppola, is the one that grabs the eye.

TIME OUT Cafés are a way of life in North Beach. **Caffe Puccini** (411 Columbus Ave.) could be Italy: Few of the staff speak English. Their caffè latte (coffee, chocolate, cinnamon, and steamed milk) and strains of Italian operas recall *Roman Holiday.* A Saturday morning must is around the corner at **Caffe Trieste** (601 Vallejo St.), where the Giotta family presents a weekly musical. Beginning at noon, the program ranges from Italian pop and folk music to favorite family operas. The Trieste opened in 1956 and quickly became headquarters for the area's beatnik poets, artists, and writers. To soak up brews and nighttime atmosphere, two pubs within a half step of City Lights—funky **Specs' Museum Cafe** (12 Adler, in the alley across the street) and colorful two-story **Vesuvio** (255 Columbus Ave.)—offer cluttered decor, a laid-back ambience, and salty patrons who seem to have lived there forever.

46 **Telegraph Hill** rises from the east end of Lombard Street to about 300 feet and is capped with the landmark Coit Tower, dedicated as a monument to the city's volunteer firefighters. Early during the gold rush, an eight-year-old who would become one of the city's most memorable eccentrics, Lillie Hitchcock Coit, arrived on the scene. Legend relates that at age 17, "Miss Lil" deserted a wedding party and chased down the street after her favorite engine, Knickerbocker No. 5, clad in her bridesmaid finery. She was soon made an honorary member of the Knickerbocker Company, and after that always signed herself "Lillie Coit 5" in honor of her favorite fire engine. Lillie died in 1929 at the age of 86, leaving the city about $100,000 of her million-dollar-plus estate to "expend in an appropriate manner . . . to the beauty of San Francisco."

Telegraph Hill residents command some of the best views in the city, as well as the most difficult ascent to their aeries. The Greenwich stairs lead up to Coit Tower from Filbert Street, and there are steps down to Filbert Street on the opposite side of Telegraph Hill. Views are superb en route, but most visitors should either taxi up to the tower or take the Muni Bus 39-Coit at Washington Square. To catch the bus from Union Square, walk to Stockton and Sutter streets, board the Muni No. 30, and ask for a transfer to use at Washington Square (Columbus Ave. and Union St.) to board the No. 39-Coit. Public parking is limited at the tower, and on holidays and weekends long lines of cars and buses wind up the narrow road.

★ 47 **Coit Tower** stands as a monument not only to Lillie Coit and the city's firefighters but also to the influence of the political and radical Mexican muralist Diego Rivera. Fresco was Rivera's medium, and it was his style that unified the work of most of the 25 artists who painted the murals of labor-union workers in the tower. The murals were commissioned by the U.S. government as a Public Works of Art project, and the artists were paid $38 a week. Some were fresh from art schools; others found no market for art in the dark depression days of the early 1930s. An illustrated brochure for sale in the tiny gift shop explains the various murals dedicated to the workers of California.

Ride the elevator to the top of the hill to enjoy the panoramic view of both the Bay Bridge and Golden Gate Bridge; directly offshore is the famous Alcatraz, and just behind it is Angel Island, a hikers' and campers' paradise. Artists are often at work in Pioneer Park, at the foot of the tower. Small paintings of the scene are frequently offered for sale at modest prices. *Discoverer of America,* the impressive bronze statue of Christopher Columbus, was a gift of the local Italian community.

Walk down the Greenwich Steps to Montgomery Street, and turn right. At the corner where the Filbert Steps intersect, you'll find the Art Deco masterpiece at 1360 Montgomery Street (*see* Off the Beaten Track, *below*). Its elegant etched-glass gazelle and palms counterpoint the silvered fresco of the heroic bridge worker—echoed by an actual view of the Bay Bridge in the distance. Descend the Filbert Steps amid roses, fuchsias, irises, and trumpet flowers—courtesy of Grace Marchant, who labored for nearly 30 years to transform a dump into one of San Francisco's hidden treasures. At the last landing before the final descent to Sansome Street, pause and sit on the bench to breathe in the fragrance of roses as you gaze at the bridge and bay below. A small bronze plaque set into the bench reads: "I have a feeling we're not in Kansas anymore."

At the foot of the hill are the Levi Strauss headquarters, a carefully landscaped $150 million complex that appears so collegial and serene it is affectionately known as LSU (Levi Strauss University). Fountains and grassy knolls complement the redbrick buildings and provide a perfect environment for brown-bag lunches; at **Uno Poco di Tutti** deli in Levi's Plaza (1265 Battery St., ☎ 415/986–0646) you'll find a little of everything.

TOUR 6: NOB HILL AND RUSSIAN HILL

If you don't mind climbing uphill, Nob Hill is within walking distance of Union Square. Once called the Hill of Golden Promise, it became Nob Hill during the 1870s when "the Big Four"—Charles Crocker, Leland Stanford, Mark Hopkins, and Collis Huntington—built their hilltop estates. It is still home to many of the city's elite as well as four of San Francisco's finest hotels.

In 1882 Robert Louis Stevenson called Nob Hill "the hill of palaces." But the 1906 earthquake and fire destroyed all the palatial mansions. The shell of one survived: The Flood brownstone (1000 California St.) was built by the Comstock silver baron in 1886 at a reputed cost of $1.5 million. In 1909 the property was purchased by the prestigious
48 **Pacific Union Club.** The 45-room exclusive club remains a bastion of the wealthy and powerful. Adjacent is a charming small park noted for its frequent art shows.

49 Neighboring **Grace Cathedral** (1051 Taylor St.) is the seat of the Episcopal church in San Francisco. The soaring Gothic structure, built on the site of Charles Crocker's mansion, took 53 years to build. The gilded bronze doors at the east entrance were taken from casts of Ghiberti's Gates of Paradise on the baptistery in Florence. The cathedral's original design called for the demolition of a four-story building to allow for a sweeping set of stairs leading up to the church, but the construction was delayed for decades, by which time preservationists began fighting to retain the structure. After what was described as "a civilized but passionate" planning commission debate, the building came down in late 1993. Architect Lewis Hobart's grand design was scheduled for completion in June 1995, to coincide with celebration of the United Nations' 50th anniversary. The cathedral's superb rose window is il-

luminated at night. There are choral evensongs on Thursday at 5:15 PM, as well as special programs during the holiday seasons.

50 The huge **Masonic Auditorium** (1111 California St.) is the site of occasional musical events, as well as conventions and seminars. The impressive lobby mosaic—commissioned for the building's 1957 opening—depicts the Masonic Fraternity's role in California history.

51 What sets the **Fairmont Hotel** (California and Mason Sts.) apart from other luxury hotels is its legendary history. Its dazzling opening was delayed a year by the 1906 quake, but since then the marble palace has hosted presidents, royalty, and local nabobs. Prices are up a bit, though: On the eve of World War I, you could get a room for as low as $2.50 per night—meals included. Nowadays, prices run as high as $6,000—this being for a night in the eight-room penthouse suite that was showcased regularly in the TV series "Hotel. " The apartment building on the corner of Sacramento Street across from the Fairmont is also a media star. In 1958 it was a major location in Alfred Hitchcock's *Vertigo* and was more recently (1993) featured in the BBC production of Armistead Maupin's homage to San Francisco, *Tales of the City.*

On the Fairmont's other flank at California and Mason streets is the
52 **Mark Hopkins Inter-Continental Hotel,** which is remembered fondly by
thousands of World War II veterans who jammed the Top of the Mark
lounge (*see* Skyline Bars *in* Chapter 7, The Arts and Nightlife) before
leaving for overseas duty. Down California at Powell Street stands the
53 posh **Stouffer Renaissance Stanford Court Hotel.** The structure is a remodeled 1909 apartment house.

54 The **Cable Car Museum,** at the corner of Washington and Mason streets, is a brief but engaging stopover on the way to Russian Hill. On exhibit are photographs, old cars, and other memorabilia from the system's 121-year history, and an overlook allows visitors to observe the cables that haul the city's cars in action. *1201 Mason St., at Washington St.,* ☎ *415/474–1887.* ☛ *Free.* ⊙ *Nov.–Mar., daily 10–5; Apr.–Oct., daily 10–6; closed some holidays.*

Just nine blocks or so from downtown, **Russian Hill** has long been home to old San Francisco families and, during the 1890s, to a group of bohemian artists and writers that included Charles Norris, George Sterling, and Maynard Dixon. An old legend says that during San Francisco's early days the steep hill (294 feet high) was the site of a cemetery for Russian seal hunters and traders. Now the hills are covered with an astounding array of housing: simple studios, sumptuous pieds-à-terre, Victorian flats, and costly boxlike condos.

From the Cable Car Museum, continue four blocks north on Mason
Street to Vallejo Street. This will put you at an ideal spot from which
to photograph Alcatraz Island and the bay. Slowly start climbing the
55 Vallejo Steps up to attractive **Ina Coolbrith Park.** An Oakland librar-
ian and poet, Ina introduced both Jack London and Isadora Duncan
to the world of books. For years she entertained literary greats in her
Macondray Lane home near the park. In 1915 she was named poet
laureate of California.

A number of buildings in this neighborhood survived the 1906 earthquake and fire and still stand today. The house at **1652–56 Taylor Street** was saved by alert firefighters who spotted the American flag on the property and managed to quench the flames using seltzer water and wet sand. A number of brown-shingle structures on Vallejo Street designed by Willis Polk, one of the city's most famous architects, also survived. For years, the Polk family resided at **1013 Vallejo Street.** Stroll past **1034–1036 Vallejo**—both buildings, tucked in between million-dollar condominium neighbors, were designed by Polk.

At this point, two secluded alleys beckon: To the north, **Russian Hill Place** has a row of Mediterranean-style town houses designed by Polk in 1915. On **Florence Place** to the south, 1920s stucco survivors reign over more contemporary construction.

Follow Vallejo Street west to Jones Street, turn right, and continue on
to Green Street. The 1000 block of Green, on one of the three crests
of Russian Hill, is one of the most remarkable blocks in San Francisco.
56 The **Feusier House** (1067 Green St.), built in 1857 and now a private
residence, is one of two octagonal houses left in the city (*see* Sightseeing Checklists, *below,* for the other—Octagon House—which is open
for tours on a limited basis). On the other side of the street (at 1088)
is the **1907 firehouse.** Local art patron Mrs. Ralph K. Davies bought
it from the city in 1956. The house, which is often used for charity benefits, has a small museum.

★ Continue west on Green Street to Hyde Street, where the **Hyde-Powell
cable car** line runs. Turn right and stroll up to Union Street. (Those who
are tired of walking may want to stop at the original Swensen's, on the
corner of Union and Hyde streets, for an ice-cream treat). Before you
continue the tour, a worthwhile detour is two blocks down Union to
Polk, where you'll find the **Alhambra Theater** auditorium—a stunning,
recently restored 1920s neo-mosque movie palace built by local architect Timothy Pfleuger. At this point you have two options: Meander down
Union Street to Jones Street, turn right, and walk a few steps down to
57 magical **Macondray Lane,** a quiet cobbled pedestrian street lined with
Edwardian cottages. From a flight of steep wooden stairs that lead down
to Taylor Street, you'll get some spectacular views of the bay. From Taylor Street, North Beach is a short walk downhill.

The other option is to keep walking north on Hyde Street three blocks
58 to **Lombard Street.** Stretching the length of just one block, San Francisco's "crookedest street" drops down the east face of Russian Hill
in eight switchbacks to Leavenworth Street. Few tourists with cars can
resist the lure of the scary descent. Pedestrians should be alert while
using the steep steps.

At the base of the steps, turn left on Leavenworth Street and then right
59 on Chestnut Street. At 800 Chestnut Street is the **San Francisco Art Institute.** Established in 1871, it occupied the Mark Hopkins home at
California and Mason streets from 1893 to 1906. The school carried
on in temporary quarters until 1926, when the present Spanish Colonial building was erected on the top of Russian Hill. Be sure to see the
impressive seven-section fresco painted in 1931 by the Mexican mas-
ter Diego Rivera; it's in the gallery to the left as you enter the institute.
There are also frequent exhibitions by students.

From here you can walk to Hyde Street and take the cable car back downtown or walk a few blocks north to Fisherman's Wharf. Hardy sorts will probably prefer to walk down to Columbus Avenue and then west on North Point or Beach streets to Ghirardelli Square, the Cannery, and Aquatic Park.

TOUR 7: PACIFIC HEIGHTS

★ **Pacific Heights** forms an east–west ridge along the city's northern flank from Van Ness Avenue to the Presidio and from California Street to the bay. Some of the city's most expensive and dramatic real estate, including mansions and town houses priced at $1 million and up, are located here. Grand old Victorians, expensively face-lifted, grace tree-lined streets—although here and there glossy, glass-walled high-rise condos obstruct the view.

Old money and some new, personalities in the limelight, and those who prefer absolute media anonymity occupy the city's most prestigious residential enclave. Few visitors see anything other than the pleasing facades of Queen Anne charmers, English Tudor imports, and baroque bastions, but strolling can still be rewarding. Notice that few of the homes in Pacific Heights feature adjoining gardens. Space has always been at a premium in San Francisco: Even in such a wealthy neighborhood, many of the structures stand close together, but extend in a vertical direction for two or more stories.

A good place to begin a tour of the neighborhood is at the corner of Webster Street and Pacific Avenue, deep in the heart of the Heights. You can get here from Union Square by taking Muni Bus 3 from Sutter and Stockton to Jackson and Fillmore streets. Head one block east on Jackson to Webster Street.

North on Webster Street, at 2550, is the massive Georgian brick mansion built in 1896 for William B. Bourn, who had inherited a Mother Lode gold mine. The architect, Willis Polk, was responsible for many of the most traditional and impressive commercial and private homes built from the prequake days until the early 1920s. (Be sure to see his 1917 Hallidie Building, 130 Sutter Street; *see* Tour 3, *above.*) Polk also designed Bourn's palatial Peninsula estate, **Filoli** (*see* The San Francisco Peninsula *in* Chapter 8, Excursions from San Francisco).

Broadway uptown, unlike its North Beach stretch, is home to some important addresses, including a consulate and, on the northwest corner,
60 two classic showplaces. **2222 Broadway** is the three-story Italian Renaissance palace built by Comstock mine heir James Flood, later donated to a religious order. Ten years later, the Convent of the Sacred Heart purchased the baroque brick Grant house (2220 Broadway) and both serve as school quarters today. A second top-drawer school, the Hamlin (2120 Broadway), occupies another Flood property.

Movie buffs may want to make the effort to travel another block west on Broadway to Steiner Street for a gander at the handsome home (at the southeast corner) used in the movie hit *Mrs. Doubtfire.*

Return east on Broadway past the Hamlin School and turn right (south) on Buchanan Street, then left on Jackson Street to Laguna Street.
61 The massive red sandstone **Whittier Mansion,** at 2090 Jackson Street, was one of the most elegant 19th-century houses in the state, built so solidly that only a chimney toppled over during the 1906 earthquake.
62 One block south on Laguna, at Washington Street, is **Lafayette Park,** a four-block-square oasis for sunbathers and dog-and-Frisbee teams. During the 1860s, a tenacious squatter, Sam Holladay, built himself a big wooden house in the center of the park. Holladay even instructed city gardeners as if the land were his own, and defied all orders to leave. The house was finally torn down in 1936.

Walking east on Washington Street along the edge of Lafayette Park, 63 the most imposing residence is the formal French **Spreckels Mansion** (2080 Washington St.). Sugar heir Adolph Spreckels's wife, Alma, was so pleased with her house that she commissioned architect George Applegarth to design the city's European museum, the California Palace of the Legion of Honor in Lincoln Park. Alma, one of the city's great iconoclasts, is the model for the bronze figure atop the Victory Monument in Union Square.

Continue east on Washington Street two more blocks to Franklin 64 Street and turn left. At 2007 Franklin is the handsome **Haas-Lilienthal House.** Built in 1886, at an original cost of $18,500, this grand Queen Anne survived the 1906 earthquake and fire and is the only fully furnished Victorian open to the public. The carefully kept rooms offer an intriguing glimpse of turn-of-the-century taste and lifestyle. A small display of photographs on the bottom floor proves that this elaborate house was modest compared with some of the giants that fell to the fire. It is operated by the Foundation for San Francisco's Architectural Heritage, whose volunteers conduct tours of the house two days a week, as well as an informative two-hour tour of the eastern portion of Pacific Heights on Sunday afternoon. ☎ *415/441–3004.* ☛ *$5 adults, $3 senior citizens and children under 12.* ⏲ *Wed. noon–4 (last tour at 3:15), Sun. 11–5 (last tour at 4:15). Pacific Heights tours ($5 adults, $3 senior citizens and children) leave the house Sun. at 12:30 PM.*

South on Franklin Street, don't be fooled by the neoclassical **Golden Gate Church** at 1901—what at first looks like a stone facade is actually redwood painted white. **1735 Franklin** is a stately brick Georgian built in the early 1900s for a coffee merchant. Looking east, at the corner of Franklin Street and California is a "tapestry brick" **Christian Science church** built in the Tuscan Revival style, noteworthy for its terra-cotta detailing.

65 The **Coleman House** at 1701 Franklin Street is an impressive twin-turreted Queen Anne mansion built for a gold-rush mining and lumber baron. At 1818 and 1834 California are two stunning **Italianate Victorians.** A block farther at 1990 California is the Victorian-era **Atherton House,** perhaps the oddest combination of architectural elements—among them Queen Anne and Stick-Eastlake—in all of Pacific Heights.

To return to downtown, walk by the side of the Atherton House to Sacramento and catch Bus 1-California (transfer to Bus 30-Stockton on Stockton Street). If you haven't ridden a cable car yet, disembark Bus 1 at Van Ness Avenue and walk one block south to the California-line terminus; the wait here is much shorter than for the Powell-Hyde line.

To see more Victorians, proceed west on California past the Atherton House another block to Laguna Street and turn left. The Italianate Victorians on the west side of the **1800 block** of Laguna Street cost only $2,000–$2,600 when they were built during the 1870s. This block is one of the most photographed rows of Victorians in the city.

Walk south on Laguna Street to Sutter and catch Bus 2, 3, or 4 to Union Square. If you still have some bounce in your step, proceed one block past Sutter to Post and walk west one block to Buchanan, where the Japantown tour begins.

TOUR 8: JAPANTOWN

Japanese-Americans began gravitating to the neighborhood known as the Western Addition prior to the 1906 earthquake; the early immigrants who arrived about 1860 named San Francisco Soko. After the 1906 fire had destroyed wooden homes in other parts of the stricken city, many survivors settled in the Western Addition. By the 1930s the pioneers had opened shops, markets, meeting halls, and restaurants and established Shinto and Buddhist temples. Japantown was virtually disbanded during World War II when many of its residents, including second- and third-generation Americans, were "relocated" in camps. Today **Japantown,** or "Nihonmachi," is centered on the slopes of Pacific Heights, north of Geary Boulevard, between Fillmore and Laguna streets. The Nihonmachi Cherry Blossom Festival is celebrated two weekends every April with a calendar of ethnic events.

To reach Japantown from Union Square, take Muni Bus 38-Geary or Bus 2, 3, or 4 on Sutter Street, westbound to Laguna. Remember to have exact change—fare is $1; paper money is accepted.

Japantown and the Western Addition are at their best during the day. Though the hotel, restaurant, and Kabuki movie complex are relatively safe in the evenings, the proximity of the often-hostile street gangs in the Western Addition poses a threat late at night, when cabs are scarce.

The buildings around the traffic-free **Japan Center Mall** between Sutter and Post streets are of the shoji screen school of architecture, and Ruth Asawa's origami fountain sits in the middle (*See* Tour 1, *above,* for more information on Ms. Asawa.) The mall faces the three-block-long,
66 5-acre **Japan Center.** In 1968 the multimillion-dollar development created by noted American architect Minoru Yamasaki opened with a three-day folk festival. The three-block cluster includes an 800-car public garage and shops and showrooms selling Japanese products: electronic products, cameras, tapes and records, porcelains, pearls, and paintings.

The center is dominated by its Peace Plaza and Pagoda located between the Tasamak Plaza and Kintetsu buildings. The original design of Professor Yoshiro Taniguchi of Tokyo, an authority on ancient Japanese buildings, has been altered greatly, mostly for the worse. Remaining from the original design are the graceful *yagura* (wooden drum tower) that spans the entrance to the mall and the copper-roofed *Heiwa Dori* (Peace Walkway) between the Tasamak Plaza and Kintetsu buildings. The five-tier, 100-foot Peace Pagoda overlooks the plaza, where seasonal festivals are held. The pagoda, which draws on the tradition of miniature round pagodas dedicated to eternal peace by Empress Koken in Nara more than 1,200 years ago, was designed by the Japanese architect Yoshiro Taniguchi "to convey the friendship and goodwill of the Japanese to the people of the United States." A cultural bridge modeled after Florence's Ponte Vecchio spans Webster Street, connecting the Kintetsu and Kinokuniya buildings.

Some 40 restaurants in the neighborhood feature a choice of Japanese, Chinese, or Korean food. Most are found in the mall, a few are on side streets, and the rest are in the center itself, concentrated on the "street of restaurants" in the Kintetsu Building. Following the practice in Japan, plastic replicas of the various dishes are on view.

Kabuki Hot Springs (1750 Geary Blvd., ☎ 415/922–6000) is a great place for a rest. Open daily, the communal bath is open for men only on Monday, Tuesday, Thursday, and Saturday, and for women only on Wednesday, Friday, and Sunday. Private baths with sauna or steam are available daily. The spa offers a number of steam, sauna, and massage packages. One, the Shogun, includes an hour of shiatsu massage, which is based on targeting pressure points in the body.

TIME OUT At **Isobune** (☎ 415/563-1030), on the second floor of the Kintetsu Building, "sushi boats" float by the customers, who take what they want and pay per boat at the end of the meal. The inexpensive but superb **Mifune** (☎ 415/922-0337), diagonally across from Isobune, serves both hot and cold noodle dishes, either boiled and served in broth or prepared toss-fried, with bits of greens and meat added for flavor.

Walk back east on Geary Boulevard's north side to Gough Street—an enclave of expensive high-rise residential towers known as Cathedral
67 Hill. Dramatic **St. Mary's Cathedral,** on the south side of Geary, was dedicated in 1971 at a cost of $7 million. The impressive Italian travertine Catholic cathedral, which was designed by a team of local architects and Pierre Nervi of Rome, seats 2,500 people around the central altar. Above the altar is a spectacular cascade made of 7,000 aluminum ribs. Four magnificent stained-glass windows in the dome represent the four elements: the blue north window, water; the light-colored south window, the sun; the red west window, fire; and the green east window, earth.

Catch Bus 38-Geary in front of the cathedral to return downtown, or get off at Van Ness Avenue and transfer to Bus 42, 47, or 49 heading south to McAllister Street. The walk takes less than 10 minutes.

TOUR 9: CIVIC CENTER

San Francisco's Civic Center stands as one of the country's great city, state, and federal building complexes with handsome adjoining cultural institutions—a realization of the theories of turn-of-the-century proponents of the "City Beautiful."

68 Facing Polk Street, between Grove and McAllister streets, **City Hall** is a French Renaissance Revival masterpiece of granite and marble, modeled after the Capitol in Washington. Its dome, which is even higher than the Washington version, dominates the area. The palatial interior, often used by locals for wedding ceremonies, will be closed for seismic upgrading at least until 1998. In front of the building are formal gardens with fountains, walkways, and seasonal flower beds. Brooks Exhibit Hall was constructed under this plaza in 1958 to add space for the frequent trade shows and other events held in the Bill Graham Civic Auditorium, on Grove Street.

Across the plaza from City Hall on Larkin Street is the main branch
69 of the **San Francisco Public Library.** (A new library is being built directly across Fulton Street; when it opens in March 1996, this site may become the new Asian Art Museum.) History buffs should visit the San Francisco History Room and Archives, where historic photographs, maps, and other memorabilia are displayed. *Main Library, ☎ 415/557-4440. ⏲ Mon. 10–6, Tues.–Thurs. 9–8, Fri. 11–5, Sat. 9–5, Sun. noon–5. For archives hrs call 415/557-4567.*

Just east of the new library, at the end of Fulton Street set on an angle
70 between Hyde and Market streets, is **United Nations Plaza,** the site of a farmers' market on Wednesday and Sunday. On the west side of City Hall, across Van Ness Avenue, are the Veterans Building, the Opera House, and Davies Symphony Hall. The northernmost of the three is
71 the **Veterans Building** (401 Van Ness Ave.), the third and fourth floors of which formerly housed the San Francisco Museum of Modern Art. Herbst Theatre, on the first floor, remains a popular venue for lectures and readings, classical ensembles, and dance performances. In 1995

the 50th anniversary of the signing of the United Nations Charter was commemorated with celebrations in the theater.

72 An ornate horseshoe carriage entrance on its south side separates the Veterans Building from the **War Memorial Opera House** (301 Van Ness Ave.), which opened in 1932. Modeled after European counterparts, the opera house has a vaulted and coffered ceiling, a marble foyer, and two balconies. The San Francisco Opera (September–December) and the San Francisco Ballet (February–May, with December *Nutcracker* performances) perform here. The Opera House will be closed for seismic retrofitting and renovation from January '96 through July '97; the ballet and opera companies will perform their regular seasons at alternative venues around town. (*See* Chapter 7, The Arts and Nightlife.)

TIME OUT For a quick pizza or a grilled chicken-breast sandwich, dash over to the bustling bistro **Spuntino** (524 Van Ness Ave., ☏ 415/861-7772). ⏲ Until midnight on Friday and Saturday, this is an excellent spot for an after-theater cappuccino. A bit down the alley that runs alongside Spuntino, celebrity chef Jeremiah Tower's **Stars** (*see* Chapter 5, Dining) offers exotic versions of California cuisine in an atmospheric room.

73 South of Grove Street, still on Van Ness, is the $37.9 million, 2,750-seat **Louise M. Davies Symphony Hall,** home of the San Francisco Symphony. The glass-encased wraparound lobby, visible from the street, is just a precursor of the sleek, futuristic wonders inside: 59 adjustable Plexiglas acoustical disks hang from the ceiling like hanging windshields. Tours are available of Davies Hall and the adjacent Performing Arts Center, which encompasses the Opera House and Herbst Theatre. *201 Van Ness Ave.,* ☏ *415/552–8338.* ☛ *$3 adults, $2 senior citizens and students. Tours of Davies Hall Wed. and Sat. by appointment. Tours of Davies Hall and the Performing Arts Center every 1/2 hr Mon. 10–2.*

74 The **San Francisco Performing Arts Library and Museum,** also known as PALM, collects, documents, and preserves the San Francisco Bay Area's rich performing-arts legacy. It houses the largest collection of its kind on the West Coast. Exhibitions often include programs, photographs, manuscripts, costumes, and other memorabilia of historic performance events. *399 Grove St., at Gough St.,* ☏ *415/255–4800.* ☛ *Free.* ⏲ *Tues.–Fri. 10–5, Sat. noon–4.*

One block south of Grove Street, Hayes Street has burgeoned since the dismantling of the freeway ramp after the Loma Prieta earthquake. Fine contemporary and ethnic art galleries, as well as boutiques and eateries line Franklin Street up to Laguna; but be careful not to stray past Gough Street after nightfall.

TOUR 10: THE NORTHERN WATERFRONT

Numbers in the margin correspond to points of interest on the Northern Waterfront: Tours 10–11 map.

For the sight, sound, and smell of the sea, hop the Powell-Hyde cable car from Union Square to the end of the line. From the cable-car turnaround, Aquatic Park and the National Maritime Museum are immediately to the west; Fort Mason, with its several interesting museums, is just a bit farther west. Those who wish to explore the more commercial attractions can head to nearby Ghirardelli Square or Fisherman's Wharf. Be sure to wear good walking shoes and a jacket or sweater for mid-afternoon breezes or foggy mists.

Begin the day with one of the early morning boat tours that depart from the Northern Waterfront piers. In clear weather (almost always), the morning light casts a warm glow on the colorful homes on Russian Hill, the weather-aged fishing boats cluttered at Fisherman's Wharf, rosy Ghirardelli Square and its fairy-tale clock tower, and the swelling seas beyond the entrance to the bay.

San Francisco is famous for the arts and crafts that flourish on the streets. Each day more than 200 of the city's innovative jewelers, painters, potters, photographers, and leather workers offer their wares for sale. You'll find them at Fisherman's Wharf, Union Square, Embarcadero Plaza, and the Cliff House. Be wary: Some of the items are from foreign factories and may be overpriced; bargaining is often a wise idea.

❶ The **National Maritime Museum** exhibits ship models, photographs, maps, and other artifacts chronicling the development of San Francisco and the West Coast through maritime history. *Aquatic Park, at the foot of Polk St., ☏ 415/556–3002 (if no answer call 415/929–0202).* ☛ *Free.* ⏲ *Daily 10–5, until 6 in summer.*

❷ The museum includes the **Hyde Street Pier** (two blocks east), where historic vessels are moored. The pier, one of the wharf area's best bargains, always bustles with activity; depending on the time of day, you might see boatbuilders at work or children manning a boat or ship as though it were still the early 1900s. The highlight of the pier is the *Balclutha,* an 1886 full-rigged, three-mast sailing vessel that sailed around Cape Horn 17 times. The *Eureka,* a side-wheel ferry, and the *C.A. Thayer,* a three-masted schooner, can also be boarded. ☏ *415/929–0202.* ☛ *$3 adults, $1 children 12–18; children under 12 and senior citizens free. (Note: Travelers with a National Park Service Golden Eagle Pass enter the pier free.)* ⏲ *Fall–spring, daily 10–5; summer, daily 10–6.*

The ***Pampanito,*** at Pier 45, is a World War II submarine. An audio tour has been installed. ☏ *415/441–5819.* ☛ *$5 adults, $4 students, $3 children 6–12, senior citizens, and active military.* ⏲ *Fall–spring, Sun.–Thurs. 9–6, Fri.–Sat. 9–8; summer, daily 9–9.*

❸ **Fort Mason,** originally a depot for the shipment of supplies to the Pacific during World War II, is a 10-minute walk west from the back of the Maritime Museum. Follow the railway tracks in back of the museum, turn right before they head into a (blocked) tunnel and then left up the fairly steep grade that leads to the complex. Fort Mason was converted into a cultural center in 1977 and now houses four nonprofit museums, a theater, and the popular vegetarian restaurant Greens (*See* Chapter 5, Dining).

The **Mexican Museum** was the first American showcase to be devoted exclusively to Mexican, Mexican-American, and Chicano art, with everything from pre-Hispanic Indian terra-cotta figures and Spanish Colonial religious images to the surrealist paintings of Frida Kahlo, wife of Diego Rivera. Limited exhibition space accommodates only a fraction of the permanent collection, including a recent 500-piece folk-art collection, a gift from the Nelson A. Rockefeller estate—but plans are underway to build a larger modern building for the museum in the downtown Yerba Buena complex by 1998. La Tienda, the museum shop, stocks colorful Mexican folk art, posters, books, and catalogues from museum exhibitions. *Fort Mason, Bldg. D,* ☏ *415/441–0404.* ☛ *$3*

Northern Waterfront: Tours 10-11

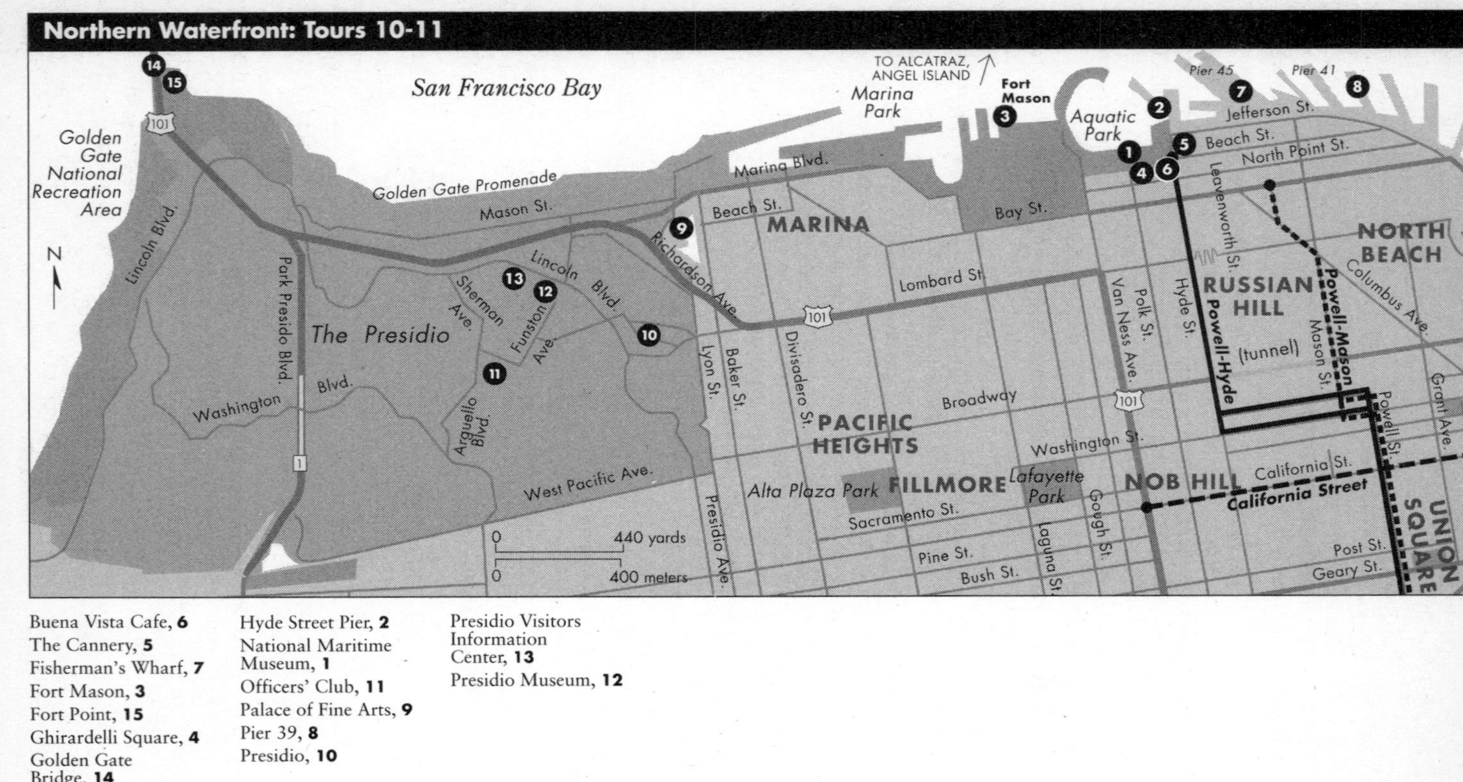

Buena Vista Cafe, **6**
The Cannery, **5**
Fisherman's Wharf, **7**
Fort Mason, **3**
Fort Point, **15**
Ghirardelli Square, **4**
Golden Gate Bridge, **14**
Hyde Street Pier, **2**
National Maritime Museum, **1**
Officers' Club, **11**
Palace of Fine Arts, **9**
Pier 39, **8**
Presidio, **10**
Presidio Visitors Information Center, **13**
Presidio Museum, **12**

adults, $2 senior citizens and students, children under 10 free; free noon–8 PM on 1st Wed. of month. ⏲ *Wed.–Sun. noon–5.*

The **Museo Italo-Americano** has permanent exhibits of works of 19th- and 20th-century Italian-American artists. Shows include paintings, sculpture, etchings, and photographs. The museum presents special exhibits, lectures, and films. *Fort Mason, Bldg. C,* ☎ *415/673–2200.* ☛ *$2 adults, $1 senior citizens and students;* ☛ *Free noon–8 PM on 1st Wed. of month.* ⏲ *Wed.–Sun. noon–5.*

The **San Francisco African-American Historical and Cultural Society** is the only museum of black culture west of the Rockies. The permanent collection includes exhibits on black California and black Civil War history. Temporary exhibits showcase current black artists of California. *Fort Mason, Bldg. C, Room 165,* ☎ *415/979–6794.* ☛ *$2 adults, 50¢ senior citizens and children 6–17.* ⏲ *Wed.–Sun. noon–5. Phone to verify schedules.*

The **San Francisco Craft and Folk Art Museum** features American folk art, tribal art, and contemporary crafts. *Fort Mason, Bldg. A,* ☎ *415/775–0990.* ☛ *$1 adults, 50¢ senior citizens and ages 12–17, children under 12 free;* ☛ *Free Sat. 10–noon and 1st Wed. of month, 11–8.* ⏲ *Tues.–Sun. 11–5, Sat. 10–5. Occasionally open Mon.; call ahead.*

Several theater companies are housed at Fort Mason. Of particular note is the **Magic Theatre** (Fort Mason, Bldg. D, ☎ 415/441–8822), known for producing the works of contemporary playwrights such as Sam Shepard, as well as local and national authors.

TIME OUT The San Francisco Zen Center operates a famous and beautiful restaurant at Fort Mason. **Greens** (Fort Mason, Bldg. A, ☎ 415/771-6222) has won international acclaim for its innovative vegetarian menu. The room is decorated with contemporary art and offers some of the finest views across the bay to the Golden Gate Bridge. Reservations are essential, but the bakery always stocks outstanding bread and pastries.

4 Spend some time strolling through **Ghirardelli Square,** which is across Beach Street from the National Maritime Museum. This charming complex of 19th-century brick factory buildings, once the home of the aromatic Ghirardelli Chocolate Company, has been transformed into a network of specialty shops, cafés, restaurants, and galleries. Two unusual shops in the Cocoa Building are **Xanadu Gallery** and **Folk Art International**: Both display museum-quality tribal art from Asia, Africa, Oceania, and the Americas. Also of interest, on the Lower Plaza level of the Cocoa Building, is the **Creative Spirit Gallery** (☎ 415/441–1537), a space sponsored and run by the National Institute of Art and Disabilities to showcase works by artists with disabilities. Nearby, in Ghirardelli's Rose court, is the **California Crafts Museum** (☎ 415/771–1919), which honors the state's craft artists.

5 Just east of the Hyde Street Pier, **The Cannery** is a three-story structure built in 1894 to house what became the Del Monte Fruit and Vegetable Cannery. Shops, art galleries, and unusual restaurants ring the courtyard today, and the **Museum of the City of San Francisco** can be found on the third floor. The first independent museum on the history of the city, it displays historical items, maps, and photographs, including the 8-ton head of the Goddess of Progress statue that toppled from City Hall just before the 1906 earthquake. *2801 Leavenworth St.,* ☎ *415/928–0289.* ☛ *Free ($2 donation suggested).* ⏲ *Wed.–Sun. 10–4.*

Just across the street, additional shopping and snacking choices are offered at the flag-festooned **Anchorage Mall.**

6 The mellow **Buena Vista Cafe** (2765 Hyde St., ☎ 415/474–5044) claims to be the first U.S. establishment to serve Irish coffee; the late San Francisco columnist Stan Delaplane is credited with importing the Gaelic concoction. The café opens at 9 AM weekdays, 8 AM weekends, and serves a great breakfast. It is always crowded, but try for a table overlooking nostalgic Victorian Park with its cable-car turntable.

7 A bit farther west, at Taylor and Jefferson streets, is **Fisherman's Wharf,** home of numerous seafood restaurants, as well as sidewalk crab pots and counters that offer take-away shrimp and crab cocktails. Ships creak at their moorings; seagulls cry out for a handout. By mid-afternoon, the fishing fleet is back to port. T-shirts and sweats, gold chains galore, redwood furniture, acres of artwork—some original—beckon visitors. Wax museums, fast-food favorites, and amusing street artists provide diversions for all ages.

TIME OUT The swingin'est place on the wharf is the airy **Lou's Pier 47 Restaurant** and bar (300 Jefferson St., ☎ 415/771-0377). You won't be able to miss this joint: the sounds of live R&B, blues and rock bands, many of them quite fine, flood the wharf. Friday and Saturday the music begins at noon, other days at 4 PM. The food at Lou's—standard American fare—is not bad either. A good place for families is **Bobby Rubino's Place for Ribs** (245 Jefferson St., ☎ 415/673-2266) across the street.

Cruises are an exhilarating way to see the bay. Among the cruises offered by the **Red and White Fleet,** berthed at Pier 43½, are frequent one-hour swings under the Golden Gate Bridge and along the Northern Waterfront. More interesting—and just as scenic—are the tours to Sausalito, Angel Island, Tiburon, Muir Woods, and the Napa Valley ★ Wine Country. Perhaps best of all is the popular tour of **Alcatraz Island.** The boat ride to the island is brief (15 minutes), but affords beautiful views of the city, Marin County, and the East Bay. The audio tour, highly recommended, features observations of guards and prisoners about life in one of America's most notorious penal colonies. A separate, ranger-led tour surveys the island's ecology. Plan your schedule to include at least three hours for the visit and boat rides combined. Advance reservations, even in the off-season, are strongly recommended. *Recorded information on all Red and White tours,* ☎ *415/546–2628.* ☛ *Alcatraz tours (including audio guide) are $9 adults and children 12–18, $8 senior citizens, $4.50 children 5–11; without audio, subtract $3.25 for adults and senior citizens, $1.25 for children 5–11. Add $2 per ticket to charge by phone at 415/546–2700.*

For a more outdoorsy adventure, consider a day at **Angel Island,** just north of Alcatraz. Discovered by Spaniards in 1775 and declared a U.S. military reserve 75 years later, the island was used from 1910 until 1940 as a screening ground for Asian immigrants, who were often held for months, even years, before being granted entry. In 1963 the government deemed Angel Island a state park: Today, picnics and hikes are its main offerings, in addition to docent-led tours that explain its history. A scenic path winds around the perimeter of the island. Twenty-five bicycles are permitted on the regular ferry on a first-come, first-served basis. *Recorded information on tours, activities, and hiking,* ☎ *415/435–1915.* ☛ *Angel Island fares are $9 adults, $8 children 12–18, $4.50 children 5–11 (includes park admission).* ⏲ *Weekends only during the off-season, daily during the summer months.*

The **Blue and Gold Fleet,** berthed at Pier 39, conducts 1¼-hour tours under both the Bay and Golden Gate bridges. Friday and Saturday night dinner-dance cruises run April–mid-December. ☎ *415/781–7877. Reservations not necessary.* ☛ *Bay Cruise: $15 adults; $8 senior citizens, active military, and children 5–18; children under 5 free. Summertime dinner-dance cruise: $40 per person (group rates available). Daily departures.*

8 **Pier 39** is the most popular of San Francisco's waterfront attractions, drawing millions of visitors each year to browse through its dozens of shops. Check out the **Disney Store,** with more Mickey Mouses than you can shake a stick at; **Left Hand World,** where left-handers will find all manner of gadgets designed with lefties in mind; and **Only in San Francisco,** the place for San Francisco memorabilia. Ongoing free entertainment, accessible validated parking, and nearby public transportation ensure crowds most days. Opening in spring 1996 is a new attraction: **Underwater World** at Pier 39. Moving walkways will transport visitors through a space surrounded on three sides by water. The focus will be on indigenous San Francisco Bay marine life, from fish and plankton to sharks. Above water, don't miss the hundreds of sea lions that bask and play on the docks on the pier's northwest side. Bring a camera.

TOUR 11: THE MARINA AND THE PRESIDIO

9 San Francisco's rosy, rococo **Palace of Fine Arts** is at the very end of the Marina, near the intersection of Baker and Beach streets. The palace is the sole survivor of the 32 tinted plaster structures built for the 1915 Panama-Pacific International Exposition. Bernard Maybeck designed the Roman Classic beauty, and in the ensuing 50 years the building fell into disrepair. It was reconstructed in concrete at a cost of $7 million and reopened in 1967, thanks to legions of sentimental citizens and a huge private donation that saved the palace from demolition. The massive columns, great rotunda, and swan-filled lagoon has been used in countless fashion layouts and recent films. Recently, travelers on package tours from Japan have been using it as a backdrop for wedding-party photos, with the brides wearing Western-style finery.

The interior houses a fascinating hands-on museum, the **Exploratorium,** which has been called the best science museum in the world. The curious of all ages flock here to play with and learn from some of the 600 exhibits. Be sure to include the dark, touchy-feely Tactile Dome in your visit, and inquire about their program of films and lectures. ☎ *415/561–0360 for general information, 415/561–0362 for required reservations for Tactile Dome.* ☛ *$9 adults, $7 students over 18 and senior citizens with ID, $5 children 6–17, $2.50 children 3–5; free 1st Wed. of month.* ⌚ *Tues.–Sun. 10–5, Wed. 10–9:30, legal Mon. holidays 10–5.*

10 If you have a car, now is the time to use it for a drive through the **Presidio.** (If not, Muni Bus 38 from Union Square will take you to Park Presidio Boulevard; from there use a free transfer to Bus 28 into the Presidio.) Now part of the Golden Gate National Recreation Area, the Presidio was a military post for more than 200 years. Don Juan Bautista de Anza and a band of Spanish settlers first claimed the area in 1776. It became a Mexican garrison in 1822 when Mexico gained its independence from Spain, until U.S. troops forcibly occupied it in 1846.

The U.S. Sixth Army was stationed here until October 1994, when the coveted space was finally transferred into civilian hands.

The more than 1,400 acres of rolling hills, majestic woods, and attractive redbrick army barracks present an air of serenity in the middle of the city. There are two beaches, a golf course, and picnic sites. The former
11 **Officers' Club** (now the Community Club) a long, low adobe built around 1776, was the Spanish commandante's headquarters and may be the oldest standing building in the city.

12 The **Presidio Museum,** housed in a former hospital built in 1863, focuses on the role played by the military in San Francisco's development. Behind the museum are two cabins that housed refugees from the 1906 earthquake and fire. Photos on the wall of one depict rows and rows of temporary shelters at the Presidio and in Golden Gate Park following the disaster. *On the corner of Lincoln Blvd. and Funston Ave., ☎ 415/556–0856. ☛ Free. ⊙ Wed.–Sun. 10–4.*

13 Four blocks west on Lincoln lies the new **Presidio Visitors Information Center,** offering maps, brochures, and schedules for guided walking and bicycle tours. *On the corner of Lincoln Blvd. and Montgomery, ☎ 415/556–0865. ☛ Free. ⊙ Daily 10–5.*

★ 14 Muni Bus 28 will take you to the **Golden Gate Bridge** toll plaza. Nearly 2 miles long, connecting San Francisco with Marin County, its art deco design is simple but powerful, made to withstand winds of over 100 miles per hour, but also to wow sightseers with its unique rust-colored beauty. Though frequently gusty and misty (walkers should wear warm clothing), the bridge offers unparalleled views of the Bay Area. The east walkway offers a glimpse of the San Francisco skyline as well as the islands of the bay. The view west confronts you with the wild hills of the Marin headlands, the curving coast south to Land's End, and the majestic Pacific Ocean. A vista point on the Marin side affords a spectacular view of the city. On sunny days sailboats dot the water, and brave windsurfers test the often-treacherous tides beneath the bridge.

15 Though **Fort Point,** designed to mount 125 cannons with a range of up to 2 miles, was constructed during the years 1853–61 to protect San Francisco from sea attack during the Civil War, it was never used for that purpose. Standing under the shadow of the Golden Gate Bridge, the national historic site is now a museum filled with military memorabilia. Guided group tours and cannon drills are offered daily by National Park Rangers. The top floor affords a superb view of the bay. *☎ 415/556–1693. ☛ Free. ⊙ Wed.–Sun. 10–5.*

From here, hardy walkers may elect to stroll about 3½ miles along the scenic Golden Gate Promenade to Aquatic Park and the Hyde Street cable-car terminus.

TOUR 12: GOLDEN GATE PARK

Numbers in the margin correspond to points of interest on the Golden Gate Park: Tour 12 map.

It was a Scotsman, John McLaren, who became manager of Golden Gate Park in 1887, transforming the brush and sand into the green civilized wilderness we enjoy today. Here you can attend a polo game or a Sunday band concert and rent a bike, boat, or roller skates. On Sunday, some park roads are closed to cars and come alive with joggers, bicyclists, skaters, museum goers, and picnickers. There are tennis courts, baseball diamonds, soccer fields, a buffalo paddock, and miles of trails for horseback riding in this 1,000-acre park.

Because it is so large, the best way for most visitors to see it is by car. Muni buses provide service, though on weekends there may be a long wait. On Market Street, board westbound Bus 5-Fulton or Bus 21-Hayes and continue to Arguello and Fulton streets. Walk south about 500 feet to John F. Kennedy Drive.

From May through October, free guided walking tours of the park are offered every weekend by the Friends of Recreation and Parks (☏ 415/221–1311).

The oldest building in the park and perhaps San Francisco's most
❶ elaborate Victorian is the **Conservatory** (☏ 415/752–8080), a copy of London's famous Kew Gardens. Originally brought around the Horn for the estate of James Lick in San Jose, the ornate greenhouse was purchased from the Lick estate with public subscription funds and erected in the park. In addition to a tropical garden, there are seasonal displays of flowers and plants and a permanent exhibit of rare orchids. ☛ *$1.50 adults, 75¢ senior citizens and children 6–12; free 1st and last 1/2 hr.* ⏲ *Daily 9–5.*

The eastern section of the park has three museums. Purchase of a $10 Golden Gate Park Cultural Pass gains you one-day admission to all three, plus the Japanese Tea Garden and the Conservatory—a substantial savings (for adults) if you are planning to visit all these attractions. Purchase your pass at any of the museums or at TIX Bay Area in Union
❷ Square. The **M. H. de Young Memorial Museum** specializes in American art, with paintings, sculpture, textiles, and decorative arts from Colonial times through the 20th century. Over 200 paintings highlight the work of American masters, including Copley, Eakins, Bingham, and Sargent. Don't miss the room of landscapes, dominated by Frederic Church's moody, almost psychedelic *Rainy Season in the Tropics,* or the wonderful gallery of American still lifes, including the trompe l'oeil paintings of William Harnett. The de Young also has a dramatic collection of tribal art from Africa, Oceania, and the Americas, including pottery, basketry, sculpture, and ritual clothing and accessories. An ongoing textile installation, *Unraveling Yarns: The Art of Everyday Life,* contains more than 60 samples of fiber art from around the world. In addition to its permanent collections, the museum hosts selected traveling shows—often blockbuster events that involve long lines and additional admission charges. The museum shop offers a wide selection of art objects, and the **Cafe de Young,** which has outdoor seating in the Oakes Garden, serves a complete menu of light refreshments until 4 PM. ☏ *415/863–3330 for 24-hr information.* ☛ *$6 adults, $4 senior citizens, $3 ages 12–17; free 1st Wed. of month. (until 5). Note: One admission charge admits you to the de Young, Asian Art, and Legion of Honor museums on the same day.* ⏲ *Wed.–Sun. 10–5, 1st Wed. of month only, 10–8:45.*

❸ The **Asian Art Museum,** located in galleries adjoining the de Young, contains a world-famous collection of more than 12,000 sculptures, paintings, and ceramics from 40 countries, illustrating major periods of Asian art. One standout permanent exhibit is the Leventritt collection of blue and white porcelains. On the second floor are treasures from Iran, Turkey, Syria, India, Tibet, Nepal, Pakistan, Korea, Japan, Afghanistan, and Southeast Asia. Both the de Young and Asian Art museums have daily docent tours. ☏ *415/668–8921.* ☛ *Collected when entering the de Young.* ⏲ *Wed.–Sun. 10–5., 1st Wed. of month 10–8:45.*

Golden Gate Park: Tour 12

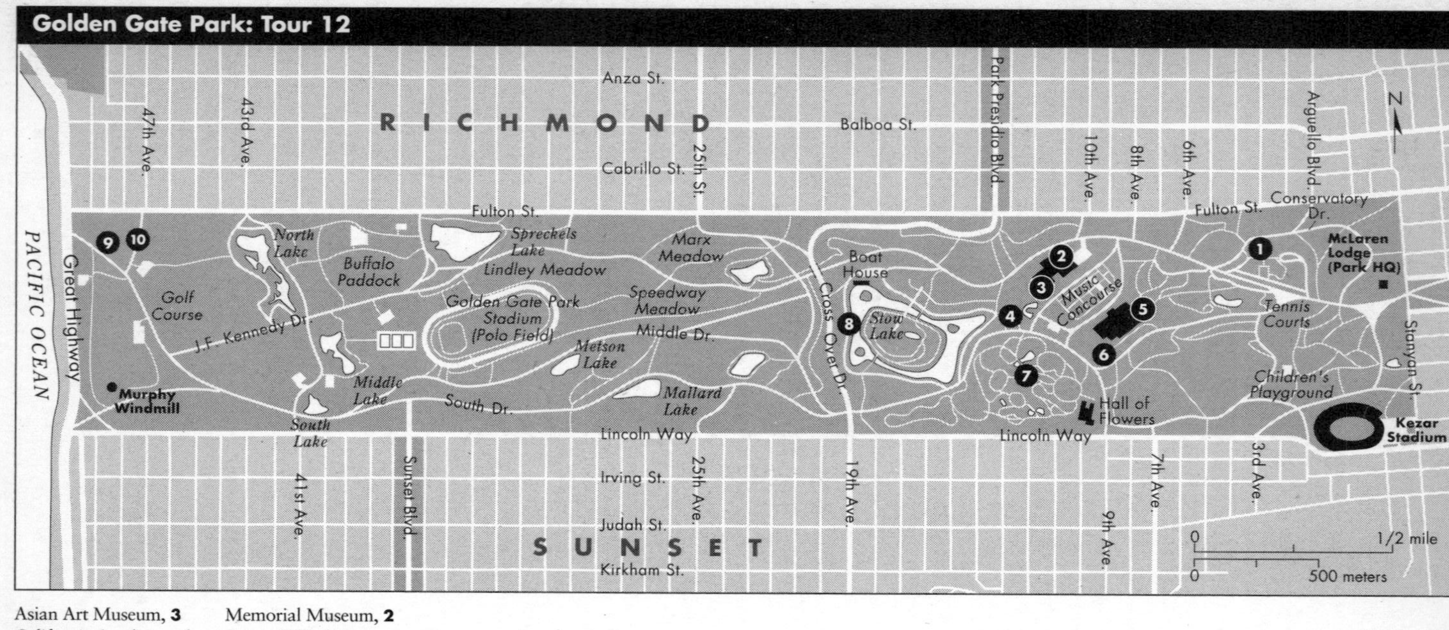

Asian Art Museum, **3**
California Academy of Sciences, **5**
Conservatory, **1**
Dutch Windmill, **9**
Japanese Tea Garden, **4**
M.H. de Young Memorial Museum, **2**
Queen Wilhelmina Tulip Garden, **10**
Shakespeare Garden, **6**
Stow Lake, **8**
Strybing Arboretum, **7**

TIME OUT ★ 4 The **Japanese Tea Garden,** next to the Asian Art Museum, is an ideal place to rest after touring the museums. This charming 4-acre village was created for the 1894 Mid-Winter Exposition. Small ponds, streams, and flowering shrubs create a serene landscape. The cherry blossoms in spring are exquisite. The Tea House, where tea and cookies are served, is popular and busy. ☎ *415/752–1171.* ☛ *$2.50 adults and children 13–17, $1.50 senior citizens and children 6–12.* ⌚ *Summer, daily 9–6; winter, daily 9–5.*

---

5 The **California Academy of Sciences,** directly opposite the de Young Museum, is one of the top five natural-history museums in the country, with both an aquarium and a planetarium. The Steinhart Aquarium, with its dramatic 100,000-gallon Fish Roundabout, is home to 14,000 creatures, including a living coral reef with colorful fish, giant clams, tropical sharks, and a rainbow of hard and soft corals. The Space and Earth Hall has an "earthquake floor" that enables visitors to experience a simulated California earthquake. The Wattis Hall presents rotating natural-history, art, and cultural exhibits. In the Wild California Hall, a 14,000-gallon aquarium tank shows underwater life at the Farallones (islands off the coast of northern California), life-size elephant-seal models, and video information on the wildlife of the state. The innovative Life Through Time Hall tells the story of evolution from the beginnings of life on earth through the age of dinosaurs to the age of mammals. A popular attraction at the Academy is the permanent display of cartoons by Far Side creator Gary Larson. There is an additional charge for Morrison Planetarium shows (depending on the show, up to $2.50 adults, $1.25 senior citizens and students, ☎ 415/750–7141 for daily schedule). Laserium (☎ 415/750–7138 for schedule and fees) presents evening laser-light shows at Morrison Planetarium, accompanied by rock, classical, and other types of music; educational shows outline laser technology. A cafeteria is open daily until one hour before the museum closes, and the Academy Store offers a wide selection of books, posters, toys, and cultural artifacts. ☎ *415/750–7145.* ☛ *$7 adults, $4 senior citizens and students 12–17, $1.50 children 6–11; $2 discount with Muni transfer; free 1st Wed. of month.* ⌚ *July 4–Labor Day, daily 10–7; Labor Day–July 4, daily 10–5.*

A short stroll from the Academy of Sciences will take you to the free
6 **Shakespeare Garden.** Two hundred flowers mentioned by the Bard, as well as bronze-engraved panels with floral quotations, are set throughout the garden.

7 **Strybing Arboretum** specializes in plants from areas with climates similar to that of the Bay Area, such as the west coast of Australia, South Africa, and the Mediterranean. 6,000 plants and tree varieties bloom in gardens throughout the grounds. *9th Ave. at Lincoln Way,* ☎ *415/661–1316.* ☛ *Free.* ⌚ *Weekdays 8–4:30, weekends and holidays 10–5. Tours leave the bookstore weekdays at 1:30, weekends at 10:30 and 1:30.*

The western half of Golden Gate Park offers miles of wooded greenery and open spaces for all types of spectator and participant sports.
8 Rent a paddleboat or stroll around **Stow Lake.** The Chinese Pavilion, a gift from the city of Taipei, was shipped in 6,000 pieces and assembled on the shore of Strawberry Hill Island in Stow Lake in 1981. At the very western end of the park, where Kennedy Drive meets the Great
9 Highway, is the beautifully restored 1902 **Dutch Windmill** and the pho-
10 togenic **Queen Wilhelmina Tulip Garden.**

TOUR 13: LINCOLN PARK AND THE WESTERN SHORELINE

No other American city provides such close-up viewing of the power and fury of the surf attacking the shore. From Land's End in Lincoln Park you can look across the Golden Gate (the name was originally given to the opening of San Francisco Bay long before the bridge was built) to the Marin Headlands. From the Cliff House south to the San Francisco Zoo, the Great Highway and Ocean Beach run along the western edge of the city.

The wind is often strong along the shoreline, summer fog can blanket the ocean beaches, and the water is cold and usually too rough for swimming. Carry a sweater or jacket and bring binoculars.

At the northwest corner of the San Francisco Peninsula is **Lincoln Park.** At one time all the city's cemeteries were here, segregated by nationality. The cemeteries have given way to an 18-hole golf course with large and well-formed Monterey cypresses lining the fairways. There are scenic walks throughout the 275-acre park, with particularly good views from **Land's End** (the parking lot is at the end of El Camino del Mar). The trails out to Land's End, however, are for skilled hikers only: Landslides are frequent, and danger lurks along the steep cliffs.

Also in Lincoln Park is the **California Palace of the Legion of Honor.** The building itself—modeled after the 18th-century Parisian original—is architecturally interesting and spectacularly situated on cliffs overlooking the ocean and the Golden Gate Bridge. The museum, which recently reopened after extensive renovations, contains 27 galleries of mostly European paintings, drawing, sculpture, tapestries, and porcelain. Collection highlights also include ancient Egyptian, Greek, and Roman art. ☎ *415/863–3330 for 24-hr information.* ☛ *$6 adults, $4 senior citizens, $3 ages 12–17; free 2nd Wed. of month. Note: One admission charge admits you to the de Young, Asian Art, and Legion of Honor museums on the same day. Tues.–Sun. 10–5 and 1st Sat. of month 10–8:45.*

★ The **Cliff House** (1066 Point Lobos Ave.), where the road turns south along the western shore, has existed in several incarnations. The original, built in 1863, and several later structures were destroyed by fire. The present building has restaurants, a pub, and a gift shop. The lower dining room overlooks Seal Rocks (the barking marine mammals sunning themselves are actually sea lions).

An adjacent attraction is the **Musée Mécanique,** a collection of antique mechanical contrivances, including peep shows and nickelodeons. The museum carries on the tradition of arcade amusement at the Cliff House. ☎ *415/386–1170.* ☛ *Free.* ⏲ *Weekdays 11–7, weekends 10–8.*

Two flights below the Cliff House are a fine observation deck and the Golden Gate National Recreation Area **Visitors Center,** which contains interesting and historic photographs of the Cliff House and the glass-roofed **Sutro Baths.** This complex, which comprised six enormous baths, 500 dressing rooms, and several restaurants, covered 3 acres just north of the Cliff House. The baths were closed in 1952 and burned in 1966. You can explore the ruins on your own or take ranger-led walks on weekends. The Visitors Center offers information on these and other trails. ☎ *415/556–8642.* ⏲ *Daily 10–4:30.*

Because traffic is often heavy in summer and on weekends, you might want to take the Muni system from the Union Square area out to the

Cliff House. On weekdays, take the Muni Bus 38-Geary Limited to 48th Avenue and Point Lobos and walk down the hill. On weekends and during the evenings, the Muni Bus 38 is marked "48th Avenue." Don't take Bus 38 bus marked "Ocean Beach," though, or you'll have to walk an extra 10 minutes to get to the Cliff House.

TIME OUT The Cliff House (☎ 415/386-3330) has several restaurants and a busy bar. The **Upstairs Room** features a light menu with a number of omelet suggestions. The lower dining room, the **Seafood & Beverage Co. Restaurant,** has a fabulous view of Seal Rocks. Reservations are recommended, but you may still have to wait for a table, especially at midday on Sunday.

Below the Cliff House are the **Great Highway** and **Ocean Beach.** Stretching 3 miles along the western (Pacific) side of the city, this is a beautiful beach for walking, running, or lying in the sun—but not for swimming. Although dozens of surfers head to Ocean Beach each day, you'll notice they are dressed head-to-toe in wet suits, as the water here is extremely cold. Across the highway from the beach is a new path that winds through landscaped sand dunes from Lincoln Avenue to Sloat Boulevard (near the zoo)—an ideal route for walking and bicycling.

At the Great Highway and Sloat Boulevard is the **San Francisco Zoo,** which was first established in 1889 in Golden Gate Park. At its present home there are 1,000 species of birds and animals, more than 130 of which have been designated endangered species. Among the protected are the snow leopard, Sumatran tiger, jaguar, and the Asian elephant. A favorite attraction is the greater one-horned rhino, next to the African elephants. Another popular zoo resident is Prince Charles, a rare white tiger and the first of its kind to be exhibited in the West.

Gorilla World, a $2 million exhibit, is one of the largest and most natural gorilla habitats of any zoo in the world. The circular outer area is carpeted with natural African Kikuyu grass, while trees and shrubs create communal play areas. The $5 million Primate Discovery Center houses 14 endangered species in atriumlike enclosures.

There are 46 "storyboxes" throughout the zoo that, when turned on with blue and red keys ($2), recite animal facts and basic zoological concepts in four languages—English, Spanish, Cantonese, and Tagalog.

The children's zoo has a minipopulation of about 300 mammals, birds, and reptiles, plus an insect zoo, a baby-animal nursery, and a beautifully restored 1921 Dentzel Carousel. A ride astride one of the 52 handcarved menagerie animals costs $1.

Zoo information, ☎ 415/753–7083. ☛ $6.50 adults, $3 children 12–15 and senior citizens, $1 children 6–12, children under 5 free when accompanied by adult; free 1st Wed. of month. ⏲ Daily 10–5. Children's zoo ☛ $1, under 3 free. ⏲ Daily 11–4.

TOUR 14: THE MISSION DISTRICT

Numbers in the margin correspond to points of interest on the Mission District: Tour 14 map.

During the 19th century the sunny weather of the then-rural Mission District made it a popular locale for resorts, racetracks, and gambling places. At 13th and Mission streets, where freeway traffic now roars overhead, stood Woodward's Gardens, a lush botanical garden with a zoo, playground, and pavilions featuring acrobatic performances.

The Mission District: Tour 14

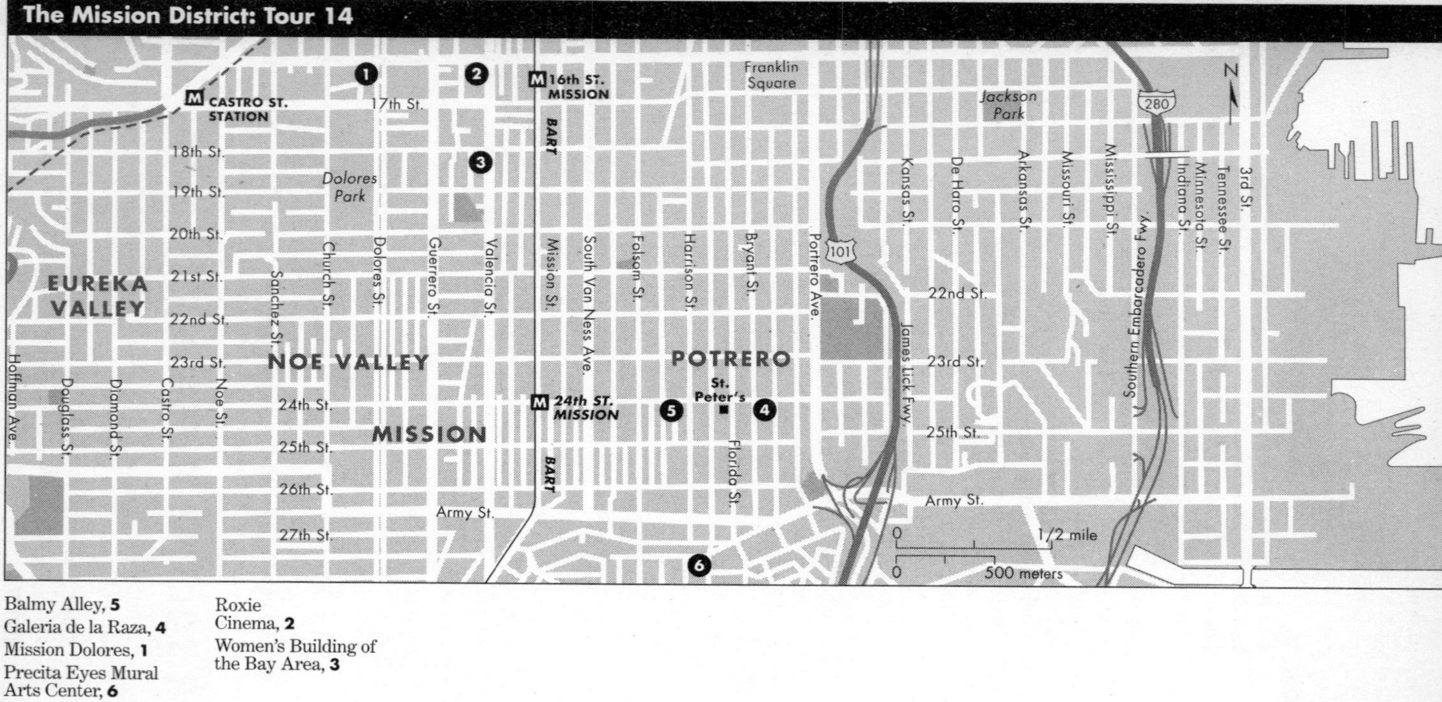

Balmy Alley, **5**
Galeria de la Raza, **4**
Mission Dolores, **1**
Precita Eyes Mural Arts Center, **6**
Roxie Cinema, **2**
Women's Building of the Bay Area, **3**

1 **Mission Dolores,** on palm-lined Dolores Street, is the sixth of the 21 missions founded by Father Junípero Serra. The adobe building, begun in 1782, was originally known as Mission San Francisco de Assisi. Completed in 1791, its ceiling depicts original Costanoan Indian basket designs, executed in vegetable dyes. There is a small museum, and the mission cemetery maintains the graves of mid-19th-century European immigrants. *Dolores and 16th Sts.,* ☎ *415/621–8203.* ☛ *$1.* ⊙ *Daily 9–4.*

Two blocks from Mission Dolores, the area around Valencia Street from 16th to 24th streets has become San Francisco's new bohemia, frequented by socialists, lesbian-feminists, new wavers, and traditional Hispanics.
2 The alternative **Roxie Cinema** (3117 16th St., ☎ 415/863–1087 for daily schedule), the disabled-adult visual-art gallery **Creativity Explored** (3245 16th St., ☎ 415/863–2103), the leftist **Modern Times Bookstore** (888 Valencia St.), the offbeat **Marsh** performance space (1062 Valencia St., ☎ 415/641–0235), the campy year-round Christmas decor at Mexican eatery **La Rondalla** (901 Valencia, ☎ 415/647–7474), and a dozen-plus cafés all contribute to the idiosyncratic atmosphere. For a walk on the (mildly) wild side, stop in at **Good Vibrations** (1210 Valencia, ☎ 415/974–8980), a friendly, brightly lit erotic literature and paraphernalia store catering to mostly female customers who wouldn't be caught dead in the traditional "adult bookstore."

The cornerstone of the women-owned and -run businesses in the neigh-
3 borhood is the **Women's Building of the Bay Area** (3543 18th St., ☎ 415/431–1180), which for more than a dozen years has held workshops and conferences of particular interest to women. It houses offices for many social and political organizations and sponsors talks and readings by such noted writers as Alice Walker and Angela Davis. The building's striking two-sided exterior mural, depicting women's peacekeeping efforts over the centuries, was completed in September 1994.

At any point on Valencia you can walk one block east to Mission. All the Mission District's resident ethnic cultures are reflected in Mission Street's businesses: Spanish-language theaters; Italian restaurants; Arab-owned clothing stores; Vietnamese markets; and Filipino, Hispanic, and Chinese restaurants and groceries. The majority of the neighborhood's Latinos are from Central America. Most of them settled here during the late 1960s and early 1970s.

On 24th Street, the area takes on the flavor of another country, with small open-air groceries selling huge Mexican papayas and plantains, tiny restaurants serving *sopa de mariscos* (fish soup), and an abundance of religious shops. Bakeries, or *panaderias* are an essential stop. Two of the best are **La Victoria** (2937 24th St.) and **Dominguez** (2951 24th St.).

4 **Galeria de la Raza,** at the east end of the street, is an important showcase for Hispanic art. It shows local and international artists and sometimes mounts larger exhibits in conjunction with other Bay Area arts groups. *2855 24th St.,* ☎ *415/826–8009.* ⊙ *Tues.–Sat. noon–6.*

Next door to the Gallery is Studio 24 Galeria Shop, which sells handicrafts from Latin America. The studio specializes in figurines from *Dia de los Muertos,* the Latin American Halloween. The aim of these brightly colored objects is to make death seem more familiar and less threatening; don't be surprised to see a skeleton calmly doing her ironing. *2857 24th St.,* ☎ *415/826–8009.* ⊙ *Tues.–Sat. noon–6.*

Art in the Mission District is not just indoors. In the tradition of the great muralist Diego Rivera, community artists have transformed the walls of their neighborhood with paintings. Two to watch for are those adorning the **St. Peter's Catholic Church** building, at 24th and Florida streets, and the **Mission**

Neighborhood Center, at 3013 24th Street. The center is on the cor-
5 ner of **Balmy Alley,** where a series of murals was begun in 1973 by a group of local children and continued by an affiliation of several dozen artists and community workers to promote peace in Central America. (Be careful in this area; the other end of the street adjoins the back of a somewhat dangerous housing project.)

6 The **Precita Eyes Mural Arts Center** gives guided walks of the Mission District's murals. The tour starts with an hour-long slide presentation, and the walk takes about an hour, visiting over 70 murals in the area. *348 Precita Ave., ☎ 415/285–2287. ☛ $4 adults, $1 students under 18. Tours every Sat. at 1:30. Walks can also be arranged by appointment for groups of 10 or more.*

The Mission District celebrates two important fiestas. The *Cinco de Mayo* (5th of May) is a weekend of music, dance, and parades. Come Memorial Day weekend, the revelers come out in earnest, when carnaval transforms the neighborhood into a western Rio for three days. Recent festivities closed Harrison Street between 16th and 22nd streets, with four stages for live music and dancers, as well as crafts and food booths. A Grand Carnaval Parade along 24th Street caps the celebration.

TIME OUT Spanish, Latin American, and Caribbean tapas (appetizers) bars are all the rage in the Mission these days. The leader of the pack is **Esperpento,** where you can mix and match mild-to-spicy specialties to create a meal. The chicken croquettes are crispy outside, creamy inside, and not to be missed. *3295 22nd St., ☎ 415/282–8867. ⏲ Weekdays 11–3 and 5–10, Sat. 11–3 and 5–10:30, Sun. noon–10.*

To continue on to the Castro, walk west on 24th Street to Castro Street, then turn right (north). The walk is steep at times, and takes about half an hour. Otherwise, take Bus 48-Quintara west on 24th Street to Castro, and transfer to Bus 24-Divisadero. To return downtown, take any Fremont, Richmond, or Concord BART train at the 24th Street and Mission station to Powell or Montgomery.

TOUR 15: THE CASTRO

Numbers in the margin correspond to points of interest on the Castro and the Haight: Tours 15–16 map.

Historians are still trying to discover what brought an estimated 100,000 to 250,000 gays and lesbians into the San Francisco area. Some point to the libertine tradition rooted in Barbary Coast piracy, prostitution, and gambling. Others note that as a huge military embarkation point during World War II, the city was occupied by tens of thousands of mostly single men. Whatever the cause, San Francisco became the city of choice for lesbians and gay men, and Castro Street, nestled at the base of Twin Peaks and just over Buena Vista hill from Haight Street, became its social, cultural, and political center.

The gay **Castro District** hosts two lively annual celebrations. In late September or early October, when San Francisco weather is at its warmest, the annual Castro Street Fair takes over several blocks of Castro and Market streets. Huge stages are set up for live music and comedy, alongside booths selling food and baubles. The weather inevitably brings off the men's shirts, and the Castro relives for a moment the permissive spirit of the 1970s. San Francisco's annual gay parade no longer originates in the Castro District. The late-June march, by far the city's largest, begins in the Civic Center and terminates at the Embarcadero.

1 Directly above the Castro Street Muni Metro station at 17th and Market streets (trains K, L, and M stop here) is **Harvey Milk Plaza,** named for the man who electrified the city in 1977 by being elected to its board of supervisors as an openly gay candidate. His high visibility accompanied demands by homosexuals for thorough inclusion in the city's life. San Francisco has responded with a tolerance found nowhere else in the United States: Gay people sit as municipal judges, police commissioners, and school board members. In the wake of Milk's assassination in 1978 by a fellow supervisor and the AIDS crisis, the Castro has become a little less flamboyant. It is still, however, the center of gay life. Gay bars abound, and gay-oriented boutiques line Castro, 18th, and Market streets.

2 Across the street from Harvey Milk Plaza is the great neon neighborhood landmark, the **Castro Theatre** marquee. Erected in 1922, the theater is the grandest of San Francisco's few remaining movie palaces. Its elaborate Spanish Baroque interior is well preserved, and a new pipe organ plays nightly, ending with a traditional chorus of the Jeanette McDonald standard, "San Francisco." The 1,500-capacity crowd can be enthusiastic and vocal, talking back to the screen as loudly as it talks to them. The Castro Theatre is the showcase for many community events, in particular the annual Gay and Lesbian Film Festival (☎ 415/703–8650), held each June.

A Different Light (489 Castro St., ☎ 415/431–0891) features books by, for, and about lesbians and gay men. The store has become the unofficial Castro community center—residents regularly phone for non-book information, and a rack in the front is chock full of fliers for local events. Book signings and readings occur several times each week.

TIME OUT There are several renowned gay chefs in San Francisco. Unfortunately, none of them work in the Castro, where a half-dozen greasy spoons do surprisingly well. Festive **Pozole,** which serves burritos, quesadillas, and other Mexican and Latin American specialties, is a welcome oasis of creative cuisine. *2337 Market St., ☎ 415/626-2666. ⏲ Mon.–Thurs. 4–11, Fri.–Sun. noon–midnight.*

3 Across Market Street, the **Names Project** (2362 Market St.) has its public workshop. A gigantic quilt made of more than 25,000 hand-sewn and -decorated panels has been pieced together by loved ones to serve as a memorial to those who have died of AIDS. People come from all over the country to work in this storefront as a labor of love and grief; others have sent panels here by mail. New additions to the quilt are always on display. **Under One Roof** (☎ 415/252–9430; open Sun.–Fri. 11–7, Sat. 10–8) is a store at the same address that sells T-shirts, posters, and other merchandise to raise funds for various AIDS organizations.

Just northwest of Castro and Market streets, an outcropping of rock provides one of the best viewing areas in the city. Walk north up Castro Street two blocks to 16th Street and turn left up a steep, rugged hill. Turn right at Flint Street; the hill to your left is variously known as Red Rock, Museum Hill, and, correctly, Corona Heights. As you climb up the path by the tennis courts along the spine of the hill, the view downtown becomes increasingly superb.

Buena Vista Park, **5**
Castro Theatre, **2**
Harvey Milk Plaza, **1**
Josephine D. Randall Junior Museum, **4**
The Names Project, **3**
Spreckels Mansion, **6**

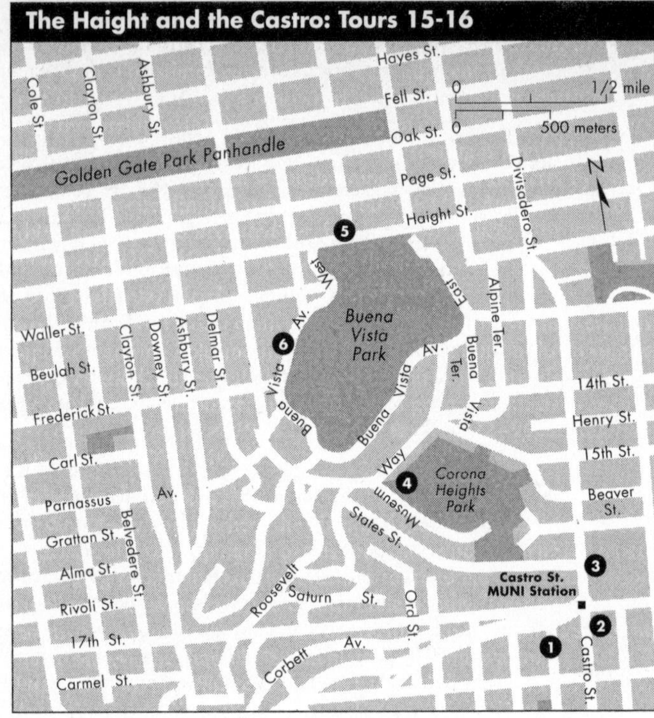

4 At the base of Corona Heights is the **Josephine D. Randall Junior Museum.** Though the Recreation and Park Department bills it as a museum for children, the Randall nevertheless has a variety of workshops and events for both young people and their parents. Highlights are an Animal Room, a library, and excellent woodworking and ceramics studios. *199 Museum Way, ☎ 415/554–9600. ⏲ Museum: Tues.–Sat. 10–5 and at night for workshops; animal room: 10:30–1 and 2–5.*

To return downtown, walk down Roosevelt Way (which intersects Museum Way) to 14th Street and turn right on Castro Street. Muni Metro is three blocks away at 17th Street. Another option is the Haight-Ashbury District, which is just seven blocks away. At Museum Way cross Roosevelt Way (watch out for the traffic on this curvy road), and head up the hill on the right side of the street, which turns into Masonic and veers off to the right after a block. Watch the signs to be sure you're still on Masonic, then head north down the street and turn left at Haight Street. Alternately, take the northbound Bus 33 from the corner of 18th Street and Castro; it takes a circuitous if still-brief route to Haight and Ashbury.

TOUR 16: THE HAIGHT

East of Golden Gate Park is the neighborhood known as "the Haight." Once home to large, middle-class families of European immigrants, the Haight began to change during the late 1950s and early 1960s. Families were fleeing to the suburbs; the big old Victorians were deteriorating or being chopped up into cheap housing. Young people found the neighborhood an affordable and exciting community in which they could live according to new precepts.

The peak of the Haight as a youth scene came in 1966, when it became the home of many rock bands. The Grateful Dead moved into a big Victorian at 710 Ashbury Street, just a block off Haight Street. Jefferson Airplane had their grand mansion at 2400 Fulton Street. By 1967, 200,000 young people with flowers in their hair and peace and civil rights on their minds were heading for the Haight.

Sharing the late-1980s fascination with events of the 1960s, many visitors to San Francisco want to see the setting of the "Summer of Love." Back in 1967, Gray Lines instituted their "Hippie-Hop," advertising it as "the only foreign tour within the continental limits of the United States," piloted by a driver "especially trained in the sociological significance of the Haight." Today's explorers can walk from Union Square to Market Street and hop aboard Muni's Bus 7-Haight.

Haight Street has once again emerged as the center of youth culture in San Francisco, though the youths it attracts today are mostly punkers, neo-hippies, and suburbanites out to spend their cash. Though it does have some upscale galleries and shops, the Haight is known for its vintage merchandise, including clothes, records, books, and a whole host of miscellaneous wonders such as incense, crystal jewelry, and candles. Nowhere else in San Francisco would the likes of **Drastic Changes Tatoo Studio** (1352 Haight, ☎ 415/431–9048) or the **Bound Together Anarchist Book Collective** (1369 Haight, ☎ 415/431–8355) seem so completely at home.

TIME OUT Island cuisine—a mix of Cajun, Southwest, and Caribbean influences—is served at **Cha Cha Cha,** which is informal and inexpensive. The decor is technicolor tropical plastic, and the food is hot and spicy. Try the spicy fried calamari or chili-spiked shrimp. *1801 Haight St., ☎ 415/386–5758. No reservations; expect to wait. No credit cards.*

Golden Gate Park provides the Haight with a variety of opportunities for recreation and entertainment. Rent roller skates, in-line skates, and skateboards at **Skates on Haight** (1818 Haight St.) and roll through the park—it's partially closed to traffic for skaters on Sunday—or, for a more genteel outing, rent bicycles at any of the shops along Stanyan Street, near the park's entrance.

The Haight's famous political spirit (it was the first neighborhood in the United States to lead a freeway revolt, and it continues to feature regular boycotts against chain stores) exists alongside some of the finest Victorian-lined streets in the city; more than 1,000 such houses occupy the Panhandle and Ashbury Heights streets.

5 Great city views can be had from **Buena Vista Park** at Haight and Lyon
6 streets. One landmark is the **Spreckels Mansion,** at 737 Buena Vista West, several blocks south of Haight Street (not to be confused with the Spreckels Mansion of Pacific Heights). The house was built for sugar baron Richard Spreckels in 1887; later tenants included Jack London and Ambrose Bierce.

WHAT TO SEE AND DO WITH CHILDREN

The attractions described in the exploring sections, above, offer a great deal of entertainment for children as well as their families. We suggest, for example, visiting the ships at the **Hyde Street Pier** and spending some time at **Pier 39,** where there is a double-decker Venetian carousel. (*See* Tour 10, *above.*)

Children will find many amusements at **Golden Gate Park,** from the old-fashioned conservatory to the expansive lawns and trails to the vintage carousel (1912) at the children's playground. The **Steinhart Aquarium** at the California Academy of Sciences has a "Touching Tide Pool," from which docents will pull starfish and hermit crabs for children or adults to feel. The winding paths and high, humpbacked bridges in the **Japanese Tea Garden** are fun for children to explore. (*See* Tour 12, *above.*)

A walk across the **Golden Gate Bridge** is another nice family excursion, if the children (and adults) are not overwhelmed by the height of the bridge and the nearby automobile traffic. (*See* Tour 11, *above.*)

Many children enjoy walking along crowded **Grant Avenue** and browsing in the souvenir shops. Unfortunately, nothing—not even straw finger wrestlers or wooden contraptions to make coins "disappear"—is as cheap as it once was. (*See* Tour 4, *above.*)

The **San Francisco Zoo,** with a children's zoo, playground, and carousel, is always a good choice and is not far from Ocean Beach. The weather and currents prohibit swimming, but it's a good place for walking and playing in the surf. (*See* Tour 13, *above.*)

The **Exploratorium** at the Palace of Fine Arts is a preeminent children's museum, amusing and informative. (*See* Tour 11, *above.*)

If you're ready to spend a day outside of the city, consider a trip to Vallejo's **Marine World Africa USA.** (*See* Chapter 8, Excursions from San Francisco.)

OFF THE BEATEN TRACK

Dark Passage

Humphrey Bogart fans can visit the fantastic Art Deco apartment and the unending stairs that were filmed in *Dark Passage,* the 1947 film in which Bogart plays a man who has been convicted of murdering his wife. To visit these sites, turn right after visiting Coit Tower on Telegraph Hill, cross the street, and walk down the brick- and ivy-lined Greenwich Steps, ending up on Montgomery Street. The famous apartment house is No. 1360. A little to the left, pick up the Filbert Steps or walk down Union Street to Grant Avenue and the North Beach attractions.

Showplace Square

A 12-block complex of renovated brick warehouses south of Market Street at the foot of Potrero Hill, Showplace Square is where more than 300 furniture wholesalers display some of the most elegant furnishings and accessories in the country. Most buildings are open for public viewing; individual showrooms set their own policies regarding retail purchase. Showplace Square is at the corner of Kansas Street (also called Henry Adams Street, in honor of the developer) and 15th Street, and has what is so sorely needed elsewhere in the city—a large parking lot.

Orchids

Orchid enthusiasts should visit **Rod McLellan's Acres of Orchids** in South San Francisco. The McLellan Company runs the largest diversified orchid nursery in the world. Two daily (free) tours of the large facility brief visitors on the propagation of orchids as well as on the history of the company (which led a nationwide fad for gardenias when refrigerated railroad cars made transportation of the delicate blossoms possible). There is also a large showroom and a gift shop with hundreds of plants. A cymbidium large enough to produce three sprays of orchids costs about \$40–\$60. The staff will give you plenty of instructions and pack your plant carefully for transportation home. *1450 El Camino Real, South San Francisco 94080,* ☎ *415/871–5655. Take I–280 south to the Hickey exit; then go east to El Camino and south (right). Showroom open daily 9–6. Free tours 10:30 and 1:30.*

SIGHTSEEING CHECKLISTS

Historic Buildings and Sites

For additional information on most of these sites, see the exploring itineraries, above.

Bank of America. The polished red-granite headquarters of this corporate giant is one of the city's most eye-catching buildings. The chic Carnelian Room on the 52nd floor offers a sweeping view of the city. *California St. at Kearny St.* (*See* Tour 3.)

The Cannery. What was once a bustling fruit and vegetable cannery now houses shops, restaurants, and the Museum of the City of San Francisco. Street artists provide entertainment in the complex's courtyard. *2801 Leavenworth St., near Fisherman's Wharf.* (*See* Tour 10.)

Chinese Six Companies. This elaborately decorated building is an example of the Chinese influence on San Francisco architecture. *843 Stockton St.* (*See* Tour 4.)

City Hall. This stunning French Renaissance Revival building is actually San Francisco's fourth city hall in the town's 150-year existence. *Entrance: Polk St. at McAllister St.* (*See* Tour 9.)

The **Cliff House.** From this historic site you can view the Pacific Ocean, Seal Rocks, and, on a clear day, the Farralon Islands, more than 30 miles away. Nearby are the ruins of the Sutro Baths. *1066 Point Lobos at the end of Geary Blvd.* (*See* Tour 13.)

Coit Tower. A gift from Lillie Hitchcock Coit, one of the city's more eccentric residents, this building showcases a series of murals painted by local artists who were influenced by Mexican painter Diego Rivera. *Greenwich St. at Kearny St.* (*See* Tour 5.)

Conservatory. Perhaps San Francisco's most elaborate Victorian, this copy of a similar structure in London's Kew Gardens has a tropical garden, plus seasonal plants and floral displays. *John F. Kennedy Dr.* (*See* Tour 12.)

Davies Hall. Home to the San Francisco Symphony, the glass-and-granite Louise M. Davies Hall is open for tours Monday, Wednesday, and Saturday. *Grove St. and Van Ness Ave.* (*See* Tour 9.)

Embarcadero Center. Offices, shops, restaurants, and two hotels are all contained in this eight-building complex. Justin Herman Plaza, near Embarcadero 5, offers views of the waterfront and the East Bay. *Off the Embarcadero between California and Clay Sts.* (*See* Tour 2.)

Fairmont Hotel. This Nob Hill landmark, under construction during the '06 earthquake, survived the catastrophe. It remains one of the city's finest hostelries. *Mason St. at California St.* (*See* Tour 6.)

Ferry Building. Another earthquake survivor, this building houses the San Francisco Port Commission. A scenic waterfront promenade extends south to the Bay Bridge. *The Embarcadero at the foot of Market St.* (*See* Tour 2.)

Fort Mason. A former military installation is now home to theaters, restaurants, galleries, and small museums. *Entrance: Marina Blvd. at Buchanan St.* (*See* Tour 10.)

450 Sutter Street. Handsome Mayan-inspired designs are used in both exterior and interior surfaces of this 1930 terra-cotta skyscraper. (*See* Tour 1.)

Ghirardelli Square. The famed chocolate was once made here; now the brick factory buildings house shops, galleries, cafés, and restaurants. *Beach St. at Polk St.* (*See* Tour 10.)

Golden Gate Bridge. The city's most famous landmark offers unparalleled views of the Bay Area. A walk across the bridge to the Marin side takes about a half hour each way. *Doyle Dr. above Fort Point.* (*See* Tour 11.)

Grace Cathedral. This 20th-century Gothic structure was designed by Lewis Hobart. The gilded-bronze doors at its east entrance were taken from casts of Ghiberti's *Gates of Paradise* on the baptistery in Florence. *1051 Taylor St. at California St.* (*See* Tour 6.)

Haas-Lilienthal House. One of the few Pacific Heights homes open to public view, the period-furnished rooms of this Queen Anne mansion offer a glimpse into turn-of-the-century taste and lifestyle. *2007 Franklin St. at Jackson St.* (*See* Tour 7.)

Hallidie Building. One of a number of Willis Polk-designed buildings in the city, this is believed to be the world's first all-glass-curtain-wall structure. *130 Sutter St.* (*See* Tour 3.)

Hammersmith Building. The small Beaux Arts structure was completed in 1907. Its extensive use of glass is noteworthy, as is the highly playful design. *301 Sutter St.* (*See* Tour 1.)

Hobart Building. This Willis Polk skyscraper, one of the architect's best, is noteworthy for its unique combination of a flat facade and oval sides. *582 Market St.* (*See* Tour 2.)

Hyde Street Pier. Three historic vessels are moored here. The highlight is the *Balclutha*, an 1886, full-rigged, three-mast sailing vessel. *The end of Hyde St., at Beach St.* (*See* Tour 10.)

Jackson Square. Some of the city's oldest buildings survive in this district, in the form of antique furniture showrooms. Walk east on Jackson from Columbus to see the original Ghirardelli Chocolate Factory and A. P. Hotaling's whiskey distillery, immortalized in verse after the '06 earthquake. (*See* Tour 3.)

Japan Center Mall. Folk crafts, antiques, kimonos, and the best udon (noodles) this side of Tokyo can all be found at this complex in the heart of Japantown. *Post St. between Laguna and Fillmore Sts.* (*See* Tour 8.)

Land's End. Views of the Golden Gate are spectacular here. The rocky trails that lead to the shoreline are for skilled hikers only. *At the end of El Camino del Mar.* (*See* Tour 13.)

Maiden Lane. What was once a notorious red-light district is now a chic shopping area. The Circle Gallery at 140 Maiden Lane, said to be a prototype for the Guggenheim Museum in New York, is the only Frank Lloyd Wright–designed building in San Francisco. *Off Stockton St. at Union Sq.* (*See* Tour 1.)

Mills Building and Tower. One of the city's outstanding prefire buildings was erected in 1891–92 and is a rare remaining example of the Chicago School of architecture. *At 220 Montgomery St. and 220 Bush St.* (*See* Tour 3.)

Mission Dolores. Originally known as the Mission San Francisco de Assisi, this historic adobe building was completed in 1791. *Dolores and 16th Sts.* (*See* Tour 14.)

Old St. Mary's Church. This brick church in Chinatown served as the city's Catholic cathedral until 1891. *Grant Ave. and California St.* (*See* Tour 4.)

Pacific Stock Exchange. Ralph Stackpole's monumental sculptural groups, *Earth's Fruitfulness* and *Man's Inventive Genius*, flank this imposing building. Don't miss the marble Art Deco lobby at the Stock Exchange Tower around the corner. *301 Pine St., at Sansome St.* (*See* Tour 3.)

Pacific Union Club. Also known as the Flood Mansion, this residence and the Fairmont Hotel, across the street, were among the few Nob Hill survivors of the 1906 quake and fire. *California St. at Mason St.* (*See* Tour 6.)

Palace of Fine Arts. A remnant of San Francisco's 1915 Panama-Pacific International Exposition, this beautiful edifice and surrounding lagoon form one of the city's signature images. *Baker and Beach Sts.* (*See* Tour 11.)

Precita Eyes Mural Arts Center. The center gives guided walks of over 40 of the Mission District's murals, and includes a half-hour slide presentation. (*See* Tour 14.)

Presidio. This 200-year-old army installation is in the process of becoming a public park. Its adobe Officer's Club is the oldest standing structure in the city. (*See* Tour 11.)

Russ Building. Its intriguing Gothic design, modeled after the Chicago Tribune Tower, distinguishes what was San Francisco's tallest building from 1927 until the early 1960s. *235 Montgomery St.* (*See* Tour 3.)

St. Mary's Cathedral. The third church to bear this name is a dramatic piece of modern architecture. Above the altar is a spectacular cascade made of 7,000 aluminum ribs. *Geary Blvd. at Gough St.* (*See* Tour 8.)

Sheraton Palace Hotel. One of the city's oldest and finest hotels has a newly restored glass-domed Garden Court and impressive original mosaic-tile floors in Oriental rug designs. Maxfield Parrish's *The Pied Piper* hangs in the bar of the same name. *2 New Montgomery St., at Market St.* (*See* Tour 2.)

Spreckels Mansion. Alma Spreckels, one of San Francisco's most iconoclastic residents, lived with husband Adolph in this palatial Pacific Heights home. Novelist Danielle Steele and husband John Traina reside here now. *2080 Washington St.* (*See* Tour 7.)

SS *Jeremiah O'Brien*. After participating in events commemorating the 50th anniversary of the D-day landing in Normandy, this World War II Liberty Ship freighter has returned to San Francisco. The steam engine and ship store operate on special "steaming weekends," usually the third of the month. Call to verify current location, as the ship periodically moves from one city pier to another. ☏ *415/441–3101.* ☛ *$5 adults, $3 senior citizens, $2 children 10–18, $1 children under 10.* ⏲ *Weekdays 9–3, weekends 9–4.*

Sutro Baths. Even the ruins of this famous landmark—100 yards north of the Cliff House—are arresting. Photographs at the site recall the glory of what was once a 3-acre entertainment complex. *Point Lobos at the end of Geary Blvd.* (*See* Tour 13.)

Union Square. The heart of San Francisco's shopping district and downtown, this urban park hosts numerous public events: fashion shows, free noontime concerts, and ethnic celebrations. *Surrounded by Stockton, Geary, Powell, and Post Sts.* (*See* Tour 1.)

Vedanta Society Headquarters. This 1905 architectural cocktail may be the most unusual structure in San Francisco: It's a pastiche of Colonial, Queen Anne, Moorish, and Hindu opulence. The highest of the six Hindu systems of religious philosophy, Vedanta maintains that all religions are paths to one goal. *2963 Webster St., at Filbert St.,* ☏ *415/922–2323.*

Victory Monument. The centerpiece of Union Square was designed by Robert Ingersoll Aitken to commemorate Commodore George Dewey's victory over the Spanish fleet in Manila in 1898. (*See* Tour 1.)

Wedding Houses. These structures were built during the late 1870s or 1880s. The romantic history of one of the houses recounts that its builder sold the property to a father as wedding presents for his two daughters. *1980 Union St., at Buchanan St.*

Westin St. Francis Hotel. The city's second-oldest hotel anchors Union Square. A ride up to the tower in a glass-walled, exterior elevator yields spectacular views of the square and beyond. *Powell St. at Union Sq.* (*See* Tour 1.)

Museums and Galleries

Ansel Adams Center. One of the best small museums in town features the works of one of America's masters, plus works of other historical and contemporary photographers. (*See* Tour 2.)

Asian Art Museum. The world-famous Avery Brundage Collection consists of more than 10,000 sculptures, paintings, and ceramics that illustrate the major periods of Asian Art. (*See* Tour 12.)

Cable Car Museum. Visitors can view the cables that run San Francisco's cable cars in action, sit in vintage cars, and learn about cable-car history. (*See* Tour 6.)

California Academy of Sciences. A natural history museum, an aquarium, and a planetarium all share space here. The Fish Roundabout is a favorite with children. (*See* Tour 12.)

Cartoon Art Museum. Rotating exhibits include comic books, plates and sketches from comic strips, film animation cels, and computer-generated imagery. *814 Mission St., Suite 200, ☎ 415/546–3922. ☛ $3.50 adults, $2.50 students and senior citizens, $1.50 children 6–17. ⏲ Wed.–Fri. 11–5, Sat. 10–5. Sun. 1–5.*

Chevron: A World of Oil. Exhibits and an audiovisual show explore the history of the oil industry. The museum is a five-minute walk from the Market-Powell Street cable-car terminus. *555 Market St., lobby level, ☎ 415/894–7700. ☛ Free. ⏲ Weekdays 9–4.*

Chinese Cultural Center. The center displays the works of Chinese and Chinese-American artists and traveling exhibits of Chinese culture. A $15 walking tour of Chinatown begins at 2 PM each Saturday. (*See* Tour 4.)

Chinese Historical Society. The society boasts the largest collection of Chinese-American artifacts in the country. Its mission is to trace the history of Chinese immigrants and their contributions to California (and American) history. (*See* Tour 4.)

De Young Memorial Museum, M.H. One of the city's premier museums showcases American art from Colonial times through the 20th century, and houses a dramatic collection of tribal art from Africa, Oceania, and the Americas. (*See* Tour 12.)

Exploratorium. Inside the Palace of Fine Arts is a fascinating hands-on museum that's fun and informative. There are 600 exhibits and a pitch-black, crawl-through Tactile Dome. (*See* Tour 11.)

Fort Point National Historic Site. This Civil War–era fortress is now a museum filled with military memorabilia. National Park Rangers offer guided group tours. (*See* Tour 11.)

Galeria de la Raza. This Mission District gallery, which shows local and international artists, showcases Hispanic art. *2855 24th St., at Hampshire St.* (*See* Tour 14.)

Jewish Community Museum. Revolving exhibits in this small, handsome museum trace important moments in Jewish history. *121 Steuart St., ☎ 415/543–8880. ☛ $3 adults; $1.50 students, children, and senior citizens. ⏲ Sun. 11–6, Mon.–Wed. noon–6, Thurs. noon–8.*

Mexican Museum. The first American showcase devoted exclusively to Mexican, Mexican-American, and Chicano art has a marvelous collection of art from pre-Hispanic Indian figures to modern Mexican masters. (*See* Tour 10.)

Museo Italo-Americano. This pleasant museum features permanent exhibits of works of 19th- and 20th-century Italian-American artists, with paintings, sculpture, etchings, and photographs. (*See* Tour 10.)

Museum of the City of San Francisco. Odd bits of San Franciscana can be viewed at this new museum in the Cannery. The centerpiece is the 8-ton Goddess of Progress's head, which she lost just before the '06 quake. (*See* Tour 10.)

National Maritime Museum. This two-floor facility exhibits ship models, photographs, maps, and other artifacts chronicling the development of San Francisco and the West Coast. (*See* Tour 10.)

Octagon House. Once thought to bring good luck, eight-sided homes were popular in the mid-19th-century. One of the two remaining examples of its kind, this one sits across the street from its original site on Gough Street. It is a treasure trove of American antique furniture and accessories from the 18th and 19th centuries. *2645 Gough St., at Union St.,* ☏ *415/441–7512.* ☛ *Free.* ⏲ *Feb.–Dec., 2nd Sun. and 2nd and 4th Thurs. of each month noon–3.*

Ripley's Believe It or Not. Of these 200 exhibits, many of them newly installed interactive displays, some actually are amazing. *175 Jefferson St.,* ☏ *415/771–6188.* ☛ *$7.95 adults; $6.75 senior citizens, students, and children 13–17; $4.50 children 5–12.* ⏲ *Sun.–Thurs. 10–10, Fri. and Sat. 10 AM–midnight.*

San Francisco Art Institute. A seven-section fresco by Diego Rivera adorns one of the galleries here. Exhibits at the Walter McBean Gallery most often feature student and alumni work. (*See* Tour 6.)

San Francisco Craft and Folk Art Museum. American folk art, tribal art, and contemporary crafts are on display in this pleasant museum. Its gift shop offers handmade items at reasonable prices. (*See* Tour 10.)

San Francisco Fire Department Museum. More than 100 years of fire-department history are documented with photographs and other memorabilia. *655 Presidio Ave., at Bush St. Take Muni Bus 38 on Geary St. to Presidio Ave.; walk 3 blocks north to Bush.* ☛ *Free.* ⏲ *Thurs.–Sun. 1–4.*

San Francisco History Room and Archives. Historic photographs, maps, and other mementos of the city are carefully documented on the third floor of the city's main library. (*See* Tour 9.)

San Francisco Museum of Modern Art. This lavish new Yerba Buena Center structure houses the Bay Area's preeminent showcase for modern painting, sculpture, graphics, photographs, and multimedia installations. (*See* Tour 2.)

San Francisco Performing Arts Library and Museum. Also known as PALM, this organization collects, documents, and preserves the San Francisco Bay Area's rich performing arts legacy. It houses the largest collection of its kind on the West Coast. (*See* Tour 9.)

Wax Museum. Visit with almost 300 wax figures of film stars, U.S. presidents, and world celebrities. Other attractions (separate admission) include a medieval dungeon and haunted gold-mine fun house. *145 Jefferson St., near Fisherman's Wharf,* ☏ *415/885–4975.* ☛ *$8.95 adults; $6.95 children 13–17, military, and senior citizens; $4.95 children 6–12.* ⏲ *Sun.–Thurs. 9 AM–10 PM, Fri. and Sat. 9 AM–midnight.*

Wells Fargo Bank History Museum. Original Western art, samples of nuggets and gold dust from major mines, and a century-old Concord stagecoach are among the attractions at this storefront museum. (*See* Tour 3.)

World of Economics. Economics is explained through videotapes, computer games, and electronic displays. Tours of the Federal Reserve Bank are given by appointment only. *101 Market St.,* ☏ *415/974–3252.*

Take Muni Bus 8 from Market and Powell Sts. to Main and Market Sts. ⏲ *Weekdays 9–4:30.*

Parks and Gardens

Alta Plaza Park. Look north to Marin, east to downtown, south to Twin Peaks, and west to Golden Gate Park from this Pacific Heights park. *Bordered by Clay, Steiner, Jackson and Scott Sts.*

Buena Vista Park. This hilly park rises above Haight Street between Baker and Central streets, offering splendid views of the city's north side and the Golden Gate Bridge. *Off Haight St., encircled by Buena Vista East and Buena Vista West Sts.*

Dolores Park. Several blocks long, this graceful grassy knoll faces downtown San Francisco. *Dolores and Church Sts., between 18th and 20th Sts.*

Dutch Windmill. Built to supply water for Golden Gate Park, this restored windmill is now powered by electric motors. It retains its charm if not its function. *Make a right turn at the end of John F. Kennedy Dr.* (*See* Tour 12.)

Golden Gate Park. Among the options here are the Japanese Tea Garden, three museums, the Conservatory, an arboretum, lawn bowling, a carousel, Stow Lake, riding stables, numerous playing fields, and a bison paddock. (*See* Tour 12.)

Ina Coolbrith Park. The Bay Bridge and Alcatraz are among the views from this restful site. *Taylor St. between Vallejo and Green Sts.* (*See* Tour 6.)

Japanese Tea Garden. Small ponds, streams, and flowering shrubs create a serene landscape. The Tea House serves a variety of teas. *Tea Garden Dr. and South Dr.* (*See* Tour 12.)

Lafayette Park. Sunbathers love the western slope of this Pacific Heights spot. Benches offer views of the neighborhood and beyond. A small playground diverts the kids. *Sacramento and Washington Sts., between Gough and Laguna Sts.* (*See* Tour 7.)

Lake Merced. There's a 6-mile jog (or drive) around this Sunset District lake. Side attractions are a golf course and a shooting range, among other things. *Bordered by Lake Merced Blvd., John Muir Dr., and Skyline Blvd.*

Lincoln Park. This 275-acre park in the city's northwest section includes the Palace of the Legion of Honor museum, a golf course, and steep cliffs that swoop down to the Golden Gate. *Entrance at 34th St. and Clement St.* (*See* Tour 13.)

Mt. Davidson Park. A huge cross that has been the subject of several court battles marks this Sunset District spot, with views (on sunny days) to the Farralon Islands. *Hillcrest Dr., off Myra Way in the Sunset District.*

Pioneer Park. At the base of Coit Tower, this eucalyptus-filled park offers views exceeded only by those of the tower itself. *Above Kearny St., near Filbert St.* (*See* Tour 5.)

Portsmouth Square. This park, now mostly cement and blacktop, dates back to the days when San Francisco was called Yerba Buena. A spot for repose in bustling Chinatown, it hosts community events. *Kearny St. and Walter U. Lum Pl., between Clay and Washington Sts.* (*See* Tour 4.)

Queen Wilhelmina Tulip Garden. This beautiful garden surrounds the base of the Dutch Windmill at the far end of Golden Gate Park. *Make a right turn at the end of John F. Kennedy Dr.* (*See* Tour 12.)

St. Mary's Park. Beniamino Bufano's 12-foot statue of Chinese leader Sun Yat-sen anchors this small Chinatown park. *Grant Ave. and California St.* (*See* Tour 4.)

Sigmund Stern Grove. This park encompasses a small valley that forms a kind of natural amphitheater. From mid-June through August, free outdoor Sunday programs feature opera, ballet, jazz, symphony, and ethnic dance. Bring a sweater, in case ocean breezes and fog roll in. *19th Ave. and Sloat Blvd., in the Sunset District. Take the Muni light rail system (M or K cars) from Powell and Market Sts. to Sloat Blvd. and West Portal; walk 3 blocks west on Sloat.*

Strybing Arboretum. Six thousand plants and tree varieties create calm, not cacophony, in the groves and gardens here. (*See* Tour 12.)

Washington Square. A great mix of people and cultures can be found at this bustling North Beach park. The church of Saints Peter and Paul overlooks the proceedings. *Columbus and Union Sts.* (*See* Tour 5.)

3 Shopping

By Sheila Gadsden

Updated by Alan Frutkin

SHOPPING IN SAN FRANCISCO means much more than driving to the local mall. Scattered among the city's diverse neighborhoods are clusters of stores of every stripe: major department stores, fine fashion boutiques, discount outlets, art galleries, and specialty stores for crafts, vintage items, and more. Most accept at least Visa and MasterCard charge cards, and many also accept American Express and Diners Club; very few accept cash only, and policies vary on traveler's checks. The *San Francisco Chronicle* and *Examiner* advertise sales; for smaller innovative shops, check the San Francisco *Bay Guardian.* Store hours are slightly different everywhere, but standard shopping times are between 10 AM and 5 or 6 PM Monday through Wednesday, Friday, and Saturday; between 10 AM and 8 or 9 PM Thursday; and from noon until 5 PM Sunday. Stores on and around Fisherman's Wharf often have longer hours in summer.

Major Shopping Districts

The Castro/Noe Valley

Often called the gay capital of the world, the Castro is a major destination for nongay travelers as well. Perhaps best known for its vintage-1922 theater, one of the grandest of its kind, the Castro is also filled with clothing boutiques, home accessory stores, and small, quirky specialty stores, including **A Different Light** (489 Castro St., ☎ 415/431–0891), one of the country's premier gay and lesbian bookstores.

Just south of Castro on 24th Street, Noe Valley is an enclave of gourmet food stores, used record shops, and clothing boutiques. Much of Armistead Maupin's *Tales of the City* was filmed in this villagelike neighborhood, whose small shops and relaxed street life evoke a '70s mood.

Chinatown

The intersection of Grant Avenue and Bush Street marks "the Gateway" to Chinatown; here hordes of shoppers and tourists are introduced to 24 blocks of shops, restaurants, markets, and a nonstop tide of activity. Racks of Chinese silks, toy trinkets, colorful pottery, baskets, and carved figurines are displayed in racks on the sidewalks, alongside herb stores that specialize in ginseng and roots. Dominating all are the sights and smells of food: crates of bok choy, tanks of live crabs, and hanging whole chickens.

Civic Center/Hayes Valley

With City Hall shut down for seismic retrofitting, a new public library being built next to the old one, and SFMOMA's recent move to Yerba Buena Gardens, the Civic Center has taken on a new face in the past few years. Although Davies Symphony Hall, the Marine Memorial Opera House, and the San Francisco Ballet are still major cultural magnets, the only real attraction for shoppers is the Opera Plaza, where **A Clean Well-Lighted Place for Books** (601 Van Ness Ave., ☎ 415/441–6670) draws a steady stream of browsers.

Hayes Valley, just southwest of Opera Plaza, is one of the city's fastest growing districts. When the Loma Prieta earthquake necessitated the removal of the shadowy freeway overpass, the newly sunny area attracted a new generation of artisans and craftspeople. A few highlights are the **San Francisco Women Artists Gallery** (370 Hayes St., ☎ 415/552–7392), the environmentally conscious clothing and home furnishings store **Worldware** (336 Hayes St., ☎ 415/487–9030), and the Mexican art shop and gallery **Polanko** (393 Hayes St., ☎ 415/252–5753).

Embarcadero Center

Five modern towers of shops, restaurants, and offices plus the Hyatt Regency Hotel make up the Embarcadero Center, downtown at the end of Market Street. What the center lacks in charm, it makes up for in sheer quantity. Its 175 establishments include such nationally known stores as **The Limited** and **Ann Taylor,** as well as West Coast–based businesses such as the **Nature Company.**

Fisherman's Wharf

San Francisco's Fisherman's Wharf is host to a number of shopping and sightseeing attractions: **Pier 39,** the **Anchorage, Ghirardelli Square,** and **The Cannery.** Each offers shops, restaurants, and a festive atmosphere as well as such outdoor entertainment as musicians, mimes, and magicians. Pier 39 includes an amusement area and a double-decked Venetian carousel. The highlights of all the centers are the view of the bay and the proximity of the cable-car lines, which can take shoppers directly to Union Square.

The Haight

Haight Street is always an attraction for visitors, if only to see the sign at Haight and Ashbury streets—the geographic center of flower power during the 1960s. These days, in addition to renascent tie-dyed shirts, you'll find high-quality vintage clothing, funky jewelry, art from Mexico, and reproductions of Art Deco accessories (*see* Vintage Fashion, Furniture, and Accessories, *below*). Used-book stores are another specialty, along with some of the best used-record stores in the city: **Recycled Records** (1377 Haight St., ☎ 415/626–4075), **Reckless Records** (1401 Haight St., ☎ 415/431–3434), and **Rough Trade** (1529 Haight St., ☎ 415/621–4395) carry classic rock and roll, obscure independent labels, and hard-to-find imports.

Jackson Square

Once the raffish Barbary Coast, tiny, now-gentrified Jackson Square is presently home to a dozen or so of San Francisco's finest retail antiques dealers, mostly located in two-story town houses. From French and English country antiques to Asian collectibles to Beidermier, every store has a specialty, and all are appointed like small museums. The shops are along Jackson Street in the Financial District, so a visit there will put you very close to the Embarcadero Center and Chinatown.

Japantown

Unlike Chinatown, North Beach, or the Mission, the 5-acre **Japan Center** (between Laguna and Fillmore Sts., and between Geary Blvd. and Post St.) is under one roof. The three-block complex, which usually feels a bit deserted, includes an 800-car public garage and shops and showrooms selling Japanese products: cameras, tapes and records, new and old porcelains, pearls, antique kimonos, tansu chests, and paintings. Among the favorites: **Soko Hardware** (1698 Post St., ☎ 415/931–5100), run by the Ashizawa merchant family since 1925, specializes in beautifully crafted Japanese tools for gardening and carpentry; **Kinokuniya,** on the second floor of the Kinokuniya Building, the center's western-most structure (1581 Webster St., ☎ 415/567–7625), may have the finest selection of English-language books on Japanese subjects in the United States. The shops in the **Tasamak Plaza Building,** east of the Peace Plaza, please souvenir shoppers with colorful flying-fish kites, delicate floral-pattern cocktail napkins, and the like.

The Marina District

Chestnut Street, one block north of Lombard Street, caters to the shopping whims of Marina District residents. A few standouts are **Lucca**

Delicatessen (2120 Chestnut St., ☎ 415/921–7873), famous for its handmade ravioli and its huge selection of Italian gourmet goods, and the **Red Rose Gallerie** (2251 Chestnut St., ☎ 415/776–6871), which specializes in "tools for personal growth," including body scents, exotic clothing, and audiotapes for rejuvenating the mind. Shops stretch from Fillmore Street to Broderick Street.

The Mission

Known as one of the city's sunniest neighborhoods, the Mission is also one of its most ethnically diverse, with a large Latino population and a sprinkling of everything else. In addition to those with a hunger for inexpensive Mexican food, the area draws bargain shoppers with its many used clothing, furniture, and alternative book stores. Shoppers can unwind with a visit to Mission Dolores, a tour of the murals at Precita Eyes Mural Arts Center, or a cup of café con leche at one of a dozen or so cafés.

North Beach

The once largely Italian enclave of North Beach grows smaller each year as Chinatown spreads northward. Sometimes called the city's answer to New York City's Greenwich Village, it is only a fraction of the size, clustered tightly around Washington Square and Columbus Avenue. Most of the businesses are small clothing stores, antiques and vintage shops, or such eccentric specialty shops as **Quantity Postcard** (1441 Grant Ave., ☎ 415/986–8866), which carries 15,000 different postcards. A number of Italian-run cafés and mom-and-pop trattorias attract Europhiles, locals, and tourists alike.

Pacific Heights

Pacific Heights residents seeking practical services head straight for Fillmore and Sacramento streets, where private residences alternate with good bookstores, fine clothing and gift shops, thrift stores, and art galleries. **Sue Fisher King Company** (3067 Sacramento St., ☎ 415/922–7276) has an eclectic collection of home accessories, and **Yountville** (2416 Fillmore St., ☎ 415/922–5050) specializes in sporty children's clothing from local and European designers. The Fillmore Street shopping area runs between Post Street and Pacific Avenue. Most shops on the western end of Sacramento Street are between Lyon and Maple streets.

South of Market

The lowest part of the city offers the lowest prices. Dozens of discount outlets, most of them open seven days a week, have sprung up along the streets and alleyways bordered by 2nd, Townsend, Howard, and 10th streets. A good place to start is the **Six Sixty Center** (660 3rd St.), two floors of shops offering everything from designer fashions to Icelandic sweaters. For more, *see* Outlets and Discount Stores, *below.*

At the other end of the spectrum are the gift shops in the new Museum of Modern Art and the Center for the Arts at Yerba Buena Gardens, both on 3rd Street between Mission and Howard. The newly opened SFMOMA shop is famous for its exclusive line of watches and jewelry, as well as its artists' monographs, contemporary gift items, and extensive book collection. The Yerba Buena shop carries an outstanding line of handmade jewelry and crafts, including an unusual selection of glass tableware.

Union Square

Serious shoppers head straight to Union Square, San Francisco's main shopping artery and the site of most department stores. Neiman Marcus, on the southeast corner of Union Square, is noted both for its high-

Downtown San Francisco Shopping

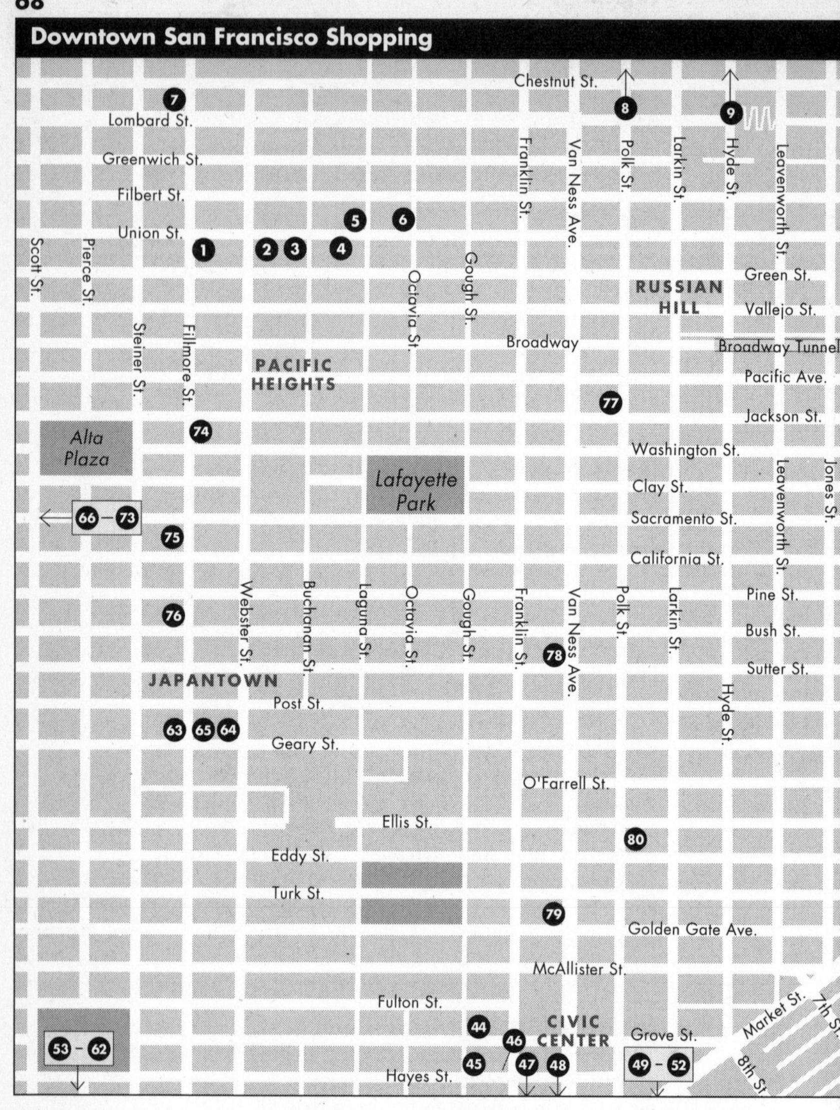

A Clean Well-Lighted Place for Books, **79**
Abitare, **11**
American Rag, **78**
Anokhi, **6**
Another Time, **47**
The Bead Store, **54**
Biordi, **15**
Brava Strada, **68**
Buffalo Exchange, **56**
Christine Foley, **52**
City Lights, **16**
Crossroads Trading Company, **76**
Designers Club, **59**
Dottie Doolittle, **71**
Esprit, **41**
Emporium, **37**
Evelyne Conquaret Antiques, **43**
Evolution, **7, 49**
F. Dorian, **45**
F.A.O. Schwarz, **36**
Fillamento, **75**
Folk Art International Gallery, **8**
Fumiki, **3**
G & M Sales, **48**
Glenda Queen Union Street Goldsmith, **4**
Green Apple Books, **73**
Gump's, **30**
Harcourts Gallery, **39**
Held Over, **57**
Hunt Antiques, **19**
Images, **46**
Imaginarium, **66**
Jade Empire, **20**
Japonesque, **18**
Jeanne Marc, **23**
Justine, **67**
Kinokuniya Bookstore, **64**
Krazy Kaps, **12**
Kris Kelly, **35**
Lang Antiques and Estate Jewelry, **24**
Loehmann's, **26**
Lombardi's, **77**

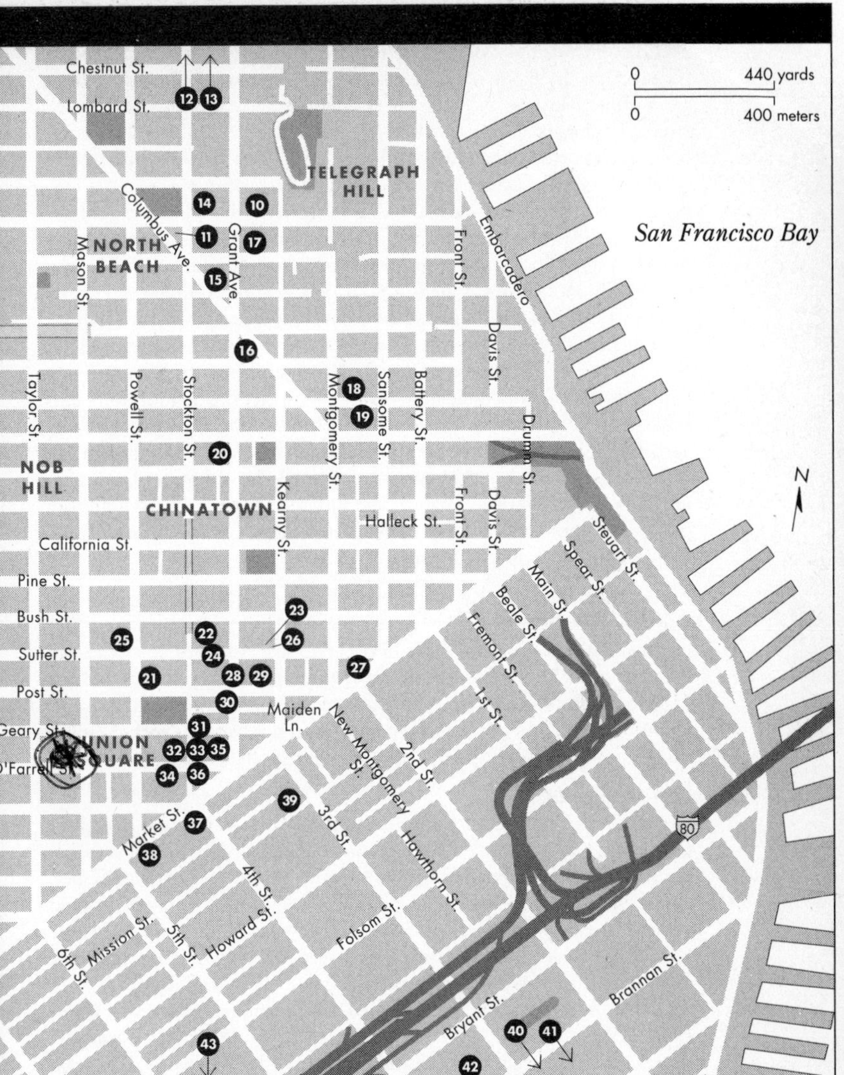

Ma-Shi'-Ko Folk Craft, **63**
Macy's, **32**
Neiman Marcus, **33**
New West, **42**
Nordstrom, **38**
North Beach Leather, **31**
North Face, **29**
Ocean Front Walkers, **17, 62**
Old and New Estates, **1**
Origins, **51**
Paris 1925, **5**
Patagonia, **9**
Peluche, **69**
Revival of the Fittest, **58**
Rolo, **50, 53**
Saks Fifth Avenue, **21**
Scheuer Linen, **22**
The Sharper Image, **8, 27**
Shige Antiques, **65**
Shreve & Co., **28**
Sierra Club Bookstore, **80**
Six Sixty Center, **40**
Small Frys, **60**
Smile: A Gallery, **25**
Telegraph Hill Antiques, **14**
Virginia Breier, **72**
Vorpal Gallery, **44**
Walker McIntyre, **70**
Whittler's Mother, **13**
Wholesale Jewelers Exchange, **34**
X-Large, **55**
Xela, **61**
Yone, **10**
Yountville, **74**
Z Gallerie, **2**

quality merchandise and its checkerboard-faced facade. Designed by Philip Johnson, the store opened in 1982 to replace a San Francisco fixture, the City of Paris; all that remains of the old building is the great glass dome. **Macy's,** with entrances on Geary, Stockton, and O'Farrell streets, has huge selections of clothing, plus extensive furniture and household accessories departments. The men's department—one of the world's largest—occupies its own building across Stockton Street. Opposite is the **F.A.O. Schwarz** children's store, with its extravagant assortment of life-size stuffed animals, animated displays, and steep prices. A half block down Stockton Street from F.A.O. Schwarz is the new **Virgin Megastore,** four floors of music, entertainment, and software in a building also housing a **Planet Hollywood** restaurant (whose owners include Demi Moore, Danny Glover, Arnold Schwarzenegger, Bruce Willis, and Sylvester Stallone). Also livening up the already lively Union Square area: a huge new **Disney Store,** selling memorabilia and other merchandise from the famous movie studio. The Disney space, across Post Street from the St. Francis Hotel, includes a 45,000-square-foot **Borders Books and Music** store. Across Powell Street from Disney, **Saks Fifth Avenue** caters to the upscale shopper. Nearby are the pricey international boutiques of Hermès of Paris, Gucci, Celine of Paris, Alfred Dunhill, Louis Vuitton, and Cartier.

Across from the cable-car turntable at Powell and Market streets is the **San Francisco Shopping Centre,** with the fashionable **Nordstrom** department store and more than 35 other shops. A big hit since the day it opened in 1992 is the two-floor **Warner Bros.** shop, which carries T-shirts, posters, and other mementos of the studio's past and present. Underneath a glass dome at Post and Kearny streets is **Crocker Galleria,** a complex of 50 shops and restaurants topped by two rooftop parks.

Union Street

Out-of-towners sometimes confuse Union Street—a popular stretch of shops and restaurants five blocks south of the Golden Gate National Recreation Area—with downtown's Union Square (*see above*). In fact, Union Street is just a short stretch of tony boutiques—a tiny, neighborhood version of Union Square. Nestled at the foot of a hill between Pacific Heights and the Marina District, the street is lined with contemporary fashion and custom jewelry shops, along with a few antiques shops and art galleries. A few local favorites are **Glenda Queen Union Street Goldsmith** (1909 Union St., ☎ 415/776–8048), known for its custom-designed jewelry, and the magical, mystical **Enchanted Crystal** (1895 Union St., ☎ 415/885–1335), where an in-house glass blower adds his wares to a large collection of jewelry, ornaments, and American crafts.

Department Stores

Since San Francisco's department stores are almost all in shopping centers—Union Square, the San Francisco Shopping Center, Six Sixty Center, and Yerba Buena Square—shoppers can hit all the majors without driving from one end of town to the next.

Emporium (835 Market St., ☎ 415/764–2222), next to the San Francisco Shopping Center, offers standard department store inventory at slightly lower prices; sales are frequent on everything from clothing to home furnishings. What the store lacks in ambience it makes up for in good value and friendly service.

Gump's (135 Post St., ☎ 415/982–1616), in business since 1910, is famous for its Christmas window displays and its high-quality collectibles. One of the city's most popular stores for bridal registries,

Gump's carries exclusive lines of dinnerware, flatware, and glassware, as well as Asian artifacts, antiques, and furniture.

Macy's (Stockton and O'Farrell Sts., ☏ 415/397–3333) is a one-stop shop, with designer fashions and an extensive array of shoes, household wares, furniture, food, and even a post office and foreign-currency exchange.

Neiman Marcus (150 Stockton St., ☏ 415/362–3900), with its gilded atrium and stained-glass skylight, offers one of the most luxurious shopping experiences in the city. Although its high-end prices raise an eyebrow or two, its biannual shoe sales—in January and July—draw a crowd.

Nordstrom (865 Market St., ☏ 415/243–8500), the store that's known for service, is housed in a stunning building with spiral escalators circling a four-story atrium. Designer fashions, shoes, accessories, and cosmetics are specialties.

Saks Fifth Avenue (384 Post St., ☏ 415/986–4300) feels like an exclusive, multilevel mall with its central escalator that ascends past a series of designer boutiques. With its extensive lines of cosmetics and jewelry, this branch of the New York–based store caters mostly to women, though there is a small men's department on the fifth floor. The restaurant, also on the fifth floor, overlooks Union Square.

Outlets and Discount Stores

A number of factory outlets in San Francisco offer clothing at bargain prices. Outlet maps are available at some of these locations for a nominal fee.

Christine Foley (430 9th St., ☏ 415/621–8126) offers discounts of up to 50% on sweaters for men, women, and children. In the small storefront showroom, pillows, stuffed animals, and assorted knickknacks sell at retail prices.

Esprit (499 Illinois St., at 16th St., south of China Basin, ☏ 415/957–2550), a San Francisco–based company, manufactures hip sportswear primarily for young women and children. Housed in a building as big as an airplane hangar, its bare-boned, glass and metallic interior feels somewhat sterile, but the discounts of 30% to 70% keep customers happy.

Loehmann's (222 Sutter St., near Union Sq., ☏ 415/982–3215), with its drastically reduced designer labels—including Lagerfeld and Krizia, is for fashion-conscious bargain hunters. This is not the place to learn who's who in the design world, as labels are often removed.

New West (426 Brannan St., at 3rd St., ☏ 415/882–4929), a spacious store, specializes in top-notch merchandise for both men and women, including Armani, Hugo Boss, and Donna Karan.

Six Sixty Center (660 3rd St., at Townsend St., ☏ 415/227–0464), a burgeoning discount complex, now offers a Tower Records Outlet with a wide selection of bargain-priced CDs, laser discs, videocassettes, and books. Nearly two dozen additional outlet stores carry apparel, accessories, and shoes for men, women, and children.

Specialty Stores

Antique Furniture

The most obvious place to look for antiques is Jackson Square. If you're feeling adventurous, try exploring the design center, where a few pubic retail showrooms are mixed in with those open only to the trade. You'll find additional miscellaneous antiques stores in almost every shopping neighborhood.

Evelyne Conquaret Antiques (Showplace Sq. W, 550 15th St., ☎ 415/552–6100), a showroom specializing in 18th- and 19th-century French antique furniture, has a large selection of lamps and accessories. At the center of the Showplace Square West interior design center, this is one of the few showrooms that is open to the public.

Fumiki (2001 Union St., ☎ 415/922–0573) offers a fine selection of Asian arts, including antiques, fine jewelry, Chinese silk paintings, and Korean and Japanese furniture, as well as antique Japanese baskets and *obis* (sashes worn with kimonos).

A Touch of Asia (1784 Union St., ☎ 415/474–3115), two blocks east on Union Street, is another good source for Asian antiques.

Hunt Antiques (478 Jackson St., ☎ 415/989–9531) feels like an English town house, with its fine 17th- to 19th-century period English furniture and its porcelains, Staffordshire pottery, prints, clocks, and paintings. In the heart of Jackson Square, Hunt is surrounded by other worthwhile shops.

Origins (680 8th St., ☎ 415/252–7089), in SoMa's Baker Hamilton Square complex in the South of Market area, imports unusual collector's items, Chinese furniture, porcelain, silk, and jade; antiques here are up to 400 years old. The complex houses more than a dozen other antique furniture shops, which cover a number of periods and styles, ranging from Thai to Art Deco to 19th-century French and English.

Shige Antiques (1825 Webster St., on Webster St. Bridge between Kinokuniya and Kintetsu Bldgs., ☎ 415/346–5567), frequented by collectors of art-to-wear, is well stocked with antique, hand-painted, silk-embroidered kimonos. Arita porcelains, silk calligraphy scrolls, tea-ceremony utensils, and dazzling lacquerware boxes are additional specialties. Downstairs in the Kinokuniya Building, **Asakichi Japanese Antiques** (1730 Geary Blvd., ☎ 415/921–2147) carries antique blue-and-white Imari porcelains and handsome tansu chests.

Telegraph Hill Antiques (580 Union St., ☎ 415/982–7055), a tiny North Beach shop, stocks paintings and diverse objets d'art, including fine china and porcelain, crystal, cut glass, Victoriana, and bronzes.

Walker McIntyre (3419 Sacramento St., ☎ 415/563–8024), which specializes in Georgian antiques and art, also offers 19th-century Japanese Imari cloisonné, lamps custom-made from antique vases, and Oriental rugs.

Art Galleries

Like small specialty stores, art galleries are ubiquitous in San Francisco. Most of the galleries surround downtown Union Square, although in recent years some have set up shop in the Hayes Valley area, near the Civic Center and South of Market. Pick up a copy of the free *San Francisco Arts Monthly* at the TIX Bay Area booth in Union Square (Stockton St. at Geary St.) for listings of other galleries in the area and elsewhere in the city. Most galleries are closed Monday.

Harcourts Gallery (460 Bush St., ☎ 415/421–3428), one of the city's best known, exhibits paintings, sculpture, and graphics by 19th- and 20th-century artists, including Picasso, Chagall, Renoir, and Miró, as well as works by contemporary artists such as Robert Rauschenberg, Sylvia Glass, and Roland Petersen.

Images (372 Hayes St., ☎ 415/626–2284) specializes in oil paintings and watercolors by northern California realist and impressionist artists. Crafts and jewelry are also on display.

Smile: A Gallery (500 Sutter St., ☎ 415/362–3436) has a whimsical, colorful collection of folk art, jewelry, and mobiles, including extraordinary life-size soft sculptures of people.

Vorpal Gallery (393 Grove St., ☎ 415/397–9200), a nationally acclaimed chain, has an excellent collection of graphic arts, postmodern paintings, drawings, and sculpture.

Booksellers

In addition to most major bookstore chains, an impressive number of small, specialty bookstores thrive in San Francisco. Most are located around other attractions, which makes bookstore browsing a convenient and popular pastime.

City Lights (261 Columbus Ave., ☎ 415/362–8193), stomping ground of the 1960s Beat poets, is the city's most famous and historically interesting bookstore. Although it is best known for poetry, contemporary literature and music, and translations of Third-World literature, City Lights also carries books on nature, the outdoors, and travel. Many titles are published in-house.

A Clean Well-Lighted Place for Books (601 Van Ness Ave., ☎ 415/441–6670), in the Opera Plaza, is a great place to while away the hours before or after a performance. Books on opera and San Francisco history are particularly well stocked, but the store bills itself as carrying "a large selection of paperbacks and hardbacks in all fields for all ages."

Green Apple Books (506 Clement St., ☎ 415/387–2272), a local favorite since 1967, has one of the largest used-book departments in the city, as well as new books in every field. Specialties are comic books, a history room, and a rare-book collection.

Kinokuniya Bookstores (Kinokuniya Bldg., 1581 Webster St., 2nd Floor, ☎ 415/567–7625), in the heart of the Japan Center, offers all sorts of books and periodicals in Japanese and English. A major attraction is the collection of beautifully produced graphics and art books.

The **Sierra Club Bookstore** (730 Polk St., ☎ 415/923–5600), has books on environmental issues, nature, and California ecology, as well as a large selection of nature calendars, cards, and T-shirts.

Children's Clothing, Toys and Gadgets

CLOTHING

Dottie Doolittle (3680 Sacramento St., ☎ 415/563–3244) is where Pacific Heights mothers buy their little girls' Florence Eiseman dresses and other traditional clothes for boys and girls, from infants to 14-year-olds. Baby furniture is sold as well.

Small Frys (4066 24th St., ☎ 415/648–3954), in the heart of Noe Valley, carries a complete range of colorful cottons for infants and children, including Oshkosh and many California labels.

Yountville (2416 Fillmore St., ☎ 415/922–5050), the upscale store for children up to eight, features California and European designs.

TOYS AND GADGETS

F.A.O. Schwarz (48 Stockton St., ☎ 415/394–8700), the San Francisco branch of the American institution, is every child's dream, with games, stuffed toys, motorized cars, model trains, and more.

Imaginarium (3535 California St., ☎ 415/387–9885; Stonestown Galleria at 19th Ave. and Winston Dr., ☎ 415/566–4111), a California-based company, manufactures its own learning-oriented games and gadgets and imports European brands that may not be found in larger stores.

Sharper Image (532 Market St., ☎ 415/398–6472; 680 Davis St., at Broadway, ☎ 415/445–6100; 900 North Point, Ghirardelli Sq., ☎ 415/776–1443) carries high-end gadgets that bring out the child in everyone. Marvel over five-language translators, super-shock-absorbent tennis rackets, state-of-the-art speaker systems, Walkman-size computers, and more.

Clothing for Men and Women

True to its reputation as the most European of American cities, San Francisco is lush with small clothing stores that sell garments and clothes by local designers. Those who shy away from malls will find plenty of other options.

Brava Strada (3247 Sacramento St., ☎ 415/567–5757) is known for its designer knitwear and accessories, Italian and other European leather goods, and one-of-a-kind jewelry from American and European artists.
Designers Club (3899 24th St., ☎ 415/648–1057), in Noe Valley, specializes in the natural fiber creations of local designer Cia Van Orden and jewelry by Audrey Daniels.
Jeanne Marc (262 Sutter St., ☎ 415/362–1121), a San Francisco designer, sells sportswear and more formal clothes in the striking prints that have become her hallmark.
Justine (3600 Sacramento St., ☎ 415/921–8548) is for Francophiles, with women's clothes by French designers Dorothée Bis, Georges Rech, and Maud Defossez.
Krazy Kaps (Pier 39, ☎ 415/296–8930) is the place to go when you're feeling a little too solemn. Their inventory, which ranges from top hats, Stetsons, and Greek fishermen's caps to silly, gimmicky hats—just might inspire you to don a tuxedo and dance.
North Beach Leather (190 Geary St., ☎ 415/362–8300), with its wavy wrought-iron walls, is itself a work of art. It's also one of the best sources for high-quality leather garments—skirts, jackets, pants, dresses, and accessories. The original store is still in business at Fisherman's Wharf (1365 Columbus Ave., ☎ 415/441–3208).
Ocean Front Walkers (1458 Grant Ave., ☎ 415/291–9727; 4069 24th St., ☎ 415/550–1980), a neighborhood store, features an eclectic mix of printed T-shirts, boxer shorts, and pajamas with graphic designs that range from animal wildlife to 1950s iconography.
Peluche (3366 Sacramento St., ☎ 415/346–6361) specializes in hand-knit, one-of-a-kind sweaters, mostly from Italy, and European fashions for women.
Rolo (2351 Market St., ☎ 415/431–4545; 450 Castro St., ☎ 415/626–7171; 1301 Howard St., ☎ 415/861–1999) is a Castro favorite, with men's and women's designer-brand denim, sportswear, shoes, and accessories that reveal a distinct European influence.
X-Large (1415 Haight St., ☎ 415/626–9573), a Los Angeles–based franchise, is run by the rap-singing Beastie Boys and features street-style clothing from hip-hop to rave. The women's clothing line, X-Girls, is overseen by Kim Gordon of the New York rock group Sonic Youth.

Handicrafts and Folk Art

One lucky consequence of San Francisco's many-layered ethnic mix is that small galleries all over the city sell crafts, pottery, sculpture, and jewelry from countries all over the world.

Anokhi (1864 Union St., ☎ 415/922–4441), small and inviting, stocks clothing, home furnishings, and accessories from East India, most of them block-printed by hand in Jaipur.
Biordi (412 Columbus Ave., ☎ 415/392–8096), in the heart of North Beach, sells Majolica dinnerware and other imported Italian handicrafts and ceramics.
Evolution (271 9th St., ☎ 415/861–6665; 2015 Chestnut St., ☎ 415/923–1938) carries an unusual selection of furniture from In-

donesia and kilims from Turkey on 9th Street, and a wide range of domestic clothing on Chestnut Street.

F. Dorian (388 Hayes St., ☎ 415/861–3191) carries cards, jewelry, and other crafts from Mexico, Japan, Italy, Peru, Indonesia, Philippines, and Sri Lanka, as well as the works of local craftsmen.

Folk Art International Gallery (Ghirardelli Sq., 900 N. Point St., ☎ 415/441–6100), whose shops fill two levels of the Cocoa Building at Ghirardelli, features an extensive contemporary folk-art collection from Mexico, China, Ecuador, France, Sri Lanka, Peru, Haiti, and other countries—masks, boxes, sculpture, baskets, toys, and textiles. Adjoining the Folk Art's upper-level gallery, **Xanadu** (☎ 415/441–5211) offers artifacts and tribal art from Asia, Africa, Oceania, and the Americas.

Japonesque (824 Montgomery St., ☎ 415/398–8577) specializes in handcrafted wooden boxes, sculpture, paintings, and handmade glass from Japan and the United States.

Ma-Shi'-Ko Folk Craft (1581 Webster St., 2nd Floor, ☎ 415/346–0748) carries handcrafted pottery from Japan, including Mashiko, the style that has been in production longer than any other. There are also masks and other handcrafted goods, all from Japan.

Virginia Breier (3091 Sacramento St., ☎ 415/929–7173), a colorful gallery of contemporary and antique crafts, represents mostly emerging artists. Every piece in the store is handpicked, from the one-of-a-kind jewelry to the Japanese tansus and cast aluminum sculptures from Brazil.

Whittler's Mother (Pier 39, Embarcadero, ☎ 415/433–3010) is a factory and store in one: Handcrafted wood trinkets are created and painted on the premises. Don't miss the carousel animals, which come both small and full-size.

Xela (3925 24th St., ☎ 415/695–1323), pronounced "Shay-La," carries merchandise from Africa, central Asia, and Bali, including jewelry, religious masks and statues, decorative wall hangings, and mukluk-slippers from Pakistan.

Housewares and Accessories

Abitare (522 Columbus St., ☎ 415/392–5800), a popular North Beach shop, has an eclectic mix of goods—soaps and bath supplies, candleholders, artsy picture frames, and one-of-a-kind furniture, artwork, and decorations.

Fillamento (2185 Fillmore St., ☎ 415/931–2224), a Pacific Heights favorite, has three floors of home furnishings, from dinnerware to bedding to bath and baby accessories. Its eclectic mix of styles ranges from the classic to the contemporary.

Z Gallerie (2071 Union St., ☎ 415/346–9000; Stonestown Galleria at 19th Ave. at Winston Dr., ☎ 415/664–7891) carries modern home furnishings and accessories: butterfly chairs, dinnerware, desks, chairs, lamps, posters, and a variety of high-tech accessories, mostly in black. Other branches are in the San Francisco Shopping Centre on Market Street and on Haight Street.

LINENS

Kris Kelly (174 Geary St., ☎ 415/986–8822), though specializing in handmade quilts from China, is primarily known for its linens, along with its handcrafted tablecloths, bedding, bath accessories, and window treatments.

Scheuer Linen (340 Sutter St., ☎ 415/392–2813), a fixture of Union Square for 40 years, draws designers and everyday shoppers with its luxurious linens for the bed, the bath, and the dining table.

Jewelry

Glenda Queen Union Street Goldsmith (1909 Union St., ☎ 415/776–8048), a local favorite since 1976, prides itself on its high-carat metals, including platinum and rare gemstones. The in-house workshop features many Bay Area artists.

Jade Empire (832 Grant Ave., ☎ 415/982–4498), one of the many fine jewelry stores in Chinatown, has fine jade, diamonds, and other gems.

Shreve & Co. (Post St. and Grant Ave., ☎ 415/421–2600), one of the city's most elegant jewelers, and the oldest retail store in San Francisco, is near Union Square.

Wholesale Jewelers Exchange (121 O'Farrell St., ☎ 415/788–2365) is the place to find gems and finished jewelry at less-than-retail prices.

ANTIQUE JEWELRY

Lang Antiques and Estate Jewelry (323 Sutter St., ☎ 415/982–2213) carries vintage jewelry and small antique objects, including fine glass, amber, and silver.

Old and New Estates (2181-A Union St., ☎ 415/346–7525) offers both antique and modern jewelry, crystal, and silver.

Paris 1925 (1954 Union St., ☎ 415/567–1925) specializes in estate pieces and vintage watches.

BEADS

The Bead Store (417 Castro St., ☎ 415/861–7332) boasts more than 1,000 kinds of unstrung beads, including stones such as lapis and carnelian, Czechoslovakian and Venetian glass, African trade beads, Buddhist and Muslim prayer beads, and even Catholic rosaries. Premade silver jewelry is another specialty, along with religious masks, figurines, and statues from India and Nepal.

Yone (478 Union St., ☎ 415/986–1424), in business since 1965, carries so many types of beads that the owner has lost track—somewhere between 5,000 and 10,000, he thinks. Ranging from plastic to bone to sterling silver, individual beads may cost up to $100. A growing collection of beads from Indonesia, Thailand, Sri Lanka, and India adds a new twist to the store.

Sporting Goods

G & M Sales (1667 Market St., ☎ 415/863–2855), a local institution since 1948, has one of the city's best selections of camping gear—with more than three dozen fully erected tents on display—and an extensive fishing department.

Lombardi's (1600 Jackson St., ☎ 415/771–0600), also in business since 1948, supplies its devoted clientele with sports clothes and equipment, outerwear, camping goods, fitness equipment, and extensive lines of athletic footwear. Merchandise is discounted on a regular basis, and ski rentals are available.

North Face (180 Post St., ☎ 415/433–3223; 1325 Howard St., ☎ 415/626–6444), a Bay Area–based company, is famous for its top-of-the-line tents, sleeping bags, backpacks, skis, and outdoor apparel, including stylish Gore-Tex jackets and pants. The Howard Street store, an outlet, sells overstocked and discontinued items, along with occasional seconds.

Patagonia (770 North Point St., near Fisherman's Wharf, ☎ 415/771–2050), a Ventura County–based company, specializes in technical wear for serious outdoors enthusiasts, including gear for rock climbing, kayaking, fly-fishing, and the like; but sportswear and casual clothing are also available.

Vintage Fashion, Furniture, and Accessories

FASHION

American Rag (1305 Van Ness Ave., ☎ 415/474–5214) stocks a huge selection of men's and women's clothes from the United States and Europe, all in excellent shape. They also carry shoes and accessories such as sunglasses, hats, belts, and scarves.

Buffalo Exchange (1555 Haight St., ☎ 415/431–7733; 1800 Polk St., ☎ 415/346–5726), part of a national chain, is one of the few stores where you can trade your own used clothes for theirs. Some new clothes are available as well.

Crossroads Trading Company (1901 Fillmore St., ☎ 415/775–8885; 2231 Market St., ☎ 415/626–8989), which carries some vintage clothing, specializes in used contemporary sportswear. Ties, belts, hats, and purses are also in stock.

Held Over (1543 Haight St., ☎ 415/864–0818) carries an extensive collection of clothing from the 1940s, '50s, and '60s.

FURNITURE AND ACCESSORIES

Another Time (1586 Market St., ☎ 415/553–8900), an Art Deco lover's delight, carries furniture and accessories by Heywood Wakefield and others. It's conveniently close to a whole host of other stores that stock vintage collectibles.

Revival of the Fittest (1701 Haight St., ☎ 415/751–8857) is a virtual bazaar, with vintage collectibles ranging from telephones, clocks, vases, dishes, and lamps to furniture and jewelry.

4 Sports, Fitness, Beaches

PARTICIPANT SPORTS AND THE OUTDOORS

By Casey Tefertiller

Updated by Dianne Aaronson

PERHAPS MORE THAN ANYWHERE ELSE, physical fitness and sports are a way of life in the Bay Area. Joggers, bicyclists, and aficionados of virtually all sports can find their favorite pastimes within driving distance, and often within walking distance, from downtown hotels. Golden Gate Park has numerous paths for runners and cyclists. Lake Merced in San Francisco and Lake Merritt in Oakland are among the most popular areas for joggers.

For information on running races, tennis tournaments, bicycle races, and other participant sports, check the monthly issues of *City Sports* magazine, available free at sporting-goods stores, tennis centers, and other recreational sites. The most important running event of the year is the *Examiner* Bay-to-Breakers race on the third Sunday in May. For information on this race, call 415/512–5000, ext. 2222.

Bicycling

Two bike routes are maintained by the San Francisco Recreation and Park Department (☎ 415/666–7201). One route goes through Golden Gate Park to Lake Merced; the other goes from the south end of the city to the Golden Gate Bridge and beyond. Many shops along Stanyan Street rent bikes.

Boating and Sailing

Stow Lake (☎ 415/752–0347) in Golden Gate Park has rowboat, pedal boat, and electric boat rentals. The lake is open daily for boating, but call for seasonal hours. San Francisco Bay offers year-round sailing, but tricky currents make the bay hazardous for inexperienced navigators. Boat rentals and charters are available throughout the Bay Area and are listed under "boat rentals" in the Yellow Pages. A selected charter is **A Day on the Bay** (☎ 415/922–0227). **Cass' Marina** (☎ 415/332–6789) in Sausalito has a variety of sailboats that can be rented or hired with a licensed skipper. Local sailing information can be obtained at the **Eagle Cafe** on Pier 39.

Fishing

Numerous fishing boats leave from San Francisco, Sausalito, Berkeley, Emeryville, and Point San Pablo. They go for salmon outside the bay or striped bass and giant sturgeon within the bay. In San Francisco, lines can be cast from San Francisco Municipal Pier, Fisherman's Wharf, or Aquatic Park. Trout fishing is possible at Lake Merced. One-day licenses, good for ocean fishing only, are available for $5.50 on the charters; sporting-goods stores sell complete state licenses—seasonal passes that permit both ocean and freshwater fishing—for $24.95. For charters, reservations are suggested. Some selected sportfishing charters are listed below. Mailing addresses are given, but telephoning is the best way to get a response. Most charters depart daily from Fisherman's Wharf during the salmon-fishing season, March through October.

Lovely Martha's Sportsfishing (156 Linden Ave., San Bruno, CA 94066, ☎ 415/871–4445).

Wacky Jacky (473 Bella Vista Way, San Francisco, CA 94127, ☎ 415/586–9800).

Fitness

Physical-fitness activities continue to be popular, but most clubs are private and visitors may have trouble finding a workout location. Several hotels have arrangements with neighborhood health clubs. A number of hotels have large health facilities of their own, including the Fairmont, Hotel Nikko, San Francisco Marriott, the Mark Hopkins Inter-Continental, the Ritz-Carlton, and the Sheraton Palace Hotel. Of these, two are open to the public: the Marriott charges a $10 drop-in fee and the Nikko $20.

The **24-hour Nautilus** center (1335 Sutter, ☎ 415/776–2200) is open to the public for a $15 drop-in fee. The clubs offer aerobics classes, a complete line of fitness equipment, sauna, Jacuzzi and steam room. The **Embarcadero YMCA** (169 Steuart St., ☎ 415/957–9622), one of the finest facilities in San Francisco, offers racquetball, an indoor track, a swimming pool, and aerobics classes. The $12 drop-in fee includes use of the sauna and whirlpool plus a magnificent view of the bay. Those preferring a "women-only" atmosphere can work out at the **Women's Training Center** (2164 Market St., ☎ 415/864–6835) for a $10 day fee which includes use of the sauna.

Golf

San Francisco has many public golf courses. Visitors can call 415/750–4653 for computerized reservations at any of the following: **Harding and Fleming Parks** (Lake Merced Blvd. and Skyline Blvd.), an 18-hole, par-72 course and a 9-hole executive course, respectively; **Lincoln Park** (34th and Clement Sts.), 18 holes, par 68; **Golden Gate Park** (47th Ave. at Fulton St.), a "pitch and putt" 9-holer; or **Sharp Park,** in Pacifica (Hwy. 1, at the foot of Sharp Park Rd.), 18 holes, par 72. **Glen Eagles Golf Course** (2100 Sunnydale Ave.), a full-size 18-holer in McLaren Park, can be reached at 415/587–2425.

Horseback Riding

Western-style horseback riding is available throughout the Bay Area. Two stables in Half Moon Bay have rentals for beach rides. Call 415/726–8550 to reserve horses at **Friendly Acres** (2150 N. Cabrillo Hwy.) and **Sea Horse Ranch** (1828 N. Cabrillo Hwy.). Other selected stables include **Sonoma Cattle Co.** (☎ 707/996–8566); **Five Brooks** (☎ 415/663–1570), in Marin County; and **Miwok Livery,** in Mill Valley (☎ 415/383–8048).

Ice-Skating

The venerable San Francisco Ice Rink closed in 1991, but two pleasant alternatives are **Berkeley Iceland** (2727 Milvia St., 4 blocks from the Ashby BART station, ☎ 510/843–8800) and **Belmont Iceland** (815 Old County Rd., ☎ 415/592–0532).

In-Line Skating

Golden Gate Park is one of the best places in the country for in-line skating, with smooth surfaces, manageable hills, and lush scenery. There's car traffic during the week and on Saturday, but the JFK Drive, which extends almost to the ocean, is closed to cars on Sunday. Within the park is a large, flat area between the Conservatory and the de Young Museum, where beginners practice stopping and artistic skaters perform their newest moves to music. **Skates on Haight** (1818 Haight St., ☎ 415/752–8376), near the Stanyan Street entrance to the park, offers free lessons and rents recreational and speed skates that fit biomechanically to your body.

For beginners, the paved path along the **Marina** offers a 1½-mile (round-trip) easy route on flat, well-paved surface and glorious views of San Francisco Bay. **SportsTech/FTC Sports** (1586 Bush St., ☎ 415/673–8363) rents and sells in-line skates and protective gear. Advanced skaters will likely want to experience the challenge and take in the brilliant views offered at **Tilden Park** (☎ 510/843–2137), in the Berkeley Hills (*see* Oakland *in* Chapter 8, Excursions from San Francisco). Follow signs to the parking lot at Inspiration Point and the trailhead for Nimitz Way, a nicely paved 8-mile (round-trip) recreational path that stretches along a ridge overlooking San Francisco Bay, the East Bay Mudlands, and Mt. Diablo.

Racquetball

Most racquetball clubs in San Francisco are private and require that drop-in guests be accompanied by a member. One exception, the **Telegraph Hill Club** (1850 Kearney St., ☎ 415/982–4700), offers day use of their courts as well as the rest of their fully equipped fitness center for a $15 day fee. (*See also* Embarcadero YMCA *in* Fitness, *above*). In addition, the San Francisco Recreation and Park Department maintains a racquetball facility at the **Mission Recreation Center** (2450 Harrison St., ☎ 415/695–5012).

Rock Climbing

The Bay Area was quick to catch on to the sport of rock climbing. Indoor enthusiasts can take a quick drive across the Bay Bridge to Emeryville, home of **City Rock** (1250 45th St., Suite 400, ☎ 510/654–2510). Experienced climbers can purchase a $14 day pass but must pass a safety test before they can climb; include an additional $6 to rent shoes and harness. Those without climbing partners can be matched with other guests at the club. Introductory lessons are offered five times per week for $35.

Swimming

The San Francisco Recreation and Park Department manages one outdoor swimming pool and eight indoor pools throughout the city. Call 415/666–7201 for information and locations.

Tennis

The San Francisco Recreation and Park Department maintains 130 free tennis courts throughout the city. The largest set of free courts is at **Dolores Park** (18th and Dolores Sts.), with six courts available on a first-come, first-served basis. There are 21 public courts in **Golden Gate Park**; reservations and fee information can be obtained by calling 415/753–7101.

Windsurfing and Gliding

Windsurfing is becoming increasingly popular in the Bay Area, with participants taking advantage of the brisk bay breezes to improve their skills. **San Francisco School of Windsurfing** (40A Loyola Terr., ☎ 415/753–3235) offers rentals, lessons for beginners on mild Lake Merced, and lessons for more advanced surfers at Candlestick Point. For adventurous types, **Airtime of San Francisco** (3620 Wawona St., ☎ 415/759–1177) offers hang-gliding lessons, para-gliding lessons, and kite rentals.

SPECTATOR SPORTS

For the sports fan, the Bay Area offers a vast selection of events—from yacht races to rodeo to baseball.

Auto Racing

Sears Point International Raceway (☎ 707/938–8448), in Sonoma at Highways 37 and 121, offers a variety of motor-sports events. The track is also the home of the Bondurant High Performance Driving School. Motor-sports events are held at various locations around the Bay Area; check local papers for details.

Baseball

The **San Francisco Giants** continue to play at chilly Candlestick Park (☎ 415/467–8000). The **Oakland A's** play at the Oakland Coliseum (☎ 510/638–0500). Game-day tickets are usually available at the stadiums. Premium seats, however, often sell out in advance. City shuttle buses marked Ballpark Special run from numerous bus stops. Candlestick Park is often windy and cold, so take along extra layers of clothing. The Oakland Coliseum can be reached by taking BART trains to the Coliseum stop.

Basketball

The **Golden State Warriors** play NBA basketball at the Oakland Coliseum Arena from October through April. Tickets are available through BASS (☎ 510/762–2277). BART trains to the Coliseum stop are the easiest method of travel.

College Sports

Major college football, basketball, and baseball are played at the University of California in Berkeley, at Stanford University on the peninsula in Palo Alto, and at San Jose State. Stanford won the College World Series in 1987 and '88, and home baseball games at sunny Sunken Diamond often sell out.

Football

The **San Francisco 49ers** play at Candlestick Park, but the games are almost always sold out far in advance, so call first (☎ 415/468–2249).

Hockey

The Bay Area welcomed the **San Jose Sharks** as its first National Hockey League team in 1991. Their popular home games can be seen at the new arena in downtown San Jose, where they began playing in the 1993–94 season. The team has been a wild success, and many of their games sell out. Call BASS (☎ 510/762–2277) for tickets.

Horse Racing

Depending on the season, horse racing takes place at **Golden Gate Fields** in Albany, at **Bay Meadows** in San Mateo, or on the northern California fair circuit. Check local papers for schedules and locations.

Rodeo

San Francisco relives its western heritage each October with the **Grand National Rodeo and Livestock Show** at the Cow Palace (☎ 415/469–6000), just south of the city limits in Daly City. The 15-3rd bus makes the trip.

Tennis

The San Jose Arena is the site of the **Cybase Open** in early February (☎ 408/287–7070). The **Virginia Slims women's tennis tour** visits the Oakland Coliseum Arena in October.

Yacht Racing

Yacht races are frequently held on the bay. Spectators can watch from the Golden Gate Bridge and other vantage points around town. Check local papers for details.

BEACHES

San Francisco's beaches are perfect for romantic sunset strolls, but don't make the mistake of expecting to find Waikiki-by-the-Metropolis. The water is cold, and the beach areas are often foggy and usually jammed on sunny days. They can be satisfactory for afternoon sunning, but treacherous currents make most areas dangerous for swimming. During stormy months, beachcombers can stroll along the sand and discover a variety of ocean treasures: glossy agates and jade pebbles, and sea-sculptured roots and branches.

Baker Beach

Baker Beach is not recommended for swimming: Watch for larger-than-usual waves. In recent years, the north end of the beach has become popular with nude sunbathers. (Though this is not legal, such laws are seldom enforced.) The beach is in the southwest corner of the Presidio, beginning at the end of Gibson Road, which turns off Bowley Street. Weather is typical for the bay shoreline: summer fog, usually breezy, and occasionally warm. Picnic tables, grills, day-camp areas, and trails are available. The mile-long shoreline is ideal for jogging, fishing, and building sand castles.

China Beach

From April through October, China Beach, south of Baker Beach, offers a lifeguard, gentler water, changing rooms, and showers. It is also listed on maps as Phelan Beach.

Half Moon Bay

The San Mateo County coast has several beaches and some nice ocean views, most notably at Half Moon Bay State Beach. A drive south on Highway 1 is scenic and will provide access to this and other county beaches. Take Highway 92 east over the mountains to I–280 for a faster but still scenic route back to the city.

Marin Beaches

The Marin headlands beaches are not safe for swimming. The cliffs are steep and unstable, making falls a constant danger. The Marin coast, however, offers two beaches for picnics and sunning: Muir and Stinson beaches. Swimming is recommended only at Stinson Beach, and only from late May to mid-September, when lifeguard services are provided. If possible, visit these areas during the week; both beaches are crowded on weekends.

Ocean Beach

South of the Cliff House, Ocean Beach stretches along the western (ocean) side of San Francisco. It has a wide beach with scenic views and is perfect for walking, running, or lying in the sun—but not for swimming.

5 Dining

By Jacqueline Killeen and Sharon Silva

SAN FRANCISCO probably has more restaurants per capita than any other city in the United States, including New York. Practically every ethnic cuisine is represented. That makes selecting some 90 restaurants to list here a difficult task indeed. We have chosen several restaurants to represent each popular style of dining in various price ranges, in most cases because of the superiority of the food, but in some instances because of the view or ambience.

Because we have covered those areas of town most frequented by visitors, this meant leaving out some great places in outlying districts such as Sunset and Richmond. The outlying restaurants we *have* recommended were chosen because they offer a type of experience not available elsewhere. All listed restaurants serve dinner and are open for lunch unless otherwise specified; restaurants are not open for breakfast unless the morning meal is specifically mentioned.

Parking accommodations are mentioned only when a restaurant has made special arrangements; otherwise you're on your own. There is usually a charge for valet parking. Validated parking is not necessarily free and unlimited; often there is a nominal charge and a restriction on the length of time.

In January 1995, smoking was banned in most Bay Area workplaces, including restaurants. Bars, however, were excluded from the ordinance.

Restaurants do change their policies about hours, credit cards, and the like. It is always best to make inquiries in advance.

The price ranges listed below are for an average three-course meal. A significant trend among more expensive restaurants is the bar menu, which provides light snacks—hot dogs, chili, pizza, and appetizers—in the bar for a cost that is often less than $15 for two.

CATEGORY	COST*
$$$$	over $50
$$$	$30–$50
$$	$20–$30
$	under $20

**per person for a three-course meal, excluding drinks, service, and 8½% sales tax*

American

Before the 1980s, it was hard to find a decent "American" restaurant in the Bay Area. In recent years, however, the offerings have grown and diversified, with fare that includes barbecue, Southwestern, all-American diner food, and that mix of Mediterranean-Asian-Latino known as California cuisine.

Civic Center

$$$ ★ **Stars.** This is the culinary temple of Jeremiah Tower, the superchef who claims to have invented California cuisine. Stars is a must on every traveling gourmet's itinerary, but it's also where many of the local movers and shakers hang out, a popular place for post-theater dining, and open till the wee hours. The dining room has a clublike ambience, and the food ranges from grills to ragouts to sautés—some daringly creative and some classical. Dinners here are pricey, but those on a budget can order a hot dog at the bar. ✕ *150 Redwood Alley,* ☎ *415/861–7827.*

Reservations accepted up to 2 wks in advance, some tables reserved for walk-ins. AE, DC, MC, V. No lunch weekends. Valet parking at night.

$-$$ **Stars Cafe.** For some years, a casual café adjacent to Stars offered a taste of Jeremiah Tower's renowned cuisine at down-to-earth prices. Now the satellite café has moved into its own orbit in much larger quarters around the corner. Both bar and table seating is available. Highlights are pizzas from the wood-burning oven and desserts by Stars' noted pastry chef Emily Luchetti. ✕ *500 Van Ness Ave.,* ☎ *415/861–4344. Reservations accepted for 5 or more for lunch, 2 or more for dinner. AE, DC, MC, V.*

Cow Hollow/Marina

$$ **Perry's.** The West Coast equivalent of P. J. Clarke's in Manhattan, this popular watering hole and meeting place for the button-down singles set serves good, honest saloon food—London broil, corned-beef hash, one of the best hamburgers in town, and a great breakfast. Brunch is served on weekends. ✕ *1944 Union St.,* ☎ *415/922–9022. Reservations accepted. AE, MC, V.*

Embarcadero North

$$ **Fog City Diner.** This is where the diner and grazing crazes began in San Francisco, and the popularity of this spot knows no end. The long, narrow dining room emulates a luxurious railroad car with dark wood paneling, huge windows, and comfortable booths. The cooking is innovative, drawing its inspiration from regional cooking throughout the United States. The sharable "small plates" are a fun way to go. ✕ *1300 Battery St.,* ☎ *415/982–2000. Reservations advised. D, DC, MC, V.*

$$ **MacArthur Park.** Year after year San Franciscans acclaim this as their favorite spot for ribs, but the oak-wood smoker and mesquite grill also turn out a wide variety of all-American fare, from steaks and hamburgers to seafood. Takeout is also available at this handsomely renovated pre-earthquake warehouse. ✕ *607 Front St.,* ☎ *415/398–5700. Reservations advised. AE, DC, MC, V. No lunch weekends and most major holidays. Valet parking at night.*

Embarcadero South

$$-$$$ **Boulevard.** Two of San Francisco's top restaurant talents teamed up in 1993 in one of the city's most magnificent landmark buildings. The culinary half of the team is nationally acclaimed chef Nancy Oakes. The design partner is Pat Kuleto. The setting is the 1889 Audiffred Building, a Parisian look-alike that was one of the few to survive the 1906 earthquake and fire. Oakes's menu is seasonally in flux, but you can be certain to find her signature juxtaposition of aristocratic fare—foie gras is a favorite—with homey comfort foods like pot roast and wood-roasted meats and fowl. For those who can't find or afford a table during regular hours, Boulevard offers a less formal weekday afternoon bar service that features pizza, oysters, burgers, or perhaps a baked potato stuffed with goat cheese. ✕ *1 Mission St.,* ☎ *415/543–6084. Reservations accepted up to 6 wks in advance. AE, D, DC, MC, V. Closed major holidays. No lunch weekends. Valet parking.*

$$-$$$ **One Market.** A giant among American chefs, Bradley Ogden gained fame at Campton Place and later at his Lark Creek Inn in Marin County. In 1993 he and partner Michael Dellar opened this huge, bustling brasserie across from the Ferry Building. The two-tiered dining room seats 170 and a large bar-café serves snacks from noon on; there's also a table for seven smack in the middle of the kitchen. With his move back to the city, Odgen's cuisine has acquired a slight Italian accent. Risotto and pasta might share the spotlight with Yankee pot roast and garlic-mashed potatoes. Jazz piano music is played on

most nights, as well as for Sunday brunch. ✕ *1 Market St.,* ☎ *415/777–5577. Reservations advised for dining room 1 wk in advance; open seating in bar-café. AE, DC, MC, V. No lunch Sat. Valet parking.*

$$ **Harry Denton's.** Every night's a party at this madcap waterfront hangout, where singles congregate in a Barbary Coast–style bar and the rugs are rolled up at 10:30 on Thursday, Friday, and Saturday nights for dancing in the dining room. Sometimes Harry himself—the city's best-known saloon keeper—dances on the bar. At lunchtime the place is quieter, attracting diners with its fine bay view and earthy menu that mixes pizza and pasta with baked oysters, pot roast, and burgers. Breakfast is served daily and extends to brunch on weekends. ✕ *161 Steuart St.,* ☎ *415/882–1333. Reservations advised. AE, DC, MC, V. Valet parking at night.*

Financial District

$$$ **Cypress Club.** Fans of John Cunin have flocked here since 1990, when Masa's longtime maître d' opened his own place, which he calls a "San Francisco brasserie." This categorizes the contemporary American cooking somewhat, but the decor defies description. It could be interpreted as anything from a parody of an ancient temple to a futuristic space war. ✕ *500 Jackson St.,* ☎ *415/296–8555. Reservations advised. AE, DC, MC, V. No lunch. Valet parking at night.*

$$$ **Rubicon.** With an investor list that includes Robin Williams, Robert de Niro, and Francis Ford Coppola, this sleek, cherry wood–lined restaurant was fated to be a destination, even if only for the chance to steal a glance at one of the bankrolling stars. Located in a stately stone building dating from 1908, Rubicon sports the dignified air of a men's club in the downstairs dining room and a somewhat less-appealing atmosphere in the more ascetic upstairs space. But chef Traci des Jardin's excellent fare, primarily dishes based on seafood, are served on both floors to Hollywood big shots and common folk, too. ✕ *558 Sacramento St.,* ☎ *415/434–4100. Reservations advised. AE, MC. V. Closed Sun. No lunch Sat. Valet parking at night.*

Nob Hill

$$–$$$ ★ **Ritz-Carlton Restaurant and Dining Room.** There are two distinctly different places to eat in this neoclassical Nob Hill showplace. The Restaurant, a cheerful, informal spot with a large garden patio for outdoor dining, serves breakfast, lunch, dinner, and a Sunday jazz brunch, with piano music at lunchtime and a jazz trio at weekend dinners. The Dining Room, formal and elegant with a harpist playing, serves only two- to five-course dinners, which are uniquely priced by the course, not by the item. Both rooms present a superb version of northern California cooking based on local ingredients with Mediterranean and Asian overtones. The culinary impresario is chef Gary Danko, who developed the menu for the Restaurant and then went on to win four-star reviews as executive chef of the Dining Room. ✕ *600 Stockton St.,* ☎ *415/296–7465. AE, D, DC, MC, V. Dining Room closed Sun. Valet parking.*

North Beach

$$ **Bix.** The owners of Fog City Diner have re-created a '40s supper club in a historic building that was an assay office in gold-rush days. Reminiscent of a theater, the restaurant has a bustling bar and dining tables downstairs, and banquettes on the balcony. Opt for the lower level; the acoustics upstairs are dreadful. The menu offers contemporary renditions of 1940s fare; there's piano music in the evenings. ✕ *56 Gold St.,* ☎ *415/433–6300. Reservations advised. AE, D, DC, MC, V. No lunch weekends. Valet parking at night.*

Acquarello, **13**
Adriano, **6**
Aioli, **48**
Alain Rondelli, **86**
Appam, **71**
Aqua, **36**
Bahia, **75**
Bardelli's, **62**
Bistro M, **61**
Bistro Roti, **43**
Bix, **26**
Boulevard, **41**
Buca Giovanni, **15**
Café Marimba, **4**
California Culinary Academy, **67**
Campton Place, **47**
Capp's Corner, **21**
Chevy's, **60**
Cypress Club, **23**
Des Alpes, **22**
Ernie's, **25**
Faz, **51**
Fleur de Lys, **66**
Fog City Diner, **18**
Fringale, **58**
Garden Court, **52**
Gaylord's, **2, 37**
Greens, **1**
Harbor Village, **38**
Harris', **12**
Harry Denton's, **44**
Hawthorne Lane, **54**
Hayes Street Grill, **77**
The Heights, **91**
Helmand, **24**
Hong Kong Flower Lounge, **81**
Hyde Street Bistro, **14**
Il Fornaio, **19**
Izzy's Steak & Chop House, **7**
Jack's, **32**
Kabuto Sushi, **84**
Khan Toke Thai House, **85**
Kuleto's, **63**
Kyo-ya, **53**
La Folie, **11**
Le Central, **49**
Le Soleil, **87**
L'Osteria del Forno, **16**
LuLu, **59**
MacArthur Park, **28**
Manora, **72, 73**
Masa's, **46**
Maykadeh, **20**
McCormick & Kuleto's, **3**
Mifune, **88**

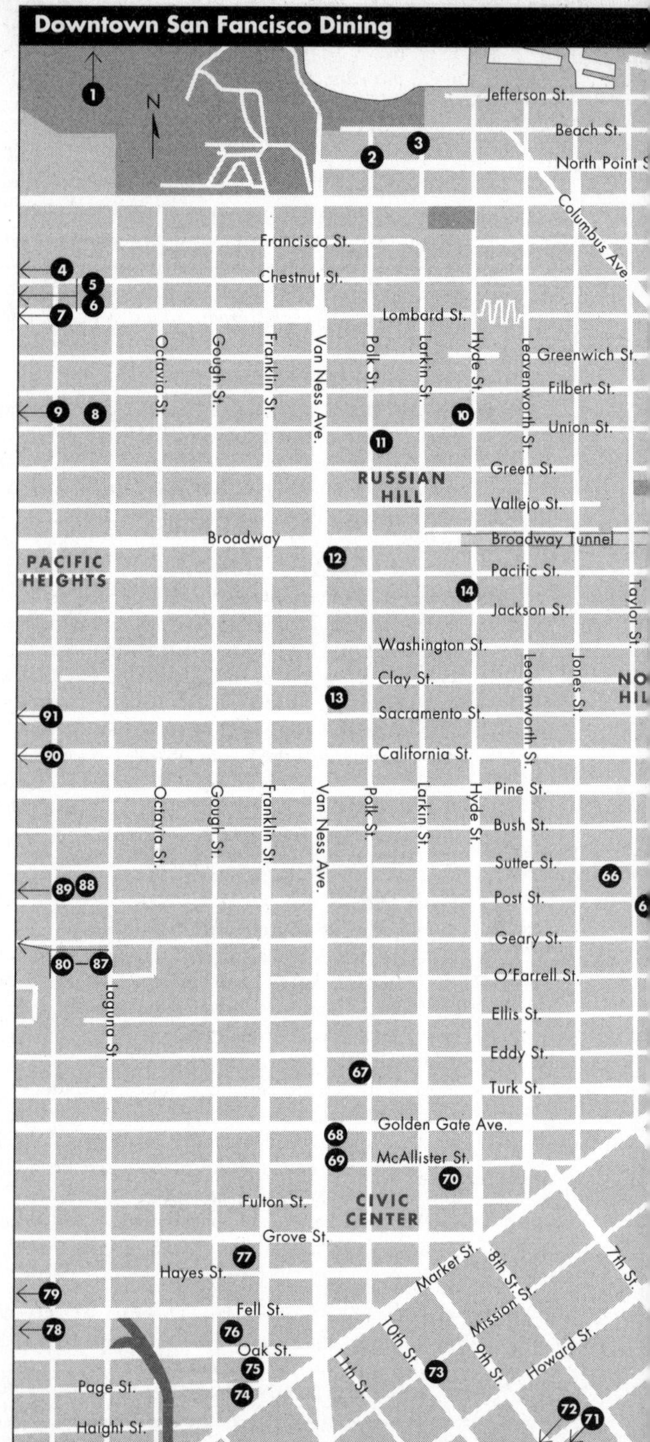

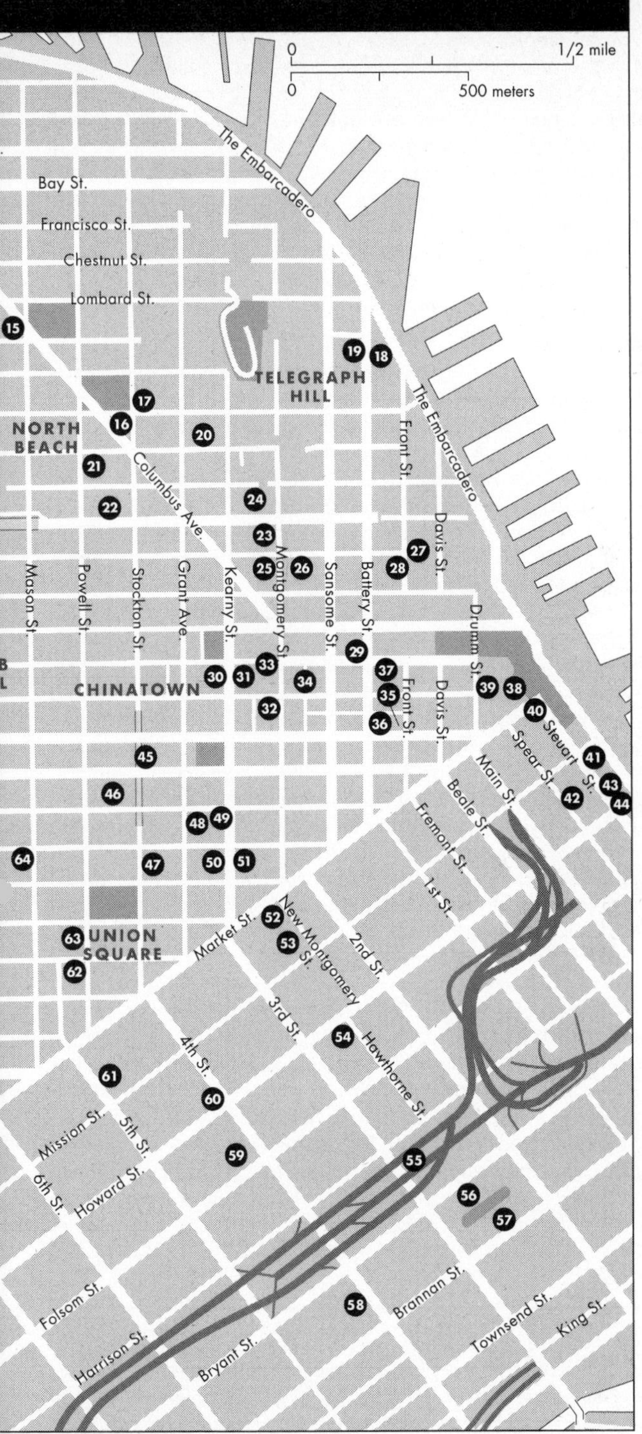

Millenium, **70**
Moose's, **17**
One Market, **40**
Pacific, **64**
Palio d'Asti, **31**
Pane e Vino, **9**
Perry's, **8**
PlumpJack Café, **5**
Postrio, **65**
R & G Lounge, **30**
Ristorante Ecco, **57**
Ritz-Carlton Restaurant and Dining Room, **45**
Rubicon, **34**
Ruby's, **55**
Rumpus, **50**
Sanppo, **89**
South Park Café, **56**
Splendido, **39**
Square One, **27**
Stars, **68**
Stars Cafe, **69**
Stoyanof's Cafe, **78**
Straits Cafe, **80**
Tadich Grill, **35**
Thepin, **76**
Ton Kiang, **82, 83**
Vertigo, **33**
Vivande Porta Via, **90**
Wu Kong, **42**
Yaya Cuisine, **79**
Yank Sing, **29**
Zarzuela, **10**
Zuni Café & Grill, **74**

South of Market

$$$ **Hawthorne Lane.** Anne and David Gingrass, two of Postrio's original trio of chefs (the other being Wolfgang Puck), have joined the booming bevy of SoMa eateries with their new spot a block from Moscone Center. The large, high-ceiling bar looks into a private courtyard and offers a selection of country-rustic bar classics like artichokes with aioli, cracked crab, and onion soup, while patrons in the intimate, light-flooded dining room have views of both courtyard and kitchen. The menu, which they describe as San Franciscan, is not unlike the East-West cuisine the Gingrasses created for Postrio (*see below*). ✕ *22 Hawthorne St.,* ☎ *415/777–9779. Reservations advised. MC, V. No lunch weekends. Valet parking.*

Union Square

$$$–$$$$ ★ **Postrio.** This is the place for those who want to see and be seen; there's always a chance to catch a glimpse of some celebrity, including Postrio's owner, superchef Wolfgang Puck, who periodically commutes from Los Angeles to make an appearance in the restaurant's open kitchen. A stunning three-level bar and dining area is highlighted by palm trees and museum-quality contemporary paintings. Attire is formal; food is Puckish Californian with Mediterranean and Asian overtones, emphasizing pastas, grilled seafood, and house-baked breads. A substantial breakfast and bar menu (with great pizza) are served here, too. ✕ *545 Post St.,* ☎ *415/776–7825. Reservations advised. AE, D, DC, MC, V. Valet parking.*

$$$ ★ **Campton Place.** This elegant, ultrasophisticated small hotel put new American cooking on the local culinary map. Chef Todd Humphries carries on the innovative traditions of opening chef Bradley Ogden with great aplomb and has added his own touches, such as embellishing traditional American dishes with ethnic flavors from recent immigrations. You might find cilantro and Szechuan peppers, for example, in his Nantucket Bay scallops. Among Humphries's most popular contemporary American dishes are such homespun fare as beef short ribs with potato purée, and a hearty chicken pot pie. Be forewarned that his sunny yellow, delightfully crumbly corn bread can be addictive. Breakfast and brunch are major events. A bar menu offers some samplings of appetizers, plus a caviar extravaganza. ✕ *340 Stockton St.,* ☎ *415/955–5555. Reservations suggested, 2 wks in advance on weekends. Jacket required. AE, D, DC, MC, V. Valet parking.*

$–$$ **Rumpus.** With Caesar salad, burgers, club sandwiches, tuna salad, and New York steak, this casual bistro has a true American menu. But there is also an utterly British bubble and squeak, a taste of home for both one of the partners and the head chef; and there's tagliatelle, *malfatti* ("badly formed" pasta), and a trio of risottos for Italophiles. Housed in a comfortable space on an old-time alley in the heart of downtown, Rumpus is always ready to deal with any hunger pangs, as the bar menu is offered all day long and late into the night. ✕ *1 Tillman Pl.,* ☎ *415/421–2300. Reservations advised. AE, MC, V. Valet parking at night.*

Chinese

For nearly a century, Chinese restaurants in San Francisco were confined to Chinatown, and the cooking was largely an Americanized version of peasant-style Cantonese. The past few decades, however, have seen an influx of restaurants representing the wide spectrum of Chinese cuisine: the subtly seasoned fare of Canton; the hot and spicy cooking of Hunan and Szechuan; the red-cooked meats, steamed buns, and braised freshwater fish of Shanghai; the northern style of Beijing, where meat and dumplings replace seafood and rice as staples; and such seldom-encountered cooking as that of the Hakkas, a Southern Chinese people known for their homey country fare such as salt-baked chicken and bean dishes. The current rage is the high-style influence of Hong Kong. These restaurants are now scattered throughout the city.

Chinatown

$-$$ **R&G Lounge.** The name conjures up an image of a dark bar with a cigarette-smoking piano player, but the restaurant, on two floors, is actually as bright as a new penny. Downstairs (entrance on Kearny Street) is a no-tablecloth dining room that is always packed at lunch and dinner. The classier upstairs space (entrance on Commercial Street), complete with shoji-lined private rooms, is a favorite stop for Chinese businessmen on expense accounts and anyone seeking exceptional Cantonese banquet fare. A menu with photographs helps diners decide among the many exotic dishes, from dried scallops with seasonal vegetables to steamed bean curd with shrimp meat. ✕ *631 B Kearny St., ☏ 415/982–7877 or 415/982–3811. Reservations accepted. AE, DC, MC, V.*

Embarcadero North

$$ ★ **Harbor Village.** Classic Cantonese cooking, dim-sum lunches, and fresh seafood from the restaurant's own tanks are the hallmarks of this 400-seat branch of a Hong Kong establishment, which sent five of its master chefs to San Francisco to supervise the initial organization of the kitchen. The setting is opulent, with Chinese antiques and teak furnishings, and the main dining room is usually crowded with business tycoons and three-generation families. A gallery of private rooms harbors large banquet tables perfect for celebrating any special occasion. ✕ *4 Embarcadero Center, ☏ 415/781–8833. Reservations not accepted for lunch on weekends. AE, DC, MC, V. Validated parking in Embarcadero Center Garage.*

Embarcadero South

$$ **Wu Kong.** Tucked away in the splashy art deco Rincon Center, Wu Kong features the cuisine of Shanghai and Canton. Specialties include dim sum, braised yellow fish, and the incredible vegetarian goose—one of Shanghai's famous mock dishes, created from paper-thin layers of dried bean-curd sheets and mushrooms. ✕ *101 Spear St., ☏ 415/957–9300. Reservations advised. AE, DC, MC, V. Validated parking at Rincon Center garage.*

Financial District

$ **Yank Sing.** The city's oldest teahouse has grown by leaps and branches with the popularity of dim sum, and each branch presently offers some 70 varieties of the little morsels each day. The Battery Street location seats 300 and the older, smaller Stevenson Street site has been rebuilt in high-tech style. ✕ *427 Battery St., ☏ 415/362–1640; 49 Stevenson St., ☏ 415/541–4949. Reservations advised. AE, DC, MC, V. No dinner. Stevenson site closed weekends.*

Richmond District

$$ **Hong Kong Flower Lounge.** Many Sinophiles swear that this outpost of a famous Asian restaurant chain serves the best Cantonese food in town. It is known in particular for its seafood—crabs, shrimp, catfish, lobsters, scallops—which is plucked straight from tanks and prepared in a variety of ways, from classic to contemporary. Indeed, the chefs here are famous for keeping up with whatever is currently hot in Hong Kong eateries. Check the prices before you order, as these denizens of the deep can be costly. A good array of dim sum is offered at midday.

✕ *5322 Geary Blvd.,* ☎ *415/668–8998. Reservations advised. AE, D, DC, MC, V.*

$ **Ton Kiang.** The lightly seasoned Hakka cuisine of south China, rarely found in this country, was introduced to San Francisco at this restaurant, with regional specialties like salt-baked chicken, braised stuffed bean curd, wine-flavored dishes, delicate fish and beef balls, and casseroles of meat and seafood cooked in clay pots. Do not overlook the seafood offerings here, such as salt-and-pepper squid or shrimp, braised catfish, or stir-fried crab. Of the two branches on Geary Boulevard, the newest, at 5821, is more stylish, and serves excellent dim sum that some aficionados consider the best in the city. ✕ *3148 Geary Blvd.,* ☎ *415/752–4440; 5821 Geary Blvd.,* ☎ *415/387–8273. Reservations advised. MC, V.*

French

French cooking has gone in and out of vogue in San Francisco since the extravagant days of the Bonanza Kings. A renaissance of the classic haute cuisine occurred during the 1960s, but in the early '90s a number of these restaurants closed. Meanwhile, nouvelle cuisine came and went, and the big draw now is the bistro or brasserie and a light, contemporary style of cooking.

Civic Center

$$–$$$ **California Culinary Academy.** This historic theater houses one of the most highly regarded professional cooking schools in the United States. Well-dressed patrons (men wear jackets) watch the student chefs at work on the double-tier stage while dining on classic French cooking offered as a prix-fixe meal or a bountiful buffet in the theaterlike Carême Room. An à la carte informal grill is located on the lower level. ✕ *625 Polk St.,* ☎ *415/771–3500. Reservations advised (2–4 wks in advance for Fri.-night buffet). AE, DC, MC, V. Closed weekends.*

Embarcadero South

$$ **Bistro Roti.** Tables in the rear of this waterfront café overlook the bay and bridge, while those at the front surround a boisterous bar. In the center, a giant wood-burning rotisserie and grill turn out succulent chops, game, and seafood. Don't miss the classic French onion soup. ✕ *155 Steuart St.,* ☎ *415/495–6500. Reservations advised. AE, DC, MC, V. Closed Dec. 25. No lunch weekends. Valet parking.*

Financial District

$$ **Le Central.** This is the quintessential bistro: noisy and crowded, with nothing subtle about the cooking. But the garlicky pâtés, leeks vinaigrette, cassoulet, and grilled blood sausage with crisp french fries keep the crowds coming. ✕ *453 Bush St.,* ☎ *415/391–2233. Reservations advised. AE, DC, MC, V. Closed Sun.*

Lower Pacific Heights

$$$ **The Heights.** Housed in a Victorian town house on an upmarket shopping street, this sophisticated French eatery is the domain of chef-owner Charles Solomon, who arrived from New York highly recommended. At comfortably spaced tables in three small but light-filled dining rooms, customers can work their way through a six-course tasting menu or choose from an à la carte menu that changes regularly. A fricassee of wild mushrooms with sweetbreads and a vegetable pot-au-feu are particularly tasty appetizers; lavender-scented roast duck atop braised pears and steelhead trout with lobster sauce may follow. Don't overlook the dessert list; the homemade ice creams and delicate puff-pastry creations are sublime.

✕ *3235 Sacramento St.,* ☏ *415/474–8890. Reservations advised. AE, D, DC, MC, V. Closed Mon. No lunch. Valet parking.*

Midtown

$$$ ★ **La Folie.** This pretty storefront café showcases the nouvelle cuisine of Roland Passot, a former sous-chef at Illinois's famous Le Français. Much of the food is edible art—whimsical presentations in the form of savory terrines, *galettes* (flat, round cakes), and napoleons—or elegant accompaniments such as bone-marrow flan. The fun spirit of the place matches the cuisine. ✕ *2316 Polk St.,* ☏ *415/776–5577. Reservations advised. AE, D, DC, MC, V. Closed Sun. No lunch.*

North Beach

$ **Des Alpes.** Basque dinners are offered here, with soup, salad, *two* entrées—sweetbreads on puff pastry and rare roast beef are a typical pair—ice cream, and coffee included in the budget price. It's a haven for trenchermen and a pleasant spot, with wood-paneled walls and bright, embroidered cloths on the tables. Service is family style. ✕ *732 Broadway,* ☏ *415/788–9900. Reservations advised on weekends. D, DC, MC, V. Closed Mon., Dec. 25. No lunch.*

Richmond District

$$–$$$ ★ **Alain Rondelli.** Hailed as one of France's top young chefs when he was at Burgundy's legendary three-star L'Esperance, Paris-born Alain Rondelli came to San Francisco to run the kitchen of Ernie's and now has opened his own beguiling little restaurant in a Richmond District storefront. The cuisine adapts Rondelli's background in classic-yet-contemporary French cooking to the agricultural abundance and Asian-Hispanic influences of California. A zap of jalapeño chili here, a bit of star anise there. Two-part entrées are a Rondelli signature: a breast of chicken followed up with a confit of the leg in a custard tart, for example. Desserts range from homey to exquisite. ✕ *126 Clement St.,* ☏ *415/387–0408. Reservations advised. MC, V. Closed Mon., Tues.*

South of Market

$$$ **Bistro M.** Ever since Bistro M opened in mid-1994, San Franciscans have been trying to identify just which local landmarks, events, and celebrities appear in the 125-foot abstract mural that swirls over two walls of the elegantly modern establishment. Out-of-towners will enjoy the guessing game, too, as well as Chef Michel Richard's distinctive French cuisine—executed with a California accent—offered at breakfast, lunch, and dinner. In the evening, the Alsatian onion tart and sardine rillettes with brioche toasts are superb first courses, followed by the imaginative oxtail in ziti terrine. Be sure to leave room for Richard's signature crunchy napoleon. ✕ *Hotel Milano, 55 5th St.,* ☏ *415/543–5554. Reservations advised. AE, D, DC, MC, V. No lunch Sun. Valet parking.*

$$–$$$ **South Park Cafe.** A bit of France tucked into oh-so-hip SoMa is how partisans of this utterly Gallic restaurant think of their favorite stop for *boudin noir* (black sausage) with sautéed apples. The chairs and tables look as if they were whisked out of a Paris café, and the occasional French-speaking waiter adds to the charm. No place in the City of Light itself serves a more authentic steak-frites than this warm, sometimes clamorous spot, which overlooks a grassy square. ✕ *108 South Park,* ☏ *415/495–7275. Reservations advised. MC, V. Closed Sun. No lunch Sat.*

$$ ★ **Fringale.** The bright-yellow paint on this dazzling bistro stands out like a beacon on an otherwise bleak industrial street, attracting a Pacific Heights–Montgomery Street clientele. They come for the French Basque–inspired creations of Biarritz-born chef Gerald Hirigoyen,

whose ultimate crème brûlée is a hallmark. ✕ *570 4th St.,* ☎ *415/543–0573. Reservations required. AE, MC, V. Closed Sun., Dec. 25. No lunch Sat.*

Union Square

$$$$ ★ **Fleur de Lys.** The creative cooking of French chef-partner Hubert Keller has brought every conceivable culinary award to this romantic spot that some consider the best French restaurant in town—any town. The menu changes constantly, but such dishes as lobster soup with lemongrass, Maryland crab cakes, and pork tenderloin with black beans bear witness to Keller's international scope. The intimate dining room, like a sheikh's tent, is encased with hundreds of yards of paisley. ✕ *777 Sutter St.,* ☎ *415/673–7779. Weekend reservations advised 2 wks in advance. Jacket required. AE, DC, MC, V. Closed Sun., most major holidays. No lunch. Valet parking.*

$$$$ ★ **Masa's.** Chef Julian Serrano carries on the tradition of the late Masa Kobayashi. In fact, some Masa regulars say her cooking is even better. Presentation is as important as the food itself in this pretty, flower-filled dining spot in the Vintage Court Hotel. ✕ *648 Bush St.,* ☎ *415/989–7154. Reservations accepted up to 2 months in advance. Jacket and tie. AE, D, DC, MC, V. Closed Sun., Mon., and 1st 2 wks of Jan. No lunch. Valet parking.*

$$$ **Pacific.** In late 1994 the kitchen of this stylish hotel dining room came under the expert culinary hand of Takayoshi Kawai, former sous-chef at San Francisco's famed Masa's restaurant. The result is a menu that draws upon French techniques and California ingredients to create sophisticated yet unstuffy dishes. The menu changes depending upon what is in the market, but the first course usually features fresh Sonoma County foie gras and seafood. For those watching their pocketbooks, a three-course prix-fixe menu offers a tasty solution, as does breakfast. ✕ *Pan Pacific Hotel, 500 Post St.,* ☎ *415/929–2087. Reservations advised. AE, DC, MC, V. Complimentary valet parking.*

Greek and Middle Eastern

The foods of Greece and the Middle East have much in common: a preponderance of lamb and eggplant dishes, a widespread use of phyllo pastry, and an abundance of pilaf.

Financial District

$$ **Faz.** Although this lovely second-story ocher dining room offers pastas and pizzas that celebrate the robust foods of the western Mediterranean, chef-owner Fazol Poursohi has not forgotten the cuisines of the eastern Mediterranean and beyond, especially in his first courses. Creamy *baba ghannooj* (eggplant spread), beef-and-rice-filled dolmas, and a Persian-inspired platter of feta cheese, pungent olives, and garden-fresh herbs are all great courses. Be sure to order the signature house-smoked fish platter, which includes salmon, trout, and sometimes sturgeon. ✕ *131 Sutter St.,* ☎ *415/362–0404. Reservations advised. MC, V. Valet parking at night. Closed Sun. No lunch Sat.*

North Beach

$–$$ **Maykadeh.** Lamb dishes with rice are the specialties in this authentic Persian restaurant, whose setting is so elegant that the modest check comes as a great surprise. ✕ *470 Green St.,* ☎ *415/362–8286. Reservations advised. MC, V. Valet parking at night.*

$ **Helmand.** Don't be put off by its location on a rather scruffy block of Broadway. The Helmand offers authentic Afghani cooking, elegant surroundings with white napery and rich Afghan carpets, and amazingly

low prices. Don't miss the *aushak* (leek-filled ravioli served with yogurt and ground beef). The lamb dishes are also exceptional. ✕ *430 Broadway, ☎ 415/362–0641. Reservations advised. AE, MC, V. No lunch weekends. Free validated parking at night at Helmand Parking, 468 Broadway.*

Sunset District

$$ **Yaya Cuisine.** Yahya Salih has brought the culinary treasures of Iraqi cuisine to a delightful storefront café and embellished them with Mediterranean and Californian touches. Of note are a first course of date-filled dumplings, and main courses of lamb *kebe* (ground lamb with raisins, pine nuts, and spices) served with a sweet-and-sour sauce, salmon *tajine* (slow-cooked in an earthenware dish), charcoal-grilled river fish, and dishes based on basmati rice, which is indigenous to Iraq. ✕ *1220 9th Ave., ☎ 415/566–6966. AE, DC, MC, V. Closed Mon.*

$ **Stoyanof's Cafe.** This light-filled Greek outpost, with an outdoor seating area that beckons on sunny days, offers large healthful salads, various phyllo-wrapped savories and sweets, kebabs, sandwiches, and other plates that conjure up balmy breezes blowing off the Aegean. The restaurant lies just steps beyond the southern border of Golden Gate Park, making it a good place to stop after a tour of the nearby Strybing Arboretum or Academy of Sciences. ✕ *1240 9th Ave., ☎ 415/664–3664. Reservations accepted. MC, V. Closed Mon.*

Indian

The following restaurants serve principally the cuisine of northern India, which is more subtly seasoned and not as hot as its southern counterparts. They also specialize in succulent meats and crispy breads from the clay-lined tandoori oven.

Northern Waterfront and Embarcadero

$$ **Gaylord's.** A vast selection of mildly spiced northern Indian food is offered here, along with meats and breads from the tandoori ovens and a wide range of vegetarian dishes. The dining rooms are elegantly appointed with Indian paintings and gleaming silver service. The Ghirardelli Square location offers bay views. ✕ *Ghirardelli Sq., ☎ 415/771–8822; Embarcadero 1, ☎ 415/397–7775. Reservations advised. AE, D, DC, MC, V. No lunch Sun. at Embarcadero. Validated parking at Ghirardelli Sq. garage and Embarcadero Center garage.*

South of Market

$$ **Appam.** A traditional north Indian cooking style, *dum pukt,* literally "breath of steam," is the specialty of this attractive restaurant, which also offers a lovely garden for sunny lunchtime dining. Curries such as a fragrant salmon *mouli,* a coconut milk–based curry, flavored with onions, tomatoes, and tamarind, or a duck leg paired with apricots, are sealed inside clay pots. The pots are then placed inside a double-walled oven, and the foods cook in their own steam. The kitchen is also capable of fine tandoori dishes and a variety of Indian breads, including the classic nan and chapati, as well as various *kulcha,* nan stuffed with traditional lamb or nontraditional goat cheese. Service can be ragged sometimes, but the unique flavors are worth the inconvenience. ✕ *1261 Folsom St., ☎ 415/626–2798. Reservations accepted. AE, MC, V. Closed Sun.*

Italian

Italian food in San Francisco spans the "boot" from the mild cooking of northern Italy to the spicy cuisine of the south. Then there is the style indigenous to San Francisco, known as North Beach Italian—such dishes as cioppino (a fisherman's stew) and Joe's special (a mélange of eggs, spinach, and ground beef).

Cow Hollow/Marina

$$ ★ **Adriano.** The daily changing Northern Italian menu in this cheerful blue-and-yellow cucina always includes one or two wonderful, seldom-encountered pastas, perhaps house-made *strongozzi* (thick spaghetti) with a spicy Umbrian tomato sauce, or *stracci* (pasta squares) with scallops; a small selection of irresistible antipasti, which might include venison carpaccio with a garlicky mayonnaise; and such tasty main courses as roast leg of lamb with eggplant purée and simply cooked sea bass. It's a neighborhood favorite. ✕ *3347 Fillmore St.,* ☎ *415/474–4180. Reservations advised. MC, V. Closed Mon. No lunch.*

$$ **Pane e Vino.** It's no easy task to snag a table in this Marina District trattoria, where roasted whole sea bass, creamy risotto, and pastas tossed with sprightly tomato sauces are among the dishes the legion of regulars can't resist. The Italian-born owner-chef concentrates on specialties from Tuscany and north, dishing them up in a charming room decorated with rustic wooden furniture and bright white walls punctuated with colorful pottery and other artifacts from the boot. ✕ *3011 Steiner St.,* ☎ *415/346–2111. Reservations accepted. MC, V. No lunch Sun.*

Embarcadero North

$$ **Il Fornaio.** An offshoot of the Il Fornaio bakeries, this handsome tile-floored, wood-paneled complex combines a café, bakery, and upscale trattoria with outdoor seating. The Tuscan cooking features pizzas from a wood-burning oven, superb house-made pastas and gnocchi, and grilled poultry and seafood. Anticipate a wait for a table, but take solace in the moderate prices. ✕ *Levi's Plaza, 1265 Battery St.,* ☎ *415/986–0100. Reservations advised. AE, DC, MC, V. Valet parking.*

Financial District

$$ **Palio d'Asti.** This moderately priced venture of restaurateur Gianni Fassio draws a lively Financial District lunch crowd. Some specialties are Piedmontese, and a good show is provided by the open kitchen and pizza oven. ✕ *640 Sacramento St.,* ☎ *415/395–9800. Reservations advised. AE, DC, MC, V. Closed Sun., some major holidays. No lunch Sat.*

Lower Pacific Heights

$$$ **Vivande Porta Via.** Located among the boutiques on upper Fillmore Street, this pricey combination Italian delicatessen-restaurant, operated by well-known chef and cookbook author Carlo Middione, draws a crowd at lunch and dinner for both its carryout and sit-down fare. Glass cases holding prosciutto di Parma, creamy balls of mozzarella, sweet-and-sour *caponatina* (eggplant antipasto), mile-high *torta rustica* (savory cheese pie), and dozens of other delicacies span one wall; the rest of the room is given over to seating and shelves laden with wines, olives oils, vinegars, dried pastas, and other Italian gourmet goods. The regularly changing menu includes half a dozen pastas and risottos, including such satisfying southern Italian plates as the classic Siclian pasta *alla Norma* (with eggplant) or spaghetti with fresh tuna and olives, and such northern specialties as risotto with radicchio, pancetta, and pine nuts. ✕ *2125 Fillmore St.,* ☎ *415/346–4430. Reservations advised. MC, V.*

Midtown

$$–$$$ **Acquarello.** This exquisite restaurant is one of the most romantic spots in town. The service and food are exemplary, and the menu covers the full range of Italian cuisine, from northern Italy to the tip of the boot. Desserts are exceptional. ✕ *1722 Sacramento St.,* ☎ *415/567–5432.*

Reservations advised. AE, D, DC, MC, V. Closed Sun., Mon., major holidays. No lunch.

North Beach

$$ **Buca Giovanni.** Giovanni Leoni showcases the dishes of his birthplace, the Serchio Valley in Tuscany, growing many of his own vegetables, olives, and herbs at his Mendocino County ranch. Pastas made on the premises are a specialty, and the calamari salad is a standout. The subterranean dining room is cozy and romantic. ✕ *800 Greenwich St.,* ☎ *415/776–7766. Reservations advised. AE, DC, MC, V. Closed Sun., Mon., Thanksgiving, Dec. 25. No lunch.*

$ **Capp's Corner.** At one of the last of the family-style trattorias, diners sit elbow to elbow at long oilcloth-covered tables to feast on bountiful, well-prepared five-course dinners. For calorie counters or the budget-minded, a simpler dinner includes a tureen of minestrone, salad, and pasta. ✕ *1600 Powell St.,* ☎ *415/989–2589. Reservations advised. AE, D, DC, MC, V. No lunch weekends. Parking validation available.*

$ **L'Osteria del Forno.** The Italian-speaking staff, the small, unpretentious dining area, and the irresistible aromas drifting from the open kitchen make customers who pass through the door of this modest storefront operation feel as if they've just crossed a threshhold in Italy. The proprietors, two northern Italian women, offer small plates of simply cooked vegetables, a few robust pastas, a roast of the day, creamy polenta, and wonderful thin-crust pizzas, including a truly memorable "white" pie topped with thin slices of porcino mushrooms and mozzarella. At lunch, try one of the delectable focaccia sandwiches. ✕ *519 Columbus Ave.,* ☎ *415/982–1124. No reservations. No credit cards. Closed Tues.*

Russian Hill

$$ **Hyde Street Bistro.** The ambience says quintessential neighborhood bistro, but the food is part *gasthaus,* part trattoria, and closely in line with the Austro-Italian tradition of Italy's northeastern Frioli region. Strudels and spaetzles are served alongside pastas and polentas, potato dumplings are paired with a Gorgonzola sauce, and the pastries belie the chef-owner's Austrian roots. ✕ *1521 Hyde St.,* ☎ *415/441–7778. Reservations advised. AE, MC, V. Closed 3 days at Christmas. No lunch. Valet parking.*

South of Market

$$ **Ristorante Ecco.** Hidden within a labyrinth of industrial sprawl is South Park, one of the city's most fashionable addresses in the 1850s. Now the tree-filled square is being gentrified with artists' and designers' lofts and one of the city's best new Italian cafés—Ecco. The cooking is robust, featuring pizza, sandwiches, and pastas at lunch, and hearty braised and grilled dishes at dinner. Ask for a seat in the main dining room, which overlooks the square. ✕ *101 South Park,* ☎ *415/495–3291. Reservations advised. AE, DC, MC, V. Closed Sun., most major holidays. No lunch Sat.*

$$ **Ruby's.** The local pizza-lovers cult claims that Ruby's cornmeal crust is the best in town, and toppings like Gorgonzola with roasted garlic, walnuts, and tomatoes keep things lively. But pizza is only part of the story here: There's also a host of creative small plates and a range of robust pastas and entrées to choose from. Save room for a memorable dessert. ✕ *489 3rd St.,* ☎ *415/541–0795. Reservations accepted for 6 or more. AE, DC, MC, V. No lunch weekends.*

Union Square

$$ **Kuleto's.** The contemporary cooking of northern Italy, the atmosphere of old San Francisco, and a terrific bar menu showcasing contempo-

rary and traditional antipasti have made this spot off Union Square a hit since it opened in the 1980s. Publike booths and a long, open kitchen fill one side of the restaurant; a gardenlike setting with light splashed from skylights lies beyond. Grilled seafood dishes are among the specialties. Breakfast is also served. ✕ *221 Powell St.,* ☎ *415/397-7720. Reservations advised. AE, D, DC, MC, V.*

Japanese

Japanese menus involve three basic types of cooking: *yaki,* marinated and grilled foods; *tempura,* fish and vegetables deep-fried in a light batter; *udon* and *soba,* noodle dishes; *domburi,* meats and vegetables served over rice; and *nabemono,* meals cooked in one pot, often at the table. Sushi bars are extremely popular in San Francisco; most offer a selection of sushi (vinegared rice with fish or vegetables) and sashimi (raw fish). Western seating refers to conventional tables and chairs; tatami seating is on mats at low tables.

Financial District

$$–$$$ ★ **Kyo-ya.** Rarely replicated outside Japan, the refined experience of dining in a fine Japanese restaurant has been introduced with extraordinary authenticity at this showplace within the Sheraton Palace Hotel. In Japan, a *kyo-ya* is a nonspecialized restaurant that serves a wide range of food types. Here, the range is spectacular—encompassing tempuras, one-pot dishes, deep-fried and grilled meats, and a choice of some three dozen sushi selections. The lunch menu is more limited than dinner, but does offer a *shokado,* a sampler of four classic dishes encased in a handsome lacquered lunch box. ✕ *Sheraton Palace Hotel, 2 New Montgomery St., at Market St.,* ☎ *415/546-5000. Reservations advised. AE, MC, V. Closed weekends.*

Japantown

$ **Mifune.** Thin, brown soba (buckwheat) and thick, white udon (wheat) are the specialties at this North American outpost of an Osaka-based noodle empire. A line often snakes out the door, but the house-made noodles, served both hot and cold and with more than a score of different toppings, are worth the wait. Seating is at rustic wooden tables, where diners can be heard slurping down big bowls of such traditional Japanese combinations as fish cake–crowned udon and *tenzaru* (cold noodles and hot tempura served on lacquered trays with gingery dipping sauce). ✕ *Japan Center Bldg., West Wing, 1737 Post St.,* ☎ *415/922-0337. No reservations. AE, D, DC, MC, V.*

$ **Sanppo.** This small place has an enormous selection of almost every type of Japanese food: yakis, nabemono dishes, domburi, udon, and soba, not to mention feather-light tempura and interesting side dishes. Western seating only. ✕ *1702 Post St.,* ☎ *415/346-3486. No reservations. MC, V. Closed Mon. No lunch Sun. Validated parking in Japan Center garage.*

Richmond District

$$ **Kabuto Sushi.** For one of the most spectacular acts in town, head out Geary Boulevard past Japantown to tiny Kabuto. Here, behind his black-lacquered counter, master chef Sachio Kojima flashes his knives with the grace of a samurai warrior. In addition to exceptional sushi and sashimi, traditional Japanese dinners are served in the adjoining dining room with both Western seating and, in a shoji-screened area, tatami seating. ✕ *5116 Geary Blvd.,* ☎ *415/752-5652. Reservations advised for dinner. MC, V. Closed Mon. No lunch.*

Mediterranean

In its climate and topography, its agriculture and viticulture, and the orientation of many of its early settlers, northern California resembles the Mediterranean region. But until quite recently no restaurant billed itself as "Mediterranean." Those that do so now primarily offer a mix of southern French and northern Italian food, but some include accents from Spain, Greece, and more distant ports of call.

Civic Center

$$–$$$ ★ **Zuni Café & Grill.** Zuni's Italian-Mediterranean menu and its unpretentious atmosphere pack in the crowds from early morning to late evening. A spacious, window-filled balcony dining area overlooks the large bar, where shellfish, one of the best oyster selections in town, and drinks are dispensed. A second dining room houses the giant pizza oven and grill. Even the hamburgers have an Italian accent—they're topped with Gorgonzola and served on herbed focaccia buns. ✕ *1658 Market St.,* ☎ *415/552–2522. Reservations advised. AE, MC, V. Closed Mon., major holidays.*

Cow Hollow/Marina

$$–$$$ **PlumpJack Café.** This clubby dining room, with its smartly attired clientele, takes its name from an opera composed by famed oil tycoon and music lover Gordon Getty, whose sons are two of the partners here. The regularly changing menu spans the Mediterranean, with grilled figs and prosciutto and crispy duck confit among the possibilities. The café is an offshoot of the nearby highly regarded wine shop of the same name, which stocks the racks that line the dining room with some of the best-priced vintages in town. ✕ *3201 Fillmore St.,* ☎ *415/346–9870. Reservations advised. AE, MC, V. Closed Sun. No lunch Sat.*

Embarcadero North

$$–$$$ ★ **Square One.** Chef Joyce Goldstein introduces an ambitious new menu daily, with dishes based on the classic cooking of the Mediterranean countries, sometimes straying to Asia and Latin America. The dining room, with its views of the open kitchen and the Golden Gateway commons, is an understated setting for some of the finest food in town—and an award-winning wine list. A bar menu is available. ✕ *190 Pacific Ave.,* ☎ *415/788–1110. Reservations advised. AE, DC, MC, V. No lunch weekends. Valet parking at night.*

$$ **Splendido.** Mediterranean cooking is the focus at this handsome restaurant. Diners here are transported to the coast of southern France or northern Italy by the artistic decor and spectacular lighting; the bay view is the only reminder of San Francisco. Among the many winners are the shellfish soup and warm goat-cheese and ratatouille salad. Desserts are truly *splendido.* A bar menu is available. ✕ *Embarcadero 4,* ☎ *415/986–3222. Reservations advised. AE, DC, MC, V. Validated parking at Embarcadero Center garage.*

Financial District

$$ **Vertigo.** Arguably San Francisco's most famous building, the Transamerica Pyramid is also home to one of the city's most stunning restaurants, a three-tier space with see-through ceilings, a parklike entrance, and an inviting French and Italian menu with Asian accents. Named for both the dizzying height of the landmark tower and for the title of the Alfred Hitchcock thriller filmed in the city, Vertigo offers a seasonal menu that combines the freshest possible ingredients—especially seafood—in creative combinations. A first course of grilled shrimp with a salad of fennel and tangerine might be followed by salmon in crunchy coriander crust, or lamb loin with goat cheese–potato gratin. A bar menu

offers afternoon snacks such as Dungeness crab cakes and corn-wheat pizzas. ✕ *600 Montgomery St.,* ☎ *415/433–7250. Reservations advised. AE, D, DC, MC, V. Valet parking. Closed Sun. No lunch Sat.*

North Beach

$$ ★ **Moose's.** Longtime San Francisco restaurateur Ed Moose's latest venture was destined to become a top celebrity hangout from the moment it opened in 1992. Politicians and media types have followed him from his former digs at Washington Square Bar & Grill just across the large, tree-shaded square. Along with a host of local luminaries, Tom Brokaw, Walter Cronkite, Tom Wolfe, and Senator Dianne Feinstein head for Moose's when they're in town. And the food impresses as much as the clientele: A Mediterranean-inspired menu highlights innovative appetizers, pastas, seafood, and grills. The surroundings are classic and comfortable, with views of Washington Square and Russian Hill from a front café area and, in the rear, facing the open kitchen, counter seats for singles. There's live music at night and a fine Sunday brunch. ✕ *1652 Stockton St.,* ☎ *415/989–7800. Reservations advised 6–8 wks in advance. AE, DC, MC, V. No lunch Mon. Valet parking.*

South of Market

$–$$ ★ **LuLu.** Since opening day in 1993, a seat at this boisterous café has been about the hottest ticket in town. Chef Reed Hearon has brought a touch of the French-Italian Riviera to a spacious and stunningly renovated San Francisco warehouse. Under the high, barrel-vaulted ceiling, beside a large open kitchen, diners feast on a signature dish of sizzling mussels roasted in an iron skillet, plus pizzas and pastas with "would you believe it" embellishments, and wood-roasted poultry, meats, and shellfish. Sharing dishes family-style is the custom here. For those who like a quieter ambience, Hearon has opened a little bistro, LuLu Bis, just next door, where four-course prix-fixe dinners are served at communal tables. ✕ *816 Folsom St.,* ☎ *415/495–5775. Reservations advised 1–2 wks in advance. AE, DC, MC, V. No Sun. lunch at LuLu. No lunch at LuLu Bis.*

Union Square

$$ **Aioli.** The food and decor of this tiny bistro are a sunny potpourri derived from the exotic locales in chef Sebastien Urbain's background, ranging from his birthplace on the French island of Réunion to cities in Africa, France, and the Middle East where he served as chef for Méridien hotels. These culinary influences are bound together with a passion for garlic, as the name of the restaurant suggests. Aioli, the garlicky sauce of Provence, embellishes an extraordinary platter of mixed seafood. Also sample the oysters baked in their shells with caramelized onions and a pungent purée of garlic. The soups are full-bodied, and the pastas outstanding. ✕ *469 Bush St.,* ☎ *415/249–0900. Reservations advised. AE, DC, MC, V.*

Mexican/Latin American/Spanish

In spite of San Francisco's Mexican heritage, until recently most south-of-the-border eateries were locked into the Cal-Mex taco-enchilada-beans syndrome. Now several restaurants offer a broader spectrum of Mexican and Latin American cooking, a well as some Spanish food.

Civic Center

$–$$ **Bahia.** An evening at this festive Brazilian café is like a quick trip to the tropics. Amid lush foliage, bold paintings, and the beat of the samba, you can feast on all the great Brazilian classics like *feijoada* (pork and black-bean stew), *bobo de camarão* (shrimp in coconut milk), and creamy chicken croquettes. There's a tapas bar in the early evening, and just down the street is Bahia's nightclub, which gyrates with the lambada until the wee hours. ✕ *41 Franklin St.,* ☏ *415/626–3306. Reservations advised. AE, MC, V.*

Cow Hollow/Marina

$$ **Café Marimba.** Chef Reed Hearon struck gold in 1993, when he and his partner Louise Clement opened both the sensationally popular LuLu (*see above*) and this casual Mexican café. Colorful folk art adorns the walls while the open kitchen turns out Hearon's contemporary renditions of regional specialties: silken *mole negro* (sauce of chiles and chocolate) from Oaxaca, served in tamales and other dishes; shrimp prepared with roasted onions and tomatoes in the style of Zihuatenejo; and chicken with a marinade from Yucatán, stuffed into one of the world's greatest tacos. Though he imparts his own imaginative touches, Hearon is devoted to authenticity—even the guacamole is made to order in a *molcajete,* the three-legged version of a pestle. His salsa repertoire is chronicled in his book, *Salsa,* another hit of 1993. ✕ *2317 Chestnut St.,* ☏ *415/776–1506. Reservations advised. MC, V. Closed Thanksgiving, Dec. 25. No lunch Mon. Valet parking.*

Russian Hill

$$ **Zarzuela.** Until the late summer of 1994, San Francisco lacked a great tapas restaurant. But Spanish-born chef Lucas Gasco changed all that when he and partner Andy Debanne opened their charming Zarzuela. The small, crowded storefront serves nearly 40 different hot and cold tapas, plus some dozen main courses. There is a tapa to suit every palate, from poached octopus atop new potatoes and hot, garlic-flecked shrimp to slabs of Manchego cheese with paper-thin slices of serrano ham. The paella of saffron-scented rice weighed down with prawns, mussels, and clams is guaranteed to make the most unsentimental Madrileño homesick. ✕ *2000 Hyde St.,* ☏ *415/346-0800. Reservations accepted for 6 or more. MC, V. Closed Sun.*

South of Market

$ **Chevy's.** Just across from Moscone center, this branch of a popular Mexican minichain is decked with funky neon signs and "El Machino" turning out flour tortillas. "Stop gringo food" is the motto here, where the emphasis is on the freshest ingredients and sauces. Of note are the fajitas, as well as the grilled quail and seafood. ✕ *4th and Howard Sts.,* ☏ *415/543–8060. Reservations accepted for 8 or more. AE, MC, V. Validated parking at garage under building (enter from Minna St.).*

Old San Francisco

Several of the city's landmark restaurants don't fit neatly into any ethnic category. Some might call them Continental or French or even American. But dating back to the turn of the century or earlier—or appearing to do so—these places all exude the traditions and aura of old San Francisco. The oldest one of them all, Tadich Grill, is listed under Seafood.

Financial District

$$$ **Garden Court.** In the Sheraton Palace hotel, this is the ultimate old San Francisco experience. From breakfast through lunch, teatime, and the early dinner hours, light splashes through the $7 million stained-glass ceiling against the towering Ionic columns and crystal chandeliers. The classic European menu highlights some famous dishes devised by Palace chefs early this century, such as Green Goddess salad, and the extravagant Sunday buffet brunch again takes center stage as one of

the city's great traditions. ✕ *Market and New Montgomery Sts., ☎ 415/546–5000. Reservations advised. Jacket and tie. AE, DC, MC, V.*

$$ **Jack's.** Little has changed in more than 100 years at this bankers' and brokers' favorite. The menu is extensive, but regulars opt for the simple fare—steaks, chops, seafood, and stews. The dining room, like the food, has an old-fashioned, no-nonsense aura, and private upstairs rooms are available for top-secret meetings. ✕ *615 Sacramento St., ☎ 415/986–9854. Reservations advised. AE, DC, MC, V. Closed Sun. No lunch Sat.*

North Beach

$$$ **Ernie's.** Founded in 1934, this venerable restaurant is a kid among the city's old-timers. But to many longtime visitors, Ernie's *is* Old San Francisco. Though redecorated in the early 1990s, the handsome interior still exudes the opulent aura of an exclusive Barbary Coast bordello with sparkling crystal and gleaming silver service plates. This is where you go to eat Caspian caviar for $40 an ounce or to watch a Caesar salad or crêpes suzettes reverently assembled tableside. Originally Italian, the menu is now contemporary French, as are many of the chefs who prepare it—although the current chef, Tony Najiola, has reintroduced some Italian dishes such as lamb carpaccio, gnocchi, and osso buco. ✕ *847 Montgomery St., ☎ 415/397–5969. Reservations advised. Jacket required. AE, DC, MC, V. No lunch. Valet parking.*

Union Square

$$ **Bardelli's.** Founded in 1906 as Charles' Oyster House, this turn-of-the-century showplace boasts vaulted ceilings, massive marble columns, and stained glass. The traditional menu mixes French, Italian, and American fare with superb fresh seafood. ✕ *243 O'Farrell St., ☎ 415/982–0243. Reservations accepted. AE, DC, MC, V. No lunch weekends. Validated parking at Downtown Center garage.*

Seafood

Like all port cities, San Francisco takes pride in its seafood, even though less than half the fish served here is from local waters. In winter and spring, look for the fresh Dungeness crab, best served cracked with mayonnaise. In summer, feast on Pacific salmon, even though imported varieties are available year-round. A recent development is the abundance of unusual oysters from West Coast beds and an outburst of oyster bars.

Civic Center

$$ **Hayes Street Grill.** Eight to 15 different kinds of seafood are chalked on the blackboard each night at this extremely popular restaurant. The fish is served simply grilled, with a choice of sauces ranging from tartar to a spicy Szechuan peanut concoction. Appetizers are unusual, and desserts are lavish. ✕ *320 Hayes St., ☎ 415/863–5545. Reservations advised several wks in advance. AE, D, DC, MC, V. Closed some holidays. No lunch weekends.*

Financial District

$$$ ★ **Aqua.** This quietly elegant and ultrafashionable spot is possibly the city's most important seafood restaurant ever. Chef-owner George Morrone has a supremely original talent for creating contemporary versions of French, Italian, and American classics: Expect mussel, crab, or lobster soufflés; lobster gnocchi with lobster sauce; shrimp and corn madeleines strewn in a salad; and ultrarare *ahi* tuna paired with foie gras. Desserts are miniature museum pieces. ✕ *252 California St., ☎ 415/956–*

9662. Reservations essential. AE, DC, MC, V. Closed Sun. No lunch Sat. Valet parking at night.

$$ **Tadich Grill.** Owners and locations have changed many times since this old-timer opened during the gold-rush era, but the 19th-century atmosphere remains, as does the kitchen's special way with seafood. Simple sautés are the best choices, or the cioppino during crab season. There is seating at both the counter and in private booths, but expect long lines for a table at lunchtime. ✕ *240 California St.,* ☎ *415/391–2373. No reservations. MC, V. Closed Sun.*

Northern Waterfront

$$ **McCormick & Kuleto's.** This seafood emporium in Ghirardelli Square is a visitor's dream come true: a fabulous view of the bay from every seat in the house; an old San Francisco atmosphere; and some 30 varieties of fish and shellfish prepared in at least 70 globe-circling ways, from tacos, pot stickers, and fish cakes to grills, pastas, and stew. The food has its ups and downs, but even on foggy days you can count on the view. ✕ *Ghirardelli Sq.,* ☎ *415/929–1730. Reservations advised. AE, D, DC, MC, V. Validated parking in Ghirardelli Sq. garage.*

Southeast Asian

In recent years San Franciscans have seen tremendous growth in the numbers of restaurants specializing in the foods of Thailand, Vietnam, Cambodia, and Singapore. The cuisines of these countries share many features, but one in particular: The cooking is generally highly spiced, and often very hot.

Civic Center

$–$$ **Thepin.** It seems as if there's a Thai restaurant on every block now, but this is the jewel in the crown. The stylish dining room sparkles with linen napery, fresh flowers, Thai artwork, and a wine list that surpasses the Asian norm. Notable are the duck dishes and the curries, each prepared with its own mixture of freshly blended spices. ✕ *298 Gough St.,* ☎ *415/863–9335. Reservations advised. AE, MC, V. Closed major holidays. No lunch weekends.*

Richmond District

$–$$ ★ **Khan Toke Thai House.** The city's first Thai restaurant has a lovely dining room furnished with low tables and cushions, and a garden view. The six-course dinners, with two entrées from an extensive list, provide a delicious introduction to Thai cooking. The seasoning is mild unless you request it hot. Classical Thai dancing on Sunday. ✕ *5937 Geary Blvd.,* ☎ *415/668–6654. Reservations advised. MC, V. No lunch.*

$–$$ ★ **Le Soleil.** The food of Vietnam is the specialty of this pastel, light-filled restaurant located in the heart of the Inner Richmond. An eye-catching painting of Saigon hangs on one wall, and the large aquarium of tropical fish near the door adds to the tranquil mood. The kitchen prepares traditional dishes from every part of the country. Try the excellent raw-beef salad; crisp, flavorful spring rolls; a simple stir-fry of chicken and aromatic fresh basil leaves; or large prawns simmered in a clay pot. ✕ *133 Clement St.,* ☎ *415/668–4848. Reservations accepted. MC, V.*

$–$$ **Straits Cafe.** This highly popular restaurant serves the unique fare of Singapore, a cuisine that combines the culinary traditions of China, India, and the Malay archipelago. That exotic mix translates into complex curries, rice cooked in coconut milk, sticks of fragrant *satay* (skewers of chicken or beef), and seafood noodle soups. On Wednesday night, a "spices and vines dinner" is offered, pairing classic Singaporean dishes with carefully selected vintages. The handsome dining room includes one wall that re-creates the old shop-house fronts of Singapore. ✕ *3300 Geary Blvd.,* ☎ *415/668–1783. Reservations advised. AE, MC, V.*

South of Market

$ **Manora.** When this homey Thai café way out on Mission Street first opened, crowds from all over town lined up for a table to try the extensive selection of carefully prepared dishes. Now the same great food is offered at a more conveniently located Manora, not far from the Performing Arts Center. Good choices are the fish cakes and curries. ✕ *3226 Mission St.,* ☎ *415/550–0856; 1600 Folsom St.,* ☎ *415/861–6224. MC, V. Closed Mon. and no lunch at Mission St.; no lunch weekends at Folsom St.*

Steak Houses

Although San Francisco traditionally has not been a meat-and-potatoes town, several excellent steak houses have opened in the past decade. You can also get a good piece of beef at most of the better French, Italian, and American restaurants.

Marina

$$ **Izzy's Steak & Chop House.** Izzy Gomez was a legendary San Francisco saloon keeper, and his namesake eatery carries on the tradition with terrific steaks, chops, and seafood, plus all the trimmings—such as cheesy scalloped potatoes and creamed spinach. A collection of Izzy memorabilia and antique advertising art covers almost every inch of wall space. ✕ *3345 Steiner St.,* ☎ *415/563–0487. Reservations accepted. AE, DC, MC, V. No lunch. Validated parking at Lombard Garage.*

Midtown

$$$ ★ **Harris'.** Ann Harris knows her beef. She grew up on a Texas cattle ranch and was married to the late Jack Harris of Harris Ranch fame. In her own large, New York–style restaurant she serves some of the best dry-aged steaks in town, but don't overlook the grilled seafood or poultry. There is also an extensive bar menu. ✕ *2100 Van Ness Ave.,* ☎ *415/673–1888. Reservations recommended. AE, DC, MC, V. No lunch. Valet parking.*

Vegetarian

Aside from the restaurants mentioned below, vegetarians should also consider the Indian and Southeast Asian restaurants, most of which generally offer a variety of meatless dishes.

Civic Center

$$ **Millenium.** Tucked into the former carriage house of the venerable Abigail Hotel, Millenium offers what it describes as "organic cuisine." That label translates to a vegetarian menu of low-fat, dairy-free dishes made with organic ingredients that keeps herbivores and carnivores alike satisfied. The kitchen looks to the Mediterranean, with pastas, polenta, and grilled vegetables among its most successful dishes. For true believers, there is *seitan* (a whole-wheat meat substitute) steak in Marsala sauce, a chocolate mousse cake made from tofu, and organic wines and beers. A Continental breakfast is served Monday through Friday and brunch is offered on Sunday. ✕ *246 McAllister St.,* ☎ *415/487–9800. Reservations accepted. MC, V.*

Marina

$$ ★ **Greens.** This beautiful restaurant with expansive bay views is owned and operated by the Zen Buddhist Center of Marin County. The din-

ing room offers a wide, eclectic, and creative spectrum of meatless cooking, and the bread promises nirvana. Dinners are à la carte on weeknights, but only a five-course prix-fixe dinner is served on Saturday. ✕ *Bldg. A, Fort Mason,* ☎ *415/771–6222. Reservations advised. MC, V. No lunch Mon., no dinner Sun. Public parking at Fort Mason Center.*

6 Lodging

By Patrick Hoctel

FEW CITIES in the United States can rival San Francisco's variety in lodging. There are plush hotels ranked among the finest in the world, renovated older buildings that have the charm of Europe, bed-and-breakfasts in the city's Victorian "Painted Ladies," and the popular chain hotels found in most cities in the United States. One of the brightest spots in the lodging picture is the transformation of handsome early 20th-century downtown high-rises into small, distinctive hotels that offer personal service and European ambience. Another is the recent addition of ultradeluxe modern hotels such as the Miyako and the Mandarin Oriental, which specialize in attentive Asian-style hospitality.

The **San Francisco Convention and Visitors Bureau** (☎ 415/391–2000) publishes a free lodging guide with a map and a listing of all hotels. Because San Francisco is one of the top destinations in the United States for tourists as well as business travelers and convention goers, reservations are always advised, especially during the May–October peak season.

To reserve a room in any property in this chapter, you can contact **Fodor's new toll-free lodging reservations hot line** (☎ 1–800–FODORS–1 or 1–800–363–6771; 0800–89–1030 in Great Britain; 0014/800–12–8271 in Australia; 1800–55–9101 in Ireland).

San Francisco's geography makes it conveniently compact. No matter what their location, the hotels listed below are on or close to public transportation lines. Some properties on Lombard Street and in the Civic Center area have free parking, but a car is more a hindrance than an asset in San Francisco.

Although not as high as the rates in New York, San Francisco hotel prices may come as a surprise to travelers from less urban areas. Average rates for double rooms downtown and at the wharf are in the $120 range. Adding to the expense is the city's 12% transient occupancy tax, which can significantly boost the cost of a lengthy stay. The good news is that because of the hotel building boom of the late 1980s, there is now an oversupply of rooms, which has led to much discounting of prices. Check for special rates and packages when making reservations.

For those in search of true budget accommodations (under $50), try the Adelaide Inn (*see* Union Square/Downtown, *below*) or the **YMCA Central Branch.** *220 Golden Gate Ave., 94102, ☎ 415/885–0460. 106 rooms, 6 with bath. Café, pool, sauna, steam room, health club. MC, V.*

An alternative to hotels and motels is staying in private homes and apartments, available through **American Family Inn/Bed & Breakfast San Francisco** (Box 420009, San Francisco 94142, ☎ 415/931–3083), **Bed & Breakfast International–San Francisco** (Box 282910, San Francisco 94128-2910, ☎ 415/696–1690 or 800/872–4500, FAX 415/696–1699), and **American Property Exchange** (170 Page St., San Francisco 94102, ☎ 415/863–8484 or 800/747–7784).

Home Exchange

This is an inexpensive solution to the lodging problem, since house swapping means living rent-free. Participants find a house, apartment, or other vacation property to exchange for their own by becoming members of a home-exchange organization, which publishes annual directories listing available exchanges. Arrangements for the actual exchange are made by the two parties to it, not by the organization. The oldest clearinghouse is **Intervac U. S./International Home Exchange** (Box 590504, San Francisco 94159, ☎ 415/435–3497 or 800/756–4663), which publishes four annual directories, including thousands of foreign and domestic homes for exchange. Membership is $65 ($60 for senior citizens), or $72 for those who would like to receive the directories but wish to remain unlisted. The **Vacation Exchange Club** (Box 650, Key West, FL 33041, ☎ 800/638–3841), also with thousands of foreign and domestic listings, publishes five annual directories plus updates; the $65 membership includes your listing. **Loan-a-Home** (2 Park La., Apt. 6E, Mount Vernon, NY 10552-3443, ☎ 914/664–7640) specializes in long-term housing; there is no charge to list your home, but directories cost $35–$45.

Apartment and Villa Rentals

If you want a home base that's roomy enough for a family and comes with cooking facilities, a furnished rental may be the solution. Most offer good value for your money, although not always—some rentals are luxury properties (economical only when your party is large). Home-exchange directories list rentals—often second homes owned by prospective house swappers—and there are services that can not only look for a house or apartment for you (even a castle if that's your fancy) but also handle the paperwork. Some send an illustrated catalogue and others send photographs of specific properties, sometimes at a charge; up-front registration fees may apply.

Among the companies are **Interhome Inc.** (124 Little Falls Rd., Fairfield, NJ 07004, ☎ 201/882–6864, FAX 201/808–1742) and **Rent a Home International** (7200 34th Ave. NW, Seattle, WA 98117, ☎ 206/789–9377 or 800/488–7368, FAX 206/789–9379). **Hideaways International** (767 Islington St., Portsmouth, NH 03801, ☎ 603/430–4433 or 800/843–4433, FAX 603/430–4444) functions as a travel club. Membership ($99 yearly per person, or for one family at the same address) includes two annual guides plus quarterly newsletters; rentals are arranged directly between members, not by the club staff.

CATEGORY	COST*
$$$$	over $175
$$$	$120–$175
$$	$80–$120
$	under $80

**All prices are for a standard double room, excluding 12% tax.*

Union Square/Downtown

The largest variety and greatest concentration of hotels is in the city's downtown hub, Union Square, where hotel guests can find the best shopping, the theater district, and convenient transportation to every spot in San Francisco.

$$$$ ★ **Campton Place Hotel.** Behind a simple brownstone facade with white awning, quiet reigns. Highly attentive, personal service—from unpacking assistance to nightly turndown—begins the moment uniformed doormen greet guests outside the marble-floored lobby. The rooms, small but well appointed, are decorated with Asian touches in subtle tones of gold and brown, with double-pane windows, Chinese armoires, and good-size writing desks. From the ninth floor up, there are only four rooms to a floor. They overlook an atrium, which lends a cozy, residential feel. The hotel is a 10-minute walk from the Moscone Center and the new Yerba Buena Center complex. The Campton Place

Restaurant, listed prominently in *Condé Nast Traveler*'s "50 American Restaurants Worth the Journey," is famed for its breakfasts. *340 Stockton St., 94108,* ☎ *415/781–5555 or 800/235–4300,* FAX *415/955–5536. 117 rooms. Restaurant, bar. AE, DC, MC, V.*

$$$$ ★ **Four Seasons Clift.** The Clift towers over San Francisco's theater district, its crisp, forest-green awnings and formal door service subtle hints of the elegance within. In the busy lobby, where dark paneling and four enormous chandeliers lend a note of grandeur, everything runs smoothly. The Clift is noted for its swift personalized service; a phone call will get you anything from complimentary limousine service to a chocolate cake. Rooms, some rich with dark woods and burgundies, others refreshingly pastel, all have large writing desks, plants, and flowers. Be sure to sample a cocktail in the famous Art Deco Redwood Room lounge, complete with chandeliers and a sweeping redwood bar. *495 Geary St., 94102,* ☎ *415/775–4700 or 800/332–3442,* FAX *415/441–4621. 329 rooms. Restaurant, lounge, exercise room, meeting rooms. AE, DC, MC, V.*

$$$$ **Westin St. Francis.** Host to the likes of Emperor Hirohito, Queen Elizabeth II, and many presidents, the St. Francis, with its imposing facade, black marble lobby, and gold-topped columns, looks more like a great public building than a hotel. The effect is softened by the columns and exquisite woodwork of the Compass Rose bar and restaurant; since its inception, this has been a retreat from the bustle of Union Square, especially for those in a romantic frame of mind. An extensive refurbishment of the entire hotel is likely to continue for several more years, but will result in a sandstone resurfacing of the exterior, and improved guest rooms. Many of the rooms in the original building are small by modern standards, but all retain their original Victorian-style moldings and bathroom tiles. The rooms in the modern tower are larger, with brighter, lacquered furniture. *335 Powell St., 94102,* ☎ *415/397–7000 or 800/228–3000,* FAX *415/774–0124. 1,200 rooms. 5 restaurants, 5 lounges, room service, exercise room, business services. AE, DC, MC, V.*

$$$ ★ **Galleria Park.** A few blocks east of Union Square, this hotel is close to the Chinatown gate and the Crocker Galleria, one of San Francisco's most elegant shopping areas. The staff is remarkably pleasant and helpful. The French country-style rooms all have floral bedspreads and white furniture that includes a writing desk. Four floors are nonsmoking. Guests are invited to enjoy the lobby's inviting fireplace or the adjacent Bentley's Seafood Grill. *191 Sutter St., 94104,* ☎ *415/781–3060 or 800/792–9639,* FAX *415/433–4409. 162 rooms, 15 suites. 2 restaurants, jogging. AE, D, DC, MC, V.*

$$$ **Holiday Inn–Union Square.** Given the rather undistinguished, '60s-style facade of this convention-oriented hotel right on the cable-car line, the charming, 19th-century English decor of the rooms comes as a surprise. Back rooms on upper floors have commanding views of the bay; from the front rooms, you can see west all the way to the avenues. Every room has a large writing desk and most have two phones. For an evening of intimacy, try the Sherlock Holmes lounge on the 30th floor—great views, two fireplaces, and the lights are kept low. *480 Sutter St., 94108,* ☎ *415/398–8900 or 800/243–1135,* FAX *415/989–8823. 400 rooms. Restaurant, lounge, health club. AE, D, DC, MC, V.*

$$$ **Inn at Union Square.** With its dark-timber double doors and its tiny but captivating lobby with trompe l'oeil bookshelves painted on the walls, this inn feels like someone's home. Comfortable, Georgian-style rooms promote indolence with sumptuous goose-down pillows; brass lion's-head door knockers are a unique touch. Complimentary Continental breakfast, afternoon tea, and evening wine and hors d'oeuvres

Downtown San Francisco Lodging

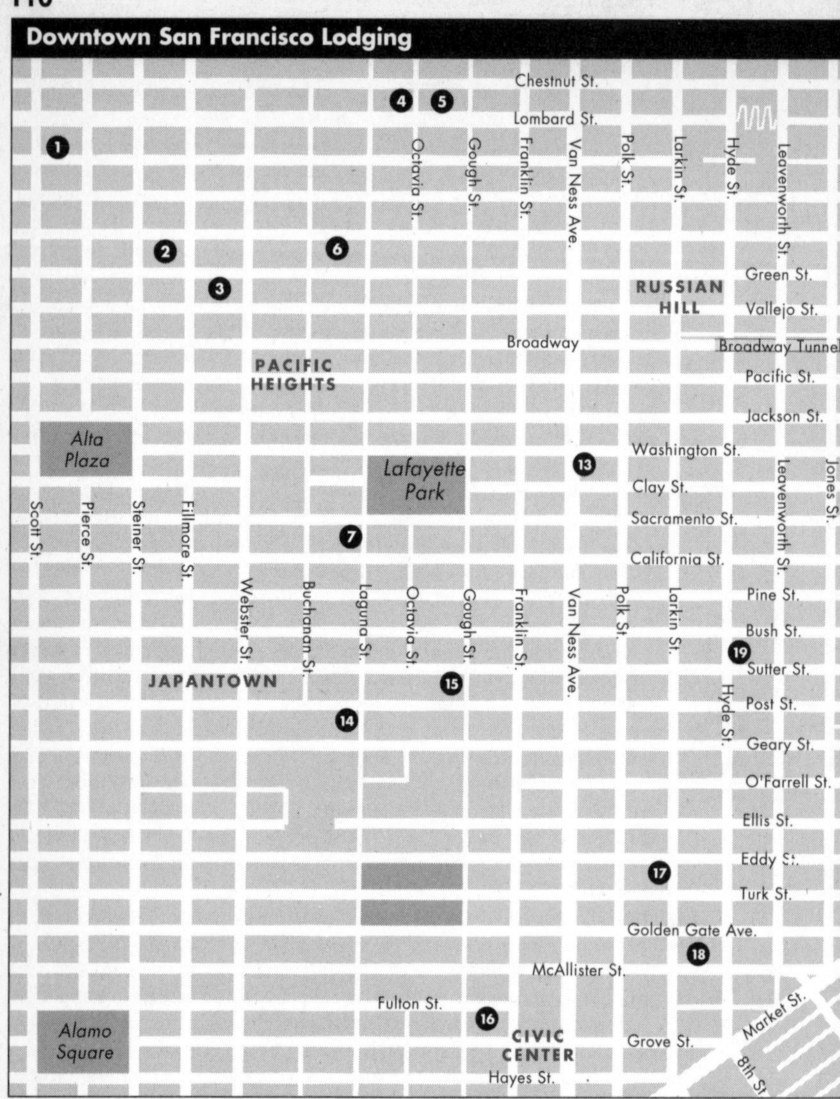

Abigail Hotel, **18**
Adelaide Inn, **20**
Bed and Breakfast Inn, **6**
Campton Place Hotel, **39**
The Cartwright, **28**
Chancellor Hotel, **36**
Clarion Hotel, **53**
Crown Sterling Suites–Burlingame, **49**
Days Inn, **55**
Edward II Inn, **1**
Fairmont Hotel and Tower, **25**
Four Seasons Clift, **32**
Galleria Park, **42**
Grant Plaza, **45**
Harbor Court, **48**
Holiday Inn–Union Square, **38**
Holiday Lodge and Garden Hotel, **13**
Hotel Diva, **30**
Hotel Majestic, **15**
Hotel Sofitel–San Francisco Bay, **50**
Huntington Hotel, **23**
Hyatt at Fisherman's Wharf, **9**
Hyatt Regency, **47**
Inn at the Opera, **16**
Inn at Union Square, **35**
King George, **33**
La Quinta Motor Inn, **56**
Mandarin Oriental, **46**
Mansion's Hotel, **7**
Marina Inn, **4**
Mark Hopkins Inter–Continental, **24**

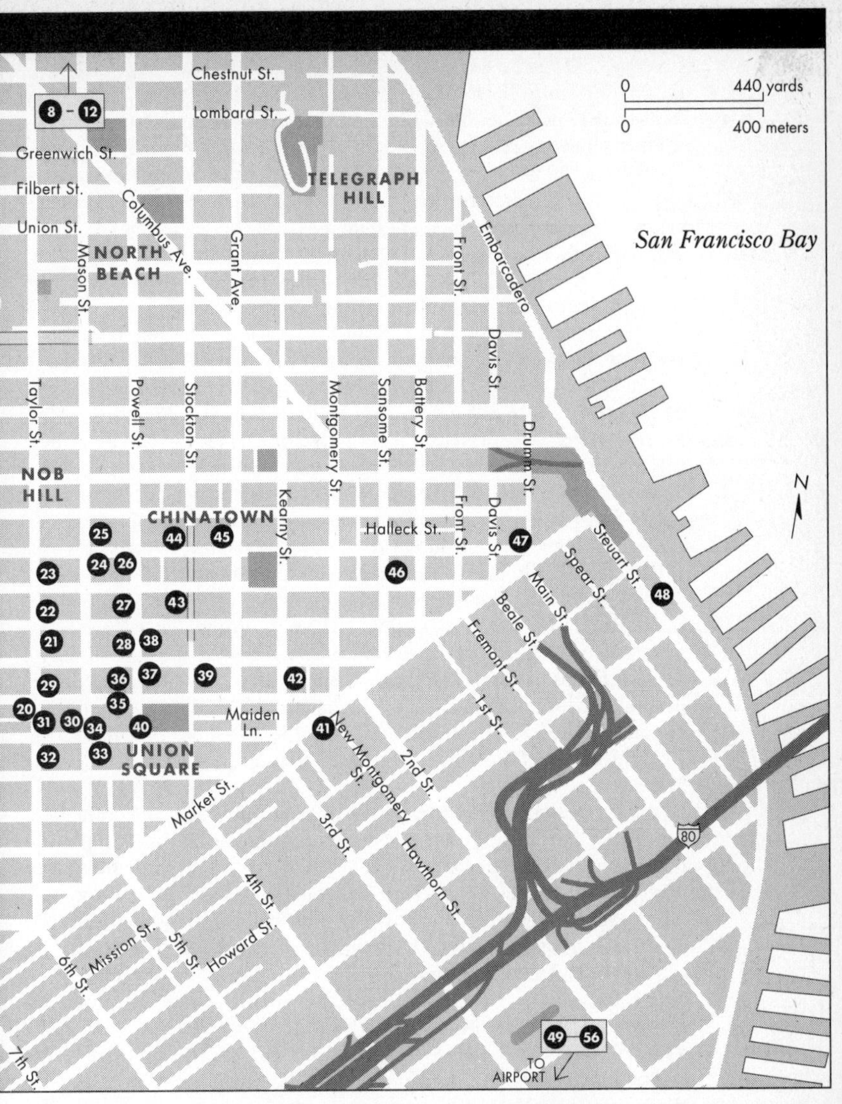

Marriot at Fisherman's Wharf, **8**
Miyako Hotel, **14**
Nob Hill Lambourne, **43**
Petite Auberge, **21**
Phoenix Inn, **17**
Prescott Hotel, **29**
Radisson Hotel, **54**
The Raphael, **34**
Ritz–Carlton, San Francisco, **44**
San Francisco Airport Hilton, **51**
San Remo Hotel, **12**
Sheraton Palace, **41**
Sherman House, **3**
Sir Francis Drake, **37**
Stouffer Renaissance Stanford Court Hotel, **26**
Town House Motel, **5**
Travelodge Hotel at Fisherman's Wharf, **11**
Tuscan Inn, **10**
Union Street Inn, **2**
Vintage Court, **27**
Warwick Regis Hotel, **31**
Westin Hotel, **52**
Westin St. Francis, **40**
White Swan Inn, **22**
York Hotel, **19**

are served in front of a fireplace in a sitting area on each floor. ☐ *440 Post St., 94102,* ☎ *415/397–3510 or 800/288–4346,* FAX *415/989–0529. 30 rooms. No smoking. AE, DC, MC, V.*

$$$ **Petite Auberge.** "The Teddy Bears' Picnic" might be an alternate name for this whimsical re-creation of a French country inn a couple of blocks uphill from Union Square. The lobby, festooned with teddies of all shapes, sizes, and costumes, sets the tone; the country kitchen and side garden create a pastoral atmosphere despite the downtown location. Rooms are small, but each has a teddy bear, bright flowered wallpaper, an old-fashioned writing desk, and a much-needed armoire—there's little or no closet space. The atmosphere borders on precious but doesn't stray past the mark. Next door, at 845 Bush Street, is a sister hotel, the 26-room **White Swan Inn,** similar in style but with an English-country flavor and larger rooms. ☐ *863 Bush St., 94108,* ☎ *415/928–6000,* FAX *415/775–5717. 26 rooms. Breakfast rooms. AE, DC, MC, V.*

$$$ **Prescott Hotel.** A gourmet's delight might be the best way to describe this plush hotel, thanks to its partnership with Wolfgang Puck's Postrio (*see* Chapter 5, Dining), which consistently hovers near the top of San Francisco's best-restaurant lists. Cuisine-conscious guests can order room service from Postrio and avoid trying to make a reservation. Thankfully, guests also have access to the health club next door at the Press Club. The Prescott's rooms, which vary only in size and shape, are traditional in style, with dark, rich color schemes. Each bed is backed by a partially mirrored wall and has a boldly patterned spread; the bathrooms have marble-top sinks and gold fixtures. The Prescott's personalized service includes complimentary limousine service to the Financial District. ☐ *545 Post St.,* ☎ *415/563–0303 or 800/283–7322,* FAX *415/563–6831. 166 rooms. Restaurant, lounge. AE, D, DC, MC, V.*

$$$ **Sir Francis Drake.** Although Beefeater-costumed doormen and dramatic red theater curtains still adorn the front of the Drake, the inside has undergone a profound change. The lobby is still opulent, with wrought-iron lion balustrades, chandeliers, and Italian marble, but guest rooms now have the flavor of a B&B, with California colonial-style furnishings and floral-print fabrics. The decor seems designed to appeal to pleasure travelers, but business travelers will appreciate the modem hookups and voice mail. Party-giver extraordinaire Harry Denton runs the renowned Starlite Roof supper club here. ☐ *450 Powell St., 94102,* ☎ *415/392–7755 or 800/268–7245,* FAX *415/391–8719. 417 rooms. 2 restaurants, meeting room. AE, D, DC, MC, V.*

$$$ **Warwick Regis Hotel.** The cherubs outside and the frescoes and columns inside lend a postmodern, neoclassical look to the facade and lobby of the Warwick, one of the finest examples of the new generation of small hotels. The large, elegant rooms, some with fireplaces, are decorated in the Louis XVI style, with French and Asian antiques and canopy beds; baths are made of Italian black marble. Soundproof windows have recently been installed in all the rooms. Continental breakfast, overnight shoe shine, and newspaper are complimentary. ☐ *490 Geary St., 94102,* ☎ *415/928–7900 or 800/827–3447,* FAX *415/441–8788. 74 rooms. Restaurant, lounge. AE, DC, MC, V.*

$$ **The Cartwright.** A block northwest of Union Square and just off the cable-car line, this conveniently located hotel's motto is "It's like being at home." This is only true, however, if your home is filled with authentic European antiques, fluffy terry-cloth robes, and floral-print bedspreads and curtains, with English tea from 4 to 6 every day in the library. Guests may choose rooms with old-fashioned carved-wood or brass beds. Complimentary Continental breakfast is served in the lobby. ☐

524 Sutter St., 94102, ☎ and fax 415/421–2865 or 800/227–3844. 114 rooms. AE, D, DC, MC, V.

$$ **Chancellor Hotel.** The three almost-floor-to-ceiling windows of the modest Chancellor Hotel lobby overlook cable cars on Powell Street en route to nearby Union Square or Fisherman's Wharf. This family-owned and -oriented hotel, although not as grand as some of its neighbors, more than lives up to its promise of comfort without extravagance—it's one of the best buys on Union Square. The moderate-sized rooms have high ceilings and Edwardian decor, with peach, green, and rose color schemes; the ceiling fans and deep bathtubs are a treat. Connecting rooms are available for couples with children. ⊞ *433 Powell St., 94102,* ☎ *415/362–2004 or 800/428–4748,* FAX *415/362–1403. 140 rooms. Restaurant, lounge. AE, D, DC, MC, V.*

$$ **Hotel Diva.** A beige awning and beaten-and-burnished silver facade give this hotel a slick, high-tech look that sets it apart from others in San Francisco. Although the Diva's proximity to the landmark Curran attracts theater folk and others of an artistic bent, it's also popular with tourists and business travelers. The black-and-silver color scheme with touches of gray extends to the nightclub-esque lobby and to the rooms, which vary in size and are comfortable but not fussy. Black-lacquered armoires, writing desks, and headboards complete the mood. ⊞ *440 Geary St., 94102,* ☎ *415/885–0200 or 800/553–1900,* FAX *415/346–6613. 125 rooms. Restaurant, lounge, exercise room, business services, meeting room. AE, D, DC, MC, V.*

$$ **King George.** The staff at the King George more than upholds this hotel's well-deserved 80-year reputation for hospitality; the desk clerks are especially adept at catering to their guests' every whim: They'll book anything from a Fisherman's Wharf tour to a dinner reservation. Behind the George's white-and-green Victorian facade, the rooms are compact but nicely furnished in classic English style, with walnut furniture and a pastel-and-earth tone color scheme. British and Japanese tourists and suburban couples seeking a weekend getaway frequent this adult-oriented hotel. ⊞ *334 Mason St., 94102,* ☎ *415/781–5050 or 800/288–6005,* FAX *415/391–6976. 144 rooms. AE, DC, MC, V.*

$$ **The Raphael.** With its own marquee proclaiming it San Francisco's "little elegant hotel," the Raphael has few pretensions to grandeur, preferring to focus its efforts on service: tour bookings, limousine service, same-day laundry, and twice-daily turndown service. The moderate-size rooms are austere, with simple, dark furnishings; each has a unique hand-painted door. The hotel restaurant, Mama's, is noted for its breakfasts and boasts room service seven days a weeks for all three meals. ⊞ *386 Geary St., 94102,* ☎ *415/986–2000 or 800/821–5343,* FAX *415/397–2447. 152 rooms. Restaurant, lounge. AE, DC, MC, V, D.*

$$ **Vintage Court.** This bit of the Napa Valley just off Union Square has lavish rooms decorated in a Wine Country theme, and each afternoon complimentary wine is served in front of a crackling fire in the lobby. Complimentary French Continental breakfast is served each morning, and for fine food, guests need go no farther than the lobby to get to Masa's (*see* Chapter 5, Dining), one of the city's most celebrated French restaurants. Guests have access to an affiliated health club one block away. ⊞ *650 Bush St., 94108,* ☎ *415/392–4666 or 800/654–1100,* FAX *415/433–4065. 106 rooms. Restaurant, lounge. AE, D, DC, MC, V.*

$$ **York Hotel.** This family-owned hotel several blocks west of Union Square is perhaps the most gay-friendly of San Francisco's more elegant hotels; it's also popular with European tourists and businesspeople who appreciate such touches as the complimentary limousine service. The gray-stone facade and ornate, high-ceiling lobby give the hotel a touch of elegance. The moderate-size rooms are a tasteful mix of Mediterranean styles, with a terra-cotta, burgundy, and forest-green color scheme. The Plush Room cabaret, where well-known entertainers perform, is the York's drawing card. ☒ *940 Sutter St., 94109,* ☎ *415/885–6800 or 800/808–9675,* FAX *415/885–2115. 96 rooms. Lounge, exercise room, nightclub. AE, D, DC, MC, V.*

$ **Adelaide Inn.** The bedspreads at this quiet retreat may not match the drapes or carpets, and the floors may creak, but the rooms are sunny, clean, and cheap: $42–$48 for a double. Tucked away in an alley, this funky European-style pension hosts many guests from Germany, France, and Italy. ☒ *5 Isadora Duncan Ct. (off Taylor between Geary and Post Sts.), 94102,* ☎ *415/441–2474 or 415/441-2261,* FAX *415/441–0161. 18 rooms share baths. Breakfast room, refrigerators. AE, MC, V.*

$ ★ **Grant Plaza.** Serious Asian-cuisine aficionados take note—this bargain hotel in the shadow of the Chinatown gate has small but clean, attractively furnished rooms from $39. The Grant stands midway between the shopping options of Union Square and the Italian cafés and restaurants of North Beach. ☒ *465 Grant Ave., 94108,* ☎ *415/434–3883 or 800/472–6899,* FAX *415/434–3886. 72 rooms. AE, MC, V.*

Financial District

High-rise growth in San Francisco's Financial District has turned it into a mini-Manhattan and a spectacular sight by night.

$$$$ **Hyatt Regency.** The gray concrete, bunkerlike exterior of the Hyatt Regency at the foot of Market Street is an unlikely introduction to the spectacular 17-story atrium lobby inside. A favorite convention site, this hotel is a good choice for business or pleasure. Besides its plethora of meeting spaces, Embarcadero Center (with its 125 shops) is right next door, and the Equinox, San Francisco's only revolving rooftop restaurant, sits atop the hotel like a crown jewel. Rooms, some with bay-view balconies, are decorated in two styles. Both have cherry-wood furniture, but one strikes a decidedly more masculine tone with a black-and-brown color scheme; the other has soft rose-and-plum combinations. ☒ *5 Embarcadero Center, 94111,* ☎ *415/788–1234 or 800/233–1234,* FAX *415/398–2567. 803 rooms. 2 restaurants, lounge. AE, D, DC, MC, V.*

$$$$ **Mandarin Oriental.** The Mandarin comprises the top 11 floors (38–48) of San Francisco's third-tallest building, the First Interstate Center, so no matter what room you're in, you'll get some of the most panoramic vistas of the city and beyond. The front and back towers of this structure are connected by a sky bridge. Rooms in the front tower fill up quickly because of their dramatic, sweeping view from the ocean all the way to the Golden Gate Bridge and beyond to Angel Island; the Mandarin Rooms in each tower are favorites because their bathtubs are flanked by windows. The California-style rooms have an Asian color scheme: light, creamy yellow with black accents and wood tones. ☒ *222 Sansome St., 94104,* ☎ *415/885–0999 or 800/622–0404,* FAX *415/433–0289. 154 rooms, 4 suites. Restaurant, lounge. AE, D, DC, MC, V.*

$$$$ **Sheraton Palace.** One of the city's grand old hotels—with a guest list that has included Enrico Caruso, Woodrow Wilson, and Al Jolson—the Palace has a pool with a skylight, a health club, and a business center. The Garden Court restaurant, with its leaded-glass, domed ceiling, is famous for its lavish buffet breakfasts. With their 14-foot ceilings, the rooms are splendid on a smaller scale. Modern amenities are carefully integrated into the classic decor, from the TV inside the mahogany armoire to the telephone in the marble bathroom. Service is the only element that is not quite up to par. ☒ *2 New Montgomery*

St., 94105, ☎ 415/392–8600 or 800/325–3535, FAX 415/543–0671. 550 rooms. 3 restaurants, 2 lounges, room service, health club. AE, D, DC, MC, V.

$$$ ★ **Harbor Court Hotel.** Within shouting distance of the Bay Bridge and the hot South of Market area with its plentiful nightclubs and restaurants, this boutique-style hotel, formerly a YMCA, is noted for the exemplary service of its warm, friendly staff. The small rooms, some with bay views, have a sage-green color scheme and partial canopy beds resting on wood casements. The adult-oriented Harbor Court attracts corporate types (especially on weekdays) as well as the average traveler. Guests have free access to YMCA facilities (including a 150-foot heated indoor pool) on one side of the hotel, and Harry Denton's Bar and Grill on the other side. There's a complimentary limousine service to the Financial District. *165 Steuart St., ☎ 415/882–1300 or 800/346–0555, FAX 415/882–1313. 131 rooms. Business services. AE, D, DC, MC, V.*

Nob Hill

Synonymous with San Francisco's high society, Nob Hill contains some of the city's best-known luxury hotels. All offer spectacular city and bay views and noted gourmet restaurants. Cable-car lines that cross Nob Hill make transportation a cinch.

$$$$ **Fairmont Hotel and Tower.** Perched atop Nob Hill and queen of all she surveys, the Fairmont, which served as the model for the St. Gregory in the TV series *Hotel,* has the most awe-inspiring lobby in the city, with a soaring, vaulted ceiling, towering, hand-painted, faux-marble columns, gilt mirrors, red-velvet upholstered chairs, and a grand, wraparound staircase. The tower rooms, which have spectacular city and bay views, reflect a more modern style than their smaller Victorian counterparts in the older building. The Tonga Room, site of San Francisco's busiest happy hour, is a must-see. *950 Mason St., 94108, ☎ 415/772–5000 or 800/527–4727, FAX 415/772–5013. 596 rooms. 5 restaurants, room service, 5 lounges, spa, health club. AE, D, DC, MC, V.*

$$$$ ★ **Huntington Hotel.** Across from Grace Cathedral and the small but captivating Huntington Park, the redbrick, ivy-covered Huntington provides a quiet alternative to the larger, more famous hotels down the street. Regulars here return year after year for the attentive personal service that is the hallmark of this hotel; the concierge calls each guest to offer complimentary sherry or tea. The management style is impeccably British in preserving the privacy of its celebrated guests. Rooms and suites, all individually appointed, reflect the Huntington's traditional style, albeit with a '90s bent. The opulent materials, such as soft leathers, raw silks and velvets, are mixed and matched in a color scheme of cocoa, gold, and burgundy. Guests have access to the health club at the Fairmont, across the street. *1075 California St., 94108, ☎ 415/474–5400 or 800/227–4683; in CA, 800/652–1539; FAX 415/474–6227. 140 rooms. Restaurant, lounge. AE, D, DC, MC, V.*

$$$$ **Mark Hopkins Inter-Continental.** The circular drive to this Nob Hill landmark across from the Fairmont leads to a lobby with floor-to-ceiling mirrors and marble floors. The rooms, with dramatic neoclassical furnishings of gray, silver, and khaki and bold leaf-print bedspreads, lead into bathrooms lined with Italian marble. Even-number rooms on high floors have views of the Golden Gate Bridge. No visit would be complete without a gander at the panoramic views from the Top of the Mark, *the* rooftop lounge in San Francisco since 1939 (Mon.–Sat. 4 PM until closing, Sun. brunch 10 AM–2 PM). *999 California St., 94108, ☎*

415/392–3434 or 800/327–0200, FAX 415/421–3302. 392 rooms. Restaurant, 2 lounges, exercise room. AE, D, DC, MC, V.

$$$$ ★ **Ritz-Carlton, San Francisco.** Rated one of the top three hotels in the world by *Condé Nast Traveler,* the Ritz-Carlton is a stunning tribute to beauty, grandeur, and warm, attentive service. Beyond the neoclassical facade, crystal chandeliers and museum-quality 18th-century oil paintings adorn an opulent lobby. Rooms are elegant and spacious, and every bath is appointed with double sinks, hair dryers, and vanity tables. A maid service cleans twice a day, and guests staying on the butler level enjoy the added luxury of their own butler. The hotel's Dining Room, presided over by renowned chef Gary Danko, is a worthy destination in its own right. *600 Stockton St., at California St., 94108, ☎ 415/296–7465 or 800/241–3333, FAX 415/291–0288. 336 rooms. 2 restaurants, 3 lounges, indoor pool, health club, shops. AE, D, DC, MC, V.*

$$$$ **Stouffer Renaissance Stanford Court Hotel.** Despite its relatively large size, the Stanford Court has a distinctly residential feeling. It's hidden from the street by a low archway that leads to an inner parking area covered by a stained-glass dome. The lobby is dominated by a similar stained-glass dome and a dramatic mural depicting scenes of early San Francisco. The moderate-size rooms feature four different styles: Montana (Southwestern), Florentine (Italian), Bentley (English), and Coulter (floral with Asian accents). The hotel's restaurant, Fournou's Ovens—famed for its Provençal decor, 54-square-foot roasting oven, and California cuisine—is usually packed. Guests have free access to the Nob Hill health club across the street. Chauffeured car service is available on weekdays. *905 California St., 94108, ☎ 415/989–3500 or 800/227–4736; in CA, 800/622–0957; FAX 415/391–0513. 402 rooms. Restaurant, lounge. AE, DC, MC, V.*

$$$ **Nob Hill Lambourne.** This urban retreat designed with the traveling executive in mind takes pride in taking care of business while offering stress-reducing pleasures. Personal computers, fax machines, personalized voice mail, laser printers, and a fully equipped boardroom help guests maintain their edge, and the on-site spa, with massages, body scrubs, herbal wraps, manicures, and pedicures, helps them take it off. Rooms have queen-size beds with divine double-padded, hand-sewn mattresses and contemporary furnishings in Mediterranean colors. A deluxe Continental breakfast is complimentary. *725 Pine St., at Stockton, 94108, ☎ 415/433–2287 or 800/274–8466, FAX 415/433–0975. 20 rooms. Kitchenettes. AE, D, DC, MC, V.*

Fisherman's Wharf/North Beach

Fisherman's Wharf, San Francisco's top tourist attraction, is also the most popular area for lodging. All accommodations are within a couple of blocks of restaurants, shops, and cable-car lines. Because of city ordinances, none of the hotels exceeds four stories; thus, this is not the area for fantastic views of the city or bay. Reservations are always necessary, sometimes weeks in advance during peak summer months, when hotel rates rise by as much as 30%. Some street-side rooms can be noisy.

$$$$ **Hyatt at Fisherman's Wharf.** Location is the key to this hotel's popularity with business travelers and families: It's within walking distance of Ghirardelli Square, the Cannery, Pier 39, Aquatic Park, and docks for ferries and bay cruises. It's also across the street from the cable-car turnaround and bus stop. The moderate-size guest rooms, a medley of greens and burgundies with dark woods and brass fixtures, have double-pane windows to keep out the often considerable street noise. Each floor has a laundry room. In the North Point Lounge, part of the

hotel's conference center, a domed Tiffany skylight crowns a small, rather expensive café with a fireplace and fountain. The Marble Works Restaurant, which still has the original facade of the 1906 Musto Marble Works, is next door and has a children's menu. *555 N. Point St., 94133, 415/563–1234 or 800/233–1234, FAX 415/563–2218. 313 rooms. Restaurant, sports bar, pool, outdoor hot tub, health club. AE, D, DC, MC, V.*

$$$ **Marriott at Fisherman's Wharf.** Behind an unremarkable sand-color facade, the Marriott strikes a grand note in its lavish, low-ceiling lobby, with marble floors and English club-style furniture. With the Transamerica Pyramid downtown to its left and the Cannery nearby on its right, the hotel is well situated for business and pleasure. Rooms, all with turquoise, blue, and white color schemes, have dark natural wood, Asian art touches, and either a king-size bed or two double beds. *1250 Columbus Ave., 94133, 415/775–7555 or 800/228–9290, FAX 415/474–2099. 255 rooms. Restaurant, lounge, health club. AE, D, DC, MC, V.*

$$$ **Tuscan Inn.** The major attraction here is the friendly, attentive staff, which provides services such as a complimentary limousine to the Financial District. The condolike exterior of the inn, made of reddish brick with white concrete, gives little indication of the charm of the relatively small, Italian-influenced guest rooms, with their white-pine furniture and floral bedspreads and curtains. Two floors are smoke-free. Room service is provided by Cafe Pescatore, the Italian seafood restaurant off the lobby. Morning coffee, tea, and biscotti are complimentary, and wine is served in the early evening. *425 N. Point St., 94133, 415/561–1100 or 800/648–4626, FAX 415/561–1199. 220 rooms. Restaurant, meeting rooms. AE, D, DC, MC, V.*

$$ **Travelodge Hotel at Fisherman's Wharf.** Taking up an entire city block, the Travelodge is the only bayfront hotel at Fisherman's Wharf and is known for its reasonable rates. The higher-priced rooms on the third and fourth floors have balconies that provide unobstructed views of Alcatraz and overlook a landscaped courtyard and pool. The rooms at this family-oriented hotel with an 80% international clientele have either a king-size bed or two double beds and are simply and brightly furnished with blond, lacquered-wood furniture, lime-green leather chairs, and Southwestern curtains and bedspreads. The nearby '50s-style Johnny Rockets diner is popular for burgers and fries. *250 Beach St., 94133, 415/392–6700 or 800/578–7878, FAX 415/986–7853. 250 rooms. 3 restaurants, pool, free parking. AE, D, DC, MC, V.*

$ ★ **San Remo Hotel.** A guest recently described a sojourn at the San Remo as being "like staying at Grandma's house." This three-story, blue-and-white Italianate Victorian just a couple of blocks from Fisherman's Wharf has reasonably priced rooms and a down-home, slightly tatty elegance. The somewhat cramped rooms are crowded with furniture: vanities, rag rugs, pedestal sinks, ceiling fans, antique armoires, and brass, iron, or wooden beds. The rooms share six black-and-white tiled shower rooms, one bathtub chamber, and six scrupulously clean toilets with brass pull chains and oak tanks. Special rates are available for longer stays. *2237 Mason St., 94133, 415/776–8688 or 800/352–7366, FAX 415/776–2811. 62 rooms, 61 with shared baths. AE, DC, MC, V.*

Lombard Street/Cow Hollow

Lombard Street, a major traffic corridor leading to the Golden Gate Bridge, stretches through San Francisco's poshest neighborhoods: Pacific Heights, Cow Hollow, and the Marina District.

$$$$ ★ **Sherman House.** This magnificent landmark mansion on a low hill in residential Pacific Heights is San Francisco's most luxurious small hotel. Rooms are individually decorated with Biedermeier, English Jacobean, or French Second Empire antiques. Tapestry-like canopies over four-poster beds, wood-burning fireplaces with marble mantels, and black-granite bathrooms with whirlpool baths complete the picture. The six romantic suites attract honeymooners from around the world, and the elegant in-house dining room serves superb French-inspired cuisine. *2160 Green St., 94123, ☎ 415/563–3600 or 800/424–5777, FAX 415/563–1882. 14 rooms. Dining room. AE, DC, MC, V.*

$$$ **Bed and Breakfast Inn.** Hidden in an alleyway off Union Street between Buchanan and Laguna, this ivy-covered, dark-green-and-white Victorian with black trim claims the title of San Francisco's first B&B. Pierre Deux and Laura Ashley are the inspirations of the English-country-style rooms, which are full of antiques, plants, and floral paintings. The Mayfair, a private flat above the main house, comes complete with a living room, kitchenette, latticed balcony, and spiral staircase leading to a sleeping loft. The Garden Suite, a larger, more deluxe flat, is a recent addition. *4 Charlton Ct., 94123, ☎ 415/921–9784. 5 rooms with bath, 4 rooms share baths, 2 flats. Breakfast room. No credit cards.*

$$ **Edward II Inn.** Banners of the English king and the state of California fly from the rooftop of this picturesque B&B. A variety of English-country-style accommodations is available, including 14 small pension rooms with private bath, 10 with shared bath; six suites with one or two bedrooms, whirlpool baths, living rooms, kitchens, and wet bars; a carriage-house annex with apartment suites; and a three-bedroom, one-bath, cottage suite perfect for traveling families. Two junior suites in the main building are especially popular, as is the pub. *3155 Scott St., at Lombard St., 94123, ☎ 415/922–3000 or 800/473–2846, FAX 415/931–5784. 31 rooms, 19 with bath. AE, MC, V.*

$$ ★ **Union Street Inn.** A retired schoolteacher transformed this ivy-draped, Edwardian, 1902 home into a delightful B&B filled with antiques and fresh flowers. The small size of the inn, which is now owned by Jane Bertorelli and David J. Coyle, affords a cozy intimacy that has made it popular with honeymooners and other romantics. Of the six rooms, one standout is the Wildrose, which has a king-size brass bed, persimmon-and-mauve decor, and a garden view that can be seen from the whirlpool tub. The very private Carriage House, which also has its own whirlpool tub, is separated from the main house by an old-fashioned English garden complete with lemon trees, a flagstone path, and a white picket fence with a gate and a rose-covered trellis overhead. An elaborate complimentary Continental breakfast is served to guests in the parlor, in the garden, or in their rooms. Special rates are available for longer stays. Off-season prices are considerably lower. *2229 Union St., 94123, ☎ 415/346–0424, FAX 415/922–8046. 6 rooms with private bath. Breakfast room. AE, MC, V.*

$ **Holiday Lodge and Garden Hotel.** This three-story, split-level hotel with a redwood-and-stone facade has a California mood. The rooms either overlook or open onto landscaped grounds with palm trees and a small, heated swimming pool. The decor has a '50s feel, with white beamed ceilings, beige wood paneling, and floral bedspreads. The lodge is two blocks from the Hard Rock Cafe, three blocks from the cable car, and within walking distance of Pacific Heights and Union Street shopping and restaurants. The Holiday's low-key atmosphere endears it to older couples, who enjoy its laid-back, West Coast style. *1901 Van Ness Ave., 94109, ☎ 415/776–4469 or 800/367–8504, FAX 415/474–7046. 76 rooms. Kitchenettes, free parking. AE, MC, V.*

$ **Marina Inn.** This inn five blocks from the marina offers B&B-style accommodations at motel prices. English-country-style rooms are sparsely appointed with a queen-size two-poster bed, private bath, small pinewood writing desks, nightstands, and armoires; the wallpaper and bedspreads are aggressively floral. Some of the rooms facing Octavia and Lombard streets have bay windows. A complimentary Continental breakfast is served in the central sitting room, and a barbershop and beauty salon are on the premises. *3110 Octavia St., at Lombard St., 94123, ☎ 415/928–1000 or 800/274–1420, FAX 415/928–5909. 40 rooms. Lounge. AE, MC, V.*

$ **Town House Motel.** What this family-oriented motel lacks in luxury and ambience it makes up for in value: The rooms are simply furnished and well kept. Like its grander neighbor, the Marina Inn, this motel is convenient to many sights of interest, although its blaring blue facade may put off some visitors. The modest, medium-size rooms have a pastel, Southwestern color scheme, lacquered-wood furnishings, and either a king-size bed or two doubles. Continental breakfast is complimentary. *1650 Lombard St., 94123, ☎ 415/885–5163 or 800/255–1516, FAX 415/771–9889. 24 rooms. Free parking. AE, D, DC, MC, V.*

Civic Center/Van Ness

The governmental heart of San Francisco, flanked by a boulevard of cultural institutions, is enjoying a renaissance that has engendered fine restaurants, fashionable nightspots, and well-situated small hotels.

$$$ ★ **Hotel Majestic.** One of San Francisco's original grand hotels, this five-story yellow-and-white Edwardian with gingerbread and scrollwork looks like a wedding cake. The lobby, with its black marble stairs, antique chandeliers, plush Victorian chairs, white marble fireplace, and red velvet sofa, manages to appear simultaneously awesome and comfortable. Most rooms contain a fireplace and either a large, hand-painted, four-poster, canopied bed or two-poster bonnet twin beds, and most have a mix of French Empire and English antiques and custom furniture. Some have original claw-foot bathtubs. The hotel's Cafe Majestic, which evokes turn-of-the-century San Francisco, has been called "San Francisco's most romantic restaurant" by *San Francisco Focus Magazine*; the menu blends California and French cuisines. *1500 Sutter St., 94109, ☎ 415/441–1100 or 800/869–8966, FAX 415/673–7331. 57 rooms. Restaurant, lounge. AE, DC, MC, V.*

$$$ ★ **Inn at the Opera.** This seven-story hotel a block or so from City Hall, Davies Hall, the War Memorial Opera Building, the War Memorial Veterans Building, Civic Auditorium, and Stars Restaurant hosts the likes of Pavarotti and Baryshnikov, as well as lesser lights of the music, dance, and opera worlds. Behind the yellow faux-marble front and red carpet are rooms of various sizes, decorated with creamy pastels and dark wood furnishings. Even the smallest singles have queen-size beds. The bureau drawers are lined with sheet music, and every room is outfitted with terry-cloth robes, microwave ovens, minibars, fresh flowers, and a basket of apples. Those in the know say the back rooms are the quietest. A major attraction here is the sumptuous, dimly lit Act

IV restaurant; stars congregate in its mahogany-and-green-velvet interior before and after performances. ☎ *333 Fulton St., 94102,* ☎ *415/863–8400 or 800/325–2708; in CA, 800/423–9610;* FAX *415/861–0821. 48 rooms. Restaurant, lounge. AE, DC, MC, V.*

$$$ Miyako Hotel. Next to the Japantown complex and near Fillmore Street, this pagoda-style hotel is frequented by Asian travelers and others with a taste for the East. Some guest rooms are in the tower building; others are in the garden wing, which has traditional seasonal gardens. Japanese-style rooms have futon beds with tatami mats; Western rooms have traditional beds with mattresses. Both types of rooms feature Japanese touches such as shojis; most have their own soaking rooms with a bucket and stool and a Japanese tub (1 foot deeper than Western tubs). A chocolate set on a haiku by the bedside awaits each guest. The hotel's Elka restaurant is nationally known for its French- and Japanese-influenced seafood dishes. *1625 Post St., at Laguna St., 94115,* ☎ *415/922–3200 or 800/533–4567,* FAX *415/921–0417. 218 rooms. Restaurant, lounge. AE, D, DC, MC, V.*

$$ Mansions Hotel. This twin-turreted Queen Anne was built in 1887 and today houses one of the most unusual hotels in the city. Rooms, which contain an odd collection of furnishings, vary in theme from the tiny Tom Thumb Room to the opulent Josephine Suite, the favorite of such celebrities as Barbra Streisand. Owner Bob Pritikin's pig paintings and other "porkabilia" are scattered throughout the hotel. Other nice touches are the sculpture and flower gardens, and the nightly concerts. Full breakfast is included. *2220 Sacramento St., 94115,* ☎ *415/929–9444,* FAX *415/567–9391. 21 rooms. Dining room, cabaret. AE, DC, MC, V.*

$$ Phoenix Inn. Dubbed the "hippest hotel" in San Francisco by *People* magazine, this turquoise-and-coral hideaway on the fringes of the Tenderloin district is a little bit south-of-the-equator and a little bit *Gilligan's Island*—probably not the place for a traveling executive, even though it bills itself as an urban retreat in a resortlike environment. Its bungalow-style rooms, decorated with casual, handmade, bamboo furniture and original art by San Francisco artists, have white beamed ceilings, white wooden walls, and vivid tropical-print bedspreads. All rooms face a pool (with a mural by Francis Forlenza on its bottom) adjacent to a courtyard and sculpture garden. An in-house cable channel plays films made in San Francisco and films about bands on the road. Miss Pearl's Jam House restaurant and bar is a good place to hear reggae and indulge in Jamaican delights. *601 Eddy St., 94109,* ☎ *415/776–1380, 415/861–1560, or 800/248–9466,* FAX *415/885–3109. 44 rooms. Restaurant, bar, lounge, pool, free parking. AE, D, DC, MC, V.*

$ Abigail Hotel. This hotel, a former B&B, retains its distinctive atmosphere with an eclectic mix of faux-stone walls, a faux-marble front desk, and an old-fashioned telephone booth in the lobby. Hissing steam radiators, sleigh beds, and antiques complete the mood. Room 211—the hotel's only suite—is the most elegant and spacious. The new Millennium Restaurant, right off the lobby, has proven to be a hit with its gourmet organic cuisine. *246 McAllister St., 94102,* ☎ *415/861–9728 or 800/243–6510,* FAX *415/861–5848. 60 rooms. Restaurant. AE, D, DC, MC, V.*

The Airport

A construction boom near San Francisco International Airport during the mid-'80s added several luxury-class hotels. Rates are about 20% less those than at in-town counterparts. Airport shuttle buses are provided by all of the following hotels. Because they cater primarily to midweek business travelers, the airport hotels often cut weekend prices drastically; be sure to inquire.

$$$ ★ **Crown Sterling Suites–Burlingame.** This California Mission–style hostelry is arguably the most lavish in the airport area. On the bay with views of planes taking off and landing, this all-suite hotel has a spectacular setting and impressive service. A black-marble, stone-floor lobby with burnt-orange roof tiles leads into a nine-story atrium and tropical garden replete with ducks, parrots, fish, and a waterfall. Suites are pink and turquoise and open onto the atrium; they have moderate-size bedrooms with either a king-size or two double beds. The suites' living rooms include a work area with a dual-line telephone and voice mail, a sleeper sofa, a wet bar, a television with cable, a microwave, and a refrigerator. Among the other amenities are a cooked-to-order breakfast and an executive business center with a meeting and catering staff to help you arrange any event, transportation to a nearby health club, and a bar with live entertainment. ☐ *150 Anza Blvd., Burlingame 94010,* ☎ *415/342–4600 or 800/433–4600,* FAX *415/343–8137. 339 suites. Restaurant, lounge, indoor pool, sauna, steam room. AE, DC, MC, V.*

$$$ **Hotel Sofitel–San Francisco Bay.** Parisian-boulevard lampposts, a Métro sign, and a kiosk covered with posters bring an unexpected bit of Paris to this bayside hotel. The French-theme public spaces—the Gigi Brasserie, Baccarat restaurant, and La Terrasse bar—have a light, open, airy feeling that extends to the room decor of light woods and pastel floral prints. In addition to the minibar, large writing desk, king or two double beds, and turndown service, rooms are equipped with pleasant extras such as a makeup mirror, complimentary Nina Ricci toiletries, a second telephone, and a rose in the bathroom. The Sofitel is tucked away in the Redwood Shores industrial park south of the airport and backs up to a lagoon. The Gigi and the Baccarat are famous locally for their joint Sunday brunches. ☐ *223 Twin Dolphin Dr., Redwood City 94065,* ☎ *415/598–9000 or 800/763–4835,* FAX *415/598–0459. 319 rooms, 28 suites. 2 restaurants, lounge, pool, spa, health club, laundry service. AE, DC, MC, V.*

$$$ **San Francisco Airport Hilton.** The only airport hotel on airport property—right off Highway 101—the Hilton provides 24-hour shuttle service to the terminal, which is walking distance away. Rooms, which have a pastel color scheme, are simply furnished with a king, a queen, or two double beds and a minibar. The courtyard and poolside areas provide respite for the weary traveler, and the pool is Olympic size. The hotel also boasts 21,000 square feet in meeting space, with a huge ballroom that can host a banquet for 720. ☐ *San Francisco International Airport, Box 8355, 94128,* ☎ *415/589–0770 or 800/445–8667,* FAX *415/589–4696. 527 rooms. 2 restaurants, lounge, pool, outdoor hot tub, exercise room. AE, DC, MC, V.*

$$$ **Westin Hotel.** This bayfront hotel, with an elegant, palm-tree-lined entrance and sparkling fountain, is geared toward business travelers and conventioneers. The 27 meeting rooms run the gamut from a grand ballroom for 700 to a lovely pool-atrium area where luncheons are sometimes held; on-site meeting managers, a catering staff, and an in-house audiovisual company are available for hire. The medium-size guest rooms have blond-wood furnishings with Asian touches and muted pink, blue, peach, and beige colors. Be sure to request a room with a bay view so you can watch the airplanes take off and land. Next door is the black-and-white tiled Bayshore Diner, with weekly burger specials, and around the corner is the rich, darkly paneled Benchmark bar and grill, known for its steaks. ☐ *1 Old Bayshore Hwy., Millbrae 94030,* ☎ *415/692–*

3500 or 800/228–3000, FAX *415/872–8111. 388 rooms. 2 restaurants, 2 lounges, indoor pool, health club. AE, DC, MC, V.*

$$ **Clarion Hotel.** This busy hotel west of the Westin, toward the freeway, is a favorite of airline personnel. Respite from the bustle in the gigantic, glass-fronted, deco-style lobby can be found in an adjoining garden area, where wrought-iron benches, a heated pool, and a whirlpool tub are set among fragrant pine trees. Although the styles and furnishings of the rooms vary—some have dark woods and brass, others are more floral—all are spacious and comfortable, with either a king-size or two double beds. *401 E. Millbrae Ave., Millbrae 94030,* ☎ *415/692–6363 or 800/223–7111,* FAX *415/697–8735. 435 rooms. 2 restaurants, lounge, spa, health club. AE, DC, MC, V.*

$$ **Radisson Hotel.** Although the '60s-style tinted-glass-and-aluminum facade and the scuffed marble floors in the lobby have seen better days, an amusing "waterfall" adds a cheery note: The water flows out of small spigots. The rather charmless guest rooms on the second and eighth floors are drably decorated in subdued shades of gray and brown; furnishings include a king, queen, or two double beds, plus a small table with two chairs. The executive-level rooms on the ninth and 10th floors have been upgraded with black, lacquered furnishings and lighter colors and accents. Freeway noise can be heard in rooms on both sides of the hotel. *1177 Airport Blvd., Burlingame 94010,* ☎ *415/342–9200 or 800/333–3333,* FAX *415/342–1655. 301 rooms. Restaurant, lounge, indoor and outdoor pools, exercise room, airport shuttle, free parking. AE, DC, MC, V.*

$ **Days Inn.** This five-story, redbrick hotel, which attracts families and business travelers, underwent an extensive renovation in late 1993; unfortunately, so did its prices. The regular rate for a room with either a queen or two double beds is $72; a king-size bed commands $82 a night. The guest rooms are modest but extremely clean, with double beds, light wood furnishings, white walls, floral bedspreads, and small circular tables with two chairs. The fancier king and queen rooms are decorated in green, pink, and burgundy with ersatz mahogany furnishings, dark green carpeting, and midsize writing desks. The sparse amenities include a vending area on each floor. *777 Airport Blvd., Burlingame 94010,* ☎ *415/342–7772 or 800/325–2525,* FAX *415/342–2635. 200 rooms. Restaurant, pool. AE, DC, MC, V.*

$ **La Quinta Motor Inn.** Literally a stone's throw from Highway 101, this Mission-style inn nonetheless provides quiet, well-insulated accommodations for the tired visitor. Weathered wood balconies and a red tile roof betray the decor inside: Guest rooms have stucco walls, Southwestern-print bedspreads and curtains, and sturdy blond-wood furniture. Each room is designated smoking or nonsmoking and comes with a king-size or two double beds; king-size rooms also have recliners. A complimentary Continental breakfast with a juice bar is served in the recently remodeled lobby until 10 AM daily; there's also a restaurant next door. *20 Airport Blvd., South San Francisco 94080,* ☎ *415/583–2223 or 800/531–5900,* FAX *415/589–6770. 174 rooms. Pool, hot tub, exercise room, coin laundry, airport shuttle service. AE, DC, MC, V.*

7 The Arts and Nightlife

THE ARTS

By Robert Taylor

THE BEST guide to arts and entertainment events in San Francisco is the "Datebook" section, printed on pink paper, in the Sunday *Examiner and Chronicle*. The *Bay Guardian* and *S.F. Weekly*, free and available in racks around the city, list more neighborhood, avant-garde, and budget-priced events. For up-to-date information about cultural and musical events, call the Convention and Visitors Bureau's *Cultural Events Calendar* (☎ 415/391–2001).

Half-price tickets to many local and touring stage shows go on sale (cash only) at 11 AM, Tuesday–Saturday, at the TIX Bay Area booth on the Stockton Street side of Union Square, between Geary and Post streets. TIX is also a full-service ticket agency for theater and music events around the Bay Area (open until 6 PM Tues.–Thurs., 7 PM Fri.–Sat.). For recorded information about TIX tickets, call 415/433–7827.

The city's charge-by-phone ticket service is **BASS** (☎ 510/762–2277 or 415/776–1999), with one of its centers in the TIX booth mentioned above and another at **Tower Records** (Bay St. at Columbus Ave.), near Fisherman's Wharf. Other agencies downtown are the **City Box Office** (153 Kearny St., Suite 402, ☎ 415/392–4400) and **Downtown Center Box Office** (in the parking garage at 325 Mason St., ☎ 415/775–2021). The opera, symphony, the ballet's *Nutcracker,* and touring hit musicals are often sold out in advance; tickets are usually available within a day of performance for other shows.

While the city's major commercial theaters are concentrated downtown, the opera, symphony, and ballet perform at the Civic Center.

Theater

San Francisco's "theater row" is a single block of Geary Street west of Union Square, but a number of commercial theaters are located within walking distance, along with resident companies that enrich the city's theatrical scene. The three major commercial theaters are operated by the Shorenstein-Nederlander organization, which books touring plays and musicals, some of them before they open on Broadway. The most venerable is the **Curran** (445 Geary St., ☎ 415/474–3800). The **Golden Gate** is a stylishly refurbished movie theater (Golden Gate Ave. at Taylor St., ☎ 415/474–3800), now primarily a musical house. The 2,500-seat **Orpheum** (1192 Market St., near the Civic Center, ☎ 415/474–3800) is used for the biggest touring shows.

The smaller commercial theaters, offering touring shows plus some local performances, are the **Marines Memorial Theatre** (Sutter and Mason Sts., ☎ 415/441–7444) and **Theatre on the Square** (450 Post St., ☎ 415/433–9500). For commercial and popular success, nothing beats *Beach Blanket Babylon,* the zany revue that has been running since 1974 at **Club Fugazi** (678 Green St., in North Beach, ☎ 415/421–4222). Conceived by imaginative San Francisco director Steve Silver, it is a lively, colorful musical mix of cabaret, show-biz parodies, and tributes to local landmarks. (*See* Cabarets *in* Nightlife, *below.*)

The city's major nonprofit theater company is the **American Conservatory Theatre (ACT),** which was founded in the mid-1960s and quickly became one of the nation's leading regional theaters. It presents a season of approximately eight plays in rotating repertory from October through late spring. ACT's ticket office is at 405 Geary Street (☎ 415/749–2228), next door to its **Geary Theatre,** which is scheduled to reopen in 1996 after a $24 million reconstruction after the 1989 earthquake. ACT may also continue performing at its interim theaters, the nearby **Stage Door Theater** (420 Mason St.) and the **Marines Memorial Theatre** (Sutter and Mason Sts.).

The leading producer of new plays is the **Magic Theatre** (Bldg. D, Fort Mason Center, Laguna St. at Marina Blvd., ☎ 415/441–8822).

The city boasts a wide variety of specialized and ethnic theaters that work with dedicated local actors and some professionals. Among the most interesting are **The Lamplighters,** the delightful Gilbert and Sullivan troupe that often gets better reviews than touring productions of musicals, performing at **Presentation Theater** (2350 Turk St., ☎ 415/752–7755); the **Lorraine Hansberry Theatre** (620 Sutter St., ☎ 415/474–8800), which specializes in plays by black writers; the **Asian American Theatre** (405 Arguello Blvd., ☎ 415/751–2600); and two stages that showcase gay and lesbian performers: **Theatre Rhinoceros** (2926 16th St., ☎ 415/861–5079) and **Josie's Cabaret & Juice Joint** (3583 16th St., ☎ 415/861–7933). The **San Francisco Shakespeare Festival** offers free performances on summer weekends in Golden Gate Park (☎ 415/666–2222).

Avant-garde theater, dance, opera, and "performance art" turn up in a variety of locations, not all of them theaters. The major presenting organization is the **Theater Artaud** (499 Alabama St., in the Mission District, ☎ 415/621–7797), which is situated in a huge, converted machine shop. Some contemporary theater events, in addition to dance and music, are scheduled at the theater in the **Center for the Arts at Yerba Buena Gardens** (3rd and Howard Sts., ☎ 415/978–2787). A more adventurous venue is George Coates Performance Works (110 McAllister St., ☎ 415/863–4130), which combines theater, film, video, and electronic music in a former church in the Civic Center.

Berkeley Repertory Theatre (☎ 510/845–4700), across the bay, is the American Conservatory Theatre's major rival for leadership among the region's resident professional companies. It performs an adventurous mix of classics and new plays in a modern, intimate theater at 2025 Addison Street near BART's downtown Berkeley station. It's a fully professional theater, with a fall–spring season. Tickets are available at the TIX booth in San Francisco's Union Square. The Bay Area's most professional outdoor summer theater, **California Shakespeare Festival,** performs in an amphitheater east of Oakland, on Gateway Boulevard just off state Highway 24 (☎ 510/548–3422).

Music

The completion of Davies Symphony Hall at Van Ness Avenue and Grove Street not only gave the San Francisco Symphony a home of its own, but also solidified the base of the city's three major performing-arts organizations—symphony, opera, and ballet—in the Civic Center. The symphony and other musical groups also perform in the smaller, 928-seat Herbst Theatre in the War Memorial Building, the Opera's "twin" at Van Ness Avenue and McAllister Street. Other musical ensembles can be found all over the city: in churches and museums, in restaurants and parks, and in outreach series in Berkeley and on the peninsula.

San Francisco Symphony (Davies Symphony Hall, Van Ness Ave. at Grove St., ☎ 415/431–5400. Tickets: $8–$65, at the box office or through BASS, ☎ 415/776–1999 or 510/762–2277). The symphony performs September through May. Young, California-born Michael Tilson Thomas, who is known for his innovative programming of 20th-century and American works, became music director in September 1994. Guest conductors often include Edo de Waart and Riccardo Muti. Soloists include artists of the caliber of Andre Watts, Peter Serkin, and Pinchas Zukerman. Special events include a summer festival built around a particular composer, nation or musical period, and summer Pops Concerts in the nearby Civic Auditorium. Throughout the season, the symphony presents a Great Performers Series of guest soloists and orchestras.

Philharmonia Baroque (Herbst Theatre, Van Ness Ave. at McAllister St., ☎ 415/391–5252. Tickets also at the TIX booth). This stylish ensemble has been called a local baroque orchestra with a national reputation, and the nation's preeminent group for performances of early music. Its season of concerts, fall–spring, celebrates composers of the 17th and 18th centuries, including Handel, Vivaldi, and Mozart.

San Francisco Chamber Symphony (various locations, ☎ 415/495–2919). This group is known for the variety of its programming, which includes composers from Handel to VillaLobos.

Kronos Quartet (Herbst Theatre and other locations, ☎ 415/731–3533). Twentieth-century works and a number of premieres make up the programs for this surprisingly avant-garde group, whose young, mainstream following debunks all conceptions of string quartets being somber affairs.

Midsummer Mozart (Herbst Theatre and occasionally at Davies Symphony Hall, ☎ 415/781–5931). This is one of the few Mozart festivals that hasn't filled its programs with works by other composers. It performs in July and August under conductor George Cleve.

Old First Concerts (Old First Church, Van Ness Ave. at Sacramento St., ☎ 415/474–1608. Tickets also at TIX booth, Union Square). This well-respected Friday evening and Sunday afternoon series of chamber music, vocal soloists, new music, and jazz takes place in a church and feels like a community gathering.

Pops Concerts (Polk and Grove Sts., ☎ 415/431–5400). Many members of the symphony perform in the July Pops series in the 7,000-seat Civic Auditorium. The schedule includes light classics, Broadway, country, and movie music. Tickets cost as little as a few dollars.

Stern Grove (Sloat Blvd. at 19th Ave., ☎ 415/252–6252). This is the nation's oldest continual free summer music festival, offering 10 Sunday afternoons of symphony, opera, jazz, pop music, and dance. The amphitheater is in a eucalyptus grove below street level; remember that summer in this area near the ocean can be cool.

There are also free band concerts on Sunday and holiday afternoons in the **Golden Gate Park** music concourse (☎ 415/666–7024) opposite the de Young Museum.

Opera

San Francisco Opera (Van Ness Ave. at Grove St., ☎ 415/864–3330). Founded in 1923, and the resident company at the War Memorial Opera House in the Civic Center since it was built in 1932, the Opera has expanded its fall season to 13 weeks. Approximately 70 performances of 10 operas are given, beginning on the first Friday after Labor Day. The Opera uses "supertitles": Translations are projected above the stage during almost all non-English operas. Long considered a major international company and the most important operatic organization in the

United States outside New York, the Opera frequently embarks on co-productions with European opera companies.

In addition to the fall season, the Opera schedules occasional summer festivals. Ticket prices range from about $35 to $100. Standing-room tickets (less than $10) are always sold at 10 AM for same-day performances, and patrons often sell extra tickets on the Opera House steps just before curtain time. Note that the Opera House will be closed in 1996 for repairs; performances will take place at the Civic Auditorium, a block east at Grove and Polk Streets, and also at the Orpheum. The full-time box office is located at 199 Grove Street, at the corner of Van Ness Avenue.

Pocket Opera (☏ 415/989–1853). This lively, modestly priced alternative to "grand" opera gives concert performances, mostly in English, of rarely heard works. Offenbach's operettas are frequently on the bill during the winter–spring season. Concerts are held at various locations.

Another operatic alternative is **The Lamplighters** (*see* Theater, *above*), which specializes in Gilbert and Sullivan but presents other light operas as well.

Dance

San Francisco Ballet (☏ 415/703–9400) has regained much of its luster under artistic director Helgi Tomasson, and both classical and contemporary works have won admiring reviews. The company's primary season runs February–May; its repertoire includes such full-length ballets as *Swan Lake* and a new production of *Sleeping Beauty,* and the annual December presentation of the *Nutcracker* is one of the most spectacular in the nation. The company also aims to reach new audiences with bold new dances, what it calls "cutting-edge works that will make you take a second look." The ballet will be performing in three Bay Area locations until December 1997, when its usual home base, the War Memorial Opera House, reopens after reconstruction. Tickets and information are available at the ballet's administration and rehearsal building, 455 Franklin Street, behind the Opera House.

Oakland Ballet (Paramount Theatre, 2025 Broadway, Oakland, near BART's 19th St. Station, ☏ 510/465–6400). Founded in 1965, this company is not simply an imitation of the larger San Francisco Ballet across the bay. It has earned an outstanding reputation for reviving and preserving ballet masterworks from the early 20th century and presenting innovative contemporary choreography, and has also re-created historic dances by such choreographers as Diaghilev, Bronislava Nininska, and Mikhail Fokine. The company, whose season begins in September, presents its own *Nutcracker* in December.

Margaret Jenkins Dance Company (Theater Artaud, 450 Florida St., ☏ 415/863–1173). The dancers in this modern troupe help shape the choreography themselves. Their repertoire, while experimental, has a broad, mainstream appeal.

Ethnic Dance Festival (Palace of Fine Arts Theatre, Bay and Lyon Sts., ☏ 415/474–3914). Approximately 30 of the Bay Area's estimated 200 ethnic dance companies and soloists perform in several programs in June. Prices are modest for the city-sponsored event.

San Francisco and the Bay Area support innumerable experimental and ethnic dance groups. Among them are **ODC/San Francisco** (☏ 415/863–6606), performing at Herbst Theatre (Van Ness Ave.); the **Joe Goode Performance Group** (☏ 415/648–4848); and **Rosa Montoya Bailes Fla-**

menco (☎ 415/931–7374), which often performs at Herbst Theatre. The **Footworks Studio** (3221 22nd St., ☎ 415/824–5044) gives many more local dancers a chance to perform.

Film

The San Francisco Bay Area, including Berkeley and San Jose, is considered one of the nation's most important movie markets. Films of all sorts can find an audience here. The area is also a filmmaking center: Documentaries and experimental works are being produced on modest budgets, feature films and television programs are shot on location, and some of Hollywood's biggest directors live here, particularly in Marin County. In San Francisco, about a third of the theaters regularly show foreign and independent films. The city is also one of the last strongholds of "repertory cinema," showing older American and foreign films on bills that change daily.

Market Street has many movie theaters, most of which screen only sex and action movies. First-run commercial movie theaters are scattered throughout the city, concentrated along Van Ness Avenue, near Japantown, and in the Marina District. All are accessible on major Muni bus routes, along with the art-revival houses. The San Francisco International Film Festival (*see below*), the oldest in the country, continues to provide an extensive selection of foreign films each spring. The Pacific Film Archive in Berkeley (*see below*) is an incomparable source for rare American and foreign films.

Foreign and Independent Films

The most reliable theaters for foreign and independent films are **Opera Plaza Cinemas** (Van Ness Ave. at Golden Gate Ave., ☎ 415/771–0102); **Lumière** (California St. near Polk St., ☎ 415/885–3200); **Clay** (Fillmore and Clay Sts., ☎ 415/346–1123); **Gateway** (215 Jackson St. at Battery St., ☎ 415/421–3353); **Bridge** (3013 Geary Blvd. near Masonic Ave., ☎ 415/751–3212); and **Castro** (Castro St. near Market St., ☎ 415/621–6120), the last working 1920s movie palace, whose extensive schedule includes many revivals.

Festivals

The **San Francisco International Film Festival** (☎ 415/931–3456) takes over several theaters for two weeks in late April at the AMC Kabuki complex at Post and Fillmore streets. The festival schedules about 75 films from abroad, many of them American premieres, along with a variety of independent American documentaries. The recent emphasis has been on films from Africa and Asia.

Other showcases for films out of the commercial mainstream include the **Roxie Cinema** (3117 16th St., ☎ 415/863–1087), which specializes in social and political documentaries; the **Cinematheque**, which splits its schedule between the San Francisco Art Institute (800 Chestnut St., ☎ 415/558–8129) and the Center for the Arts at Yerba Buena Gardens; and the **Phyllis Wattis Theatre** at the San Francisco Museum of Modern Art (151 3rd St., ☎ 415/357–4000.)

The most extensive screening schedule for both American and foreign, old and new films is the **Pacific Film Archive** at the University Art Museum (2625 Durant Ave., Berkeley, ☎ 510/642–1124), which often shows films from New York's Museum of Modern Art collection.

NIGHTLIFE

By Daniel Mangin

Updated by Dennis Harvey

San Francisco provides a tremendous potpourri of evening entertainment, from ultrasophisticated cabarets to bawdy bistros that reflect the city's gold-rush past. With the exception of the hotel lounges and discos noted below, casual dress is the norm. Bars generally close between midnight and 2 AM. Bands and performances usually begin between 8 and 10 PM. The cover charge at smaller clubs ranges from $3 to $7, and credit cards are rarely accepted. At the larger venues the cover may go up to $30, and tickets can often be purchased through BASS (☎ 415/776–1999 or 510/762–2277).

For information on who is performing where, check the following sources: The Sunday San Francisco *Examiner and Chronicle*'s pink "Datebook" insert lists major events and cultural happenings. The free alternative weeklies, the *Bay Guardian* and *SF Weekly,* are terrific sources for current music clubs and comedy. Another handy reference for San Francisco nightlife is *Key* magazine, offered free in most major hotel lobbies. For a phone update on sports and musical events, call the Convention and Visitor Bureau's *Events Hotline* (☎ 415/391–2001).

Although San Francisco is a compact city with the prevailing influences of some neighborhoods spilling into others, the following generalizations should help you find the kind of entertainment you're looking for. **Nob Hill** is noted for its plush piano bars and panoramic skyline lounges. **North Beach,** infamous for its topless and bottomless bistros, also maintains a sense of its beatnik past and this legacy lives on in atmospheric bars and coffeehouses. **Fisherman's Wharf,** while touristy, is great for people-watching and attracts plenty of street performers. **Union Street** is home away from home for singles in search of company. South of Market (**SoMa,** for short) has become a hub of nightlife, with a bevy of highly popular nightclubs, bars, and lounges in renovated warehouses and auto shops. Gay men will find their scene at **Castro** and **Polk Streets.**

No-Fault Nightspots

Detailed descriptions of the following clubs can be found within listings for each category.

Rock/Pop/Folk/Blues: Slim's, which books the top artists in each of these areas, is almost risk-free; for rock, **Bottom of the Hill** is hot with the locals right now.

Jazz: The best bargain is **Jazz at Pearl's**; supermodel Christy Turlington bought into the already hoppin' **Up and Down Club,** and it has become superhip.

Cabaret: Club Fugazi's *Beach Blanket Babylon* revue has been going strong for more than 20 years—they must be doing something right.

Comedy: Go where your favorite comics are; **Cobb's Comedy Club** is a good bet.

Dancing Emporiums: Salsa weekends are hot at **Cesar's Latin Palace**; the trendy young and restless love **Harry Denton's.**

Piano Bars: The **Redwood Room** is plush; featuring top talent, **Club 36** is an entertainment bargain—with a view.

Singles Bars: Johnny Love's, without question.

Skyline Bars: The **Carnelian Room** is the classiest; **Top of the Mark** is regaining its reputation as a lively yet romantic room with a view.

Rock, Pop, Folk, and Blues

The hip SoMa scene of a few years ago has mellowed a bit of late; the clubs still feature fine music, but the trendies have bailed out. Musical offerings in this part of town and elsewhere run from mainstream to way, way out.

The **Blue Lamp** (561 Geary St., ☎ 415/885–1464), a downtown "hole in the wall," has an aura of faded opulence. Fare ranges from '20s blues to original rock and roll.

Bottom of the Hill (1233 17th St., at Texas St., ☎ 415/626–4455), "two minutes south of SoMa" in the Potrero Hill District, showcases some of the city's best local alternative rock and blues. The atmosphere is ultra low-key, though even these cool folks start a-buzzin' when the occasional rock or pop star drops in to check out the scene.

Brave New World (1751 Masonic St., at Fulton St., ☎ 415/441–1751), lures a fancifully garbed, heavily pierced clientele. Bands like Jack Killed Jill and the Mental Pigmies (sic) enthrall the assembled youngsters most nights; Tuesdays feature exotic dancers, while Sundays offer a free jazz program.

DNA Lounge (375 11th St., near Harrison St., ☎ 415/626–1409), a longtime, two-floor SoMa haunt, was recently revamped to include new murals and a larger VIP lounge. Alternative independent rock, funk, and rap are the music of choice here. Live bands play most nights at 10 PM; other nights the club is open for dancing to recorded music—until 4 AM on weekends.

The Fillmore (1805 Geary Blvd., at Fillmore St., ☎ 415/346–6000), one of San Francisco's most famous rock music halls, reopened in 1994 after several years of retrofitting. Today it serves up a varied menu of national and local acts: rock, reggae, grunge, jazz, comedy, folk, acid house, and more; ticket prices range from $12.50 to $22.50. On the empty lot nearby there was once another famous landmark, Jim Jones's People's Temple.

Freight and Salvage Coffee House (1111 Addison St., Berkeley, ☎ 510/548–1761), one of the finest folk houses in the country, is worth a trip across the bay. Some of the most talented practitioners of folk, blues, Cajun, and bluegrass perform here, among them Taj Mahal, Iris DeMent, Laurie Lewis, and Greg Brown. Be prepared to shell out as much as $18 to get in.

Great American Music Hall (859 O'Farrell St., between Polk and Larkin Sts., ☎ 415/885–0750) is one of the great eclectic nightclubs, not only in San Francisco but in the entire country. Here you will find truly top-drawer entertainment, running the gamut from the best in blues, folk, and jazz to alternative rock with a sprinkling of outstanding comedians. The colorful marble-pillared emporium (built in 1907 as a bordello) will also accommodate dancing to popular bands. Past headliners include B. B. King, Van Morrison, the Spin Doctors, and George Clinton.

Jack's Bar (1601 Fillmore St., ☎ 415/567–3227), a smoky R&B dive (in every sense of the word), has been serving up hot music since 1932, with dancing seven nights a week in a soulful atmosphere. The club's Sunday jam sessions are legendary. Tuesday is Comedy Night. It's best to take a cab to and from this place.

Last Day Saloon (406 Clement St., between 5th and 6th Aves., ☎ 415/387–6343) offers an attractive setting of wooden tables and potted plants, along with major entertainers and a varied schedule of blues, Cajun, rock, and jazz. Illustrious performers of the past have included Taj Mahal, Big Head Todd & the Monster, Motherhips, Maria Muldaur, and Pride and Joy.

Lou's Pier 47 (300 Jefferson St., Fisherman's Wharf, ☎ 415/771–0377) features cool music and hot food on the waterfront.

Paradise Lounge (1501 Folsom St., ☎ 415/861–6906), a quirky lounge with two stages for eclectic live music and dancing, also has an upstairs cabaret featuring offbeat local and national performers. 21 and over only.

Pier 23 (Embarcadero and Pier 23, across from Fog City Diner, ☎ 415/362–5125), a waterfront restaurant by day, turns into a packed club by night, with a musical spectrum ranging from Caribbean, salsa, and jazz to Motown and reggae. Get here early in the evening for dinner and you can keep your table after the music starts.

The Saloon (1232 Grant St., near Columbus Ave. in North Beach, ☎ 415/989–7666) is a favorite blues spot among locals in the know. Local R&B favorites Johnny Nitro and the Doorslammers play here every Sunday and most Fridays.

Slim's (333 11th St., ☎ 415/621–3330), one of SoMa's most popular nightclubs, specializes in what it labels "American roots music"—blues, jazz, classic rock, and the like. The club has expanded its repertoire in recent years, with national touring acts playing alternative rock and roll and a series of "spoken word" concerts. Co-owner Boz Scaggs helps bring in the crowds and famous headliners. The box office doubles as a general BASS ticket outlet.

The Warfield (982 Market St., ☎ 415/775–7722), once a movie palace, is one of the city's largest rock-and-roll venues. There are tables and chairs downstairs, and theater seating upstairs. Such contemporary acts as the Jerry Garcia Band, Smashing Pumpkins, Public Enemy, and Nancy Griffith have played here recently.

Jazz

Jazz options run the gamut from mellow restaurant cocktail lounges to hip SoMa venues to stylish showcases for top acts.

Cafe du Nord (2170 Market St., at Sanchez St., ☎ 415/861–5016), once a Basque restaurant, now hosts some of the liveliest jam sessions in town. The atmosphere in this basement poolroom/bar is decidedly casual, but the music, provided mostly by local talent, is strictly top-notch.

Eleven (374 11th St., ☎ 415/431–3337), an Italian restaurant–cum–casual jazz showcase, joined the ranks of SoMa hot spots at the end of 1993. The various funky, salsafied, and trad sounds here are called "Live Loft Jazz," because the stage is 12 feet off the ground.

Heart and Soul (1695 Polk St., ☎ 415/673–6788), a sleek, plush "1940s big-city retro room," captures the ambience of another era with just a hint of lounge-revival irony. The kitchen serves excellent appetizers and meals, while local and national combos and vocalists play jazz from 1940s through the '60s.

Jazz at Pearl's (256 Columbus Ave., near Broadway, ☎ 415/291–8255) is one of the few reminders of North Beach's days as a hot spot for cool tunes. Sophisticated and romantic, the club's picture windows overlook City Lights Bookstore across the street. The talent level is remarkably high, especially considering that there is rarely a cover.

Kimball's East (5800 Shellmound St., Emeryville, ☎ 510/658–2555), in a shopping complex in Emeryville just off Highway 80 near Oakland, hosts jazz greats such as Wynton Marsalis and Hugh Masekela and popular vocalists such as Lou Rawls and Patti Austin. With an elegant interior and fine food, it's one of the Bay Area's most luxurious supper clubs.

Moose's (1652 Stockton St, in North Beach, ☎ 415/989–7800), one of the city's hottest restaurants since 1992, also features great sounds in its small but stylish bar area.

New Orleans Room (Mason and California Sts., ☎ 415/772–5259), in the Fairmont Hotel, gained popularity when it switched from Dixieland to jazz around 1991. Its new stars include Stanley Turrentine, Joe Williams, and others.

Pasand Lounge (1875 Union St., ☎ 415/922–4498), a popular Indian restaurant, offers jazz and R&B on a small stage in the back.

330 Ritch Street (330 Ritch at Townsend, ☎ 415/541–9574), a new SoMa supper club, blends stylish modern decor with an extensive tapas menu, a dance floor, two pool tables, and progressive live jazz combos most nights of the week.

Up and Down Club (1151 Folsom St., ☎ 415/626–2388), a hip restaurant and club whose owners include supermodel Christy Turlington, books up-and-coming jazz artists downstairs Wednesday through Monday. There's a bar and dancing to a DJ upstairs Wednesday through Saturday.

Yoshi's (Jack London Sq., Oakland, ☎ 510/652–9200), which will move back to its home on Jack London Square in March 1996, continues to be one of the Bay Area's best jazz venues. Jazz greats including J. J. Johnson, Betty Carter, local favorite Kenny Burrell, Joshua Redman, and Cecil Taylor play here, along with blues and Latin performers.

Cabarets

Traditional cabaret is in short supply in San Francisco, but two longtime favorite spots and a couple of alternative venues offer a range of entertainment.

Club Fugazi (678 Green St., ☎ 415/421–4222) is most famous for *Beach Blanket Babylon,* a wacky musical revue that has become the longest-running show of its genre. A send-up of San Francisco moods and mores, *Beach Blanket* has now run for two decades, outstripping the Ziegfeld Follies by years. While the choreography is colorful and the songs witty, the real stars of the show are the exotic costumes—worth the price of admission in themselves. Order tickets as far in advance as possible; the revue has been sold out up to a month in advance. Those under 21 are admitted only to the Sunday matinee.

Coconut Grove (1415 Van Ness Ave., ☎ 415/776–1616) has a chic, '40s supper-club ambience. Tom Jones, Connie Stevens, Diahann Carroll, and other pop icons are among the past headliners.

Eichelberger's (2742 17th St., ☎ 415/863–4177), named by its native New Yorker owners after the late Manhattan performance artist Ethyl Eichelberger, has a bar downstairs and a "classic supper club with a San Francisco twist" above. The "twist" is presumably its full schedule of cabaret acts after dining hours upstairs. Ranging from drag chanteuses to veteran jazz stylists, the entertainment attracts a primarily gay clientele.

Finocchio's (506 Broadway, ☎ 415/982–9388), an amiable, world-famous club, has been generating confusion with its female impersonators since 1936. The scene at Finocchio's is decidedly retro, which for the most part only adds to its charm.

Josie's Cabaret and Juice Joint (3583 16th St., at Market St., ☎ 415/861–7933), a small, stylish café and cabaret in the predominantly gay Castro District, books performers who reflect the countercultural feel of the neighborhood. National talents stopping through have included Lypsinka, lesbian comic Lea Delaria, and transsexual performance artist Kate Bornstein.

The Marsh (1062 Valencia St., ☏ 415/641–0235), in the Mission District, books an eclectic mix of alternative/avant-garde theater, performance, comedy, and musical acts.

Comedy Clubs

In the '80s it seemed as if every class clown or life-of-the-party type was cutting it up at a comedy club. The stand-up boom, like others from the decade, has gone bust, except for the two fine clubs listed below.

Cobb's Comedy Club (2801 Leavenworth St., at the corner of Beach St., ☏ 415/928–4320), in the Cannery, books super stand-up comics such as Margaret Smith, Dana Gould, Jake Johannsen, and Dom Irrera.

Punch Line (44-A Battery St., between Clay and Washington Sts., ☏ 415/397–7573), a launching pad for the likes of Jay Leno and Whoopi Goldberg, features some of the area's top talents—several of whom are certain to make a national impact. Note that weekend shows often sell out; it is best to buy tickets in advance at BASS outlets (☏ 510/762–2277) or from the club's new charge line (☏ 415/397-4337). Eighteen and over only.

Other comedy possibilities: Josie's and the Marsh (*see* Cabarets, *above*) often book, respectively, gay and avant-garde comics. The Fillmore and the Great American Music Hall (*see* Rock, Pop, Folk, and Blues, *above*) are also apt to have an occasional favorite comic onstage.

Dancing Emporiums

Some of the rock, blues, and jazz clubs listed above sport active dance floors. Some also feature DJ dancing when live acts aren't on the stage. Below are eight spots devoted solely to folks out to shake a tail feather.

Cesar's Latin Palace (3140 Mission St., ☏ 415/648–6611), in the Mission District, lures all kinds of dancers with its salsa-style Latin music. Latin dance lessons from 9 to 10 PM are included in the price of admission Friday and Saturday nights. Sunday is Brazilian Night. Note: no alcohol is served here.

Club DV8 (540 Howard St., ☏ 415/957–1730), one of SoMa's largest, has two huge dance floors with DJs mixing up funk, flashback, Euro HiNRG, house, techno, industrial, and even "French video and dance night."

Metronome Ballroom (1830 17th St., ☏ 415/252–9000) is at its most lively on weekend nights, when ballroom dancers come for lessons and revelry. The ambience is lively but mellow at this smoke- and alcohol-free spot.

Oz (335 Powell St., between Geary and Post Sts., ☏ 415/774–0116), on the top floor of the St. Francis Hotel—accessible via glass elevator—has marble floors and a splendid panorama of the city. Dancers can recharge on cushy sofas and bamboo chairs. The fine sound system belts out progressive house music.

Sound Factory (525 Harrison St., ☏ 415/543–1300) became an instant hit when it opened in SoMa in 1993. Musical styles change with the night and sometimes the hour. Depending on who's up in the DJ booth, you're likely to hear anything from garage and deep house to '70s disco. Two "virtual reality pods" offer refuge; live bands also perform at special events. Some nights the venue becomes an alcohol-free, after-hours club.

If none of the above tickles your fancy, give the events hot line of one of these clubs a jingle: **Miss Pearl's Jam House** (☎ 415/775–5267), **El Rio** (☎ 415/282–3325), or **Avenue Ballroom** (☎ 415/681–2882; no smoking, no alcohol).

Piano Bars

You only have eyes for her. Or him. Six quiet spots with talented tinklers provide the perfect atmosphere for holding hands and making plans.

Act IV Lounge (333 Fulton St., near Franklin St., ☎ 415/553–8100), in the Inn at the Opera Hotel, is a popular spot for a romantic rendezvous. The focal point of this tastefully appointed lounge is a crackling fireplace.

Club 36 (345 Stockton St., ☎ 415/398–1234), on the top floor of the Grand Hyatt, offers piano music and jazz combos, and a view of North Beach and the Bay.

Masons (California and Mason Sts., ☎ 415/772–5233), an elegant restaurant in the Fairmont Hotel, features fine jazz and show standards by local talents.

Redwood Room (Taylor and Geary Sts., ☎ 415/775–4700), in the Four Seasons Clift Hotel, is a classy Art Deco lounge with a low-key but sensuous ambience. Klimt reproductions grace the walls, and mellow sounds fill the air.

Ritz-Carlton Hotel (600 Stockton St., ☎ 415/296–7465) has a tastefully appointed lobby lounge where a harpist plays during high tea, daily from 2:30 to 5 PM. The lounge shifts to piano (with occasional vocal accompaniment) for cocktails until 11:30 weeknights and 1:30 AM weekends.

Washington Square Bar and Grill (1707 Powell St., on Washington Sq., ☎ 415/982–8123), affectionately known as the "Washbag" among San Francisco politicians and newspaper folk, hosts pianists performing jazz and popular standards.

Skyline Bars

San Francisco is a city of spectacular vistas. Enjoy drinks, music, and sometimes dinner with 360-degree views at any of the bars below.

Carnelian Room (555 California St., ☎ 415/433–7500), on the 52nd floor of the Bank of America Building, offers what is perhaps the loftiest view of San Francisco's magnificent skyline. Enjoy dinner or cocktails at 781 feet above the ground; reservations are a must for dinner.

Cityscape (Mason and O'Farrell Sts., ☎ 415/771–1400), in the tower of the Hilton Hotel, offers dancing to Top 40, rock, and pop nightly from 10 to 1.

Club 36. (*See* Piano Bars, *above.*)

Crown Room (California and Mason Sts., ☎ 415/772–5131), the aptly named lounge on the 29th floor of the Fairmont Hotel, is one of the most luxurious of the city's skyline bars. Just riding the glass-enclosed Skylift elevator is a drama in itself.

Equinox (5 Embarcadero Center, ☎ 415/788–1234), on the 22nd floor of the Hyatt Regency, is known for its revolving 360-degree views of the city. You can sightsee, eat, and drink, all from the comfort of your own chair.

Phineas T. Barnacle (1090 Point Lobos Ave., ☏ 415/386–3330), inside the Cliff House, offers a unique panorama of seal rocks and the horizon of the Pacific Ocean.

Top of the Mark (California and Mason Sts., ☏ 415/392–3434), in the Mark Hopkins Hotel, was immortalized by a famous magazine photograph as a hot spot for World War II service people on leave or about to ship out. Now folks can dance to the sounds of that era on weekends. There's live music Wednesday through Saturday night, and dancing to standards from the '20s, '30s, and '40s Friday and Saturday. The view is superb seven nights a week.

View Lounge (777 Market St., ☏ 415/896–1600), on the 39th floor of the San Francisco Marriott since 1989, is one of the loveliest of the city's skyline lounges. Live piano music is played Monday–Saturday, along with an R&B band Friday and Saturday from 9 PM to 1 AM.

Singles Bars

Ever notice how everyone looks so much better when you visit another town? Here's where the magic will happen for you:

Balboa Cafe (3199 Fillmore St., ☏ 415/921–3944), a jam-packed hangout for the young and upwardly mobile crowd, is famous for its burgers and single clientele.

Gordon Biersch Brewery and Restaurant (2 Harrison St., ☏ 415/243–8246), inside the old Hill Brothers coffee factory, is a favorite of the swinging twentysomething set.

Hard Rock Cafe (1699 Van Ness St., ☏ 415/885–1699), part of the famous chain of youth-oriented bars, is filled with a collection of rock-and-roll memorabilia that won't disappoint fans.

Harry Denton's (161 Steuart St., ☏ 415/882–1333), one of San Francisco's liveliest, most upscale saloons, is packed with well-dressed young professionals. There are live bands and dancing after 10 PM nightly except Sunday. Its location on the Embarcadero, where the freeway came down after the '89 quake, affords stunning views of the bay from the back bar.

Holding Company (2 Embarcadero Center, ☏ 415/986–0797), one of the most popular weeknight Financial District watering holes, is where scores of office workers gather to enjoy friendly libations. The spanking-new kitchen and bar are open seven nights a week.

Johnny Love's (1500 Broadway, at Polk St., ☏ 415/931–8021) has been a hit ever since it was opened by the popular Mr. Love, former patron of Harry Denton's. At the base of Russian Hill, it's one of *the* places to be seen. Live music (heavy on the R&B) is offered nightly.

Perry's (1944 Union St., at Buchanan St., ☏ 415/922–9022), the most famous of San Francisco's singles bars, is usually jam-packed. You can dine here on great hamburgers as well as more substantial fare.

San Francisco's Favorite Bars

Locals patronize all of the places listed above, but there are several joints they hold near and dear:

Buena Vista (2765 Hyde St., ☏ 415/474–5044) the Wharf area's most popular bar, introduced Irish coffee to the New World—or so they say. Because it has a fine view of the waterfront, it's usually packed with tourists.

Cypress Club (500 Jackson St., off Columbus Ave., ☏ 415/296–8555) is an eccentric restaurant-bar where sensual, '20s-style opulence clashes with Fellini/Dali frivolity. The decor alone makes it worth a visit, but it's also a fine spot for a before-dinner or after-theater chat. Raymond Chandler's *The Big Sleep* inspired the club's name.

Edinburgh Castle (950 Geary St., near Polk St., ☎ 415/885–4074), cherished by Scots all over town, pours out happy and sometimes baleful Scottish folk tunes the likes of which can be heard nowhere for miles; Fridays feature bagpipe performances. There are plenty of Scottish brews from which to choose. You can work off your fish-and-chips with a turn at the dart board.

Harrington's (245 Front St., ☎ 415/392–7595), an Irish drinking saloon, is *the* place to be on St. Patrick's Day.

House of Shields (39 New Montgomery St., ☎ 415/392–7732), a saloon-style bar, attracts an older, Financial District crowd after work. It closes at 8 PM weekdays, 6 PM Saturday.

Peer Inn (Pier 33 at the Embarcadero, ☎ 415/788–1411) is a bit less touristed than other bars on the Wharf. It also has an adjacent restaurant.

Spec's (12 Adler Pl., just south of Broadway, ☎ 415/421–4112), a hidden hangout for artists, poets, and seamen, is worth looking for. It's a good, old-fashioned watering hole, reflecting a sense of the North Beach of days gone by.

Tosca Café (242 Columbus Ave., ☎ 415/391–1244), like Spec's and Vesuvio nearby, holds a special place in San Francisco lore. It's got an Italian flavor, with opera and Italian standards on the jukebox and an antique espresso/cappuccino machine that's nothing less than a work of art. Known as a hangout for filmmaker Francis Ford Coppola, playwright/actor Sam Shepard, and ballet star Mikhail Baryshnikov (when they're in town), this place positively breathes a film noir atmosphere.

Vesuvio Cafe (255 Columbus Ave., between Broadway and Pacific Ave., ☎ 415/362–3370), near the legendary City Lights Bookstore, is little altered since its heyday as a haven for the Beat poets.

Gay and Lesbian Nightlife

In the days before the gay liberation movement, bars were more than mere watering holes. They also served as community centers where members of a mostly undercover minority could network and socialize. In the 1960s, they became hotbeds of political activity. The Tavern Guild of San Francisco, comprising the town's major gay establishments, achieved several of the community's first political victories, waging and winning a legal and public-relations battle to end police harassment. Even teetotaling gays benefited from the confrontation. By the 1970s, other social opportunities became available to gay men and lesbians, and the bars' importance as centers of activity decreased. Old-timers wax nostalgic about the vibrancy of pre-AIDS, '70s bar life, but plenty of fun is still to be had today. The one difference is that some of the best clubs operate only once a week, in clubs that cater to a different (sometimes straight) clientele on other nights..

The one-night-a-week clubs tend to come and go, so it's best to pick up one of the two main gay papers: the *Bay Area Reporter* (☎ 415/861–5019) or the *San Francisco Bay Times* (☎ 415/626–8121). Both, plus *Odyssey,* a club-info and gossip sheet, are usually available at the clubs listed below.

The papers reveal something else: There's more to gay nightlife than the bars. Most nights, **Theatre Rhinoceros** (☎ 415/861–5079) offers plays or solo shows on two stages and **Josie's Cabaret** features work by cutting-edge performance, comedy, and theater artists. Members of the Tavern Guild (☎ 415/752–2366) and Japantown Bowling (☎ 415/921–6200) leagues compete Monday–Thursday nights. City College's Gay and Lesbian Studies Department (☎ 415/239–3876) holds classes Monday through Thursday (6:30–9:30 PM) in film, literature, and other topics at Everett Middle School, 17th Street at Church (drop-ins are normally allowed). Check the gay papers' extensive calendar listings for other activities.

Lesbian Bars

For a place known as a "gay" mecca, San Francisco has always suffered a surprising drought of seven-days-a-week women's bars; instead, it has just a few reliable one-nighters (call ahead to be sure they are still operating). Younger lesbians and gays, some of whom prefer to call themselves "queers," don't segregate themselves quite as much as the older set; you'll find mixed crowds at a number of the bars listed under Gay Male Bars, below.

The Box (715 Harrison St., ☎ 415/647–8258), a long-running one-nighter, moved to new digs in 1994, but "Mixtress" Page Hodel still keeps the dressed-to-sweat crowd in constant motion with house, hip-hop, and funk sounds. Expect to find a mixed, increasingly male crowd.
Club Q (177 Townsend St., ☎ 415/647–8258), a dance party from Page Hodel's One Groove Productions, is geared to "women and their friends."
G-Spot (Harrison and 9th Sts., ☎ 415/863–6623), at the Stud, is a hot spot (aka Girlspot) on Saturday night, when a mostly lesbian crowd dances to pop (Whitney Houston, etc.,) with a bit of techno-beat.
Luna Sea (2940 16th St. #216C, at S. Van Ness Ave., ☎ 415/863–2989), a newcomer amid the burgeoning Mission District arts scene, is a women's gallery/theatre space featuring an ever-changing lineup of visual-arts displays, performance art, and readings. Some events are for women only.
Red Dora's Bearded Lady Café and Cabaret (485 14th St., at Guerrero St., ☎ 415/626–2805), a neighborhood venue, serves a predominantly lesbian and gay clientele. It's also a gallery with mostly women's work, and a music outlet for local independent labels. The kitchen serves inexpensive vegetarian fare.
The Stud. *See* The SoMa Scene, *below,* for women's nights at this formerly male-oriented bar.
Wild Side West (424 Cortland St., ☎ 415/647–3099), its name notwithstanding, is a mellow, mixed neighborhood bar, way off the beaten path in Bernal Heights.

Gay Male Bars

"A bar for every taste, that's the ticket," was how the curious "documentary" *Gay San Francisco* described late-'60s nightlife here. Leather bars, drag-queen hangouts, piano bars, and bohemian cafés were among the many options for gay men back then. The scene remains just as versatile today. Unless otherwise noted, there is no cover charge at these establishments.

THE SOMA SCENE

Esta Noche (3079 16th St., below Valencia St., ☎ 415/861–5757), a longtime Mission District establishment, draws a steady crowd of Latino gays, including some of the city's wildest drag queens.
SF-Eagle (12th and Harrison Sts., ☎ 415/626–0880) is one of the few SoMa bars that remain from the days before AIDS and gentrification. International leather legend Mister Marcus (to you) often drops by to judge the Mr. SF Leather, Mr. Leather Calendar, and innumerable other contests, most of which are AIDS benefits.
The Stud (Harrison and 9th Sts., ☎ 415/863–6623) is still going strong since 1966. Its always-groovin' DJs mix up-to-the-minute music with carefully chosen highlights from the glory days of gay disco. Thurs-

day and Saturday nights draw a mostly lesbian crowd; Friday is "Club Jesus," catering to the pierced and tattooed set of all persuasions.

IN THE CASTRO

The Café (2367 Market St., at 17th St., ☎ 415/861–3846), formerly Café San Marcos, is in the heart of the gay Castro district. Always comfortable and often crowded, it's a place where you can chat quietly or cut the rug as you please.

Café Flore (2298 Market St., ☎ 415/621–8579) attracts poets, punks, and poseurs, who mingle day and night at open-air tables or inside the glass walls, over beer, wine, coffee, and tea. A separate concessionaire serves surprisingly tasty food until 10 PM, though most people come only for drinks or dessert.

Detour (2348 Market St., ☎ 415/861–6053) attracts a crowd that's youngish and a bit surly (in a sexy sort of way). The music is loud but well selected.

Elephant Walk (Castro St., at 18th St., no ☎), one of the Castro's cozier bars, is among the few (along with Moby Dick, at 18th and Hartford streets, and Twin Peaks, at 17th and Castro streets) where the music level allows for easy conversation.

The Metro (3600 16th St., at Market St., ☎ 415/703–9750), more upscale than the nearby Detour, has a balcony that overlooks the intersection of Noe, 16th, and Market streets. "Guppies" (gay yuppies) love this place, especially since it has a fairly good restaurant adjoining the bar.

Midnight Sun (4067 18th St., ☎ 415/861–4186), one of the Castro's longest-standing and most popular bars, has giant video screens riotously programmed. Don't expect to hear yourself think.

ON/NEAR POLK STREET

The Cinch (1723 Polk St., ☎ 415/776–4162), a neighborhood bar with country-western music, is one of several hosts of the gay San Francisco Pool Association's weekly matches.

Giraffe Video Lounge (1131 Polk St., ☎ 415/474–1702) is a lively bar with multiple TV screens playing the latest music videos.

Kimo's (1551 Polk St., ☎ 415/885–4535), a laid-back club, has floor-to-ceiling windows that provide a great view of Polk Street action.

N Touch (1548 Polk St., ☎ 415/441–8413), a tiny dance bar, has long been popular with Asian-Pacific Islander gay men. Video screens alternately play mildly erotic videos and MTV.

AROUND TOWN

Alta Plaza Bar & Grill (2301 Fillmore St., ☎ 415/922–1444) is an upper Fillmore restaurant-bar that caters to nattily dressed guppies and their admirers.

Lion Pub (2062 Divisadero St., at Sacramento St., ☎ 415/567–6565), one of the community's older enterprises, is a cozy neighborhood bar with an ever-changing but always singular decor.

8 Excursions from San Francisco

SAUSALITO

By Robert Taylor

THE SAN FRANCISCO Convention and Visitors Bureau describes Sausalito's location as "the Mediterranean side of the Golden Gate." With its relatively sheltered site on the bay in Marin County, just 8 miles from San Francisco, it appeals to Bay Area residents and visitors for the same reason: It is so near and yet so far. As a hillside town with superb views, an expansive yacht harbor, the aura of an artist's colony, and ferry service, Sausalito might be a resort within commuting distance of the city. It is certainly the primary excursion for visitors to San Francisco, especially those with limited time to explore the Bay Area. Mild weather encourages strolling and outdoor dining, although morning fog and afternoon winds can roll over the hills from the ocean, funneling through the central part of town once known as Hurricane Gulch.

There are substantial homes, including Victorian mansions, in Sausalito's heights, but the town's raffish reputation predates them. Discovered in 1775 by Spanish explorers and named Saucelito (Little Willow) for the trees growing around its springs, Sausalito was a port for whaling ships during the 19th century. In 1875 the railroad from the north connected with ferryboats to San Francisco and the town became an attraction for the fun-loving. Even the chamber of commerce recalls the time when Sausalito sported 25 saloons, gambling dens, and bordellos. Bootleggers flourished during Prohibition in the 1920s, and shipyard workers swelled the town's population during the 1940s, when tour guides divided the residents into "wharf rats" and "hill snobs."

Ensuing decades brought a bohemian element with the development of an artists' colony and a houseboat community. Sausalito has also become a major yachting center, and restaurants attract visitors for fresh seafood as well as spectacular views. Sausalito remains a friendly and casual small town, although summer traffic jams can fray nerves. If possible, visit on a weekday—and take the ferry.

Exploring

Numbers in the margin correspond to points of interest on the Sausalito map.

Bridgeway is Sausalito's main thoroughfare and prime destination, with the bay, yacht harbor, and waterfront restaurants on one side, and more restaurants, shops, hillside homes, and hotels on the other. It is only a few steps from the ferry terminal to the tiny landmark park in the cen-
1 ter of town: the **Plaza Vina del Mar,** named for Sausalito's sister city in Chile. The park features a fountain and two 14-foot-tall statues of elephants created for the 1915 Panama-Pacific International Exposition in San Francisco.

2 Across the street to the south is the Spanish-style **Sausalito Hotel,** which has been refurbished and filled with Victorian antiques. Between
3 the hotel and the **Sausalito Yacht Club** is another unusual historic landmark, a drinking fountain inscribed with the words, "Have a Drink on Sally." It's in remembrance of Sally Stanford, the former San Francisco madam who later ran Sausalito's Valhalla restaurant and became the town's mayor—although, as suggested by a sidewalk-level bowl that reads, "Have a Drink on Leland," the fountain may actually be in remembrance of her dog.

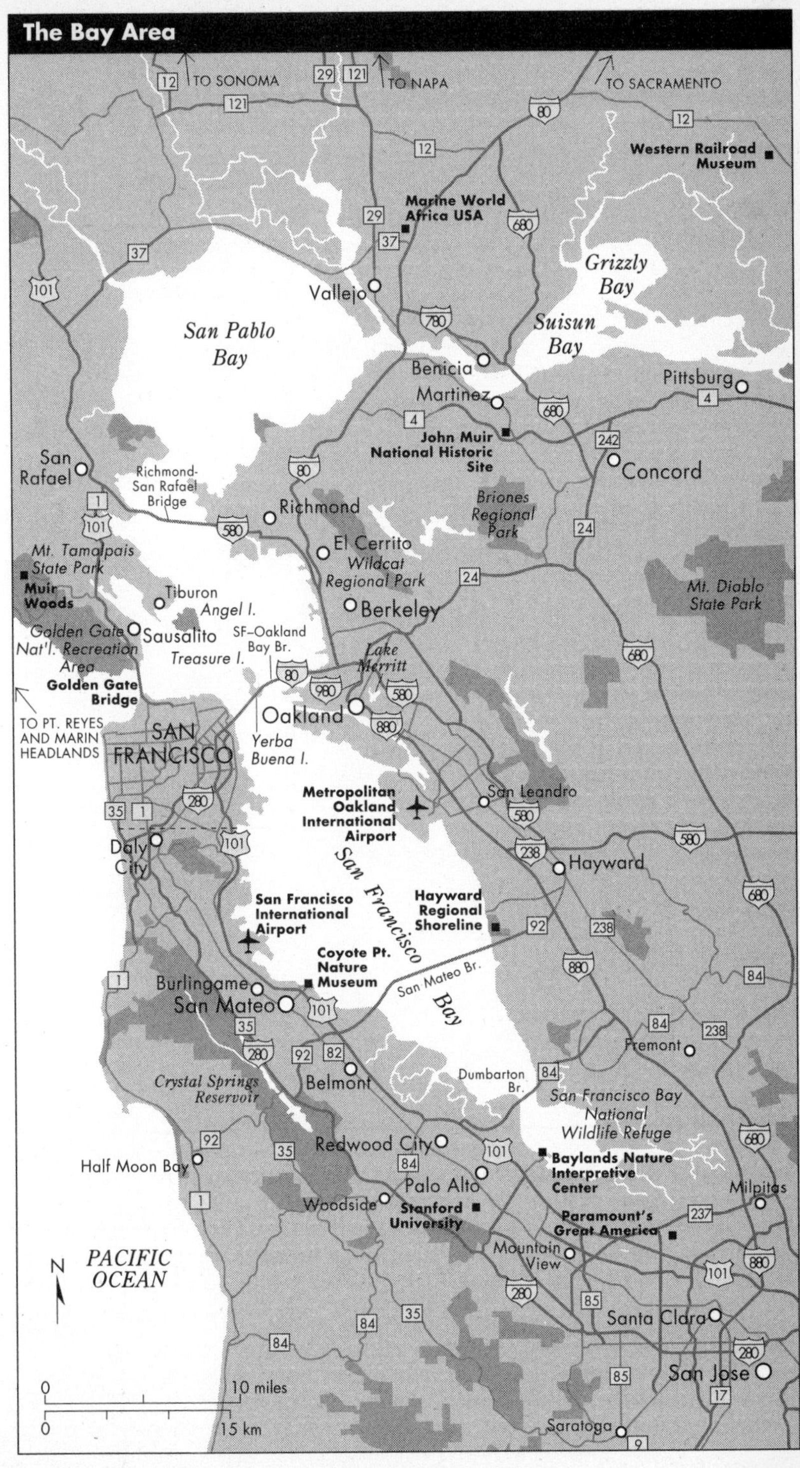
The Bay Area
TO SONOMA
TO NAPA
TO SACRAMENTO
Western Railroad Museum
Marine World Africa USA
Grizzly Bay
Vallejo
San Pablo Bay
Suisun Bay
Benicia
Martinez
Pittsburg
John Muir National Historic Site
San Rafael
Richmond-San Rafael Bridge
Concord
Richmond
Briones Regional Park
El Cerrito
Mt. Tamalpais State Park
Wildcat Regional Park
Muir Woods
Tiburon
Angel I.
Berkeley
Mt. Diablo State Park
Golden Gate Nat'l. Recreation Area
Sausalito
SF–Oakland Bay Br.
Treasure I.
Lake Merritt
Golden Gate Bridge
TO PT. REYES AND MARIN HEADLANDS
SAN FRANCISCO
Oakland
Yerba Buena I.
Metropolitan Oakland International Airport
San Leandro
Daly City
Hayward
San Francisco Bay
San Francisco International Airport
Hayward Regional Shoreline
Coyote Pt. Nature Museum
San Mateo Br.
Burlingame
San Mateo
Fremont
Crystal Springs Reservoir
Belmont
Dumbarton Br.
San Francisco Bay National Wildlife Refuge
Redwood City
Half Moon Bay
Baylands Nature Interpretive Center
Palo Alto
Milpitas
Woodside
Stanford University
Paramount's Great America
PACIFIC OCEAN
N
Mountain View
Santa Clara
San Jose
Saratoga
0
10 miles
0
15 km

Alta Mira Hotel, **5**
Bay Model, **7**
Plaza Vina del Mar, **1**
Sausalito Hotel, **2**
Sausalito Yacht Club, **3**
Valhalla, **4**
Village Fair, **6**

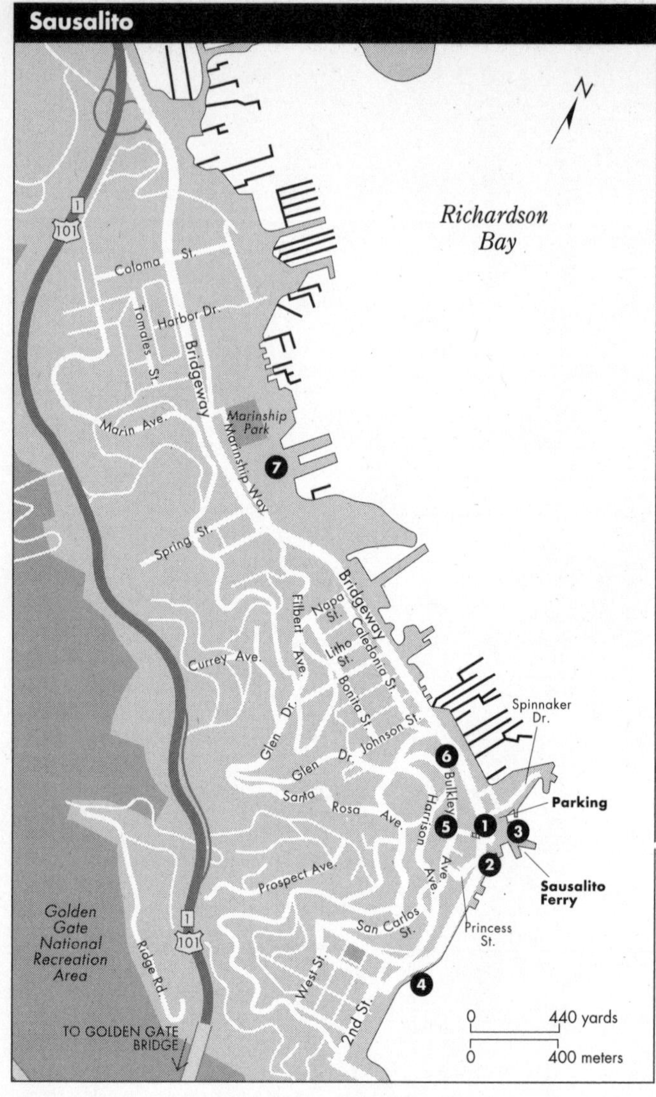

South on Bridgeway, toward San Francisco, an esplanade along the water affords picture-perfect views. Farther south are a number of restaurants on piers, including—near the end of Bridgeway at Richardson

4 Street—what was the **Valhalla** and is the oldest restaurant in Sausalito. Built in 1893 as "Walhalla," it was one of the settings for the film *The Lady from Shanghai* in the 1940s, Sally Stanford's place in the 1950s, and most recently a Chart House restaurant.

North on Bridgeway from the ferry terminal are yacht harbors and, parallel to Bridgeway a block to the west, the quieter Caledonia Street, with its own share of cafés and shops. There is a pleasant, grassy park with a children's playground at Caledonia and Litho streets, with a food shop nearby for picnic provisions.

Along the west side of Bridgeway are flights of steps that climb the hill to Sausalito's wooded, sometimes rustic and sometimes lavish residential

neighborhoods. The stairway called Excelsior, just across the street from
5 Vina del Mar Park, leads to the **Alta Mira,** a popular Spanish-style hotel and restaurant with a spectacular view (*see* Dining, *below*).

Where there isn't a hillside house or a restaurant or a yacht in Sausalito, there is a shop. Mostly along Bridgeway and Princess Street, they offer a wide assortment of casual and sophisticated clothing, posters and paintings, imported and handcrafted gifts, and the expected vari-
6 ety of T-shirts, ice cream, cookies, and pastries. The **Village Fair** (777 Bridgeway) is a four-story former warehouse that has been converted into a warren of clothing, craft, and gift boutiques. Crafts workers often demonstrate their talents in the shops, and a winding brick path—Little Lombard Street—connects various levels. The shopping complex is a haven during wet weather.

Sausalito's reputation as an art colony is enhanced by the **Art Festival** held during the three-day Labor Day weekend in September. It attracts more than 35,000 visitors to the waterfront area, and ferry service is extended to the site during the festival. Details are available from the Sausalito Chamber of Commerce (333 Caledonia St., 94965, ☎ 415/332–0505).

7 North on Bridgeway, within a few minutes' drive, is the **Bay Model,** a 400-square-foot replica of the entire San Francisco Bay and the San Joaquin–Sacramento River delta, which is used by the U.S. Army Corps of Engineers to reproduce the rise and fall of tides, the flow of currents, and the other physical forces at work on the bay. Housed in a former World War II shipyard building, the Bay Model is next to a display of shipbuilding history. At the same site is the Wapama, a World War I–era steam freighter being restored by volunteers. *2100 Bridgeway,* ☎ *415/332–3871.* ☛ *Free.* ⏲ *Tues.–Fri. 9–4, weekends 10–6; closed Sun. in winter.*

Along the shore of Richardson Bay, between the Bay Model and U.S. 101, are some of the 400 houseboats that make up Sausalito's "floating homes community." In the shallow tidelands, most of them float only about half the time, but their constant presence ensures a trademark view of the rustic, the eccentric, the flamboyant, and the elegant.

Just south of Sausalito, facing a cove beneath the Golden Gate Bridge, the **Bay Area Discovery Museum** fills five former military buildings with entertaining and enlightening hands-on exhibits. Youngsters and their families can crew on a boat, explore in and under a house, and make multitrack recordings. From San Francisco take the Alexander Avenue exit from U.S. 101 and follow signs to East Fort Baker. ☎ *415/487–4398.* ☛ *$5.* ⏲ *Wed.–Sun. 10–5, and Tues. 10–5 in summer; closed major holidays.*

Dining

Restaurants by the bay or perched on Sausalito's hillside feature prime views and fare that covers the waterfront. Most menus contain at least one heart-healthy pick on every menu. Casual dress is acceptable.

CATEGORY	COST*
$$$$	over $30
$$$	$20–$30
$$	$10–$20
$	under $10

**per person for a three-course meal, excluding drinks, service, and 7¼% sales tax*

$$$ **Gate Five.** The 80% seafood menu at this cozy, East Coast–style harborside restaurant includes Maine lobster, New England clam chowder, and fresh mussels. Ask to sit near one of the two fireplaces. ✕ *305 Harbor Dr., ☏ 415/331–5355. AE, DC, MC, V.*

$$$ **Mikayla.** Part of a hotel complex that includes a classic Victorian, a cluster of cottages, and terraced gardens stepping down the hillside, this upscale restaurant serves up fine American cuisine with French overtones and all-star views of the bay. The light, airy dining terrace with retractable roof and sliding glass walls is a great spot to splurge on a Sunday brunch buffet. ✕ *801 Bridgeway, ☏ 415/331–5888. Reservations advised. AE, D, DC, MC, V. No lunch Mon.–Sat.*

$$–$$$ **Alta Mira.** This Sausalito landmark, in a Spanish-style hotel a block above Bridgeway, has spectacular views of the bay from the heated front terrace and the windowed dining room. It's a favored destination Bay Area–wide for Sunday brunch (try the famed eggs Benedict and Ramos Fizz), an alfresco lunch, or cocktails at sunset. The California-Continental cuisine includes succulent rack of lamb, duckling, seafood salad, and a stellar Caesar salad. ✕ *125 Bulkley Ave., ☏ 415/332–1350. Reservations advised. AE, DC, MC, V.*

$$ **Spinnaker.** Spectacular bay views, homemade pastas, and seafood specialties like fresh grilled salmon are the prime attractions in this contemporary building on a point beyond the harbor, near the yacht club. You may see a pelican perched on one of the pilings just outside. ✕ *100 Spinnaker Dr., ☏ 415/332–1500. Reservations advised. Sun. brunch. AE, DC, MC, V.*

$–$$ **Margaritaville.** Exotic drinks and every Mexican favorite you'd ever crave from fajitas and enchiladas to *camarones ranchero* (fresh Pacific prawns sautéed in a flavorful red sauce) are on the bill of fare in a tropically hip setting with views of the marina and the bay. ✕ *1200 Bridgeway, ☏ 415/331–3226. Reservations accepted for 6 or more. AE, DC, MC, V.*

$ **Lighthouse Coffee Shop.** This budget-priced coffee shop serves breakfast and lunch (omelets, sandwiches, and burgers) every day from 6:30 (7 on weekends). Most find the down-to-earth atmosphere and simple fare (including Danish meatballs, herring, and salmon open-faced sandwiches) a welcome break from tourist traps and seafood extravaganzas. ✕ *1311 Bridgeway, ☏ 415/331–3034. No reservations. No credit cards. No alcohol.*

Sausalito Essentials

Arriving and Departing

BY BUS

Golden Gate Transit (☏ 415/332–6600) travels to Sausalito from 1st and Mission streets and other points in the city.

BY CAR

Cross the Golden Gate Bridge and head north on U.S. 101 to the Sausalito exit, then go south on Bridgeway to municipal parking near the center of town. The trip takes 20 to 45 minutes one-way. (Bring change for the parking lots' meters.)

BY FERRY

Golden Gate Ferry (☏ 415/332–6600) crosses the bay from the Ferry Building at Market Street and the Embarcadero; **Red and White Fleet** (☏ 415/546–2896) leaves from Pier 41 at Fisherman's Wharf. The trip takes 15–30 minutes.

Guided Tours

Most tour companies include Sausalito on excursions north to Muir Woods and the Napa Valley Wine Country. Among them are **Gray Line** (☎ 415/558–9400) and **Great Pacific Tour Co.** (☎ 415/626–4499).

TIBURON

Located on a peninsula called Punta de Tiburon (Shark Point) by the Spanish explorers, this Marin County community has maintained its village atmosphere. The harbor faces Angel Island across Raccoon Strait, and San Francisco is directly south, 6 miles across the bay—which makes the view from the decks of restaurants on the harbor a major attraction. More low-key than Sausalito, Tiburon has always been a waterfront settlement, beginning in 1884 when ferryboats from San Francisco connected here with a railroad to San Rafael. Whenever the weather is pleasant, and particularly during the summer, the ferry is the most relaxing way to visit and avoid traffic and parking problems.

Exploring

Tiburon's main street is indeed called **Main Street.** It's lined on the bay side with restaurants that overlook the harbor and offer views of San Francisco from outdoor decks. Sunday brunch is especially popular. On the other side of the narrow street are shops and galleries that sell casual clothing, gifts, jewelry, posters, and paintings. One gallery is devoted to a visual celebration of food. West along Main Street is **Ark Row.** During the 19th century these buildings were houseboats on the bay. Later they were beached and transformed into shops; now they are antiques and specialty stores along a tree-lined walk. On a hill above town is **Old St. Hilary's Historic Preserve,** a Victorian-era church operated by the Landmarks Society as a historical and botanical museum. The surrounding area is a wildflower preserve. *Esperanza and Alemany Sts., ☎ 415/435–1853. ☛ Free. ⌚ Apr.–Oct., Wed. and Sun. 1–4.*

Between Tiburon Boulevard and Richardson Bay, in a wildlife sanctuary on the route into town, is the 1876 **Lyford House** (☎ 415/388–2524), a Victorian fantasy that is now the western headquarters for the National Audubon Society. House tours are conducted on Sunday afternoon.

Dining

Tiburon's restaurants specialize in prime bay views and seafood prepared simply or with Mexican, Italian, or Chinese touches. The informal dining and drinking cafés along Main Street also serve a wide variety of lunch and brunch fare. Dress is casual.

CATEGORY	COST*
$$$$	over $30
$$$	$20–$30
$$	$10–$20
$	under $10

**per person for a three-course meal, excluding drinks, service, and 7¼% sales tax*

$$ Guaymas. This large open kitchen churns out regional Mexican dishes such as *pato de granja* (roasted duck with pumpkin-seed sauce), *carnitas ropa* (slowly roasted pork with salsa and black beans), and *pollo en mole* (chicken with chocolate sauce, chilis, and 29 spices). Steaming tortillas and three different kinds of salsa are a welcome alternative to chips. Adobe walls are whitewashed and decorated with colorful

Mexican toys, and the heated terrace bar has spectacular views of the bay. ✕ *5 Main St., at the ferry terminal,* ☎ *415/435–6300. Reservations advised. Sun. brunch. DC, MC, V.*

$$ **Mr. Q's.** Located on an upper level over the harbor, this casual and crowded restaurant is best known for the view from its deck, which extends farther onto the bay than those of its competitors. Jazz and rock groups play on weekends. Steaks, ribs, chicken, salads, and fresh seafood are popular here; pasta, sandwiches, salads, and a variety of drinks are offered for lunch and dinner. Brunch is served every day. ✕ *25 Main St.,* ☎ *415/435–5088. Reservations advised for dinner, not accepted for lunch. AE, DC, MC, V.*

$$ **Sam's Anchor Cafe.** Perhaps the most well-known restaurant in Tiburon, Sam's is a major draw for tourists and locals who flock to its outside deck for bay views and beer. A college hangout since 1921, the informal restaurant has mahogany wainscoting, old photos on the walls, and crayons and a color-in menu for the kids. Burgers, fresh seafood, sandwiches, soups, and salads are the bill of fare; you can also eat popcorn straight out of an old-fashioned popper. ✕ *27 Main St.,* ☎ *415/435–4527. Reservations for dinner only. AE, D, DC, MC, V.*

$ **Sweden House Bakery & Café.** This dollhouse-like, painted-wood café is a cozy place for pastries and coffee or sandwiches (shrimp salad, chicken salad with walnuts, and Swedish meat loaf are good choices). The secluded deck outside is nice on sunny days (although a sign warns, "Please Watch Your Food or the Birds Will Eat It"). A takeout bakery caters to those on the run. ✕ *35 Main St.,* ☎ *415/435–9767. No reservations. No dinner. MC, V.*

Tiburon Essentials

Arriving and Departing

BY BUS

Golden Gate Transit (☎ 415/332–6600) sends buses to Tiburon from 1st and Mission streets and other points in San Francisco and also from Sausalito.

BY CAR

Take U.S. 101 north to the Tiburon Boulevard exit. The trip takes 30 minutes to one hour one-way.

BY FERRY

Red and White Fleet (☎ 415/546–2896) ferries depart weekdays in the early morning, late afternoon, and evening from the Ferry Building. Ferries also depart midday on weekdays and all day on weekends from Pier 41. The trip takes a half hour. Ferry service is available across the strait from Tiburon to Angel Island (☎ 415/435–2131).

THE MARIN HEADLANDS

"The Golden Gate" originally referred not to a bridge painted "international orange" but to the grassy and poppy-strewn hills flanking the passageway into San Francisco Bay. This is the one break in the Coast Range Mountains that allows the rivers of California's 400-mile-long Central Valley to reach the ocean. The most dramatic scenery is on the north side of the gate—the Marin Headlands. Once the site of military installations, they are now open to the public as part of the Golden Gate National Recreation Area. The most spectacular photographs of San Francisco are taken from the headlands, with the Golden Gate Bridge in the foreground and the city skyline on the horizon. There are remarkable views east across the bay, north along the coast, and out to sea, where the Farallon Islands are visible on a clear day.

Exploring

Although they are only a short distance from San Francisco, the headlands are a world apart—a vast expanse of wild and open terrain. There are windswept ridges, stretches of shrubs and wildflowers, protected valleys, and obscure beaches. The views can be breathtaking, even when fog is rushing over the hills into the bay. The weather can change dramatically within a few hours, however. Dress warmly and wear appropriate shoes for walking. Stay on marked paths and park in designated areas.

The **Marin Headlands Visitors Center** at Fort Cronkhite is the center for exploring the region, which includes Rodeo Beach, Rodeo Lagoon, and the Point Bonita lighthouse. ☎ *415/331–1540.* ⏲ *Daily 9:30–4:30.*

Also at Fort Cronkhite is the **California Marine Mammal Center** (☎ 415/289–7325), which rescues and rehabilitates sick and injured seals and sea lions. Campsites are available, and at nearby Fort Barry there is the Golden Gate Hostel (☎ 415/331–2777). For advance planning, detailed maps are available at the Golden Gate National Recreation Area headquarters in Fort Mason, Bay and Franklin streets, in San Francisco (☎ 415/556–0560).

Conzelman Road offers the most spectacular views of the gate, and craggy **Hawk Hill** is the best place on the West Coast from which to watch the migration of eagles, hawks, and falcons as they fly south for the winter from mid-August to mid-December. As many as 1,000 have been sighted in a single day. The viewing area is about 2 miles up Conzelman Road; look for a sign denoting former military Battery 129.

The Marin Headlands Essentials

Arriving and Departing

BY BUS

San Francisco Muni (☎ 415/673–6864) Bus 76 runs hourly from 4th and Townsend streets on Sundays and holidays only. The trip takes 45 minutes one-way.

BY CAR

The headlands are a logical side trip on the way to Sausalito, but reaching them can be tricky. Take U.S. 101 across the Golden Gate Bridge to the first exit, Alexander Avenue, just past Vista Point. Then take the first left turn through a tunnel under the highway and look for signs to Fort Barry and Fort Cronkhite. Conzelman Road follows the cliffs that face the gate; Bunker Road is a less spectacular route through Rodeo to the headlands headquarters at Fort Cronkhite.

MUIR WOODS

One hundred and fifty million years ago, ancestors of redwood and sequoia trees grew throughout the United States. Today the *Sequoia sempervirens* can be found only in a narrow, cool coastal belt from Monterey to Oregon. (*Sequoiadendron gigantea* grows in the Sierra Nevada.) **Muir Woods National Monument,** 17 miles northwest of San Francisco, is a 550-acre park that contains one of the most majestic redwood groves in the world. Some redwoods in the park are nearly 250 feet tall and 1,000 years old. This grove was saved from destruction in 1908 and named for naturalist John Muir, whose campaigns helped to establish the National Park system. His response: "This is the best tree-lover's monument that could be found in all of the forests of the world. Saving these woods from the axe and saw is in many ways the most notable service to God and man I have heard of since my forest wandering began."

Exploring

Muir Woods is a pedestrian's park; no cars are allowed in the redwood grove itself. Beginning from the park headquarters, 6 miles of easy trails cross streams and pass through ferns and azaleas as well as magnificent stands of redwoods, including Bohemian Grove and the circular formation called Cathedral Grove. The main trail along Redwood Creek is 1 mile long, paved, and wheelchair accessible. All the trails connect with an extensive network of hiking tails in Mt. Tamalpais State Park. No picnicking or camping is allowed, but snacks are available at the visitor center, along with a wide selection of books and exhibits. The weather is usually cool and often wet, so dress warmly and wear shoes appropriate for damp trails. Pets are not allowed. ☎ *415/388–2595.* ⏲ *Daily 8 AM–sunset.*

Muir Woods Essentials

Arriving and Departing

BY CAR

Take U.S. 101 north to the Mill Valley–Muir Woods exit. The trip takes 45 minutes one-way when the roads are clear, but allow extra time for traffic on summer weekends. The park staff recommends visiting before 10 AM and after 4 PM to avoid congestion. Note that the narrow, winding entrance road cannot accommodate some larger recreation vehicles.

Guided Tours

Most tour companies include Muir Woods on excursions to the Wine Country, among them **Gray Line** (☎ 415/558–9400) and **Great Pacific Tour Co.** (☎ 415/626–4499).

MT. TAMALPAIS STATE PARK

Although the summit of Mt. Tamalpais is less than ½-mile high, the mountain rises practically from sea level and dominates the topography of Marin County. Located about 18 miles northwest of San Francisco, adjacent to Muir Woods National Monument, Mt. Tamalpais offers views of the entire Bay Area and west to the Pacific Ocean from its summit. On foggy days lower elevations are sometimes blanketed by the fog, with other peaks just visible above. For years this 6,400-acre park has been a favorite destination for hikers. There are 50 miles of trails, some rugged but many developed for easy walking through meadows, grasslands, and forests, and along creeks.

Exploring

Panoramic Highway—the winding "Pan Toll Road" was once a toll road—leads to the three peaks and the 2,571-foot summit of Mt. Tamalpais. Along the route are numerous parking areas, picnic spots, scenic overlooks, and trailheads. The **Mountain Theater,** a natural amphitheater with terraced stone seats, is used for plays and musicals in May and June. The relatively gentle **West Point Trail** begins here. A map of hiking trails is available from the ranger station, about 4 miles from the intersection of Panoramic Highway and the road down the hill to Muir Woods. ☎ *415/388–2070.* ⏲ *Daily 7–6.*

Mt. Tamalpais State Park Essentials

Arriving and Departing

BY BUS

Golden Gate Transit (☏ 415/332–6600) departs from 1st and Mission streets and other points in the city on Saturday, Sunday, and holidays only.

BY CAR

Take U.S. 101 north over the Golden Gate Bridge to the Mill Valley–Muir Woods exit. From this road (Shoreline Highway), take Panoramic Highway into the park. The trip takes one hour one-way.

POINT REYES

By Dan Spitzer

Point Reyes frames the northern end of Drake's Bay. When Sir Francis sailed down the California coast in 1579 he missed the Golden Gate and San Francisco Bay, but he did land at what he described as a convenient harbor. It may have been Drake's Bay, Bolinas Bay, Bodega Bay, or somewhere else along Point Reyes. With its high rolling grassland above spectacular cliffs, Point Reyes probably reminded him of Scotland. Today Point Reyes National Seashore is a spectacularly beautiful park and a favorite spot for whale-watching.

Exploring

Past the turnoff for Muir Woods, Highway 1 takes you past the town of **Stinson Beach,** which takes its name from one of the longest (4,500 feet) and most popular stretches of sand in Marin County. Along Bolinas Lagoon, just north of Stinson Beach, you'll find the **Audubon Canyon Ranch,** a 1,000-acre bird sanctuary. During the spring the public is invited to view great blue heron and great egret tree nests. There is also a small museum with a picnic area and displays on the geology and natural history of the region. ☏ *415/868–9244.* ☛ *Free.* ⏲ *Mid-Mar.–mid-July, weekends and holidays only 10–4.*

At the northern edge of Bolinas Lagoon, a couple of miles beyond the Audubon Canyon Ranch, follow the unmarked road running west from Highway 1. This leads to the sleepy town of **Bolinas.** Some residents are so wary of tourism that whenever the state tries to post signs, they tear them down. Birders should take Mesa Road until they reach the **Point Reyes Bird Observatory,** a sanctuary that harbors nearly 350 species. ☏ *415/868–0655.* ☛ *Free.* ⏲ *Daily 9–5.*

As you drive back to Bolinas, go right on Overlook Drive and right again on Elm Avenue until you come to Duxberry Reef, known for its fine tide pools.

Returning to Highway 1, you will pass a number of horse farms. About ⅓ mile past Olema, look for a sign marking the turnoff for **Point Reyes National Seashore's Bear Valley Visitors Center.** The center has some fine exhibits of park wildlife, and helpful rangers can advise you on beaches, visits to the lighthouse for whale-watching (the season for gray-whale migration is mid-December–March), as well as on hiking trails and camping. Camping is free, but reservations should be made through the visitor center. A brilliantly reconstructed Miwok Indian Village is situated a short walk from the center. It provides insight into the daily lives of the first inhabitants of this region. The lighthouse is a very pretty, 30–40-minute drive from the visitor center, across rolling hills that resemble Scottish heaths. On busy weekends, parking at the lighthouse may be difficult. If you don't care to walk down—and back up—hundreds of steps, you may want to skip the descent to the lighthouse itself. You *can* see whales from the cliffs above the lighthouse, but it's worth the effort to get the lighthouse view. ☎ *415/663–1092.* ☛ *Free.* ⌚ *Daily 9–5.*

Dining

Fresh seafood and local produce are best bets on a trip up to Point Reyes, and most of the following restaurants make good use of these ingredients in their meals. This area is also perfect for picnicking. So if you prefer the great outdoors, consider packing a lunch to take along on your wanderings. Restaurants hereabouts are generally casual and have no dress code.

CATEGORY	COST*
$$$	$15–$20
$$	$10–$15
$	under $10

**per person for a three-course meal, excluding drinks, service, and 7¼% sales tax*

$$$ Manka's. Regional cuisine featuring fresh-caught fish and wild game (venison, caribou, elk, quail) is served with style in this renovated 1917 hunting lodge. Candlelight, lush floral bouquets, food quotes on the wood-paneled walls, and a large fireplace provide an inimitable intimate atmosphere. Vegetarian specials are always available, and the small-plate menu on Monday is a bargain. ✕ *30 Callendar Way, corner of Callendar Way and Argyll Way, Inverness,* ☎ *415/669–1034. Reservations advised. AE, MC, V. Dinner Thurs.–Mon. Closed Thurs. in Jan. and Feb.*

$$ Buckeye Roadhouse. The atmosphere here is a blast from the past with a '90s twist: mahogany paneling, huge stone fireplace, hunting-lodge decor, and a view of Richardson Bay. Traditional American fare includes seafood, baby back ribs, lamb shank, and New Orleans gumbo. The Buckeye also uses prime native-Marin ingredients in dishes like smoked Petaluma duck with wild rice. ✕ *15 Shoreline Hwy., Mill Valley,* ☎ *415/331–2600. Reservations advised. Sun. brunch. D, DC, MC, V.*

$$ Sand Dollar. The owner is the local fire chief and this is the only bar in town, so you're sure to meet lots of locals lingering inside by the fire on foggy days or out on the deck when the sun breaks through. Burgers and fries, salads, and sandwiches are a good bet at lunch; fresh fish selections and pastas with scallops, mussels, and clams are great for dinner; the homemade soups and sinfully sweet mud pie are a hit anytime. ✕ *3458 Hwy. 1, Stinson Beach,* ☎ *415/868–0434. Reservations advised on weekends. Sun. brunch. MC, V.*

$–$$ Pelican Inn. Hearty English fare—from fish-and-chips to prime rib and Yorkshire pudding—is served with a fine selection of imported beers and ales. Old farm tools hang above a large open hearth in the wood-paneled dining room, and the bar has the convivial ambience of a pub in the Cotswolds. Ask the hostess if you can peek at the antiques-filled rooms upstairs; you'll think you're in England. ✕ *10 Pacific Way, Muir Beach (off Hwy. 1),* ☎ *415/383–6000. Reservations advised for 6 or more. Sun. brunch buffet. MC, V. Closed Mon. except to guests.*

$–$$ Station House Cafe. Prints by local photographers decorate the light-filled, rust-and-green interior of this local favorite, and a garden offers alfresco dining in good weather. Breakfast, lunch, and dinner are served. The grilled chicken and salmon specialties and seafood pasta dishes like fettuccine and barbecued oysters are a predictable hit. ✕ *11180 Hwy. 1, Point Reyes Station,* ☎ *415/663–1515. Reservations advised. MC, V.*

$ **Grey Whale.** This is a good place for pizza, salad, vegetarian lasagna, pastries and coffee, for lunch or dinner. The patio overlooks the parking lot, but a view of paradise, complete with bay and mountains, lies just beyond. ✕ *Sir Francis Drake Blvd. in the center of Inverness,* ☎ *415/669–1244. No reservations. MC, V.*

Point Reyes Essentials

Arriving and Departing

Take U.S. 101 north over the Golden Gate Bridge to the Mill Valley–Muir Woods exit and take Highway 1 north. You'll pass the turnoffs for Muir Woods and Mt. Tamalpais. If you have the energy for a long day of exploring, you can combine a trip to Point Reyes with a trip to Muir Woods or Mt. Tamalpais, but you'll need well over an hour to get to the visitor center and two hours to get all the way from San Francisco to the end of the point.

BERKELEY

By Robert Taylor

Berkeley and the University of California are not synonymous, although the founding campus of the state university system dominates the city's heritage and contemporary life. But the city of 100,000 facing San Francisco across the bay has other interesting features for visitors. Berkeley is culturally diverse and politically adventurous, a breeding ground for social trends, a continuing bastion of the counterculture, and an important center for Bay Area writers, artists, and musicians. Indeed, the city's liberal reputation and determined spirit have led detractors to describe it in recent years as the People's Republic of Berkeley.

Named for George Berkeley, the Irish philosopher and clergyman who crossed the Atlantic to convert the Indians and wrote "Westward, the course of empire takes its way," the city grew with the university. The latter was created by the state legislature in 1868 and established five years later on a rising plain of oak trees split by Strawberry Canyon. The central campus occupies 178 acres of the scenic 1,282-acre property, with most buildings located from Bancroft Way north to Hearst Street and from Oxford Street east into the Berkeley Hills. The university has more than 30,000 students and a full-time faculty of 1,600. It is considered one of the nation's leading intellectual centers and a major site for scientific research.

Exploring

Numbers in the margin correspond to points of interest on the Berkeley map.

❶ The visitor center (☎ 510/642–5215) in **University Hall** at University Avenue and Oxford Street is open weekdays 8:30–4:30. There are maps and brochures for self-guided walks; 1½-hour student-guided tours leave Monday, Wednesday, and Friday at 10 AM and 1 PM.

❷ At **Sproul Plaza,** just inside the campus at Telegraph Avenue and Bancroft Way, the lively panorama of political and social activists, musicians, class-bound students, and food vendors along Bancroft Way give credence to U.C. Berkeley's reputation as a "university within a park."

TIME OUT Some people insist that without its cafés Berkeley would simply collapse. No fewer than 55 peacefully coexist within 1 square mile of the U.C. campus. Cafés of all persuasions serve every kind of coffee concoction, along with light meals. They are where people read, discuss, and debate, or eavesdrop on others doing the same. A few among the many: **Caffe Mediterraneum** (2475 Telegraph Ave., ☎ 510/549-1128) is a relic of '60s-era Berkeley but far enough from campus to pull in a mostly nonstudent crowd. Allen Ginsberg wrote while imbibing here. **Caffe Strada** (2300 College Ave., ☎ 510/843-5282) has a sprawling patio where frat boys, sorority sisters, and foreigners meet and greet; try the iced white-chocolate mocha. The **Musical Offering** (2430 Bancroft Way, ☎ 510/849-0211) serves light meals and coffee; in back there's a music store specializing in classical CDs and cassettes.

The university's suggested tour circles the upper portion of the central
campus, past buildings that were sited to take advantage of vistas to
the Golden Gate across the bay. The first campus plan was proposed
by Frederick Law Olmsted, who designed New York's Central Park;
over the years the university's architects have also included Bernard
Maybeck and Julia Morgan (who designed Hearst Castle at San
3 Simeon). Beyond Sproul Plaza is the bronze **Sather Gate,** built in 1909,
and the former south entrance to the campus; the university expanded
a block beyond its traditional boundary in the 1960s. Up a walkway
4 to the right is vine-covered **South Hall,** one of two remaining buildings
that greeted the first students in 1873.

5 Just ahead is **Sather Tower,** popularly known as the Campanile, the campus landmark that can be seen for miles. The 307-foot tower was modeled on St. Mark's tower in Venice and was completed in 1914. The carillon, which was cast in England, is played three times a day. In the lobby of the tower is a photographic display of campus history. An elevator takes visitors 175 feet up to the observation deck. ☛ *50¢.* ⏲ *Daily 10–3:15.*

6 Opposite the Campanile is **Bancroft Library,** with a rare-book collection and a changing series of exhibits that may include a Shakespeare first folio or a gold-rush diary. On permanent display is a gold nugget purported to be the one that started the rush to California when it was discovered on January 24, 1848.

7 Across University Drive to the north is the **Earth Sciences Building,** with
a seismograph for measuring earthquakes. Another scientific wonder
8 is the **Paleontology Museum,** whose public displays line the lobby and
hall of the Valley Life Sciences Building south of University Drive. The
casted skeleton of a 40-foot Tyrannosaurus rex hangs in the building's
three-story atrium. ☎ *510/642–1821.* ☛ *Free.* ⏲ *When the univer-*
sity is in session, weekdays 8–5, Sat. 1–4.

The university's two major museums are on the south side of campus
9 near Bancroft Way. The **Phoebe Apperson Hearst Museum of Anthro-**
pology (formerly the Lowie), in Kroeber Hall, has a collection of more
than 4,000 artifacts. Items on display may cover the archaeology of ancient America or the crafts of Pacific Islanders. The museum also houses
the collection of artifacts made by Ishi, the lone survivor of a California Indian tribe who was brought to the Bay Area in 1911. ☎ *510/642–*
3681. Nominal ☛ *charge.* ⏲ *Tues.–Fri. 10–4:30, weekends noon–4:30.*

10 The **University Art Museum** is a fan-shaped building with a spiral of ramps and balcony galleries. It houses a collection of Asian and Western art, including a major group of Hans Hofmann's abstract paintings, and also displays touring exhibits. On the ground floor is the Pacific Film Archive, which offers daily programs of historic and contemporary films. *2626 Bancroft Way,* ☎ *510/642–0808; for film-program information, 510/642–1124.* ☛ *Museum: $6, $4 senior citizens.* ⏲ *Museum: Wed. and Fri.–Sun. 11–5, Thurs. 11–9.*

Bancroft Library, **6**
Botanical Garden, **13**
Cody's Books, **15**
Earth Sciences Building, **7**
Faculty Glade, **11**
Hearst Greek Theatre, **12**
Lawrence Hall of Science, **14**
Leopold Records, **17**
Moe's, **16**
Paleontology Museum, **8**
Phoebe Apperson Hearst Museum of Anthropology, **9**
Sather Gate, **3**
Sather Tower, **5**
South Hall, **4**
Sproul Plaza, **2**
University Art Museum, **10**
University Hall (Visitors Center), **1**

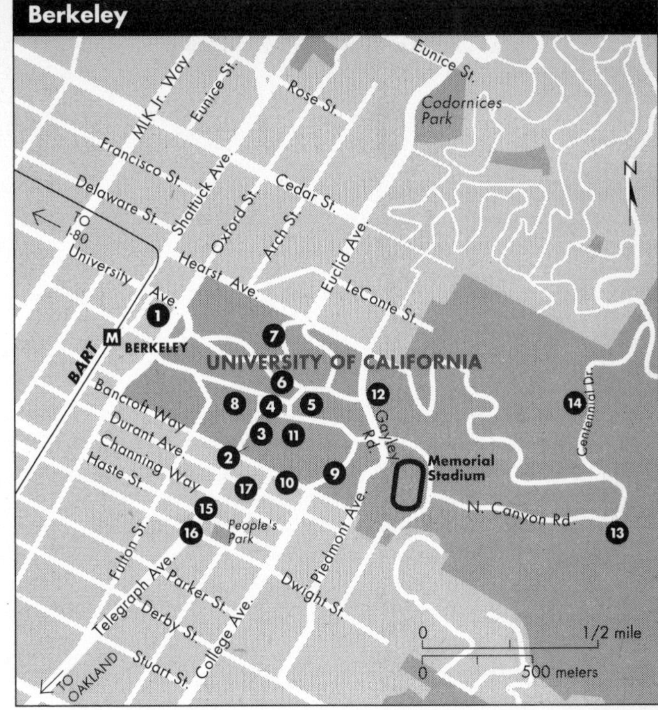

Many of the university's notable attractions are outdoors. Just south
11 of the Campanile near the rustic Faculty Club is **Faculty Glade** on the south fork of Strawberry Creek, one of the best examples of the university's attempt to preserve a parklike atmosphere. East of the cen-
12 tral campus, across Gayley Road, is the **Hearst Greek Theatre,** built in 1903 and seating 7,000. Sarah Bernhardt once performed here; now it is used for major musical events.

13 Above the Greek Theatre in Strawberry Canyon is the 30-acre **Botanical Garden,** with a collection of some 25,000 species. It's a relaxing gathering spot with benches and picnic tables. ⏲ *Daily 9–4:45.*

Perched on a hill above the campus on Centennial Drive is the fortresslike
14 **Lawrence Hall of Science,** which is a laboratory, a science education center, and—most important to visitors—a dazzling display of scientific knowledge and experiments. Displays are updated regularly. On weekends there are additional films, lectures, and demonstrations, especially for children. ☎ *510/642–5132.* ☛ *$6 adults, $4 senior citizens and students.* ⏲ *Weekdays 10–5.*

Beyond the university, Berkeley is a rewarding city to explore. Just south of the campus on **Telegraph Avenue** is the busy student-oriented district, full of cafés, bookstores, poster shops, and street vendors with traditional and trendy crafts items. Shops come and go with the times,
15 but among the neighborhood landmarks are **Cody's Books** (2454 Tele-
16 graph Ave.), with its adjacent café; **Moe's** (2476 Telegraph Ave.), with a huge selection of used books; and three of the Bay Area's best music
17 stores: Amoeba Music (2455 Telegraph Ave.), **Leopold Records** (2518 Durant Ave.), and Rasputin's Records (2350 Telegraph Ave.). This district was the center of student protests during the 1960s, and on the street it sometimes looks as if that era still lives (it can be unruly at

night). People's Park, one of the centers of protest, is just east of Telegraph between Haste Street and Dwight Way.

Downtown Berkeley around University and Shattuck avenues is nondescript. However, there are shops for browsing along College Avenue near Ashby Avenue south of campus and in the Walnut Square development at Shattuck and Vine streets northwest of campus. Shingled houses line the tree-shaded streets near College and Ashby avenues, and hillside homes with spectacular views can be seen on the winding roads near the intersection of Ashby and Claremont avenues, around the Claremont Hotel (*see* Exploring *in* Oakland, *below*). At the opposite side of the city, on 4th Street north of University Avenue, an industrial area has been converted into a pleasant shopping street with several popular eateries.

Dining

Food is a priority in Berkeley, where specialty markets, cheese stores, charcuteries, coffee vendors, produce outlets, innovative restaurants, and ethnic eateries abound. The most popular gourmet ghetto is along Shattuck Avenue, a few blocks north of University Avenue. University Avenue itself has become a corridor of good Indian, Thai, and Cambodian restaurants. You'll find lots of students, interesting coffeehouses, and cheap eats on Telegraph, Durant, and Berkeley avenues near the campus. Casual dress is considered politically correct wherever you dine.

CATEGORY	COST*
$$$$	over $30
$$$	$20–$30
$$	$10–$20
$	under $10

**per person for a three-course meal, excluding drinks, service, and 8¼% sales tax*

$$–$$$$ **Chez Panisse Café & Restaurant.** President Clinton has joined the ranks of luminaries who have dined at this legendary eatery, but like anyone else without a reservation, he sat in the upstairs café. Alice Waters is still the mastermind behind the culinary wizardry, with Jean-Pierre Moullé lending hands-on talent as head chef. In the downstairs restaurant, where redwood paneling, a fireplace, and lavish floral arrangements create the ambience of a private home, dinners are prix fixe and pricey, but the cost is lower on weekdays and almost halved on Monday. The daily-changing menu includes local rock cod with ginger sauce, sirloin roast with red wine sauce, pasta specialties, and roast truffled breast of guinea hen. Upstairs in the café the atmosphere is informal, the crowd livelier, the prices lower, and the menu more simple, with dishes such as calzone with goat cheese, mozzarella, prosciutto, and garlic. ✕ *1517 Shattuck Ave., north of University Ave. Restaurant (downstairs):* ☎ *510/548–5525; reservations required; no lunch. Café (upstairs):* ☎ *510/548–5049; same-day reservations; Fri. and Sat. dinner, walk-ins only. 15% service charge added to each bill. AE, D, DC, MC, V. Closed Sun.*

$$$ **Rivoli.** Husband and wife team Wendy Rucker and Roscoe Skipper use native California ingredients in French- and Italian-inspired dishes for a menu that changes weekly. Highlights are linguine with scallops; braised veal stew; ricotta tart with prosciutto, figs, salsa verde, and mizuna; and rigatoni with eggplant, olives and feta cheese. Desserts include a pear granita with ginger snaps, bittersweet chocolate *tiramisù* with expresso crème anglaise, and home-style hot-fudge sundae. ✕ *1539 Solano Ave.,* ☎ *510/526–2542. Reservations recommended. AE, MC, V. No lunch.*

$$ **Spenger's Fish Grotto.** This rambling, boisterous seafood restaurant is known for hearty portions of fairly ordinary food. It's a wildly popular place, though, so expect a wait in their combination oyster/sports bar, or opt for the take-out section next door and eat your fish alfresco on the Berkeley pier at the foot of University Avenue. ✕ *1919 4th St., near University Ave. and I–80,* ☏ *510/845–7771. Reservations for 5 or more. AE, D, DC, MC, V.*

$$ **Venezia Caffe & Ristorante.** This family-friendly eatery was one of the first to serve fresh pasta in the Bay Area, and it continues to offer a wide range of tasty selections (don't miss their house-made chicken sausage). The large dining room looks like a Venetian piazza, with a fountain in the middle, murals on the walls, and laundry hanging overhead. Children get their own menu, free antipasti, and crayons. ✕ *1799 University Ave.,* ☏ *510/849–4681. Reservations advised. AE, DC, MC, V. No lunch weekends.*

Berkeley Essentials

Arriving and Departing

BY CAR

Take I–80 east across the Bay Bridge, then the University Avenue exit through downtown Berkeley to the campus, or take the Ashby Avenue exit and turn left on Telegraph Avenue to the traditional campus entrance; there is a parking garage on Channing Way. The trip takes a half hour one-way (except in rush hour).

BY PUBLIC TRANSPORTATION

BART (☏ 415/992–2278) trains run under the bay to the downtown Berkeley exit; transfer to the Humphrey GoBart shuttle bus to campus. The trip takes from 45 minutes to one hour one-way.

OAKLAND

Originally the site of ranches, farms, a grove of redwood trees, and, of course, clusters of oaks, Oakland has long been a warmer and more spacious alternative to San Francisco. By the end of the 19th century, Mediterranean-style homes and gardens had been developed as summer estates. With swifter transportation, Oakland became a bedroom community for San Francisco; then it progressed to California's fastest-growing industrial city. In recent decades, Oakland has struggled to upgrade its image as a tourist destination. However, the major attractions remain the same as they ever were: the parks and civic buildings around Lake Merritt, which was created from a tidal basin in 1898; the port area, now named Jack London Square, where the author spent much of his time at the turn of the century; and the scenic roads and parks along the crest of the Oakland-Berkeley hills. Also in the hills is the castlelike Claremont Resort Hotel, a landmark since 1915, as well as more sprawling parks with lakes and miles of hiking trails.

Exploring

Numbers in the margin correspond to points of interest on the Oakland map.

❶ If there is one reason to visit Oakland, it is to explore the **Oakland Museum of California,** an inviting series of landscaped buildings that display the state's art, history, and natural science. It is the best possible introduction to a tour of California, and its dramatic and detailed exhibits can help fill the gaps on a brief visit. The natural-science department displays a typical stretch of California from the Pacific Ocean to the

Nevada border, including plants and wildlife. A breathtaking film, *Fast Flight,* condenses the trip into five minutes. The museum's sprawling history section includes everything from Spanish-era artifacts and a gleaming fire engine that battled the flames in San Francisco in 1906 to 1960s souvenirs of the "summer of love." The California Dream exhibit recalls a century of inspirations. The museum's art department includes mystical landscapes painted by the state's pioneers, as well as contemporary visions. There is a pleasant museum café for lunch and outdoor areas for relaxing. *1000 Oak St., at 10th St.,* ☎ *510/834–2413.* ☛ *$4 adults, $2 children 7–18, free children under 7.* ⌚ *Wed.–Sat. 10–5, Sun. noon–7.*

2 Near the museum, **Lake Merritt** is a 155-acre oasis surrounded by parks and paths, with several outdoor attractions on the north side.
3 The **Natural Science Center and Waterfowl Refuge** attracts birds by the hundreds during winter months. *At the foot of Perkins St.,* ☎ *510/238–3739.* ⌚ *Daily 10–5.*

4 **Children's Fairyland** is a low-key amusement park with a puppet theater, small merry-go-round, and settings based on nursery rhymes. *Grand Ave. at Park View Terr.,* ☎ *510/452–2259. Nominal admission charge.* ⌚ *Summer, daily 10–4:30; winter, weekends 10–4:30.*

5 The **Lakeside Park Garden Center** has a Japanese garden and many native flowers and plants. *666 Bellevue Ave.,* ☎ *510/238–3208.* ☛ *Free.* ⌚ *Daily 10–3 or later in summer; closed Thanksgiving, Dec. 25, Jan. 1.*

Jack London, although born in San Francisco, spent his early years in Oakland before shipping out for adventures that inspired *The Call of the Wild, The Sea Wolf, Martin Eden,* and *The Cruise of the Snark.* He
6 is commemorated with a bronze bust on what is now called **Jack Lon-**
7 **don's Waterfront,** at the foot of Broadway. A livelier landmark is **Heinhold's First and Last Chance Saloon,** one of his hangouts. Next door is the reassembled Klondike cabin in which he spent a winter. Restaurants cluster around the plaza, and the nearby Jack London Village has specialty shops and restaurants. The best local collection of the author's letters, manuscripts, and photographs is in the Jack London Room at the Oakland Main Library (125 14th St., ☎ 510/238–3134). Oakland's downtown has been undergoing redevelopment for many years, and is finally becoming a destination for visitors and residents alike. A number of community events have settled down at the plaza at Jack London Square, ranging from boat and auto shows to a farmers' market every Sunday. Other areas for shopping, browsing, or just relaxing at a café can be found on Lake Shore Avenue northeast of Lake Merritt, Piedmont Avenue near the Broadway exit from I–580, and College Avenue west of Broadway in North Oakland, which neighbors BART's Rockridge station. From the station, the local Bus 51 will take visitors to the University of California campus, about 1½ miles away in Berkeley.

The East Bay Regional Park District (☎ 510/562–7275) offers 46 parks in an area covering 60,000 acres to residents and visitors. In the Oakland hills is **Redwood Regional Park,** accessible from Joaquin Miller Road off Highway 13, to which Ashby Avenue will lead you. In the Berkeley hills is the 2,000-acre **Tilden Park,** which includes a lake and children's playground and is accessible from Grizzly Peak Boulevard off Claremont Avenue. There are scenic views of the Bay Area from roads that link the hilltop parks: Redwood Road, Skyline Boulevard, and Grizzly Peak Boulevard. Parks are open daily during daylight hours.

Children's Fairyland, **4**
Heinhold's First and Last Chance Saloon, **7**
Jack London's Waterfront, **6**
Lake Merritt, **2**
Lakeside Park Garden Center, **5**
Natural Science Center and Waterfowl Refuge, **3**
Oakland Museum of California, **1**

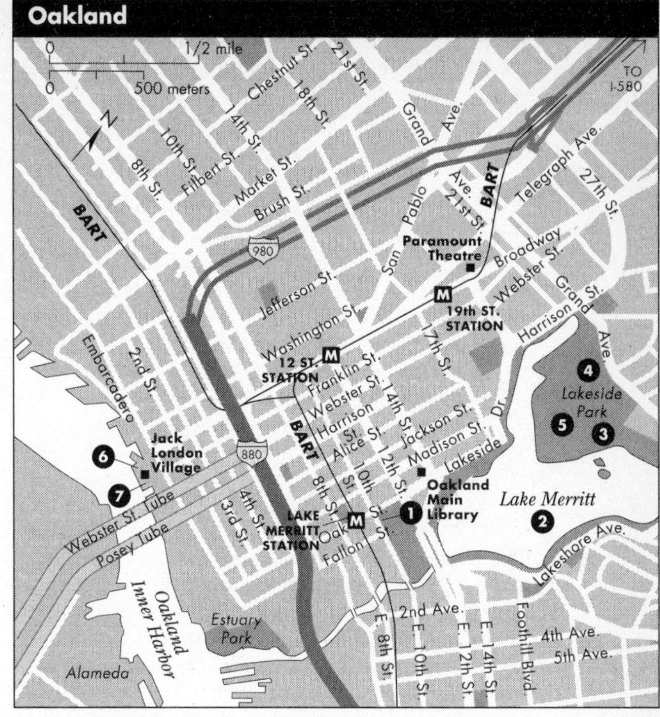

Off the Beaten Track

Given the city's reputation for Victorian and Craftsman housing, visitors to Oakland are generally surprised by the profusion of Art Deco architecture in the neighborhood around the 19th Street BART station downtown. Some of these buildings have fallen into disrepair, but the **Paramount Theater** (2025 Broadway, ☎ 510/465–6400) is a masterpiece of the Art Deco style and remains open and operating as a venue for concerts and performances of all kinds. For $1 you can take a two-hour tour of the building, given the first and third Saturday of each month. For information about performances, check the free weekly *East Bay Express,* or call the box office.

In the years just after the Second World War, Oakland gave birth to the gritty, hurts-so-bad-I-think-I'm-gonna-die soulful music known as West Coast blues, and the style still flourishes in clubs and bars all over town. One consistently good spot for blues is **Eli's Mile High Club** (3629 Martin Luther King Jr. Way, ☎ 510/655–6661). Reputedly *the* birthplace of West Coast blues, it's a small, basic club with a pool table, soul food, and music Wednesday–Sunday. At **Your Place Too** (5319 Martin Luther King Jr. Way, ☎ 510/652–5837) there are 50¢ beers and a warped pool table (complete with resident pool shark), along with nightly blues and the occasional hard-core band.

A drive through the Oakland Hills is spectacular, although a wide area north from Broadway is still recovering from the devastating 1991 firestorm. One landmark that was saved is the **Claremont Hotel** (Ashby and Domingo Aves., ☎ 510/843–3000). From a distance, the sprawling white building with towers and gables looks like a castle. Surrounded by 22 acres of lush grounds tucked into the south Berkeley hills, the Claremont is on the Oakland–Berkeley border, and for years both cities have claimed it. When a new entrance was built on a different side of the building, the address changed from Berkeley to Oakland. The 1915 hotel has been restored and refurbished and turned into a resort spa facility. To get there, drive north on Claremont Avenue to Ashby Avenue and on up the hill to the hotel.

Dining

Oakland's ethnic diversity is reflected in its restaurants and cafés. There is a thriving Chinatown a few blocks northwest of the Oakland Museum, a number of seafood restaurants at Jack London Square, and fare to fit any palate, penchant, or pocketbook on Piedmont and College Avenues. Dress is casual.

CATEGORY	COST*
$$$$	over $30
$$$	$20–$30
$$	$10–$20
$	under $10

**per person for a three-course meal, excluding drinks, service, and 8¼% sales tax*

$$–$$$ **Bay Wolf.** A favorite for 20 years, this converted home has a redwood deck out front, elegantly understated dining rooms inside, and a kitchen garden out back. The menu changes frequently to feature fresh seasonal ingredients and Mediterranean cuisine with a twist: Try pork loin salad with stuffed squash; grilled eggplant, peppers, and couscous; or pan-roasted salmon with artichokes, asparagus, spring carrots, and sorrel sauce. ✕ *3853 Piedmont Ave.,* ☎ *510/655–6004. Reservations advised. MC, V. No lunch weekends.*

$$–$$$ **Claremont Resort and Spa.** The dining room is large and elegant, with pressed linen, large contemporary paintings, and views across the bay to San Francisco and the peninsula and north to Mt. Tamalpais. Fresh seafood is a Sunday brunch special, and the creative dinner menu includes such seasonal specials as roast rack of lamb with tomato chutney, and salmon with passion-fruit essence. ✕ *Ashby and Domingo Aves.,* ☎ *510/843–3000. Reservations required. AE, D, DC, MC, V.*

$–$$$ **Oliveto Café & Restaurant.** This is one of the East Bay's most interesting Italian restaurants, fashioned after a rustic stucco casa in Tuscany and situated on the corner of a bustling gourmet marketplace. In the formal dining room upstairs, gourmets indulge in chef Paul Bertolli's tagliatelle with smoked ham, ravioli with pumpkin, or chicken cooked under a brick. The café at street level is the place to see and be seen sipping wine or espresso, or snacking on pizzas and pastries. ✕ *5655 College Ave.,* ☎ *510/547–5356. Reservations advised for restaurant. AE, DC, MC, V. No lunch weekends in restaurant.*

$$ **ZZA's Trattoria.** Pizzas, salads, house-smoked chicken, and homemade pasta, ravioli, and lasagna are served in this fun, family-oriented restaurant on the shore of Lake Merritt. There's a wild neon sign over the open kitchen, along with butcher-paper table covers and crayons, and customers' artwork on the walls. ✕ *552 Grand Ave.,* ☎ *510/839–9124. Same-day reservations for 6 or more. MC, V. No lunch Mon., Tues., weekends.*

$–$$ **Lantern Restaurant.** Fine Hong Kong cuisine can be had downstairs at the oldest restaurant in Oakland's Chinatown, but the dim sum (steamed dumplings, spring rolls, and assorted exotic delicacies) served in the enormous upstairs dining room is the big deal here. Point to what you want as the carts roll by and pay by the plate. ✕ *814 Webster St.,* ☎ *510/451–0627. D, DC, MC, V.*

$–$$ **Rockridge Cafe.** This casual café is known for burgers, breakfasts, and mighty fine pie. ✕ *5492 College Ave.,* ☎ *510/653–1567. Reservations for 6 or more. MC, V. Sun. brunch.*

Oakland Essentials

Arriving and Departing

BY CAR

Take I–80 across the Bay Bridge, then I–580 to the Grand Avenue exit for Lake Merritt. To reach downtown and the waterfront, take the I–980 exit from I–580. The trip takes 45 minutes.

BY PUBLIC TRANSPORTATION

Take the BART to Oakland City Center station or to Lake Merritt station for the lake and Oakland Museum. The trip takes 45 minutes one-way.

THE SAN FRANCISCO PENINSULA

During the morning and evening rush hours, the peninsula south of San Francisco resembles nothing so much as a vast commuter corridor. At other times and on the network of less-traveled roads, the area offers a remarkable variety of scenic attractions. Redwood forests still stand, though they were heavily logged during the 19th century. In San Mateo and Half Moon Bay there are small adobe houses from California's Spanish and Mexican eras.

The peninsula's most dramatic development came later with the grand country estates built by the "bonanza kings" who made their fortunes in mining and transportation. Many mansions survive: Ralston Hall, built by the owner of San Francisco's Palace Hotel, now the College of Notre Dame on Ralston Avenue in Belmont; La Dolphine on Manor Drive in Burlingame, inspired by Le Petite Trianon at Versailles; and the Uplands, built by banker C. Templeton Crocker, now the Crystal Springs School for Girls on Uplands Drive in Burlingame. The only estate open to the general public is Filoli, in Woodside, which has 16 acres of gardens. Another major attraction is Stanford University, in Palo Alto, with a campus that stretches from the flatlands of the Santa Clara Valley into the Santa Cruz Mountains.

Exploring

One of the few great country houses in California that remains intact in its original setting is **Filoli** in Woodside. Built for wealthy San Franciscan William B. Bourn in 1916–19, it was designed by Willis Polk in a Georgian style, with redbrick walls and a tile roof. The name is not Italian but Bourn's acronym for "fight, love, live." As interesting to visitors as the house (which you might remember from the television series *Dynasty*) are the 16 acres of formal gardens. The gardens were planned and developed over a period of more than 50 years and preserved for the public when the last private owner, Mrs. William P. Roth, deeded Filoli to the National Trust for Historic Preservation.

The gardens rise south from the mansion to take advantage of the natural surroundings of the 700-acre estate and its vistas. Among the designs are a sunken garden, walled garden, woodland garden, yew alley, and a rose garden developed by Mrs. Roth with more than 50 shrubs of all types and colors. A focal point of the garden is a charming teahouse designed in the Italian Renaissance style. Spring is the most popular time to visit, but daffodils, narcissi, and rhododendrons are in bloom as early as February, and the gardens remain attractive in October and November. *Cañada Rd., near Edgewood Rd., Woodside,* ☎ *415/364–2880.* ☛ *$8 adults, $4 children.* ⏲ *For tours mid-Feb.–mid-Nov., Tues.–Sat. Reservations necessary; spring tours may fill several wks in advance. Call for openings. Filoli is often open for unguided visits and nature hikes on the estate; call for information.*

Stanford University, 30 miles south of San Francisco, also has its roots among the peninsula's estates. Originally the property was former California governor Leland Stanford's farm for breeding horses. For all its stature as one of the nation's leading universities, Stanford is still known as "the Farm." Founded and endowed by Leland and Jane Stanford in 1885 as a memorial to their son, Leland, Jr., who died of typhoid fever, the university was opened in 1891. Frederick Law Olmsted conceived the plan for the grounds and Romanesque sandstone buildings, joined by arcades and topped by red-tile roofs. Variations on this solid style persist in newer buildings, which, along with playing fields, now cover about 1,200 acres of the 8,200-acre campus. The center of the university is the inner quadrangle, a group of 12 original classroom buildings later joined by Memorial Church, whose facade and interior walls are covered with mosaics of biblical scenes.

The university is organized into seven schools made up of 70 departments. In addition, there are several institutes on campus, including the Hoover Institution on War, Revolution, and Peace. Its 285-foot tower is a landmark; an elevator leads to an observation deck. Except for the central cluster of buildings, the campus is remarkably uncongested—enrollment is only about 15,000. Free walking tours leave daily at 11 AM and 3:15 PM from the **Visitor Information Booth** (☎ 415/723–2560 or 415/723–2053) at the front of the quadrangle. The main campus entrance, Palm Drive, is an extension of University Avenue from Palo Alto.

The **Stanford Art Gallery,** to the right of Hoover Tower near the campus entrance, features visiting shows, some student works, and a selection of the university's historical artifacts. At the Stanford Museum of Art on Lomita Drive, ¾ mile northwest of the Art Gallery, you can view a collection of Rodin bronzes in a garden outside. The museum, with its collection of 18th- and 19th-century art, has been closed for renovation since it was damaged in the 1989 Loma Prieta earthquake. It is expected to reopen in 1997. *Art Gallery* ☎ *415/723–3469. Donation requested.* ⏲ *Tues.–Fri. 10–5, weekends 1–5.*

Two miles west of the main campus, on Sand Hill Road, is the **Stanford Linear Accelerator** (☎ 415/926–2204). Tours reveal the workings of the 2-mile-long electron accelerator, which is used for elementary-particle research.

Just north of the main campus, facing El Camino Real, is the **Stanford Shopping Center,** one of the Bay Area's first and still one of the most pleasant and inviting. The Nature Company has a fascinating collection of artifacts and gadgets concerning the natural world, a large collection of natural-history books, and a good poster selection. The Palo Alto Coffee Roasting Company roasts a variety of coffees in three strengths. Crate and Barrel has a large selection of moderately priced kitchenwares and housewares.

Dining

El Camino Real (Highway 82) is the peninsula's major commercial thoroughfare, lined with cafés, restaurants, and fast-food franchises. Palo Alto also has its fair share of pleasant cafés, some with outdoor dining, mostly along University Avenue and its cross streets, just east of El Camino Real. The Stanford Shopping Center has a variety of upscale cafés: Gaylord's serves moderately priced Indian food in a relaxed and elegant atmosphere, and the nearby Fresh Choice has perhaps the biggest salad bar on the Peninsula.

CATEGORY	COST*
$$$$	over $30
$$$	$20–$30
$$	$10–$20
$	under $10

**per person for a three-course meal, excluding drinks, service, and 8¼% sales tax*

$$–$$$ **Flea Street Cafe.** Floral decor evokes a romantic, intimate country inn, and the fare is imaginative, featuring fresh organic produce and home-baked breads. Specialties change seasonally and may include herb-roasted Cornish game hen with sage jalapeño gravy and red-onion cornbread stuffing, fettuccine with duck sausage and pippin apples, and—for Sunday brunch—house-baked buttermilk biscuits, homemade jams, and seductive pancake, egg, and omelet creations. Young diners have access to a fully stocked toy chest. ✕ *Alameda de las Pulgas, Menlo Park (take Sand Hill Rd. west from the Stanford shopping center or east from I–280, turn right on Alameda),* ☏ *415/854–1226. Reservations advised. MC, V. Closed Mon. No lunch Sat.*

$$–$$$ **Il Fornaio Cucina Italiana.** Situated in a gorgeous Italianate setting on the ground floor and back patio of the Garden Court Hotel, this popular eatery has a casually rustic look, with food as the visual focus. Buy gourmet fare to go or stay here to sample superb antipasti, pizza, pasta, and calzone baked to perfection in a wood-burning oven. Italian breads and irresistible bread sticks, biscotti, cakes, and tortes are prime attractions. There is also a charming café area just inside the front door for coffee and snacks. ✕ *520 Cowper St., Palo Alto,* ☏ *415/853–3888. Reservations strongly advised. Weekend brunch. AE, DC, MC, V.*

$$–$$$ **MacArthur Park.** This classic steak house, favored by the Stanford crowd, specializes in oakwood-smoked ribs. Tasty renditions of chicken and fish entrées are also available, but those who like to send their cholesterol counts soaring will opt for ribs and finish off with mud pie (a chocolate cookie topped with ice cream, hot fudge, and chopped nuts). ✕ *27 University Ave. (west side of the Caltrain station), Palo Alto,* ☏ *415/321–9990. Reservations advised. Sun. brunch. AE, DC, MC, V. No lunch Sat.*

$$–$$$ **Village Pub.** In this pleasant restaurant near Filoli, patrons elbow up to a carved oak bar to sample the ale, or relax in the stylishly simple modern dining room to savor creative California-rustic renditions of duck, fresh seafood, steak, and pasta. ✕ *2967 Woodside Rd. (¾ mi from I–280W), Woodside,* ☏ *415/851–1294. Reservations advised. AE, DC, MC, V. No lunch weekends.*

$ **Vicolo Pizzeria.** An upscale little hangout (hungry Stanford students come here for breakfast, lunch, and dinner), Vicolo has whimsical, faux-Italian decor, more than 30 varieties of gourmet toppings on tasty cornmeal crust, and sidewalk seating in good weather. ✕ *473 University Ave. (near Cowper St.), Palo Alto,* ☏ *415/324–4877. No reservations. No credit cards.*

The San Francisco Peninsula Essentials

Arriving and Departing

BY CAR

The most pleasant direct route down the peninsula is I–280, the Junipero Serra Freeway, which passes along Crystal Springs reservoir. Take the Edgewood Road exit for Filoli, and Alpine Road for Stanford. U.S. 101 along the bay shore can be congested, but from there take Highway 93 west to Filoli, and University Avenue or Embarcadero Road to Stanford. Skyline Boulevard (Highway 35), which begins near the San Francisco Zoo, is the most scenic route through the peninsula, following the crest of the Santa Cruz Mountains and offering views of both the bay and the Pacific Ocean. Highway 1 follows a relatively unknown section of the coast from San Francisco to Santa Cruz, a route including rugged cliffs, public beaches, former fishing villages such as Pescadero, and several 19th-century lighthouses.

BY PUBLIC TRANSPORTATION

Take the **CalTrain** (☎ 800/660–4287) from 4th and Townsend streets to Palo Alto, then the shuttle bus to Stanford campus. Other attractions on the peninsula are difficult to reach except by car.

SILICON VALLEY

By Claudia Gioseffi

Like many famous rock bands, Silicon Valley began in a garage. In the spring of 1938, Dave and Lucile Packard, joined by William Hewlett, made room in back of their house for what would eventually become Hewlett-Packard, a pioneer company in the high-tech and electronics revolutions. Another milestone was marked 39 years later when Steve Jobs and Steve Wozniak emerged from a small garage in Cupertino with something called Apple. Ultimately these computer companies, and others such as Intel, Tandem, and Microsystem, grew big enough to replace sleepy Santa Clara County's fruit growers and cattle ranchers with an industry that changed the world. Although some companies have now relocated to less expensive regions of the country, Silicon Valley remains the undisputed home of the tiny chips that support the Information Superhighway.

The Valley is a sprawling community of spanking-new office parks, business-lined highways, shopping malls, and Spanish-style homes—their red-tiled roofs peeking through dense junipers and magnolias. El Camino Real, Highway 101, and the more picturesque I–280 link the area's key towns: Sunnyvale, Cupertino, Santa Clara, and San Jose. Green hills that turn khaki under the summer sun surround the valley. Many of the sights here are suitable for a day trip from San Francisco, but the region's attractions warrant a closer look. Moderate year-round temperatures make Silicon Valley ideal for viticulture—and for enjoying the great outdoors. Take a weekend, rent a car, open the windows or fold down the top, and head south.

The center of the Valley is San Jose—California's first town, and now the state's third largest city. Despite its reputation as a charmless, suburban Los Angeles of the north, San Jose is buffered by city parks and gardens, and in addition to the industrial parks, computer companies, and corporate headquarters, it is home to museums, symphonies, theaters, and wineries.

Exploring

Santa Clara

Santa Clara's offerings include two major attractions at opposite ends of the sightseeing spectrum: the mission, founded in 1777, and Paramount's Great America, northern California's answer to Disneyland.

In **Paramount's Great America** 100-acre theme park, on the edge of San Francisco Bay, each section of the park recalls a familiar part of North America: Hometown Square, Yukon Territory, Yankee Harbor, County Fair, and Orleans Place. The double-decker carousel just inside the entrance, the "Columbia," is fairly tame, but the park's other rides would tempt Evel Knievel. There are six roller coasters, a triple-arm Ferris wheel, and several exciting water rides. The latest rides are the "Rip Roaring Rapids," which takes you on a white-water river in oversize inner tubes; the "Vortex" stand-up roller coaster; a movie-themed *Top Gun* roller coaster, whose cars travel along the outside of a 360-degree loop track; a *Days of Thunder* racing-simulator theater, which combines film, a giant-screen image, special effects, and moving seats to simulate a stock-car race; and a Nickelodeon-style interactive amusement arena based on the cable network's popular kids show *Double Dare*. Star Trek characters wander around the grounds, and movie and TV references are everywhere. The park is served by Santa Clara County Transit and BART (the Fremont station). *Great America Pkwy., between U.S. 101 and Hwy. 237 (6 mi north of San Jose),* ☏ *408/988–1776.* ☛ *$25.95 adults, $18.95 senior citizens, $12.95 children 3–6. Parking $5.* ⏲ *Weekends Mar.–May and Sept. –Oct., daily in summer. Opens at 10 AM; closing times vary with season. AE, MC, V.*

After a day at the park, you may be in the mood for some intellectual stimulation. Visitors to the **Intel Museum,** just a couple miles south of the Great America park, can learn how computer chips are made, and follow the development of Intel Corporation's microprocessor, memory, and systems product lines. Although the tour is designed to be self-guided, guided tours are available by reservation. *Robert Noyce Bldg., 2200 Mission College Blvd.,* ☏ *408/765–0503.* ☛ *Free.* ⏲ *Weekdays 8–5.*

Downtown Santa Clara's attractions are on or near the green campus of Santa Clara University. Founded in 1851 by Jesuits, this was California's first college.

Right in the center of the campus is the **Mission Santa Clara de Assis,** the eighth of 21 California missions founded under the direction of Father Junipero Serra. The mission has a dramatic history. The present site was the fifth chosen, after the first four were flooded by the Guadelupe River. In 1926 the permanent mission chapel was destroyed by fire. Roof tiles of the current building, a replica of the original, were salvaged from earlier structures, which dated from the 1790s and 1820s. Early adobe walls and a garden remain as well, as does a wooden **Memorial Cross** from 1777 set in front of the Santa Clara Mission church. In the mid-1770s, Franciscan friars raised grapes here for sacramental wines; the olive and fig trees they planted at this time remain. Also on the campus is a notable art museum, the **de Saisset,** with a permanent collection that includes California mission artifacts. The museum also has a full calendar of temporary exhibits. *Campus: 500 El Camino Real. Mission:* ☏ *408/554–4023;* ☛ *Free;* ⏲ *Weekdays 8–6. De Saisset Museum:* ☏ *408/554–4528;* ☛ *Free;* ⏲ *Tues.–Sun. 11–4.*

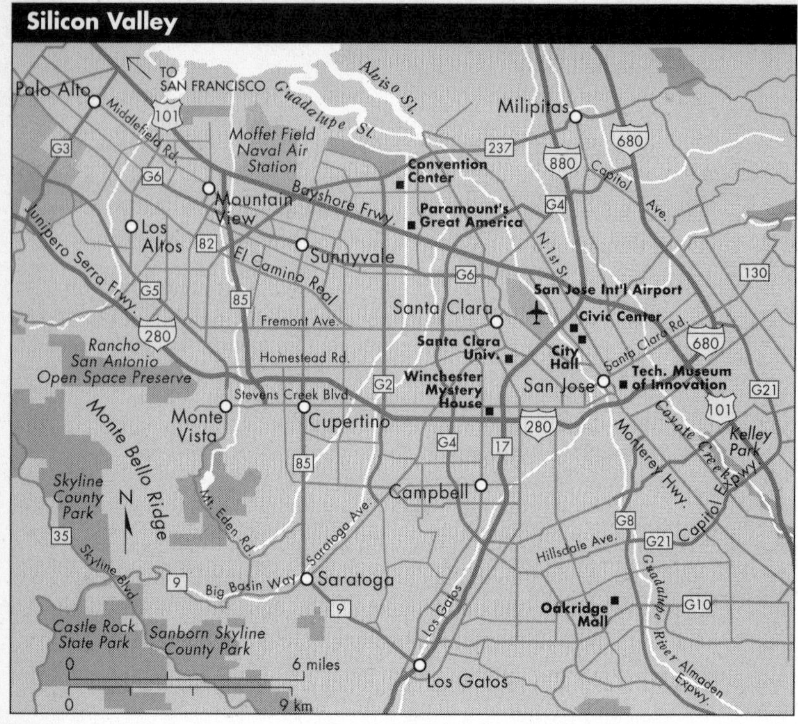

Several blocks east of campus is the **Carmelite Monastery,** a fine example of Spanish Ecclesiastical architecture. Built in 1917, it's on the grounds of a historic ranch. The church and grounds are open from 7:15 to 4 daily; to see inside the chapel, ring the bell. Mass is held at 7:15 AM Monday through Saturday, and 10:30 AM on Sunday, and is open to the public. *1000 Lincoln St., ☎ 408/296–8412. ☛ Free.*

From the monastery, a stroll up Lincoln Street will bring you to Civic Center Park to see a **statue of Saint Clare,** the patron saint of Santa Clara. The sculpture was cast in Italy in 1965 by Anne Van Kleeck, who used an ancient wax process. It was then shipped around Cape Horn and dedicated on this site in 1985. *Civic Center Park, Lincoln St. at El Camino Real.*

Across from the Civic Center, skylights cast natural light for viewing the exhibitions in the **Triton Museum of Art.** A permanent collection of 19th- and 20th-century sculpture by artists from the Bay Area is displayed in a 7-acre garden, which you can see through a curved-glass wall at the rear of the building. Indoors there are rotating exhibits of contemporary works in a variety of media and a permanent collection of 19th- and 20-century American artists, many from California. *1505 Warburton Ave., ☎ 408/247–3754. ☛ Free for most exhibitions. ⌚ Tues. 10–9, Wed.–Fri. 10–5, weekends noon–5.*

The **Santa Clara Historic Museum,** next door, exhibits artifacts and photos that trace the history of the region. *1509 Warburton Ave., ☎ 408/248–2787. ☛ Free. ⌚ Daily 1–4.*

Walk over to the grounds of City Hall to see noted San Francisco sculptor Benny Bufano's primitive *Universal Child,* facing the museum.

The statue, which depicts the children of the world standing as one, stands 85 feet tall.

The **Harris-Lass Historic Museum** is built on Santa Clara's last farmstead. A restored house, summer kitchen, and barn convey a sense of life on the farm from the early 1900s through the 1930s. *1889 Market St.,* ☎ *408/249–7905.* ☛ *$3 adults, $2 senior citizens over 60, $1 children 6–12.* ⏲ *Weekends noon–4; guided tours every ½ hr, last tour at 3:30.*

San Jose

As part of its plans to attract tourists and increase convention business, San Jose has embarked on a massive project to redevelop its city center. A 20-mile light-rail transportation system, a convention center, a 17,000-seat arena for the San Jose Sharks hockey team, and a major addition to the San Jose Museum of Art are all part of the new trend. The city has also begun to restore the few remaining 19th-century buildings downtown, marrying existing Old West and mission architecture with modern styles and materials. One product of these efforts is a very traditional small-town clock tower constructed from marble and stainless steel.

A good way to explore is to hop on the light rail that connects San Jose State University on one end with the Center for Performing Arts on the other; its route will give you a good overview of the city, and the convention center stop will drop you in the center of downtown, where you can explore on foot.

The **Children's Discovery Museum,** near the convention center, exhibits interactive installations on space, technology, the humanities, and the arts. Children can dress up in period costumes, create jewelry from recycled materials, or play on a real fire truck. *180 Woz Way, at Auzerais St.,* ☎ *408/298–5437.* ☛ *$6 adults, $5 senior citizens, $4 children 2–18.* ⏲ *Tues.–Sat. 10–5, Sun. noon–5.*

The **Tech Museum of Innovation,** across from the convention center, presents high-tech information through hands-on lab exhibits that are fun and accessible, allowing visitors to discover and demystify disciplines such as microelectronics, biotechnology, robotics, and space exploration. *145 W. San Carlos St.,* ☎ *408/279–7150.* ☛ *$6 adults, $4 students and senior citizens.* ⏲ *Tues.–Sun. 10–5.*

In collaboration with New York's Whitney Museum, the **San Jose Museum of Art** is exploring the development of 20th-century American art with exhibits of pieces from the permanent collections of both. The series will run through the year 2000, and will include works by such American artists as Andrew Wyeth, Edward Hopper, and Georgia O'-Keeffe. Housed in a former post office building, the museum also has a permanent collection that includes paintings, large-scale multimedia installations, photographs, and sculptures by local and nationally known artists. *110 S. Market St.,* ☎ *408/294–2787.* ☛ *$5 adults; $3 senior citizens, students, and children 6–17.* ⏲ *Tues.–Wed. 10–5, Thurs. 10–8, Fri.–Sun. 10–5.*

The following attractions are on the outskirts of town; the easiest way to reach them is by car.

On the north end of town lies the **Winchester Mystery House.** Convinced that spirits would harm her if construction ever stopped, firearms-heiress Sarah Winchester constantly added to her house. For 38 years beginning in 1884, she kept hundreds of carpenters working around the clock, creating a bizarre, 160-room Victorian labyrinth with stairs going nowhere and doors that open into walls. The brightly painted house and well-tended gardens are a favorite family attraction, and though the grounds are no longer dark and overgrown, the place retains an air of mystery. An extensive firearms collection is on exhibit as well. *525 S. Winchester Blvd. (between Stevens Creek Blvd. and I–280), ☎ 408/247–2101. ☛ $12.50 adults, $9.50 senior citizens, $6.50 children 6–12. ⏲ Daily 9:30–4; later in summer.*

The **Egyptian Museum and Planetarium** offers some mysteries of its own in the West Coast's largest collection of Egyptian and Babylonian antiquities, including mummies and an underground replica of a pharaoh's tomb. The museum's entrance is a reproduction of the Avenue of Ram Sphinxes from the Temple at Karnak in Egypt, and the complex is surrounded by a garden filled with palms, papyrus, and other plants recalling ancient Egypt. The planetarium offers programs like the popular "Celestial Nile," which describes the significant role astrology played in ancient Egyptian myths and religions. *1600 Park Ave., at Naglee Ave., ☎ 408/947–3636. ☛ Museum only: $6 adults, $4 senior citizens and students, $3.50 children 7–15. Planetarium admission and show times vary. ⏲ Daily 9–5; planetarium open weekdays only.*

On 176 acres of rolling lawns on the east side of San Jose, off I–280, is **Kelley Park,** a haven for families and picnickers. On the grounds is the creative **Happy Hollow Park & Zoo,** with theme rides, puppet shows, a riverboat replica, and events specially planned for children from two to 10 years old. Also in the park is the **Japanese Friendship Garden,** with fish ponds and a teahouse inspired by Japan's Korakuen Garden. Occupying 25 acres of the park is the **San Jose Historical Museum,** which recreates San Jose in the 1880s with a collection of original and replicate Victorian homes and shops, a firehouse, and a trolley line. The dusty Main Street recalls small-town America without the brightly painted gloss of amusement-park reproductions. *Kelley Park: 1300 Senter Rd.; ☛ Free, parking $3 on holidays and in summer. Happy Hollow Park: ☎ 408/295–8383; ☛ $3.50, $3 senior citizens, free for visitors under 2 and over 75; ⏲ Apr.–Oct., Mon.–Sat. 10–5, Sun. 11–6; Nov.–Mar., Mon.–Sat. 10–5, Sun. 10–5. Historical Museum: ☎ 408/287–2290; ☛ $4 adults, $3 senior citizens, $2 children 4–17; ⏲ Weekdays 10–4:30, weekends noon–4:30.*

On the sandy shores of Lake Cunningham, **Raging Waters,** off the Capitol Expressway, attracts kids of all ages. Among the many water-related attractions are several children's wading pools and a water slide with a heart-stopping, 7-foot free fall. *Lake Cunningham Park, 2333 S. White Rd., ☎ 408/270–8000. ☛ $18.95, $12.95 after 3 PM. ⏲ Mid-May–mid-June, weekends 10–6; mid-June–Labor Day, daily 10–7.*

Saratoga

Saratoga, 10 miles west of San Jose, is a quaint former artists' colony chock-full of antiques shops, upscale jewelry stores, and art galleries. The Zen-style **Hakone Gardens** are nestled on a steep hillside just south of downtown. Designed in 1918 by a man who had been an imperial gardener in Japan, the gardens have been carefully maintained, with *koi* (carp) ponds and sculptured shrubs. *21000 Big Basin Way, ☎ 408/741–4994. ☛ Free. Parking: $3 Mon., Wed.–Fri.; $5 weekends; free Tues. ⏲ Weekdays 10–5, weekends 11–5.*

Off the Beaten Track

The small town of **Gilroy,** known as the Garlic Capital of the World, is 30 miles south of San Jose on U.S. 101, surrounded by rolling countryside and crisscrossed by picturesque back roads. Multitudes follow their noses here every July when the world-renowned **Gilroy Garlic Fes-**

tival kicks off. The recipe for the three-day extravaganza calls for more than 4 tons of garlic. Contact the Gilroy Visitors Bureau (☎ 408/842–6436).

Wineries

Although most people don't think of wine in connection with Silicon Valley, the area's vintages are gaining attention. Many of the wineries represent generations of vintners, whose families began making wine in Europe long before coming to California.

Cupertino

Ridge Vineyards is perched on Montebello Ridge in the Santa Cruz Mountains overlooking San Francisco Bay. Founded in 1959, the winery adheres to traditional wine-making techniques. *17100 Montebello Rd., Cupertino,* ☎ *408/867–3233. Tasting Sat. and Sun. 11–3.* ☛ *Free.*

Fellom Ranch Vineyards, a bit farther down Montebello Road, is nestled on a terraced hillside at a 2,000-foot elevation, with panoramic views of the valley. When the Fellom family purchased the ranch in the 1920s, it consisted of a small vineyard of zinfandel grapes; today—thanks to its high elevation, its nonirrigated vines, and the unique microclimate of the Montebello mountain—the winery produces some of the finest cabernet sauvignon grapes in the world. *17075 Montebello Rd., Cupertino,* ☎ *408/741–0307. Tours and tasting, by appointment only, most weekends, depending on the season.* ☛ *Free.*

Los Gatos

Byington Winery and Vineyards is one of the newest wineries in the region. Eight acres of pinot noir grapes are planted on an 80-acre estate with breathtaking views of the Pacific and Monterey Bay and a pastoral picnic area. The Italian-style chateau has a veranda and a tasting room with a fireplace. *21850 Bear Creek Rd.,* ☎ *408/354–1111. Tasting daily, 11–5. Tours $5, by appointment only.*

Mirassou Champagne Cellars, located in the hills of Los Gatos and run by members of the Mirassou family, is one of the pioneers of champagne-making in California. The winery offers samples of its award-winning sparkling wines, including a blanc de noir and a brut. Tours offer an in-depth look at production methods and let you explore the property's century-old cellars. *300 College Ave.,* ☎ *408/395–3790.* ⏲ *Wed.–Sun. noon–5, tours at 1:30 and 3:30.* ☛ *Free.*

San Jose

J. Lohr Winery is on the site of the old Falstaff and Fredericksburg breweries. Most of the winery's more than 1,000 acres of vineyards are located on California's central coast, in Monterey; the rest are in the Napa Valley and the Sacramento Delta. J. Lohr produces many varietals but is best known for its Estate chardonnay, cabernet sauvignon, Johannisberg Riesling, and gamay. On the brief tours of the facility, tanks and bottling facilities are displayed, and production methods explained. *1000 Lenzen Ave.,* ☎ *408/288–5057. Tasting daily 10–5, tours Sat. and Sun. at 11 and 2.* ☛ *Free.*

Mirassou Vineyards, run by America's oldest wine-making family, has been in operation for 130 years and has produced several award-winning wines in the last few years. They include a reserve pinot noir, a chardonnay, a cru gamay, and a Petite Syrah. Mirassou also hosts three annual events, the Epicurean Fare in June, an American Pops Concert in July, and the Holiday Festival in November, in addition to a series of Bistro and Candlelight Dinners. (*See* Arts and Nightlife, *below.*) *3000 Aborn Rd.,* ☎ *408/274–4000.* ⏲ *Daily noon–5, tours Mon.–Sat. 1:30 and 3:30, Sun. 1 and 3.* ☛ *Free.*

Sport and the Outdoors

Participant Sports

GOLF

Sunnyvale Golf Course (605 Macara La., ☎ 408/738–3666), **San Jose Municipal Golf Course** (1560 Oakland Rd., ☎ 408/441–4653), and **Santa Clara Golf & Tennis Club** (5155 Stars & Stripes Dr., ☎ 408/980–9515) are all 18-hole municipal courses. For serious golfers who are willing to travel farther afield, Pebble Beach courses are about 90 minutes from San Jose. Many greens there are world-class: **Poppy Hills** (☎ 408/625–2035), **Spyglass Hill** (☎ 408/625–8563), and the **Links at Spanish Bay** (☎ 408/624–3811). Tee times can be difficult to get despite high greens fees—$75 to $225—depending on the course.

HORSEBACK RIDING

Garrod Farms Stables (22600 Mount Eden Rd., Saratoga, ☎ 408/867–9527), has horse and pony rentals. Farther afield, **Molera Trail Rides** (Box 167, Big Sur, ☎ 408/625–8664) caters to experienced riders.

SWIMMING

The International Swim Center is a competitive swim facility open to adults 18 years and older. Olympian swimmers occasionally use it, but public lap-swimming times are scheduled, and lessons are available. Take Homestead Avenue to the Santa Clara Public Library parking lot; the pool is just behind it. *2625 Patricia Dr., Santa Clara, ☎ 408/246–5050. $3 drop-in fee. ⏲ Daily 5:30–8 AM for adults, 3–7 for children ages 4–19, and 6–7 PM for adults.*

Spectator Sports

Home to the San Jose Sharks hockey team, the 20,000-seat **San Jose Arena,** completed in 1993, looks like a giant hothouse with its glass entrance and skylight ceiling. The venue also hosts tennis matches, basketball games, concerts, and other events. *Santa Clara St. at Autumn St., San Jose, ☎ 408/287–9200. Ticket office open weekdays 9:30–5:30, Sat. 9:30–1, or call BASS at 408/998–2277.*

Beaches

About 45 minutes south of San Jose on Route 17 is the **Santa Cruz Beach and Boardwalk** (☎ 408/426–7433)—part Asbury Park and part Coney Island—with its huge weekend crowds of sun-scorched surfers and Bay Area residents. The mile-long boardwalk, lined with rides, amusements, and arcades, runs along Beach Street.

The San Mateo County coast state beaches run from Pacifica, just south of San Francisco, down to Big Basin Redwoods State Park. A 20–30 minute drive west over the mountains from just north of Santa Clara leads to the beaches at Half Moon Bay and others along the coast. The **Half Moon Bay State Parks District Office** (☎ 415/726–8800) has information on the state parks and beaches from Montara to Año Nuevo.

Shopping

The malls of Silicon Valley are a mind-blowing maze of shopping habitats: **Valley Fair Shopping Center** (2855 Stevens Creek Blvd., ☎ 408/248–4451) is in Santa Clara; **Pavilion Shops** (150 S. 1st St., ☎ 408/286–2076) and **Eastridge Mall** (Capitol Expressway and Tully Rd., ☎ 408/274–0360) are in San Jose.

In downtown **Los Gatos,** restored buildings dating from California's younger years now house boutiques, antiques shops, and restaurants. Call the **Los Gatos Chamber of Commerce** (☎ 408/354–9300) for details.

The **Factory Outlets at Gilroy** (8300 Arroyo Circle, ☎ 408/842–3729) and **Pacific West Outlet Center** (8375 Arroyo Circle, No. 46, ☎ 408/847–4155) are both in Gilroy, 45 minutes south of San Jose. There, bargain shoppers will find discounts of up to 75% on clothing and gear by Esprit, Brooks Brothers, Anne Klein, Nike, and Eddie Bauer.

The **San Jose Flea Market** looks, feels, and smells like Mexico's festive and colorful *mercados,* on a larger scale. Some 2,700 booths spread over 125 acres sell handicrafts, leather, jewelry, furniture, produce, and more. As in markets south of the border, it's smart to examine merchandise before buying. *Berryessa Rd. between I-680 and Hwy. 101, ☎ 408/453–1110. ☛ Free. Parking $3 on weekends, $1 weekdays. ⏲ Wed.–Sun. dawn to dusk.*

Dining

Though Silicon Valley's billboard-strewn highways lined with motels and fast-food franchises can look like a surreal suburban landscape, the Bay Area's reputation as a world-class culinary center remains intact at its southernmost tip.

CATEGORY	COST*
$$$$	over $30
$$$	$20–$30
$$	$10–$20
$	under $10

**per person for a three-course meal, excluding drinks, service, and 8¼% sales tax*

SAN JOSE

$$$$ ★ **Emile's.** Swiss chef and owner Emile Mooser is well versed in the classic marriage of food and wine, and will make your wine selection from the restaurant's extensive list for you. House specialties include house-cured gravlax and rack of lamb. Romantic lighting and walls hand-painted with gold leaves create an intimate and elegant backdrop. ✕ *545 S. 2nd St., ☎ 408/289–1960. Reservations advised. AE, MC, V. Closed Sun. and Mon. Lunch Fri. only.*

SARATOGA

$$$$ **Le Mouton Noir.** Anything but the black sheep that its name suggests, this romantic French-country restaurant is filled with aspiring and established foodies and wine connoisseurs, and the kitchen turns out classic, contemporary French cuisine. Fine examples of the seasonal menu are the seafood dishes and the roast rack of lamb with a light, caramelized fennel and raspberry sauce. ✕ *14560 Big Basin Way, near Hwy. 9, ☎ 408/867–7017. Reservations recommended. AE, DC, MC, V. No lunch Sun. and Mon.*

SAN JOSE

$$$ **Paolo's Restaurant.** Not far from the cultural centers, this casual eatery caters to those with curious palettes. The bar menu offers small plates that give you several different tastes in a hurry—great for a snack before or after the theater. Try the eggplant sandwich, antipasto plate, or the mixed salad topped with a hearty serving of shrimp. The Italian entrées and the parklike dining room—filled with plants and overlooking a patio, lush greenery, and the Guadalupe River—deserve more leisurely appreciation. ✕ *333 W. San Carlos St., ☎ 408/294–2558. Reservations advised. AE, D, DC, MC, V. No lunch weekends.*

SANTA CLARA

$$$ **Birk's.** Silicon Valley's business people come to this sophisticated American grill to unwind after a hard day of paving the way to the future. High-tech sensibilities will appreciate the modern open kitchen and streamlined, multilevel dining area. Yet the menu is traditional, strong on grilled and smoked meat, fish, and fowl. Try the smoked prime rib, served with garlic mashed potatoes and creamed spinach, or the rotisserie-grilled chicken or ribs. ✕ *3955 Freedom Circle at Hwy. 101 and Great America Pkwy.,* ☎ *408/980–6400. Reservations advised. AE, DC, MC, V. No lunch weekends.*

SAN JOSE

$$ **Henry's World Famous Hi-Life.** This vintage rib-and-steak joint is where the Sharks eat after each game. Located in a 120-year-old building two blocks from San Jose Arena, it has been owned and operated by the same family since 1960. The interior is funky and rustic, the atmosphere friendly and fun. Try the sweet barbecue sauce. ✕ *301 W. St. John St.,* ☎ *408/295–5414. Reservations for 8 or more. MC, V. No lunch Sat.–Mon.*

$$ **Scott's Seafood Grill & Bar.** Young, upwardly mobile types fill the clean-lined, oak-and-brass dining room here. Seafood and shellfish are the specialties; the fresh calamari (dusted with flour and lightly fried in garlic, lemon butter, and wine) and the oyster bar are noted attractions. Meat eaters will appreciate the juicy steaks. ✕ *185 Park Ave., 6th Floor,* ☎ *408/971–1700. Reservations accepted. AE, D, DC, MC, V. No lunch weekends.*

SAN JOSE

$ **Original Joe's.** Hearty Italian specialties, along with steaks, chops, and hamburgers, are served in large portions until 1:30 AM in a warm cognac-and-green dining room with seating in cozy booths, and at a convivial counter overlooking the open kitchen. This downtown favorite has been in business since 1956. ✕ *301 S. 1st St.,* ☎ *408/292–7030. No reservations. AE, D, MC, V.*

SANTA CLARA

$ **Pizzeria Uno.** Some say that eating at one is eating at them all. Still, Pizzeria Uno is consistent, reliable, and tasty. You can get the same gourmet deep-dish pizzas here as in the Chicago flagship, classic pies that predate Wolfgang Puck's versions by 45 years. ✕ *2570 El Camino Real,* ☎ *408/241–5152. Reservations for 10 or more. AE, D, DC, MC, V.*

Lodging

All the big hotel chains are represented in the valley: Best Western, Howard Johnson, Marriott, Days Inn, Hilton, Holiday Inn, Quality Inn, and Sheraton. Many dot the King's Highway—El Camino Real. If character is more important than luxury, seek out a smaller inn.

CATEGORY	COST*
$$$$	over $175
$$$	$110–$175
$$	$75–$110
$	under $75

**All prices are for a standard double room, excluding 9½% room tax (10% in San Jose).*

$$$$ **Fairmont Hotel.** If you're accustomed to the best, this is the place to stay. Affiliated with the famous San Francisco hotel of the same name, this downtown gem opened in 1987, and offers the utmost in luxury and sophistication. Get lost in the lavish lobby sofas under dazzling chandeliers while waiting for your Louis Vuitton collection to be delivered to your room, or dip your well-traveled feet in the fourth-floor pool, making rings in the exotic palms mirrored in the water. The rooms have every imaginable comfort, from down pillows and custom-designed comforters to oversize bath towels changed twice a day. The hotel has accessible rooms for travelers with disabilities. *170 S. Market St., at Fairmont Pl., San Jose 95113, 408/998–1900 or 800/527–4727, FAX 408/287–1648. 500 rooms, 41 suites. 4 restaurants, lounge, no-smoking floors, room service, fitness center, business services, valet parking. AE, D, DC, MC, V.*

$$$ **Hotel De Anza.** This lushly appointed French Mediterranean–style hotel, opened in 1931, has an art deco facade, hand-painted ceilings, and an enclosed terrace with towering palms and dramatic fountains. You'll also find many business amenities, including computers, cellular phones, and secretarial services. *233 W. Santa Clara St., San Jose 95113, 408/286–1000 or 800/843–3700, FAX 408/286–0500. 100 rooms. Restaurant, jazz club, exercise room, breakfast buffet, complimentary late-night snacks, valet parking. AE, DC, MC, V.*

$$$ ★ **Inn at Saratoga.** This five-story, European-style inn is actually only 10 minutes from the cultural action of Saratoga, yet with its aura of calm, it feels far from bustling Silicon Valley. All rooms have secluded sitting alcoves overlooking a peaceful creek, and the hotel's sun-dappled patio provides a quiet retreat. Modern business conveniences are available but discreetly hidden. *20645 4th St., Saratoga 95070, 408/867–5020 or 800/338–5020; in CA, 800/543–5020; FAX 408/741–0981. 46 rooms. Business services, meeting room. AE, DC, MC, V.*

$$ **Biltmore Hotel & Suites.** This hotel's central Silicon Valley location makes it a popular choice for business travelers. In the past several years, the atrium lobby has been enclosed and the ballroom expanded. Other attractions are a sports bar and 16 meeting rooms. *2151 Laurelwood Rd., Santa Clara 95054, 408/988–8411 or 800/255–9925, FAX 408/988–0225. 128 rooms, 134 suites. Restaurant, lounge, pool, hot tub, fitness center, airport shuttle, parking. AE, D, DC, MC, V.*

$$ **Madison Street Inn.** At this refurbished Queen Anne Victorian, complimentary breakfast and afternoon tea are served on a brick garden patio with a bougainvillea-draped trellis. As one of the few bed-and-breakfasts in Silicon Valley, the inn has a distinctive look, with a blue- and red-trimmed facade and the look of a private home. *1390 Madison St., Santa Clara 95050, 408/249–5541, FAX 408/249–6676. 5 rooms, 3 with private baths. Pool, hot tub, meeting room. AE, D, DC, MC, V.*

$$ **Sundowner Inn.** Exploiting the Valley's passion for high-tech machinery, this contemporary hotel offers voice mail, computer data ports, and remote-control televisions with ESPN, HBO, CNN, Nintendo, and VCRs, which you can use to play complimentary tapes from the library of 500. There's also a fleet of mountain bikes and a library full of best-sellers you can borrow. The complimentary breakfast buffet is served poolside. *504 Ross Dr., Sunnyvale 94089, 408/734–9900 or 800/223–9901, FAX 408/747–0580. 105 rooms, 12 suites. Restaurant, no-smoking rooms, pool, sauna, exercise room, laundry, meeting room. AE, D, DC, MC, V.*

$ **Motel 6.** Everything the name suggests, Motel 6 is the quintessential highway motel—basic and conveniently located. *3208 El Camino Real, Santa Clara, 95051, 408/241–0200 or 800/437–7486. 99 rooms. Pool, parking. AE, D, DC, MC, V.*

The Arts and Nightlife

Because of its size, it's not surprising that San Jose offers the richest mix of performing arts and other cultural attractions in Silicon Valley.

The city's calendar is packed with everything from film festivals to jazz festivals, and there are many nightclubs and dance floors within the larger hotels. Throughout the rest of the valley there is plenty to do after the sun goes down.

Arts

If you're traveling in summer, try not to miss the **Mountain Winery Concert Series** (14831 Pierce Rd., Box 1852, Saratoga 95070, ☎ 408/741–5181), where music is performed under the moon and stars on a stage surrounded by grapevines. The series hosts internationally known country, jazz, blues, and opera acts. Be sure to buy tickets well in advance, as shows always sell out.

Mirassou Vineyards (☎ 408/274–4000) hosts a series of Pops Concerts each summer. The winery also offers four-course **Bistro Dinners** of informal, peasant fare ($45 per person) as well as more elegant, eight-course **Candlelight Dinners,** accenting food and wine pairings ($75 per person).

The **Flint Center at DeAnza College** (21250 Stevens Creek Blvd., Cupertino, ☎ 408/864–8816) showcases nationally known dance, music, and theater acts. There is also a top-notch lecture series with celebrity speakers from the worlds of entertainment, education, and politics. Designed by the Frank Lloyd Wright Foundation, the **Center for Performing Arts** (255 Almaden Blvd., San Jose) is the venue for performances of the **San Jose Civic Light Opera** (1717 Technology Dr., ☎ 408/453–7108), the **San Jose Symphony** (99 Almaden Blvd., Suite 400, ☎ 408/288–2828), and the **San Jose Cleveland Ballet** (Almaden Blvd. and Woz Way, ☎ 408/288–2800). The **San Jose Repertory Theatre** (1 N. 1st St., Suite 1, ☎ 408/291–2255), the only professional resident theater in Silicon Valley, performs at the **Montgomery Theater** (corner of San Carlos and Market). For schedules and tickets, call the companies directly or phone BASS (☎ 408/998–2277). The season generally runs from September through June.

Nightlife

ComedySportz (3428 El Camino Real, Santa Clara, ☎ 408/725–1356) is a comedy club and sports bar combined. The **Plumed Horse** (14555 Big Basin Way, Saratoga, ☎ 408/867–4711; Mon.–Sat.) is known for good jazz and blues. Try the **New West Melodrama and Comedy Vaudeville Show** (157 W. San Fernando St., San Jose, ☎ 408/295–7469) for a fresh take on the Old West.

Silicon Valley Essentials

Arriving and Departing

BY CAR

U.S. 101, I–280 (the Junipero Serra Freeway), and I–880 (Highway 17) connect the Valley with the San Francisco Bay Area. The drive south from San Francisco to San Jose on I–280 takes 60 minutes depending on traffic, which gets heavy during rush hour. The drive north from Monterey on U.S. 101 takes about 90 minutes. Highway 1, which runs along the California coast, takes longer, but is far more scenic.

BY PLANE

San Jose International Airport (☎ 408/277–4759), just 3 miles from downtown San Jose, is served by the light-rail system in addition to airport shuttle services such as **Express Airport Shuttle** (☎ 408/378–6270) and **South & East Bay Airport Shuttle** (☎ 408/559–9477).

BY PUBLIC TRANSPORTATION

Although Silicon Valley is as much a car culture as Los Angeles, commuter services are available. **CalTrain** (☎ 800/660–4287) runs from 4th and Townsend streets in San Francisco to San Jose's light-rail system; **Amtrak** (☎ 800/872–7245), **BART** (Bay Area Rapid Transit, ☎ 415/992–2278), and **Greyhound Lines** (☎ 800/231–2222) also provide public transportation.

Getting Around

In San Jose, **light-rail vehicles** serve most major attractions, shopping malls, historic sites, and downtown. Service is every 10 to 15 minutes between 4:30 AM and 1:30 AM on weekdays, every 15 to 30 minutes between 5:45 AM and 1:30 AM on weekends. **Historic trolleys** also operate in downtown San Jose from 11 to 7 during the summer, and on some holidays throughout the year. Buy tickets for both the light rail and the trolleys at vending machines in any transit station. Tickets for the light rail are valid for two hours; prices vary with destination. Trolley fare is 50¢ for all ages. For more information call or visit the **Transit Information Center** (4 N. 2nd St., San Jose, ☎ 408/321–2300).

Guided Tours

Royal Coach Tours (644 Stockton Ave., San Jose, ☎ 408/279–4801 or 800/443–7433) plans custom tours for individuals as well as groups.

Visitor Information

For information about recreational events, contact the **Santa Clara Chamber of Commerce and Convention & Visitors Bureau** (2200 Laurelwood Rd., Santa Clara, 95054, ☎ 408/970–9825) or the **Visitor Information Center** (1515 El Camino Real, Box 387, Santa Clara, 95050, ☎ 408/296–7111). The **San Jose Visitor and Business Center** (☎ 408/283–8833) publishes a bimonthly calendar of ethnic festivals and outdoor events, and the **San Jose Convention and Visitors Bureau** (333 W. San Carlos St., Suite 1000, San Jose 95110, ☎ 408/295–9600) produces an annual events calendar. For schedules of around-the-clock activities, call the **San Jose Tourist Bureau's FYI Hotline** (☎ 408/295–2265).

ON AND AROUND THE BAY

A ferry ride to Sausalito or Tiburon or a drive across the Golden Gate or Bay bridges are just two of the many opportunities to enjoy and explore San Francisco Bay and its nearby waterways. The bay, 60 miles long and between 3 and 13 miles wide, was the area's transportation hub before there were passable roads and rails. Shipping and sailing were plentiful here in the 1830s, as described by Richard Henry Dana in his classic *Two Years Before the Mast.* Now the bay is an equally thriving destination for weekend and vacation excursions. Around the bay are miles of shoreline parks and wildlife refuges, easily accessible but almost never seen by travelers on the busy Bayshore and East Shore freeways.

Yerba Buena Island provides the center anchorage for the Bay Bridge. It is connected by a causeway to man-made Treasure Island, which has a military museum and relics of the island's 1939 World's Fair. Excursions are available to the Farallon Islands, 23 miles outside the Golden Gate, where wildlife is abundant. Other boating excursions explore the bay and the delta's maze of waterways as far as Stockton and Sacramento. Back on land, about an hour's drive northeast of San Francisco, the town of Benicia is an early state capitol that has been meticulously restored. Across Carquinez Strait is the former home of naturalist John

Muir. Scenic river roads, particularly Highway 160, offer slower-paced alternatives to freeway travel between the Bay Area and Sacramento.

Exploring

Every day 250,000 people pass through **Yerba Buena Island** on their way across the San Francisco–Oakland Bay Bridge, yet it remains a mystery to most of them. Yerba Buena and the adjacent Treasure Island are primarily military bases, but they are accessible to the public. **Treasure Island** provides a superb bay-level view of the San Francisco skyline. The **Navy–Marine Corps–Coast Guard Museum** focuses on the military role in the Pacific; it is housed in one of the remaining buildings from the 1939 Golden Gate International Exposition. *Bldg. 1, Treasure Island,* ☎ *415/395–5067.* ☛ *Free.* ⏲ *Daily 10–3:30.*

Recently developed wildlife refuges offer welcome access to the bay's shore, which can appear to be a congested commercial strip from surrounding freeways. Among the best of the free public parks are **Coyote Point Nature Museum,** just off U.S. 101, south of San Francisco Airport (☎ 415/342–7755; open Tues.–Sat. 10–5, Sun. noon–5); the **Baylands Nature Interpretive Center** (☎ 415/329–2506; open Tues. and Wed. 10–5, Thurs. and Fri. 2–5, weekends 1–5), in the marshes at the east end of Embarcadero Road in Palo Alto; the **San Francisco Bay National Wildlife Refuge,** on Thornton Avenue in Fremont, at the east end of the Dumbarton Bridge/Highway 84 (☎ 510/792–0222; open Tues.–Sun. 10–5); and the **Hayward Regional Shoreline** (open daily 6 AM–sunset; for guided walks, call the Interpretive Center, ☎ 510/881–6751), the largest marsh restoration project on the West Coast, on West Winton Avenue at the east end of the San Mateo Bridge/Highway 92.

Another major wildlife center, outside the bay, is the **Gulf of the Farallones National Maritime Sanctuary.** Though the islands are off-limits to visitors, rare nesting birds and passing seals and whales are visible from cruise boats. Oceanic Society Expeditions operates cruises from June to November (☎ 415/474–3385). Fares are $49–$58.

Houseboats can be rented to explore the 1,000 miles of delta waterways. Boats accommodate up to 14 persons, and a "test drive" with an operator is included in the rental; prices are about $600–$2,000 a week. "The California Adventure Guide," covering houseboating, white-water rafting, and hot-air ballooning, is available from the California Office of Tourism (801 K St., Suite 1600, Sacramento 95814, ☎ 800/862–2543).

The historic port city of **Benicia** is worth a detour for travelers on I–80 between San Francisco and Sacramento. (Take the I–780 exit in Vallejo, then Benicia's East 2nd Street exit.) The old town center is on 1st Street, and at the foot of the street there is a fishing pier with a view through Carquinez Strait to San Pablo Bay. Benicia was named for the wife of General Mariano Vallejo, who owned the surrounding 99,000 acres. It was the state capital in 1852 and 1853, and the handsome brick Greek Revival **capitol** has been splendidly restored. *1st and W. G Sts.,* ☎ *707/745–3385.* ☛ *Nominal fee.* ⏲ *Daily 10–5.*

A pleasant garden and Federal-style home next door to the capitol is open to the public. Nearby are scattered historic buildings, art galleries, crafts workshops, and antiques stores. The **Chamber of Commerce** (601 1st St.) distributes a helpful map and guide to the old waterfront district—including a list of former brothels. The Union Hotel (401 1st

St., ☎ 707/746–0100) has been brilliantly restored, and its restaurant is the area's finest.

Just across Carquinez Strait from Benicia is Martinez, another historic port city that has become increasingly industrial. Martinez is said to be the birthplace of the martini, which according to legend was invented as the "Martinez cocktail" and was later slurred into its present designation. Visitors to the town can view the **John Muir National Historic Site,** the Victorian-era residence of conservationist John Muir. Carefully restored and maintained, it sits atop a hill and is still surrounded by orchards and gardens. *Alhambra Ave., near Hwy. 4,* ☎ *510/228–8860.* ☛ *Nominal fee.* ⌚ *Wed.–Sun. 10–4:30.*

North of the delta, about halfway between San Francisco and Sacramento, is the **Western Railway Museum,** which has collected and restored more than 100 pieces of railway equipment, including steam engines, suburban railroad commuter cars, and a variety of streetcars that make excursions around the 25-acre site. *Hwy. 12 at Rio Vista Junction, 10 mi east of Fairfield,* ☎ *707/374–2978.* ☛ *$2–$5.* ⌚ *11–5 weekends and most holidays.*

MARINE WORLD AFRICA USA

One of northern California's most popular attractions, this 160-acre wildlife theme park has been a phenomenal success since moving in 1986 from a crowded site south of San Francisco to Vallejo, about an hour's drive northeast. Animals of the land, sea, and air perform in shows, roam in natural habitats, and stroll among park visitors with their trainers. Among the "stars" are killer whales, dolphins, camels, elephants, sea lions, chimpanzees, and a troupe of human water-skiers (April–October). The newest attraction, "Shark Experience," takes visitors on a walk through an acrylic tunnel that traverses a 300,000-gallon coral reef habitat with 15 species of sharks and rays and 100 species of tropical fish.

Owned by the Marine World Foundation, a nonprofit organization devoted to educating the public about the world's wildlife, the park is a family attraction, with entertaining but informative shows and close-up looks at exotic animals. For additional sightseeing, visitors can reach the park on a high-speed ferry from San Francisco, a trip that offers unusual vistas through San Francisco Bay and San Pablo Bay. *Marine World Pkwy., Vallejo,* ☎ *707/643–6722.* ☛ *$24.95 adults, $20.95 senior citizens 60 and over, $16.95 children 4–12.* ⌚ *Summer, daily 9:30–6:45; rest of year and some school holidays, Wed.–Sun. 9:30–5.*

Marine World Africa USA Essentials

Arriving and Departing

BY BUS

Greyhound Lines (☎ 800/231–2222) runs buses from downtown San Francisco to Vallejo. You can take the **BART** train (415/992–2278) to El Cerrito Del Norte Station and transfer to **Vallejo Transit** line (☎ 707/648–4666) to get to the park.

BY CAR

Take I–80 east to Marine World Parkway in Vallejo. The trip takes one hour one-way. Parking is $4 at the park.

BY FERRY

Blue and Gold Fleet's (☎ 415/705–5444) high-speed ferry departs mornings each day that the park is open, from Pier 39 at Fisherman's Wharf. It arrives in Vallejo an hour later. Round-trip service allows five hours to visit the park. Excursion tickets cost $22.50–$39 and include park admission.

9 The Wine Country

Updated by Claudia Gioseffi

IN 1862, after an extensive tour of the wine-producing areas of Europe, Count Agoston Haraszthy de Mokcsa reported a promising prognosis to his adopted California: "Of all the countries through which I passed, not one possessed the same advantages that are to be found in California. . . . California can produce as noble and generous a wine as any in Europe; more in quantity to the acre, and without repeated failures through frosts, summer rains, hailstorms, or other causes."

The "dormant resources" that the father of California's viticulture saw in the balmy days and cool nights of the temperate Napa and Sonoma valleys are in full fruition today. While the wines produced here are praised and savored by connoisseurs throughout the world, the area continues to be a fermenting vat of experimentation, a proving ground for the latest techniques of grape growing and wine making.

Ever more competitive, the vintners constantly hone their skills, aided by the scientific know-how of graduates of the nearby University of California at Davis, as well as by the practical knowledge of the grape growers. They experiment with planting the vine stock closer together and with canopy management of the grape cluster, as well as with cold fermentation in stainless-steel vats, and new methods of fining, or filtering, the wine.

For many, wine making is a second career—since any would-be wine maker can rent the cumbersome, costly machinery needed to stem and press the grapes. Many say making wine is a good way to turn a large fortune into a small one, but that hasn't deterred the doctors, former college professors, publishing tycoons, and airline pilots who come to try their hand at it.

Twenty years ago, Napa Valley had no more than 20 wineries; today there are almost 10 times that number. In Sonoma County, where the web of vineyards is looser, there are more than 100 wineries, and development is now claiming the cool Carneros region at the head of the San Francisco Bay, deemed ideal for growing the chardonnay grape. Grape growers now produce their own wines instead of the selling their grapes to larger wineries. As a result, smaller producers can make excellent, reasonably priced wines, while the larger wineries consolidate land and expand their varietals.

In the past, the emphasis was on creating wines to be cellared, but today so-called drinkable wines, which can be enjoyed relatively rapidly, are more commonly produced. These are served in the first-class restaurants that have proliferated in the Valley as a result of the thriving tourist industry.

In addition to state-of-the-art viticulture and dining, the Wine Country is steeped in California history. The town of Sonoma is filled with remnants of Mexican California and the solid, ivy-covered, brick wineries built by Haraszthy and his disciples. Calistoga is a virtual museum of Steamboat Gothic architecture, replete with the fretwork and clapboard beloved of gold-rush prospectors and late 19th-century spa goers. St. Helena is home to a later architectural fantasy, the beautiful Art Nouveau mansion of the Beringer brothers; and the latter-day postmodern extravaganza of Clos Pegase is in Calistoga.

Tourism's growth has produced tensions, and some residents look askance at projects like the Wine Train between Napa and St. Helena.

Still, the area's natural beauty, recalling the hills of Tuscany and Provence, will always draw tourists—from the spring, when the vineyards bloom yellow with mustard flowers, to the fall, when fruit is ripening. Haraszthy was right: This is a chosen place.

EXPLORING

Three major paths cut through the Wine Country: U.S. 101 north from Santa Rosa, Highways 12 and 121 through Sonoma County, and Highway 29 north from Napa.

Like the wines they produce, each of the regions within the Wine Country has its own flavor. Napa Valley is larger, more commercial, and a bit more sophisticated than Sonoma County; with more than 200 wineries, it is the undisputed capital of American wine production. Still, the valley has its fair share of small, quirky towns. Calistoga feels like an Old West frontier town, with wooden-plank storefronts and people in cowboy hats; St. Helena is posh, with tony shops and elegant restaurants; Yountville is small, concentrated, and redolent of American history.

While Napa Valley is upscale and elegant, Sonoma County is overalls-and-corduroy, with an air of rustic innocence; and yet its Alexander, Dry Creek, and Russian River valleys are no less productive of award-winning vintages. Here, family-run wineries treat visitors like personal friends, and tastings are usually free. The Sonoma countryside also offers excellent opportunities for hiking, biking, camping, and fishing.

Since there are more than 400 wineries in and around the valley, it pays to be selective when planning your visit. Better to mix up the wineries with other sights and diversions—a picnic, a trip to the village museum, a ride in a hot-air balloon—than to try to visit them all in one day.

Numbers in the margin correspond to wineries on the Wine Country map.

Unless otherwise noted, visits to the wineries listed are free.

Napa Valley

The town of **Napa** is the gateway into the valley that's famed for its unrivaled climate and neat rows of vineyards. The towns in the valley are small, and their Victorian Gothic architecture makes the area feel like a distant world.

Yountville

1 A few miles north of Napa is the small town of **Yountville.** Turn west off Highway 29 at the Veterans Home exit and then up California Drive to **Domaine Chandon,** owned by the French champagne producer Moet-Hennessy and Louis Vuitton. Tours of the sleek modern facilities on this beautifully maintained property include sample flutes of the méthode champenoise sparkling wine. Champagne is $3–$4 per glass, hors d'oeuvres are complimentary, and an elegant restaurant beckons gourmets. *California Dr., Yountville,* ☎ *707/944–2280. Restaurant closed Mon. and Tues. Nov.–Apr. and closed entirely Jan. 1–25. No dinner Mon. and Tues. May–Oct. Tours daily 11–5, except Mon. and Tues. Nov.–Apr. Closed major holidays.*

Vintage 1870, a 26-acre complex of boutiques, restaurants, and gourmet stores, is on the east side of Highway 29. The vine-covered brick buildings were built in 1870 and originally housed a winery, livery stable, and distillery. The original mansion of the property is now

Benziger Family Winery, **18**
Beringer Vineyards, **4**
Buena Vista Carneros Winery, **15**
Charles Krug Winery, **5**
Chateau Montelena, **9**
Clos du Bois, **26**
Clos du Val, **10**
Clos Pegase, **8**
Cuvaison, **13**
Davis Bynum Winery, **21**
Domaine Chandon, **1**
Dry Creek Vineyard, **23**
Freemark Abbey Winery, **6**
Gloria Ferrer Champagne Caves, **16**
Hop Kiln Winery, **22**
Kenwood Vineyards, **19**
Korbel Champagne Cellars, **20**
Lytton Springs Winery, **25**
Piper Sonoma, **27**
Robert Mondavi, **2**
Robert Stemmler Winery, **24**
Rutherford Hill Winery, **12**
Sebastiani Vineyards, **14**
Stag's Leap Wine Cellars, **11**
Sterling Vineyards, **7**
V. Sattui, **3**
Viansa, **17**

The Wine Country

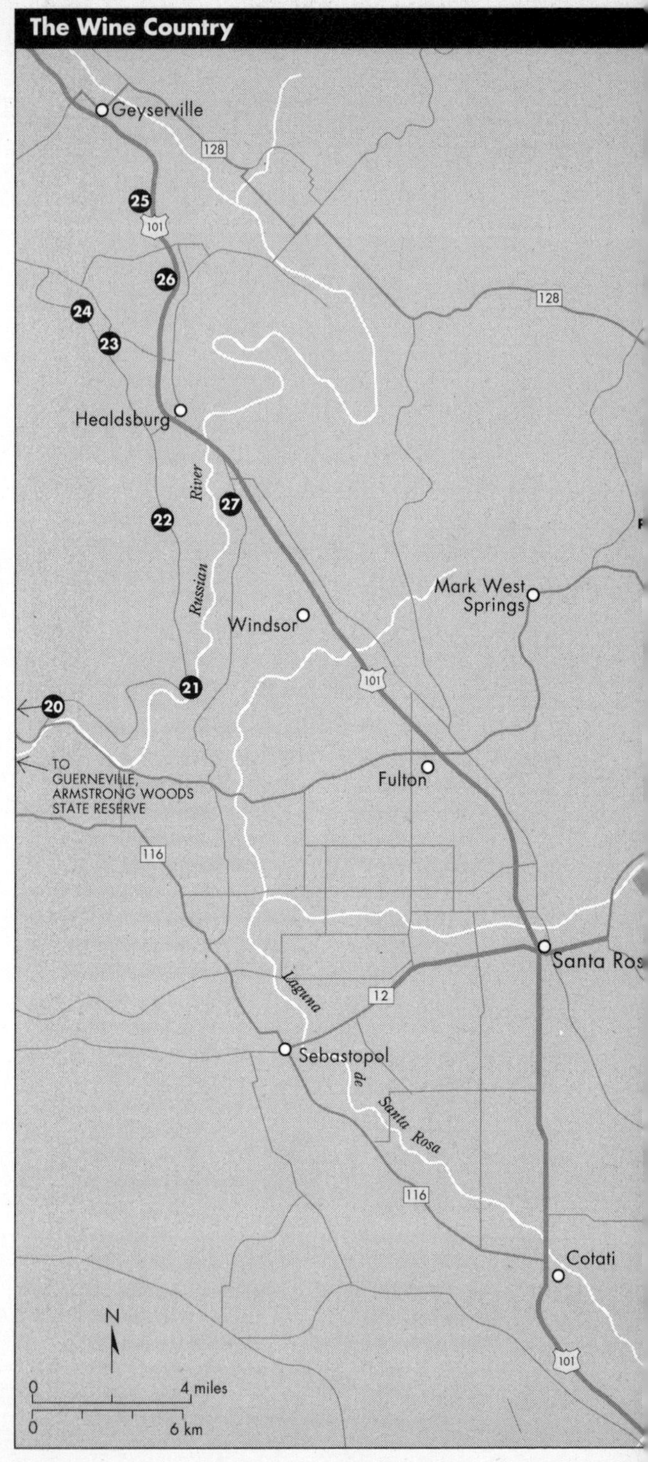

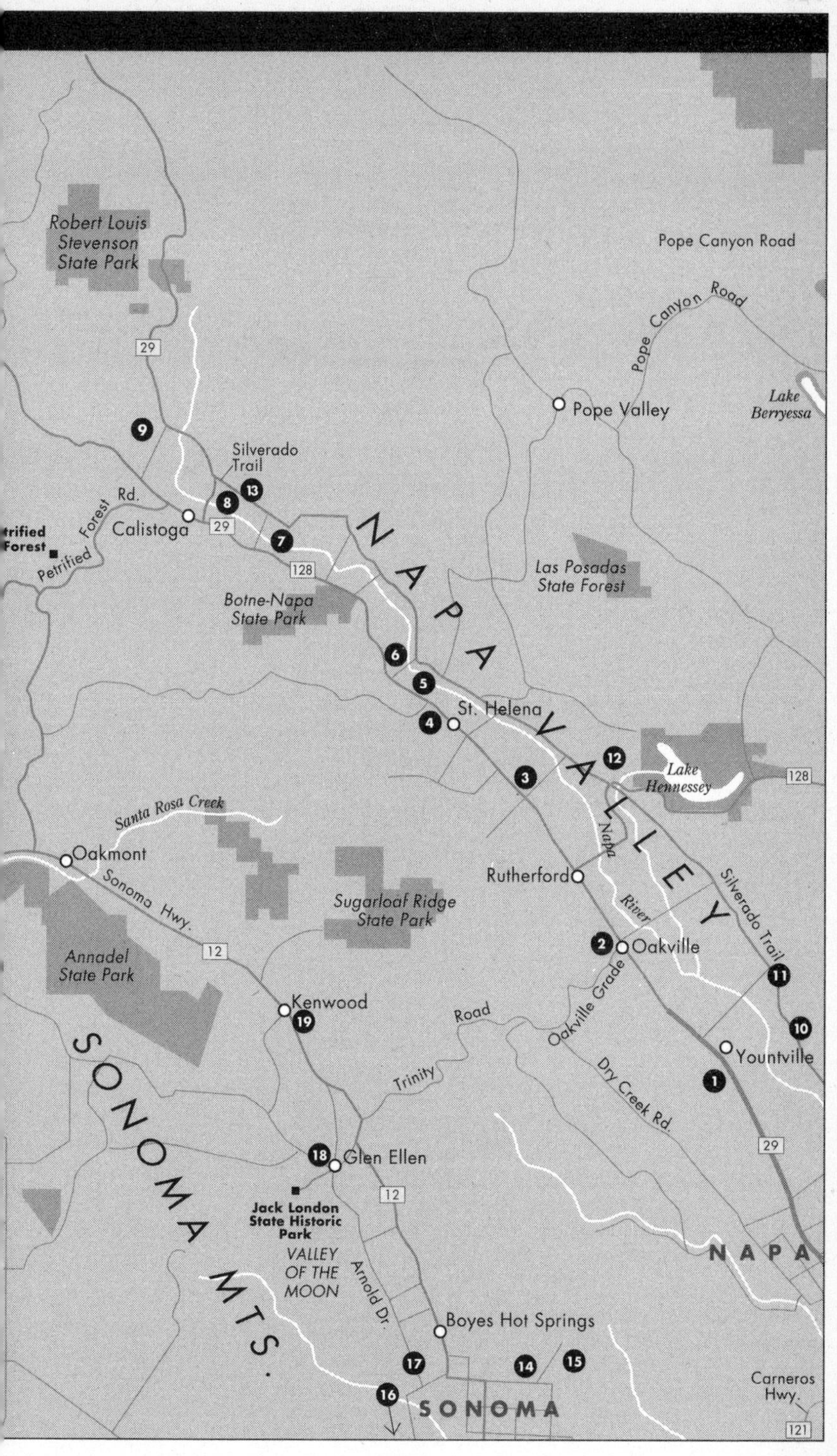

Robert Louis Stevenson State Park
29
9
Silverado Trail
13
8
Rd.
Forest
Petrified
trified Forest
Calistoga
29
7
128
NAPA VALLEY
Botne-Napa State Park
6
5
4
St. Helena
3
12
Lake Hennessey
128
Pope Canyon Road
Pope Canyon Road
Pope Valley
Lake Berryessa
Las Posadas State Forest
Santa Rosa Creek
Oakmont
Sonoma Hwy.
12
Annadel State Park
Sugarloaf Ridge State Park
Rutherford
Napa River
Silverado Trail
2
Oakville
11
10
Yountville
1
Oakville Grade
Dry Creek Rd.
Kenwood
19
Road
Trinity
SONOMA MTS.
18
Glen Ellen
12
Jack London State Historic Park
VALLEY OF THE MOON
Arnold Dr.
Boyes Hot Springs
17
14
15
16
SONOMA
29
NAPA
Carneros Hwy.
121

Compadres Bar and Grill, and the adjacent **Red Rock Cafe** is housed in the train depot Samuel Brannan built in 1868 for his privately owned Napa Valley Railroad. The remodeled railroad cars now accommodate guests at the Napa Valley Lodge (*see* Lodging, *below*).

Washington Square, at the north end of Yountville, is a complex of shops and restaurants; **Pioneer Cemetery,** birthplace of the town's founder, George Yount, is across the street.

St. Helena

Many premier wineries lie along the route from Yountville to St. Helena.

2 At **Robert Mondavi,** tasters are encouraged to take the 60-minute production tour with complimentary tasting before trying the reserved wines ($1–$5 per glass). In-depth, three- to four-hour tours and gourmet lunch tours are also popular. Afterwards, visit the art gallery, and look for the summer concerts that are held on the grounds. *7801 St. Helena Hwy., Oakville,* ☎ *707/259–9463. Reservations advised in summer.* ⏲ *May–Oct., daily 9–5:30; Nov.–Apr., daily 9:30–4:30; closed major holidays.*

3 The wine made at **V. Sattui** is sold only on the premises; the tactic draws crowds, as does the huge gourmet delicatessen with its exotic cheeses and pâtés. Award-winning wines include dry Johannisberg Rieslings, zinfandels, and Madeiras. *1111 White La., St. Helena,* ☎ *707/963–7774.* ⏲ *Daily 9–5; closed Dec. 25.*

4 **Beringer Vineyards** has been operating continually since 1876. Tastings are held in the Rhine House mansion, where hand-carved oak and walnut furniture and stained-glass windows feature Belgian Art Nouveau at its most opulent. The Beringer brothers, Frederick and Jacob, built the mansion in 1883 for the princely sum of $30,000. Tours are given every 30 minutes, and include a visit to the deep limestone tunnels in which the wines mature. *2000 Main St., St. Helena,* ☎ *707/963–4812.* ⏲ *Daily 9:30–4; summer hrs are sometimes extended to 5; closed major holidays.*

5 The **Charles Krug Winery** opened in 1861 when Count Haraszthy loaned Krug a small cider press. The oldest winery in the Napa Valley, it is run by the Peter Mondavi family. The gift shop stocks everything from gourmet food baskets with local produce and "grape" pasta to books about the region and its wines. *2800 N. Main St., St. Helena,* ☎ *707/963–5057.* ⏲ *Daily 10:30–5; closed major holidays.*

The town of St. Helena boasts many Victorian buildings. Don't overlook the **Silverado Museum,** two blocks east from Main Street on Adams. Its Robert Louis Stevenson memorabilia consist of more than 8,000 artifacts, including first editions, manuscripts, and photographs. *1490 Library La.,* ☎ *707/963–3757.* ☛ *Free.* ⏲ *Tues.–Sun. noon–4; closed major holidays.*

6 **Freemark Abbey Winery** was founded in the 1880s by Josephine Tychson, the first woman to establish a winery in California. *3022 St. Helena Hwy. N, St. Helena,* ☎ *707/963–9694.* ⏲ *Mar.–Dec., daily 10–4:30; Jan. and Feb., Thurs.–Sun. 10–4:30. 1 tour daily at 2 PM.*

The **Hurd Beeswax Candle Factory** is next door, with two restaurants and a gift shop that specializes in handcrafted candles made on the premises.

Calistoga

Calistoga, at the head of the Napa Valley, is noted for its mineral water, hot mineral springs, mud baths, steam baths, and massages. The Calistoga Hot Springs Resort was founded in 1859 by maverick entrepreneur Sam Brannan, whose ambition was to found "the Saratoga of California." He tripped up the pronunciation of the phrase at a formal banquet—it came out "Calistoga"—and the name stuck. One of his cottages, preserved as the **Sharpsteen Museum,** has a magnificent diorama of the resort in its heyday. *1311 Washington St., ☎ 707/942–5911. Donations accepted. ⏲ May–Oct., daily 10–4; Nov.–Apr., daily noon–4.*

7 The **Sterling Vineyards** sits on a hilltop to the east near Calistoga. The pristine white Mediterranean-style buildings are reached by an enclosed gondola from the valley floor; the view from the tasting room is superb and the gift shop is one of the best in the valley. *1111 Dunaweal La., Calistoga, ☎ 707/942–3300. Tram fee: $6 adults, children under 16 free. ⏲ Daily 10:30–4:30; closed major holidays.*

8 At **Clos Pegase,** neoclassicism sets the tone. The winery, designed by architect Michael Graves, the exemplar of postmodernism, and commissioned by Jan Schrem, a publisher and art collector, pays homage to art, wine, and mythology. *1060 Dunaweal La., Calistoga, ☎ 707/942–4981. ⏲ Daily 10:30–5; closed major holidays.*

9 **Chateau Montelena** is a vine-covered 1882 building set amid Chinese-inspired gardens, complete with a lake, red pavilions, and arched bridges. It's a romantic spot for a picnic, but be sure to reserve in advance. *1429 Tubbs La., Calistoga, ☎ 707/942–5105 or 800/222–7288. ⏲ Daily 10–4. Tours at 11 and 2 by appointment only.*

Calistoga Gliders gives participants a bird's-eye view of the entire valley. On clear days, visibility extends to the San Francisco skyline, the snowcapped Sierra peaks, and the Pacific Ocean. *1546 Lincoln Ave., ☎ 707/942–5000. Fees: $110–$150 for 2 passengers, depending on length of ride. ⏲ Daily 9 AM–sunset (weather permitting); closed Thanksgiving and Dec. 25.*

Although paying to wallow in mud may sound like an odd thing to do, it's a chic and popular pastime in the Napa Valley. At **Indian Springs,** $85 entitles enthusiasts to "The Works": a mud bath, a mineral-water shower, and a mineral-water whirlpool, followed by time in the steam room, a blanket wrap, and a half-hour massage. An extra half-hour massage costs $93, and a straight mud bath without any frills costs $45. *1507 Lincoln Ave., Calistoga, ☎ 707/942–4102. Reservations recommended. ⏲ Daily 8–3:30.*

Silverado Trail

The **Silverado Trail,** which runs parallel to Highway 29 north from Napa, takes you away from the crowds to some distinguished wineries.

10 At **Clos du Val,** on the Silverado Trail, French owner Bernard Portet produces a celebrated cabernet sauvignon. *5330 Silverado Trail, ☎ 707/259–2200. ⏲ Daily 10–5.*

11 In 1993 the World Wine Championships gave **Stag's Leap Wine Cellars** a platinum award for their 1990 Reserve Chardonnay, designating it the highest-ranked premium chardonnay in the world. Their proprietary red table wine, Cask 23, consistently earns accolades from *Connoisseur* and *The Wine Spectator* as well. *5766 Silverado Trail, ☎ 707/944–2020. Tasting fee: $3. Tours by appointment. ⏲ Daily 10–4; closed major holidays.*

12 The wine at **Rutherford Hill Winery** is aged in French oak barrels stacked in more than 30,000 square feet of caves—the largest such caves in the nation. Tours of the caves can be followed by a picnic in the orchards: choose among oak, olive, or madrone. *200 Rutherford Hill Rd. (off the Silverado Trail), Rutherford,* ☎ *707/963–7194.* ⏲ *Weekdays 10–4:30, weekends 10–5. Tour times vary seasonally; call for detailed information.*

13 A Swiss-owned winery, **Cuvaison** specializes in chardonnay, merlot, and cabernet sauvignon for the export market. Two small picnic areas on the grounds look out over Napa Valley. *4550 Silverado Trail,* ☎ *707/942–6266.* ⏲ *Daily 10–5. Tours by appointment.*

Sonoma

Rustic Sonoma is anchored by its past. As the site of the last and the northernmost of the 21 missions established by the Franciscan order of Fra Junipero Serra, its central plaza includes the largest group of old adobes north of Monterey. The **Mission San Francisco Solano,** whose chapel and school were used to bring Christianity to the Indians, is now a museum with a fine collection of 19th-century watercolors. *114 Spain St. E,* ☎ *707/938–1519.* ☛ *$2 adults, $1 children 6–12; includes the Sonoma Barracks on the central plaza and General Vallejo's home, Lachryma Montis (*see below*).* ⏲ *Daily 10–5; closed major holidays.*

TIME OUT The four-block **Sonoma Plaza** is an inviting array of shops and food stores that overlook the shady park and attract gourmets from miles around. You can pick up the makings for a first-rate picnic here. The **Sonoma French Bakery** (466 1st St. E, ☎ 707/996–2691) is famous for its sourdough bread and cream puffs. The **Sonoma Cheese Factory** (2 Spain St., ☎ 707/996–1000), run by the same family for four generations, makes Sonoma jack cheese and a tangy Sonoma Teleme. Great swirling baths of milk and curds are visible through the windows, along with flat-pressed wheels of cheese.

A few blocks west (and quite a hike away) is the tree-lined approach to **Lachryma Montis,** which General Mariano Vallejo, the last Mexican governor of California, built for his large family in 1851. The Victorian Gothic house is secluded in the midst of beautiful gardens; opulent Victorian furnishings, including a white marble fireplace in every room, are particularly noteworthy. The state purchased the home in 1933. *Spain St. W,* ☎ *707/938–1519.* ☛ *$2 adults, $1 children 6–12.* ⏲ *Daily 10–5; closed major holidays.*

14 The **Sebastiani Vineyards,** originally planted by Franciscans of the Sonoma Mission in 1825, were bought by Samuele Sebastiani in 1904. The Sebastianis are renowned producers of red wines, and Sylvia Sebastiani has recorded her good Italian home cooking in a family recipe book, *Mangiamo,* to complement them. Tours include a look at an unusual collection of impressive carved oak casks. *389 4th St. E,* ☎ *707/938–5532.* ⏲ *Daily 10–5; last tour at 4:30; closed major holidays.*

15 The landmark **Buena Vista Carneros Winery** (follow signs from the plaza), set among towering trees and fountains, is a must-see in Sonoma. It was here, in 1857, that Count Agoston Haraszthy de Mokcsa laid the basis for modern California wine making, bucking the conventional wisdom that vines should be planted on well-watered ground by instead planting on well-drained hillsides. Chinese laborers dug tunnels 100 feet into the hillside, and the limestone they extracted was used to build the main house. Although their wines are produced elsewhere

in the Carneros region today, the winery offers tours, a gourmet shop, an art gallery, and great picnic spots. *18000 Old Winery Rd.,* ☎ *707/938–1266.* ⏲ *Daily 10:30–4:30.*

Carneros

In the Carneros region of the Sonoma Valley, south of Sonoma, the
16 wines at **Gloria Ferrer Champagne Caves** hearken back to a 700-year-old stock of Ferrer grapes. The wines here are aged in a "cava," or cellar, where several feet of earth maintain a constant temperature—an increasingly popular alternative to temperature-controlled warehouses. *23555 Carneros Hwy. 121,* ☎ *707/996–7256. Tasting fees by the glass and the type of champagne.* ⏲ *Daily 10:30–5:30. Tours every hr from 11 to 4.*

17 One of the newer wineries in Sonoma Valley is **Viansa,** opened by a son of the famous Sebastiani family who decided to strike out on his own. Reminiscent of a Tuscan villa, the winery's ocher-colored building is surrounded by olive trees and overlooks the valley. Inside is an Italian food and gift market. *25200 Arnold Dr., Sonoma,* ☎ *707/935–4700.* ⏲ *Daily 10–5.*

Glen Ellen and Kenwood

Continue north on Highway 12 through lush Sonoma Valley, where writer Jack London lived for many years; much around here has been named for him. The drive along Highway 12 takes you through orchards and rows of vineyards, with oak-covered mountain ranges flanking the valley. Some 2 million cases of wine are bottled in this area annually, and the towns of Glen Ellen and Kenwood are rich in history and lore. **Glen Ellen,** with its century-old Jack London Bar, is nestled at the base of the hill leading to Jack London State Park and the Benziger Family Winery. Nearby is Grist Mill Inn, a historic landmark with shops, and Jack London Village, with a charming bookstore filled with London's books and memorabilia. **Kenwood** is home to several important wineries, a historic train depot, and several eateries and shops specializing in locally produced gourmet products.

In the hills above Glen Ellen—known as the Valley of the Moon—lies **Jack London State Historic Park.** The House of Happy Walls is a museum of London's effects, including his collection of South Sea artifacts. The ruins of Wolf House, which London designed and which mysteriously burned down just before he was to move in, are nearby, and London is buried on the property. *2400 London Ranch Rd.,* ☎ *707/938–5216. Parking: $5 per car, with discounts for senior citizens. Park open daily 9:30–sunset, museum daily 10–5. Museum closed major holidays.*

18 The **Benziger Family Winery** specializes in premium estate and Sonoma County wines. Their Imagery Series is a low-volume release of unusual red and white wines distributed in bottles with art labels by well-known artists from all over the world. *1883 London Ranch Rd., Glen Ellen,* ☎ *707/935–3000. Complimentary tasting of Sonoma County wines; tasting fees vary.* ⏲ *Daily 10–4:30.*

19 The beautifully rustic grounds at **Kenwood Vineyards** complement the attractive tasting room and the artistic bottle labels. While Kenwood produces all premium varietals, they are best known for their signature Jack London Vineyard reds—pinot noir, zinfandel, cabernet and merlot, and a unique Artist Series Cabernet. *9592 Sonoma Hwy., Kenwood,* ☎ *707/833–5891. Free tasting, no tours.* ⏲ *Daily 10–4:30.*

Santa Rosa, Healdsburg, and Guerneville

Santa Rosa is the Wine Country's largest city and a good bet for moderately priced hotel rooms, especially for those who have not reserved in advance. Healdsburg, with its pastoral treasures, remains undeveloped and relatively untrafficked. Guerneville is a sleepy little hamlet that seems straight out of a cops-and-robbers film.

The **Luther Burbank Home and Gardens** commemorate the great botanist who lived and worked on these grounds for 50 years, singlehandedly developing the modern techniques of hybridization. Arriving as a young man from New England, he wrote: "I firmly believe . . . that this is the chosen spot of all the earth, as far as nature is concerned." The Santa Rosa plum, the Shasta daisy, and the lily of the Nile agapanthus are among the 800 or so plants he developed or improved. In the music room of his house, a Webster's Dictionary of 1946 lies open to a page on which the verb "burbank" is defined as "to modify and improve plant life." *Santa Rosa and Sonoma Aves., ☎ 707/524–5445. ☛ Gardens free; ⏲ Nov.–Mar., daily 8–5; Apr.–Oct., daily 8–7. ☛ Guided tours of the house and greenhouse: $2, children under 12 free; tours Apr.–Oct., Wed.–Sun. 10–4.*

The wineries of Sonoma County, located along winding roads, are not immediately obvious to the casual visitor; a tour of the vineyards that lie along the Russian River is a leisurely and bucolic experience. For a free map of the area, contact **Russian River Wine Road** (Box 46, Healdsburg 95448, ☎ 707/433–6782).

20 For a historical overview, start at the imposing **Korbel Champagne Cellars,** which displays photographic documents of the North West Railway in a former train stop on its property. *13250 River Rd., Guerneville, ☎ 707/887–2294. ⏲ Oct.–Apr., daily 9–4:30; May–Sept., daily 9–5. Tours on the hr 10–3.*

Armstrong Woods State Reserve, just outside of Guerneville, contains 752 acres of virgin redwoods and is the best place in the Wine Country to see California's most famous trees. More redwood country lies west of Guerneville, along the Russian River Road (Highway 116), which leads to the Pacific Ocean and the rugged Sonoma coast. A string of small towns along this are loaded with bed-and-breakfasts, seafood restaurants, and interesting sights. **Duncan Mills** is an old logging and railroad town with a complex of shops and a small museum in an old train depot. At the coast is **Jenner,** where the Russian River meets the Pacific. A colony of harbor seals makes its home here March through June.

East of Guerneville, turn left off the River Road onto Westside Road, which winds past a number of award-winning wineries.

21 **Davis Bynum Winery,** in business since 1965, specializes in Russian River Valley wines and are noted for their merlots and pinot noirs. *8075 Westside Rd., Healdsburg, ☎ 707/433–5852. ⏲ Daily 10–5.*

22 The **Hop Kiln Winery** is in an imposing hops-drying barn, which was built during the early 1900s and used as the backdrop for such films as the 1960 *Lassie* with James Stewart. *6050 Westside Rd., Healdsburg, ☎ 707/433–6491. ⏲ Daily 10–5.*

23 **Dry Creek Vineyard** is one of California's leading producers of white wines and well known for its fumé blanc. Their reds, especially zinfandels and cabernets, have also begun to earn notice. Flowering magnolia and redwood trees provide an ideal setting for a picnic. *3770 Lambert Bridge Rd., Healdsburg, ☎ 707/433–1000. ⏲ Daily 10:30–4:30.*

24 The **Robert Stemmler Winery,** which draws on German traditions of wine making, specializes in pinot noir. Picnic facilities, available by appointment only, are small and private, shaded by towering redwood trees. *3805 Lambert Bridge Rd., Healdsburg (Dry Creek Rd. exit from Hwy. 101, northwest 3 mi to Lambert Bridge Rd.), ☎ 707/433–6334. ⏲ Weekdays by appointment only; weekends 10:30–4:30.*

25 **Lytton Springs Winery** produces the archetype of Sonoma zinfandel, a dark, fruity wine with high alcohol content. Though the origin of this varietal is still disputed—some claim it was transplanted from stock in New England—the vines themselves are distinctive—gnarled and stocky, many of them over a century old. *650 Lytton Springs Rd., Healdsburg, ☎ 707/433–7721. ⏲ Daily 11–4.*

26 Five miles north of Healdsburg, **Clos du Bois** produces the fine estate chardonnays of the Alexander and Dry Creek valleys that have been mistaken for great French wines. *19410 Geyserville Ave., Box 940, Geyserville, ☎ 707/857–3100 or 800/222–3189. ⏲ Daily 10–4:30. No tours.*

27 South of Healdsburg, off U.S. 101, is **Piper Sonoma,** a state-of-the-art winery specializing in méthode champenoise sparkling wines. *11447 Old Redwood Hwy., Healdsburg, ☎ 707/433–8843. ⏲ Daily 10–5.*

TIME OUT Once you've seen, heard about, and tasted enough wine for one day, head over to **Kozlowski's Farms** (5566 Gravenstein, Hwy. 116N, ☎ 707/887–1587), in Forestville, where jams are made from every berry imaginable. Originally in Forestville but now located in Santa Rosa, **Brother Juniper's** (463 Sebastopol Ave., Santa Rosa, ☎ 707/542–9012) makes a heavenly "Struan" bread of polenta, malted barley, brown rice, buttermilk, wheat bran, and oats.

What to See and Do with Children

In the **Bale Grist Mill State Historic Park,** a partially restored 1846 flour mill is powered by a 36-foot overshot waterwheel. Short paths lead from the access road to the mill and the old pond site. *3 mi north of St. Helena on Hwy. 29, ☎ 707/942–4575. Day use: $2 adults, $1 children 6–17. ⏲ Daily 10–5. Waterwheel demonstrations most weekends. Call ahead for schedule and other special tour arrangements.*

Old Faithful Geyser of California blasts a 60-foot tower of steam and vapor about every 40 minutes; the pattern is disrupted if there's an earthquake in the offing. One of just three regularly erupting geysers in the world, it is fed by an underground river that heats to 350°F. The spout lasts three minutes. Picnic facilities are available. *1299 Tubbs La., 1 mi north of Calistoga, ☎ 707/942–6463. ☛ $5 adults, $4 senior citizens, $2 children 6–11. ⏲ Daily 9–6 during daylight saving time, 9–5 in winter. Call first if you're traveling from a distance to make sure the geyser will be active when you arrive.*

The **Petrified Forest** contains the remains of the volcanic eruptions of Mount St. Helena 3.4 million years ago. The force of the explosion uprooted the gigantic redwoods, covered them with volcanic ash, and infiltrated the trees with silicas and minerals, causing petrification. Explore the museum, then picnic on the grounds. *4100 Petrified Forest Rd., 5 mi west of Calistoga, ☎ 707/942–6667. ☛ $3 adults, $2 senior citizens, $1 children 4–11. ⏲ Summer, daily 10–6; winter, daily 10–4:30.*

The **Redwood Empire Ice Arena** in Santa Rosa is a skating rink with a twist. It was built by local resident Charles Schulz, creator of *Peanuts.*

The Snoopy Gallery and gift shop, with Snoopy books, clothing, and life-size comic strip characters, is delightful. *1667 W. Steele La.,* ☎ *707/546-7147. Public skating daily, times vary.*

A steam train at **Train Town** runs for 20 minutes through a forested park with trestles, bridges, and small animals. *20264 Broadway (Hwy. 12), 1 mi south of Sonoma Plaza,* ☎ *707/938-3912.* ☛ *$3.50 adults, $2.50 children under 16 and senior citizens.* ⌚ *Mid-June–Labor Day, daily 10:30–5; Sept.–mid-June, Fri.–Sun. 10:30–5 (weather permitting); closed Dec. 25.*

Howarth Memorial Park, in Santa Rosa, has a lake where canoes, rowboats, paddleboats, and small sailboats can be rented for $6 an hour. The children's area has a playground, pony rides, a petting zoo, a merry-go-round, and a miniature train. Fishing, tennis, and hiking trails are also available. *Summerfield Rd. off Montgomery Rd.,* ☎ *707/543-3282.* ☛ *Amusements: 75¢–$1.* ⌚ *Park: daily in good weather; children's area: summer, Wed.–Sun.; spring and fall, weekends.*

Off the Beaten Track

Breathtaking views of both the Sonoma and Napa valleys are evident from all of the hairpin turns of the **Oakville Grade,** which twists along the range dividing the two valleys. The surface of the road is good, and those who are comfortable with mountain driving will enjoy this half-hour excursion. Driving the road at night, however, can be difficult. Trucks are advised not to attempt it at any time.

Robert Louis Stevenson State Park, on Highway 29, 3 miles northeast of Calistoga, encompasses the summit of Mount St. Helena. It was here, in an abandoned bunkhouse of the Silverado Mine, that Stevenson and his bride, Fanny Osbourne, spent their honeymoon in the summer of 1880. The stay inspired Stevenson's "The Silverado Squatters," and Spyglass Hill in *Treasure Island* is thought to be a portrait of Mount St. Helena. The park's 3,000 acres are undeveloped except for a fire trail leading to the site of the cabin, which is marked with a marble tablet, and then on to the summit. Picnicking is permitted, but fires are not.

SHOPPING

Don't expect bargains at the wineries, where prices are generally as high as at retail outlets. Residents report that the area's supermarkets stock a wide selection of local wines at lower prices. For connoisseurs seeking extraordinary values, the **All Seasons Cafe Wine Shop** (☎ 707/942-6828) in Calistoga is a true find. Gift shops in the larger wineries offer the ultimate in gourmet items. Most wineries will ship purchases.

SPORTS AND THE OUTDOORS

Ballooning

This whimsical pastime has fast become part of the scenery in the Wine Country, and many hotels arrange excursions. Most flights take place soon after sunrise, when the calmest, coolest time of day offers maximum lift and soft landings. Prices depend on the duration of the flight, number of passengers, and services (some companies provide extras such as pickup at your lodging or champagne brunch after the flight). Expect to spend about $165 per person. Companies that provide flights include **Balloons Above the Valley** (Box 3838, Napa 94558, ☎ 707/253-2222 or 800/464-6824 in CA), **Napa Valley Balloons** (Box 2860, Yountville 94599, ☎ 707/944-0228 or 800/253-2224 in CA),

American Balloon Adventures (Box 795, Calistoga 94515, ☎ 707/942–6546 or 800/333–4359), **Once in a Lifetime** (Box 795, Calistoga 94515, ☎ 707/942–6541 or 800/659–9915), and **Napa's Great Balloon Escape** (Box 795, Calistoga 94515, ☎ 707/253–0860 or 800/564–9399), featuring a catered brunch finale at the Silverado Country Club, overlooking the golf course.

Bicycling

One of the best ways to experience the countryside is on two wheels, and the Eldorado Bike Trail is considered one of the best. Reasonably priced rentals are available in most towns.

Golf

Although the weather is mild year-round, rain may occasionally prevent your teeing off in the winter months. Call to check on greens fees at **Fountaingrove Country Club** (1525 Fountaingrove Pkwy., Santa Rosa, ☎ 707/579–4653), **Oakmont Golf Club** (west course: 7025 Oakmont Dr., Santa Rosa, ☎ 707/539–0415; east course: 565 Oak Vista Ct., Santa Rosa, ☎ 707/538–2454), **Silverado Country Club** (1600 Atlas Peak Rd., Napa, ☎ 707/257–0200), or the **Chardonnay Club** (2555 Jameson Canyon Rd., Napa, ☎ 707/257–8950), a favorite among Bay Area golfers.

DINING

Restaurants in the Wine Country have traditionally reflected the culinary heritage of early settlers from Italy, France, and Mexico. Star chefs from urban areas are the most recent influx of immigrants, bringing creative California cuisine, seafood, and an eclectic range of American-regional and international fare. Food now rivals wine as the prime attraction in the region, with restaurants offering fresh produce, meats, and prime ingredients from local farms. Those on a budget will find an appealing range of reasonably priced eateries. Gourmet delis offer superb picnic fare, and brunch is a cost-effective strategy at high-end restaurants.

With few exceptions (which are noted), dress is informal. Where reservations are indicated to be essential, you may need to reserve a week or more ahead; during the summer and early fall harvest seasons you may need to book several months ahead.

CATEGORY	COST*
$$$$	over $40
$$$	$25–$40
$$	$16–$25
$	under $16

**per person for a three-course meal, excluding drinks, service, and 7½% sales tax*

Calistoga

$$$$ **All Seasons Cafe.** Bistro cuisine has a California spin in this sun-filled setting with marble tables and a black-and-white checkerboard floor. A seasonal menu featuring organic greens, wild mushrooms, local game birds, house-smoked beef and salmon, and homemade breads, desserts, and ice cream from their on-site ice-cream plant, is coupled with a superb listing of local wines at bargain prices. For lunch there's a tempting selection of pizza, pasta, and sandwiches. ✕ *1400 Lincoln Ave.,* ☎ *707/942–9111. Reservations advised on weekends. Brunch Fri.–Sun. MC, V. Closed Wed.*

$$$ **Catahoula Restaurant and Saloon.** Inside the Mount View Hotel and Spa, this homey new restaurant, named after Louisiana's state dog, is the brainchild of chef Jan Birnbaum, whose credentials include stints at the Quilted Giraffe in New York and at the Campton Place in San Francisco. Using a large wood-burning oven as a stove, Birnbaum churns out California-Cajun dishes such as spicy gumbo Ya Ya with andouille sausage, oven braised lamb shank with red beans, whole roasted fish, and oven-roasted chili squid salad with honey caramelized endive. Save room for tantalizing desserts such as chocolate-sour cherry bread pudding or a wood-fired chocolate s'more that will bring you back to the campfire. Sit at the counter and watch the chef cook—it's the best entertainment in town. ✕ *1457 Lincoln Ave.* ☎ *707/942–2275. Reservations required. MC, V. Closed Tues.*

$–$$ **Silverado Restaurant & Tavern.** In a setting straight out of a spaghetti western, savvy locals and seasoned wine connoisseurs linger over an award-winning wine list with over 700 selections priced just above retail. The eclectic menu includes egg rolls, chicken-salad sandwiches, Caesar salad, and great burgers. ✕ *1374 Lincoln Ave.,* ☎ *707/942–6725. Reservations advised. MC, V. Closed Thurs.*

$ **Boskos Ristorante.** Set in a restored sandstone building that dates back to the 1800s, this family-style eatery dishes up homemade pasta, pizza, and garden-fresh salads. *Glorioso* (pasta shells with garlic, mushrooms, and red chilies), is a favorite entrée. Leave room for the homemade chocolate cheesecake. ✕ *1364 Lincoln Ave.,* ☎ *707/942–9088. No reservations. No credit cards.*

Geyserville

$–$$ **Château Souverain Café.** A spectacular view of Alexander Valley vineyards, an outdoor terrace for tranquil summer lunches, and reasonable prices make chef Martin Courtman's French country menu triply irresistible. Try braised lamb shanks, garlic and black pepper penne pasta, or grilled buckwheat polenta with Gorgonzola cheese. ✕ *400 Souverain Rd. (Independence La. exit west from Hwy. 101),* ☎ *707/433–3141. Reservations advised. AE, MC, V. Closed Mon.–Thurs. and Jan.*

Healdsburg

$$$$ **Restaurant at Madrona Manor.** This country inn with 21 rooms serves breakfast to guests only, but others can sample great food from the brick oven, smokehouse, orchard, and kitchen garden, including local Sonoma produce, Campbell lamb, and choice seafood. Chef Todd Muir turns out dishes fit for a wine baron: smoked lamb salad, Dungeness crab mousse, acorn squash soup, oven-roasted pork tenderloin, and Grand Marnier crème caramel. The 1881 Victorian mansion, surrounded by 8 acres of wooded and landscaped grounds, provides a storybook setting for a candlelight dinner or brunch on the outdoor deck. The seasonal menu is à la carte. ✕ *1001 Westside Rd. (take central Healdsburg exit from Hwy. 101, turn left on Mill St.),* ☎ *707/433–4231. Reservations advised. Sun. brunch Apr.–Oct. AE, D, DC, MC, V. No lunch.*

$–$$ **Bistro Ralph.** Ralph Tingle, once executive chef of the defunct Fetzer Vineyards Sun Dial Grill in Mendocino, has created a culinary hit with his California homestyle cuisine. The small, frequently changing menu includes Szechuan pepper calamari, braised lamb shanks with mint essence (using locally ranched Bruce Campbell lamb), and sea bass braised with ginger and carrot juice. Wine is used liberally in the cooking and the wine list features picks from small local wineries. The stark industrial setting is tempered by a couple of trees perched incongruously on the bar and an exceedingly friendly wait staff. ✕ *109 Plaza St.,* ☎ *707/433–1380. Reservations advised. MC, V. No lunch weekends.*

$–$$ **Samba Java.** This lively café manages to fit a lot of tables, colorful decor, and culinary action into a very small space. The menu, which represents an eclectic range of California cuisine, is based largely on

Sonoma ingredients and changes daily. Breads and preserves are made in-house, as are the succulent roasted pork loin with a sweet-potato *galette* (razor-thin slices layered with olive oil and herbs) and wilted bitter greens, and the mocha swirl cheesecake. ✕ *109A Plaza St.,* ☎ *707/433–5282. Reservations accepted for dinner; lunch reservations for 6 or more only. Breakfast served weekends. AE, MC, V. No lunch Mon., no dinner Sun.–Wed.*

Napa

$$$ **Silverado Country Club.** There are two restaurants and a bar and grill at this large, famous resort. The elegant Vintner's Court, with Pacific Rim cuisine, serves dinner only; there is a seafood buffet on Friday night and a champagne brunch on Sunday. Royal Oak serves steak and seafood for dinner nightly. The bar and grill is open for breakfast and lunch year-round; in the summer, lunch offerings include an outdoor barbecue with chicken and hamburgers. ✕ *1600 Atlas Peak Rd. (follow signs to Lake Berryessa),* ☎ *707/257–0200. Reservations required for 2 restaurants only. AE, D, DC, MC, V. Vintner's Court closed Mon. and Tues. No dinner Sun.*

$$–$$$ **La Boucane.** Chef-owner Jacques Mokrani has created a gorgeous little gem of a restaurant in a restored 1885 Victorian decorated with period antiques. Classic French cuisine (rack of lamb, champagne-crisp duck) is delivered with style in a candlelit dining room enhanced by silver, linen, and a red rose on each table. ✕ *1778 2nd St. (at Jefferson St. in downtown Napa),* ☎ *707/253–1177. Reservations advised. MC, V. Closed Sun. and Jan. No lunch.*

$–$$ **Bistro Don Giovanni.** Rumor has it that Alice Waters' first venture in the Wine Country, Table 29, failed because there weren't enough Napa Valley selections on the wine list. Giovanni and Donna Scala, the culinary couple behind the success of Ristorante Piatti, have avoided this problem, with a wine list that's as locally representative as their menu is eclectic. The ambience is casual Mediterranean, with terra-cotta tile floors, high ceilings, and a full bar stocked with Napa Valley wines, as well as a spacious outdoor patio with an expansive view of the valley. Ingredients such as pesto, goat cheese, and shrimp top individual pies from the wood-burning pizza oven. The carpaccio is a standout. Winning items include pastas and grilled entrées such as pork chops with garlic-infused mashed potatoes. Don't miss the delectable fruit-crisp dessert, which changes daily. ✕ *4110 St. Helena Hwy. 29,* ☎ *707/224–3300. Reservations advised. AE, DC, MC, V.*

$ **Jonesy's Famous Steak House.** This spacious and informal local favorite with a children's menu has been providing entertainment for aviation buffs, steak lovers, and kids of all ages since 1946. One entire wall has an expanse of windows with a prime view of the Napa County Airport landing strip. Inside, prime steaks, weighted down with Sacramento River rocks to keep juices in, are seared over a dry grill. Roasted chicken, homemade soups, and fresh fish round out the fare. ✕ *2044 Airport Rd. (halfway between Napa and Vallejo, off Hwy. 29),* ☎ *707/255–2003. Reservations advised. AE, D, DC, MC, V. Closed Mon. and 1 wk at Christmas.*

Oakville

$$ **Stars Oakville Cafe.** Jeremiah Tower, father of California Cuisine, and Peter Hall have transformed an old building next to the Oakville Grocery store into a country café with glazed tile floors, white walls, lots of flowers, and picture windows that look into the kitchen. Wood-burning ovens turn out rustic fare for a daily-changing menu that features roasted leg of lamb, roast salmon, and roast pumpkin-filled pasta with white truffle oil. The wine list is stellar, and desserts (brownie-steamed

pudding, pumpkin cheesecake) are sublime. Space heaters on the tented outdoor patio add comfort to alfresco dining, and the adjacent garden with olive and lemon trees, lavender, and an antique aviary is the perfect setting for an after-dinner stroll. ✕ *7848 St. Helena Hwy. 29 (corner of Hwy. 29 and Oakville Crossroad),* ☎ *707/944–8905. Reservations required weekends, advised weekdays. AE, D, DC, MC, V. No lunch Tues. and Wed.*

Rutherford

$$–$$$$ **Auberge du Soleil.** The dining room of this 50-room inn is a setting of Mediterranean elegance: earth tones, wood beams, and outdoor deck with panoramic views of the valley. The frequently changing menu, which features local produce, includes roasted lobster sausage and rosemary-roasted rack of lamb. A moderately priced bar menu offers slow-roasted garlic with homemade pretzels and pan-seared salmon sandwiches, and the extensive wine list represents French, Italian, and Napa Valley wines. ✕ *180 Rutherford Hill Rd. (off Silverado Trail just north of Rte. 128),* ☎ *707/963–1211. Reservations advised. AE, D, MC, V.*

St. Helena

$$$$ **Restaurant at Meadowood.** This sprawling resort looks like a scene from an F. Scott Fitzgerald novel, complete with croquet lawns, and provides the perfect setting for weekend brunch. Refined French cuisine with a California twist is offered on a prix fixe in either a dining room with a cathedral ceiling, a fireplace, and lush greenery, or outdoors on a terrace overlooking the golf course. A lighter menu of pizzas and spa food can be had at breakfast and lunch (and early dinners Friday and Saturday) at a second, less formal and less expensive Meadowood restaurant, the Grill. ✕ *900 Meadowood La.,* ☎ *707/963–3646. Reservations required. AE, D, DC, MC, V.*

$$$$ **Terra.** The delightful twosome who own this lovely, unpretentious restaurant housed in a century-old stone foundry learned their culinary skills at the side of chef Wolfgang Puck. Hiro Sone was head chef at L.A.'s Spago, and Lissa Doumanie was the pastry chef. Together, they offer an enticing array of southern French and northern Italian favorites, highlighting Hiro's Japanese-French-Italian finesse. Favorites are pear and goat cheese salad with warm pancetta and sherry vinaigrette, and fillet of salmon with Thai red-curry sauce and basmati rice. Save room for Lissa's desserts. ✕ *1345 Railroad Ave.,* ☎ *707/963–8931. Reservations advised. MC, V. Closed Tues. No lunch.*

$$$$ **Trilogy.** Chef-owner Diane Pariseau pairs one of the best and most extensive contemporary wine lists in the valley with superb renditions of California-French cuisine on a prix-fixe menu that changes daily. Pariseau deftly juxtaposes flavors and textures; her all-star entrées, such as grilled chicken breast on a nest of sautéed apples and green peppercorns, or grilled tuna steak with olive oil and sweet red pepper puree, are artfully presented. The secluded dining room feels like a gracious country home, with a mere 10 tables. ✕ *1234 Main St.,* ☎ *707/963–5507. Reservations required. MC, V. Closed Mon. and 3 wks in Dec. No lunch weekends.*

$$$ **Showley's.** In a building that dates from 1860, this homey, family-run restaurant has two dining rooms, the smaller of which has a bar. The seasonal menu reflects the owner-chef's interest in international flavors as well as local products (there's a fig tree out back that inspired an annual fig menu in late summer). Fresh fish and meats are noteworthy, especially the garlic chicken, tenderloin of pork, and roast monkfish with garlic-mashed potatoes. Starters are equally well-prepared, especially the *chile en nogada,* which is stuffed with pork, pine nuts,

and chutney and served with a walnut–crème fraîche sauce. Desserts to try are the famous chocolate phyllo pastry "hoo hoo" layered with Valrhona chocolate pastry cream and fresh raspberries, or the homemade ice creams that change flavors each season. ✕ *1327 Railroad Ave.,* ☎ *707/963–1200. Reservations recommended. AE, D, MC, V.*

$$ **Brava Terrace.** Owner and chef Fred Halpert was one of the instigators of the culinary renaissance in the Wine Country. American-born, French-trained Halpert has created a menu that features produce plucked from the restaurant's own garden to enliven his trademark pasta, risotto, and cassoulet dishes. The chocolate-chip crème brûlée provides a grand finale. Brava has a comfortably casual ambience with a full bar, a large stone fireplace, a romantic outdoor terrace, and a heated deck with views of the valley floor and Howell Mountain. ✕ *3010 St. Helena Hwy. (Hwy. 29, ½ mi north of St. Helena),* ☎ *707/963–9300. Reservations advised. AE, D, DC, MC, V. Closed Wed. Nov.–Apr. and Jan. 16–25.*

$$ ★ **Tra Vigne.** This Napa Valley fieldstone building has been transformed into a striking, extremely popular trattoria with a huge wood bar, impossibly high ceilings, and plush banquettes. Homemade mozzarella, olive oil, and vinegar, and house-cured pancetta and prosciutto contribute to a one-of-a-kind tour of Tuscan cuisine. Although getting a table without a reservation is sometimes difficult, drops-ins can sit at the bar. The outdoor courtyard in summer is a sun-splashed Mediterranean vision of striped umbrellas and awnings, crowded café tables, and rustic pots overflowing with flowers. The Cantinetta delicatessen in the corner of the courtyard offers wine by the glass and gourmet picnic fare. ✕ *1050 Charter Oak Ave. (off Hwy. 29),* ☎ *707/963–4444. Reservations suggested in dining room. D, DC, MC, V.*

Santa Rosa

$$$ **Cafe Lolo.** Voted the best new restaurant in Sonoma County by the *Press Democrat* and winner of the best Sonoma County wine list award at the 1994 Sonoma County Harvest Fair, this small, clean, downtown café also caught the eye of *The Wine Spectator* and the *San Francisco Chronicle* that same year. Tables are elegantly dressed in white linen, but the mood is casual. Chef/owner Michael Quigley's menu lunch and dinner menus include fresh seafood, daily changing risotto and pasta dishes, free-range chicken, rabbit, and lots of goat cheese and local produce. ✕ *620 5th St.,* ☎ *707/576–7822. Reservations advised. AE, MC, V. Closed Sun. No lunch Sat.*

$$–$$$ **John Ash & Co.** The thoroughly regional cuisine here emphasizes beauty, innovation, and the seasonal availability of food products grown in Sonoma County and in the restaurant's organic garden. In spring, local lamb is roasted with hazelnuts and honey; in fall, farm pork is roasted with fresh figs and Gravenstein apples. Desserts are delicious and the wine list extensive. With patio seating outside and a cozy fireplace indoors, the slightly formal restaurant looks like a Spanish villa amid the vineyards, and is a favorite spot for Sunday brunch. ✕ *4330 Barnes Rd. (River Rd. exit west from Hwy. 101),* ☎ *707/527–7687. Reservations advised. AE, MC, V. No lunch Mon.*

$–$$ **Lisa Hemenway's.** A shopping center on the outskirts of town seems an unlikely location for a restaurant find, but Hemenway, who trained under John Ash (*see* John Ash & Co., *above*) has created a light and airy eatery with soft wine-country colors and a garden view from the patio. The fare, which is updated every four months, represents American and international cuisine, from grilled sea bass with Singapore curry to red chili crepes and tapas. The adjacent café, Tote Cuisine, has a vast selection of tempting takeouts for picnickers. ✕ *714 Village Ct.*

Mall (east on Hwy. 12, at Farmer's La. and Sonoma Ave.), ☎ *707/526–5111. Reservations advised. Sun. brunch. AE, MC, V.*

$ **Mixx.** Great service and an eclectic "mix" of dishes define this small restaurant with large windows, booth and table seating, high ceilings, and French blown-glass chandeliers. Nightly homemade pasta and seafood dishes are offered, along with regional specialties such as grilled Cajun prawns and New Mexican stuffed chilies—all based on locally grown ingredients and served with Napa Valley wine. ✕ *135 4th St. (at Davis behind the mall on Railroad Sq.),* ☎ *707/573–1344. Reservations advised. No lunch weekends. AE, MC, V.*

$ **Omelette Express.** As the name implies, some 300 omelet possibilities are offered in this friendly, no-frills eatery in the historic Railroad Square. ✕ *112 4th St.,* ☎ *707/525–1690. No reservations weekends. No dinner. MC, V.*

Sonoma

$$$ **Grille at Sonoma Mission Inn & Spa.** There are two restaurants at this famed resort (*see* The Cafe, *below*). The Grille offers formal dining in a light, airy setting with original art on the walls, French windows overlooking the pool and gardens, and a patio for alfresco dining. Wine Country cuisine changes seasonally to feature favorites like Sonoma leg of lamb and basil-roasted chicken with garlic-mashed potatoes. On weekends, a prix-fixe menu pairs each course with the appropriate wine from the restaurant's extensive selection. A special spa menu caters to health-conscious gourmets. ✕ *18140 Hwy. 12 (2 mi north of Sonoma at Boyes Blvd.),* ☎ *707/938–9000. Reservations strongly advised. Sun. brunch. AE, DC, MC, V.*

$$ **Eastside Oyster Bar & Grill.** Chef-owner Charles Saunders, renowned for his stint at the Sonoma Mission Inn (*see above*), has received rave reviews for his creative culinary flair and health-conscious approach. Accordingly, the California fare here is made from fresh and local ingredients only, including the fish, meat, and poultry, and the produce comes from an organic kitchen garden. Specialties include a surprisingly delicate hangtown fry (plump oysters on a bed of greens and beets with a Sonoma mustard vinaigrette), creative renditions of roast chicken or Sonoma lamb, and stellar salads and vegetarian dishes. Inside, the restaurant has a fireplace and an intimate bistro atmosphere; outside there's a wisteria-draped terrace where diners enjoy a picture-window view into the pastry kitchen. ✕ *133 E. Napa St. (just off downtown plaza square),* ☎ *707/939–1266. Reservations advised. Sun. brunch. AE, DC, MC, V.*

$$ **Kenwood Restaurant & Bar.** This is where Napa and Sonoma chefs eat on their nights off. Both in tastes and looks it evokes the mood of a sunny hotel dining room in the south of France. Patrons indulge in country French cuisine such as braised rabbit and warm sweetbread salad in the airy dining room, or head through the French doors to the patio, which affords a memorable view of the vineyards. ✕ *9900 Hwy. 12, Kenwood,* ☎ *707/833–6326. Reservations advised. MC, V. Closed Mon.*

$$ **Ristorante Piatti.** On the ground floor of the remodeled El Dorado Hotel, a 19th-century landmark building, this is the Sonoma cousin of the Yountville Piatti (*see below*). Pizza from the wood-burning oven and northern Italian specials (spit-roasted chicken, ravioli with lemon cream) are served in a rustic Italian setting with an open kitchen and bright wall murals, or on the award-winning outdoor terrace, "one of the five best in northern California," according to the San Francisco Chronicle. ✕ *405 1st St. W (facing the plaza),* ☎ *707/996–2351. Reservations advised. AE, MC, V.*

$ The Cafe. This is Sonoma Mission Inn's (*see above*) second restaurant, with an informal bistro atmosphere, overstuffed booths, ceiling fans, and an open kitchen renowned for its country breakfasts, pizza from the wood-burning oven, and tasty California renditions of northern Italian cuisine. ✕ *18140 Sonoma Hwy. (2 mi north of Sonoma on Hwy. 12 at Boyes Blvd.),* ☎ *707/938–9000. Reservations recommended at dinner; accepted for 6 or more for breakfast and lunch. Weekday brunch. AE, DC, MC, V.*

$ La Casa. Whitewashed stucco, red tile, and serapes adorn this restaurant just around the corner from Sonoma's plaza. There's bar seating, a patio out back, and an extensive menu of traditional Mexican food: chimichangas and snapper Veracruz for entrées, sangria to drink, and flan for dessert. ✕ *121 E. Spain St.,* ☎ *707/996–3406. Reservations advised. AE, DC, MC, V.*

Yountville

$$$$ Domaine Chandon. Part of the world-renowned winery, this large, formal dining room caters to wine and food aficionados with a daily-changing menu of expertly prepared, artfully presented, French-inspired California cuisine. Sonoma duck breast is served with polenta and green-olive sage juice; venison is wrapped in pancetta and drizzled with huckleberry sauce. Desserts are a must: Try the hot, gooey chocolate cake with double-vanilla ice cream, or the daily-made sorbets. The cavernous room looks out over miles of vineyards and native oaks. There is also outdoor service on a tree-shaded patio. ✕ *California Dr. (Yountville exit off Hwy. 29, toward Veterans' Home),* ☎ *707/944–2892. Reservations essential. Jacket required. AE, D, DC, MC, V. No lunch Mon. and Tues. Nov.–Apr.*

$$$$ French Laundry. Though it dates back to 1977, this intimate, cottage-style restaurant only recently entered Wine Country stardom, under Thomas A. Keller's ownership. Inside an old converted brick building surrounded by lush gardens, fresh flowers, and gentle lighting make patrons feel like well-tended houseguests being treated to an exquisite meal. The prix-fixe menu, which costs $46 for five courses, $38 for four (lunch is $33 for four courses and $28 for three), includes canapés such as "bacon and eggs"—quail eggs paired with bacon and served atop tiny silver spoons; entres such as pan-roasted Virginia striped bass with sweet peppers and black olives, or thyme-scented eggplant with potato gnocchi; and for dessert, "coffee and doughnuts" (cinnamon sugared doughnuts with cappuccino ice cream), or warm chocolate truffle cake with caramel cream. ✕ *6640 Washington St.,* ☎ *707/944-2380. Reservations recommended. AE, MC, V. Closed Mon.*

$$ Anesti's Grill and Rotisserie. Specialties at this spacious, cheerful restaurant include leg of lamb, duckling roasted on the only French rotisserie in Napa, and rack of lamb from the mesquite grill. The open kitchen provides entertainment indoors; a patio offers alfresco dining and vistas of vineyards and hills. ✕ *6518 Washington St.,* ☎ *707/944–1500. Reservations advised. AE, D, DC, MC, V.*

$$ Mustard's Grill. Grilled fish, steak, local fresh produce, and an impressive wine list are offered in a boisterous, noisy bistro with a black-and-white marble floor and upbeat artwork. Expect to encounter a crowd, since this is a wine makers' hangout. ✕ *7399 St. Helena Hwy., Napa Valley (Hwy. 29, 1 mi north of Yountville),* ☎ *707/944–2424,* FAX *707/944–0828. Reservations advised well in advance. D, DC, MC, V.*

$$ Ristorante Piatti. A small, stylish trattoria with a pizza oven and open kitchen, this cheery place is full of good smells and happy people. Its authentic regional Italian cooking—from antipasti to grilled chicken to *tiramisù*—is the perfect cure for a jaded appetite. The homemade pastas are the best bet. ✕ *6480 Washington St.,* ☎ *707/944–2070. Reservations advised. AE, MC, V.*

$ **The Diner.** One of the best-known and most-appreciated stop-offs in the Napa Valley, this breakfast-centric eatery has local sausages and house potatoes that are not to be missed. Healthful versions of Mexican and American classics are served for dinner. ✕ *6476 Washington St.,* ☎ *707/944–2626. Reservations accepted for 6 or more; expect a wait for seating. No credit cards. Closed Mon.*

LODGING

Not surprisingly, staying in the Wine Country is expensive. Most inns, hotels, and motels are exquisitely appointed, and many are fully booked long in advance of the summer season. Since Santa Rosa is the largest population center in the area, it has the largest selection of rooms, many at moderate rates. Try there if you've failed to reserve in advance or have a limited budget. For those seeking something more homey (and also a bit more expensive), check out the dozens of bed-and-breakfast inns that have been established in the Victorian homes and old hotels of the Wine Country (the tourist bureaus of Sonoma and Napa counties both provide information and brochures). Breakfast, which is included in the price of B&Bs, often features local produce and specialties. Families should note, however, that small children are often discouraged as guests at B&Bs. For all accommodations in the area, rates are lower on weeknights and about 20% less in the winter.

CATEGORY	COST*
$$$$	over $100
$$$	$80–$100
$$	$50–$80
$	under $50

**All prices are for a standard double room, excluding 12% tax.*

Calistoga

$$$–$$$$ ★ **Brannan Cottage Inn.** This exquisite Victorian cottage with lacy white fretwork, large windows, and a shady porch is the only one of Sam Brannan's 1860 resort cottages still standing on its original site. Rooms, which have private entrances, are adorned with elegant stenciled friezes of stylized wildflowers. Full breakfast is included. 🏨 *109 Wapoo Ave., 94515,* ☎ *707/942–4200. 6 rooms. Breakfast room. MC, V (for room payment; reservations held by mailed check only).*

$$$–$$$$ **Mount View Hotel.** Once simply a refurbished 1930s hotel with character, the Mount View is now one of the valley's most elegant places to stay. A full-service European spa offers state-of-the-art pampering, and three cottages are each equipped with private redwood deck, Jacuzzi, and wet bar. Catahoula's, the popular restaurant/saloon, offers southern-inspired American cuisine (*see* Dining, *above*). 🏨 *1457 Lincoln Ave., 94515,* ☎ *707/942–6877,* FAX *707/942–6904. 33 rooms with bath. Restaurant, pool, spa. AE, MC, V.*

$$–$$$ **Dr. Wilkinson's Hot Springs.** This hot-springs spa resort has been in operation since 1952. Reserve ahead for weekends, when there are separate fees for mud baths, massages, facials, and steam rooms. Midweek packages include room and full spa services. 🏨 *1507 Lincoln Ave., 94515,* ☎ *707/942–4102,* FAX *707/942–6110. 42 rooms. 3 mineral baths. AE, MC, V.*

$$ **Comfort Inn Napa Valley North.** All the rooms in this motel have one king- or two queen-size beds, and many have vineyard views. Continental breakfast is included. There are rooms for nonsmokers and travelers with disabilities and discounts for senior citizens. Guests have access (for a fee) to a full-scale spa across the street. ☎ *1865 Lincoln Ave., 94515,* ☎ *707/942–9400 or 800/228–5150,* FAX *707/942–5262. 54 rooms with bath. Pool, hot tub, sauna, steam room. AE, D, DC, MC, V.*

$$ **Mountain Home Ranch.** This rustic ranch, established in 1913, is set on 300 wooded acres, with hiking trails, a creek, and a fishing lake. The seven cabins spread over the grounds are ideal for families; each has a full kitchen and bath, and the majority have wood-burning fireplaces. There is just one TV, in the dining room, and no phones. In summer, the modified American plan (full breakfast and dinner) is used; otherwise, Continental breakfast is included. Special children's rates are available. *3400 Mountain Home Ranch Rd., 94515 (north of town on Hwy. 128, left on Petrified Forest Rd., right on Mountain Home Ranch Rd., to end; 3 mi from Hwy. 128),* ☎ *707/942–6616,* FAX *707/942–9091. 6 rooms in main lodge; 11 cabins, all with private bath. 2 pools, tennis court. MC, V. Closed Dec. and Jan.*

Glen Ellen

$$$–$$$$ **Beltane Ranch.** On a slope of the Mayacamas range on the eastern side of the Sonoma Valley lies this 100-year-old house built by a retired San Francisco madam. Part of a working cattle and grape-growing ranch—the nearby Kenwood Winery has a chardonnay made from the ranch's grapes—the Beltane is surrounded by miles of trails through oak-studded hills. Innkeeper Rosemary Woods and her family, who have lived on the premises for 50 years, have stocked the comfortable living room with dozens of books on the area. The rooms, all with private baths and antique furniture, open onto the building's wraparound porch. *11775 Sonoma Hwy. (Hwy. 12), 95442,* ☎ *707/996–6501. 4 rooms. Tennis court, hiking, horseshoes. No credit cards, but personal checks accepted.*

$$$–$$$$ **Glenelly Inn.** Just outside the hamlet of Glen Ellen, this sunny little establishment, built as an inn in 1916, offers all the comforts of home—including a hot tub in the garden. Mother and daughter innkeepers Ingrid and Kristi Hallamore serve breakfast in front of the common room's cobblestone fireplace and local delicacies in the afternoons. On sunny mornings, guests may eat outside, under the shady oak trees. *5131 Warm Springs Rd., 95442,* ☎ *707/996–6720. 8 rooms. Breakfast room, outdoor hot tub. MC, V.*

Healdsburg

$$$$ **Healdsburg Inn on the Plaza.** This 1900 brick building on the town plaza has a bright solarium and a roof garden. The rooms, most with fireplaces, are spacious, with quilts and pillows piled high on antique beds. In the bathrooms, claw-foot tubs are outfitted with rubber ducks. Full breakfast, afternoon coffee and cookies, and early evening wine and popcorn are included. *110 Matheson St., Box 1196, 95448,* ☎ *707/433–6991. 10 rooms. Breakfast room. MC, V.*

$$$$ **Madrona Manor.** A splendid, three-story, 1881 Victorian mansion, carriage house, and outbuildings sit on 8 wooded and landscaped acres. Mansion rooms are recommended: All nine have fireplaces, and five contain the antique furniture of the original owner. The approach to the mansion leads under a stone archway and up a flowered hill; the house overlooks the valley and vineyards. Full breakfast is included, and a fine restaurant on the premises serves dinner (*see* Dining, *above*). Pets are allowed. *1001 Westside Rd., Box 818, 95448,* ☎ *707/433–4231 or 800/258–4003,* FAX *707/433–0703. 21 rooms with bath. Restaurant, pool. AE, D, DC, MC, V.*

$$ **Best Western Dry Creek Inn.** Continental breakfast and a bottle of wine are complimentary at this three-story Spanish Mission–style motel, and there's also a coffee shop next door. Small pets are allowed. Midweek discounts are available, and direct bus service from San Francisco Airport can be arranged. ✉ *198 Dry Creek Rd., 95448,* ☎ *707/433–0300 or 800/528–1234; in CA, 800/222–5784;* FAX *707/433–1129. 102 rooms with bath. Pool, hot tub, coin laundry. AE, D, DC, MC, V.*

Napa

$$$$ **Napa Valley Marriott.** Since Marriott took over this former Sheraton motel, the lounge has been redecorated in Marriott's trademark sports-bar-and-grill style. A convenient restaurant remains on the premises, and live music is still featured in the lounge. Rooms are available for travelers with disabilities, and all guests are entitled to a pay-per-movie service. ✉ *3425 Solano Ave., 94558 (1 block west off Hwy. 29; take Redwood-Trancas exit),* ☎ *707/253–7433 or 800/228–9290,* FAX *707/258–1320. 191 rooms. Pool, hot tub, 2 tennis courts. AE, D, DC, MC, V.*

$$$$ **Silverado Country Club.** This luxurious 1,200-acre resort in the hills east of the town of Napa offers cottages, kitchen apartments, and one- to three-bedroom efficiencies, many with fireplaces. There are also two dining rooms, a lounge, a sundries store, eight pools, 22 tennis courts, and two championship golf courses designed by Robert Trent Jones. Fees are charged for golf, tennis, and bike rentals. ✉ *1600 Atlas Peak Rd., 94558 (6 mi east of Napa via Hwy. 121),* ☎ *707/257–0200 or 800/532–0500,* FAX *707/257–2867. 277 condo units. 3 restaurants. AE, D, DC, MC, V.*

$$$–$$$$ **Best Western Inn.** This immaculate modern redwood motel with spacious rooms has a restaurant on the premises, and same-day laundry and valet service. Suites are available, as are rooms for nonsmokers and travelers with disabilities. Small pets are allowed. ✉ *100 Soscol Ave., 94558 (from the direction of the Golden Gate Bridge, take Imola Ave./Hwy. 121 exit east from Hwy. 29 to junction of Hwy. 121 and Soscol),* ☎ *707/257–1930 or 800/528–1234,* FAX *707/255–0709. 68 rooms. Pool, spa, free parking. AE, D, DC, MC, V.*

$$$–$$$$ **John Muir Inn.** Continental breakfast and in-room coffee are complimentary at this well-equipped, three-story inn, which has kitchenettes, refrigerators, movies, valet service, and some whirlpool tubs. Discounts for senior citizens and rooms for nonsmokers and guests with disabilities are available. ✉ *1998 Trower Ave., 94558 (corner of Hwy. 29),* ☎ *707/257–7220 or 800/522–8999,* FAX *707/258–0943. 59 rooms. Pool, spa. AE, D, DC, MC, V.*

$$$ **Chateau Hotel.** This French country inn–style modern motel offers Continental breakfast, in-room refrigerators, facilities for travelers with disabilities, and discounts for senior citizens. ✉ *4195 Solano Ave., 94558 (west of Hwy. 29; exit at Trower Ave.),* ☎ *707/253–9300 or 800/253–6272 in CA. 115 rooms. Refrigerators, pool, hot tub. AE, D, DC, MC, V.*

Rutherford

$$$$ ★ **Auberge du Soleil.** As you sit on a wisteria-draped deck sipping a late-afternoon glass of wine, with acres of terraced olive groves and rolling vineyards at your feet, you'll swear you're in Tuscany. The Mediterranean spell lingers inside, where Santa Fe accents create an atmosphere of irresistible indolence. The hotel's renowned restaurant is not to be missed (*see* Dining, *above*). ✉ *180 Rutherford Hill Rd., 94573,* ☎ *707/963–1211 or 800/348–5406,* FAX *707/963–8764. 50 rooms. Pool, hot tub, massage, steam room, 3 tennis courts, exercise room. AE, D, MC, V.*

$$$$ **Rancho Caymus Inn.** California-Spanish in style, this inn has well-maintained gardens and large suites with kitchens and whirlpool baths. Well-chosen details include decorative handicrafts, beehive fireplaces, tile murals, stoneware basins, and llama-hair blankets. Also of note are the home-baked breads. ☎ *1140 Rutherford Rd., Box 78, 94573 (junction of Hwys. 29 and 128),* ☎ *707/963–1777 or 800/845–1777,* FAX *707/963–5387. 26 rooms. 2-night minimum Apr.–Nov. AE, DC, MC, V.*

St. Helena

$$$$ **Harvest Inn.** This Tudor-style inn with 47 fireplaces overlooks a 14-acre vineyard and hills beyond. Although the property is set close to a main highway, the lush landscaping and award-winning brick and stonework create an illusion of remoteness. Most rooms have wet bars, refrigerators, antique furnishings, and fireplaces. Pets are allowed in certain rooms for a $20 fee. Complimentary breakfast is served in the breakfast room and on the patio overlooking the vineyards. ☎ *1 Main St., 94574,* ☎ *707/963–9463 or 800/950–8466,* FAX *707/963–4402. 55 rooms. 2 pools, 2 hot tubs. AE, D, MC, V.*

$$$$ **Meadowood Resort.** Set on 256 wooded acres, with a golf course, croquet lawns, and hiking trails, this is a vacation getaway. The hotel is a rambling country lodge reminiscent of a turn-of-the-century New England seaside cottage, and separate bungalow suites are clustered on the hillside. Half the suites and some rooms have fireplaces. ☎ *900 Meadowood La., 94574,* ☎ *707/963–3646 or 800/458–8080,* FAX *707/963–3532. 82 rooms. 2 restaurants, bar, room service, 2 pools, hot tub, massage, sauna, steam room, 9-hole golf course, 7 tennis courts, croquet, health club. AE, D, DC, MC, V.*

$$$$ ★ **Wine Country Inn.** Surrounded by a pastoral landscape of vineyards and hills dotted with old barns and stone bridges, this New England–style inn feels peaceful. Rural antiques fill all of the rooms, most of which overlook the vineyards with either a balcony, patio, or deck. Most rooms have fireplaces, and some have private hot tubs. A hearty country breakfast is served buffet-style in the sun-splashed common room, and wine tastings are scheduled in the afternoons. With no TV, this is a place for readers and dreamers. ☎ *1152 Lodi La., 94574,* ☎ *707/963–7077 or 800/473–3463,* FAX *707/963–9018. 24 rooms with bath. Pool, hot tub. MC, V.*

$$$–$$$$ **El Bonita Motel.** Hand-painted grapevines surround the windows at this roadside motel, and flower boxes overflow with new colors every season. While most rooms have private whirlpools, the outdoor pool is available only in summer. There are 16 rooms in the main motel and six smartly furnished garden rooms with kitchenettes. ☎ *195 Main St., 94574,* ☎ *707/963–3216 or 800/541–3284,* FAX *707/963–8838. 42 rooms. Kitchenettes, pool, hot tub, sauna. AE, D, DC, MC, V.*

$$$–$$$$ **Hotel St. Helena.** The oldest standing wooden structure in St. Helena, this restored 1881 hostelry aims at Old World comfort. It is completely furnished with antiques and decorated in rich, appealing tones of burgundy. Complimentary Continental breakfast is included. Smoking is discouraged—the only evidence of the New World. ☎ *1309 Main St., 94574,* ☎ *707/963–4388,* FAX *707/963–5402. 14 rooms with bath, 4 rooms with shared bath. AE, DC, MC, V.*

$$–$$$$ **Cinnamon Bear Bed and Breakfast.** Built in 1904 in the classic Arts and Crafts style, this house is decorated with the 1920s in mind. The beds are covered with antique quilts and the rooms are filled with toys of the period. Claw-foot tubs and a cozy fireplace in the parlor complete the mood. Full breakfast is included. Rooms for nonsmokers are available. ☎ *1407 Kearney St., 94574 (from Main St., Hwy. 29, turn* *west on Adams St., then 2 blocks to Kearney),* ☎ *707/963–4653. 3 rooms with bath. MC, V.*

Santa Rosa

$$$$ **Vintner's Inn.** Set on 50 acres of vineyards, this French provincial inn has large rooms, many with wood-burning fireplaces, and a trellised sundeck. Breakfast is complimentary, and the noteworthy John Ash & Co. (*see* Dining, *above*) tempts guests to other meals. Guests can get discounted passes to an affiliated health club nearby, and VCRs can be rented for a small fee. *4350 Barnes Rd., 95403 (River Rd. exit west from U.S. 101),* ☎ *707/575–7350 or 800/421–2584,* FAX *707/575–1426. 44 rooms. Restaurant, hot tub. AE, DC, MC, V.*

$$–$$$$ **Doubletree Hotel.** Many rooms in this large, modern, hilltop hotel look out on the valley and vineyards; the Burgundy, Cabernet, Chardonnay, Chablis, and Riesling buildings have especially fine views. Work-size desks and functional, comfortable furnishings make the spacious rooms feel like home. Rooms are available for nonsmokers and travelers with disabilities. In addition to a jogging path, golf and tennis are available at the adjacent Fountaingrove Country Club for additional fees. *3555 Round Barn Blvd., 95401 (exit Mendocino Ave. from U.S. 101),* ☎ *707/523–7555 or 800/528–0444,* FAX *707/545–2807. 247 rooms with bath, 14 suites. Restaurant, bar, pool, hot tub. AE, D, DC, MC, V.*

$$$ ★ **Fountaingrove Inn.** A redwood sculpture and a wall of cascading water are the focal points of this elegant, comfortable inn in the heart of the Sonoma valley. Rooms have work spaces with modem jacks. Buffet breakfast is included, and an elegant restaurant offers a piano and a stellar menu. Guests have access to a nearby 18-hole golf course, a tennis court, and a health club nearby, for a fee. Golf packages are available, as are discounts for senior citizens. *101 Fountaingrove Pkwy. (near U.S. 101), 95403,* ☎ *707/578–6101 or 800/222–6101,* FAX *707/544–3126. 85 rooms. Restaurant, room service, pool, hot tub, meeting rooms. AE, DC, MC, V.*

$$–$$$ ★ **Los Robles Lodge.** This pleasant, relaxed motel has comfortable rooms overlooking a pool set into a grassy landscape. Rooms are available for people with disabilities and for nonsmokers. Pets are allowed, except in executive rooms, which have whirlpools. *1985 Cleveland Ave., 95401 (Steele La. exit west from Hwy. 101),* ☎ *707/545–6330 or 800/255–6330,* FAX *707/575–5826. 104 rooms. Restaurant, coffee shop, pool, outdoor hot tub, nightclub, coin laundry. AE, D, DC, MC. V.*

$$ **Best Western Hillside Inn.** Ten of the rooms at this small, cozy, landscaped motel have balconies or patios. Kitchenettes and suites are available. *2901 4th St., 95409 (at Farmers La., 2 mi east off U.S. 101 on Hwy. 12),* ☎ *707/546–9353 or 800/528–1234. 35 rooms. Restaurant, pool, sauna, shuffleboard. AE, DC, MC, V.*

Sonoma

$$$$ **Sonoma Mission Inn & Spa.** This classy 1920s resort blends Mediterranean and old-California architecture for a look that's early Hollywood: Gloria Swanson would fit right in. Despite its unlikely location off the main street of tiny, down-home Boyes Hot Springs, the hotel's extensive spa facilities and treatments attract guests from all over. Ask for a room in one of the newer buildings: They are much larger and more attractive than the smallish standard rooms in the main building. Don't miss the pool, which is heated by warm mineral water pumped from underground wells, or the well-equipped fitness pavilion. *18140 Hwy. 12 (just north of Sonoma), Box 1447, 95476,* ☎ *707/938–9000 or 800/358–9022; in CA, 800/862–4945;* FAX *707/996–5358. 170 rooms.*

2 restaurants, 2 bars, coffee shop, 2 pools, 2 hot tubs, sauna, steam room, 2 tennis courts, health club. AE, DC, MC, V.

$$$$ **Thistle Dew Inn.** A half block from Sonoma Plaza, this turn-of-the-century Victorian home is filled with collector-quality arts-and-crafts furnishings. Owners Larry and Norma Barnett live on the premises, and Larry cooks up creative, sumptuous breakfasts and serves hors d'oeuvres in the evenings. Four of the six rooms have private entrances and decks, and all have queen-size beds with antique quilts, private baths, and air-conditioning. Welcome bonuses include a hot tub and free use of the inn's bicycles. Smoking is not permitted indoors. *171 W. Spain St., 95476, ☎ 707/938–2909 or 800/382–7895 in CA. 6 rooms. AE, MC, V.*

$$$–$$$$ **Best Western Sonoma Valley Inn.** Just one block from the historical town plaza, this comfortable hotel features balconies, handcrafted furniture, wood-burning fireplaces, and whirlpool baths. Continental breakfast and complimentary quarter bottles of wine are included. Kitchenettes and rooms for nonsmokers and travelers with disabilities are available. *550 2nd St. W, 95476, ☎ 707/938–9200 or 800/334–5784, FAX 707/938–0935. 72 rooms. Pool, hot tub, coin laundry. AE, D, DC, MC, V.*

$$$–$$$$ ★ **El Dorado Hotel.** In 1990 Claude Rouas, the owner of Napa's acclaimed Auberge du Soleil, opened this small hotel with its popular restaurant, Ristorante Piatti (*see* Dining, *above*). Rooms reflect Sonoma's mission era, with Mexican-tile floors and white walls. The best rooms are numbers 3 and 4, which have big balconies overlooking Sonoma Plaza. Only four of the rooms—the ones in the courtyard by the pool—have bathtubs; the rest have showers only. *405 1st St. W (on Sonoma Plaza), ☎ 707/996–3030 or 800/289–3031, FAX 707/996–3148. 27 rooms. Restaurant, pool. AE, MC, V.*

$$–$$$ **Vineyard Inn.** Built as a roadside motor court in 1941, this inn with red-tile roofs brings a touch of Mexican village charm to an otherwise lackluster location—at the junction of two main highways. Set in the heart of Sonoma's Carneros region, across from two vineyards, it is the closest lodging to Sears Point Raceway. Rooms have queen-size beds. Continental breakfast is provided. *23000 Arnold Dr. (at the junction of Hwys. 116 and 121), 95476, ☎ 707/938–2350 or 800/359–4667. 9 rooms, 3 suites with wet bar, 1 resident suite with kitchenette. Breakfast room. AE, MC, V.*

Yountville

$$$$ **Napa Valley Lodge.** Spacious rooms overlook the vineyards and the valley in this hacienda-style lodge, which has a tile roof, covered walkways, balconies, patios, and colorful gardens. Freshly brewed coffee is provided to guests, along with a Continental breakfast and the morning paper. Some rooms have fireplaces, others have wet bars. *2230 Madison St. at Hwy. 29, 94599, ☎ 707/944–2468 or 800/368–2468, FAX 707/944–9362. 55 rooms. Refrigerators, pool, hot tub, sauna, exercise room. AE, D, DC, MC, V.*

$$$$ **Vintage Inn.** All the rooms at this luxurious inn have fireplaces, whirlpool baths, refrigerators, private verandas or patios, hand-painted fabrics, window seats, and shuttered windows. A welcome bottle of wine, Continental breakfast with champagne, and afternoon tea are all complimentary. In season, bike rentals and hot-air ballooning are available. *6541 Washington St., 94599, ☎ 707/944–1112 or 800/351–1133, FAX 707/944–1617. 80 rooms with bath. Pool, spa, tennis court. AE, D, DC, MC, V.*

THE ARTS AND NIGHTLIFE

Galleries throughout the Wine Country display the work of local artists: painters, sculptors, potters, and jewelry makers. The **Luther Burbank Performing Arts Center** in Santa Rosa (50 Mark West Springs Rd., 95403, ☎ 707/546–3600; box office open Mon.–Sat. noon–6 and approximately 1 hr before most events) offers a full events calendar featuring concerts, plays, and other performances by locally and internationally known artists. Send away for the calendar in advance if you're planning a trip. For the symphony, ballet, and other live theater performances throughout the year, call the **Spreckels Performing Arts Center** in Rohnert Park (☎ 707/584–1700 or 707/586–0936; box office open Tues.–Sat. noon–5). The most highly recommended theater groups among the valley's 30 ensembles include: Cinnebar in Petaluma (☎ 707/763–8920), Main Street Theatre in Sebastopol (☎ 707/823–0177), SRT (Summer Repertory Theatre) in Santa Rosa (☎ 707/527–4307), and the Actors Theatre also in Santa Rosa (☎ 707/523–4185). In addition to the sounds at local music clubs and the larger hotels, wineries often schedule concerts and music festivals during the summer. Popular music aficionados might also try the Mystic Theatre in Petaluma, where Chris Isaak sometimes plays (☎ 707/765–6665), and movie lovers can take in a foreign or first-run film at the Raven Theatre in Healdsburg (☎ 707/433–5448). The Sebastiani Theatre, on historic Sonoma square, (☎ 707/996–2020) features first-run movies and hosts special events during the year.

Many believe that the best way to savor evenings in the Wine Country is to linger over an elegant dinner, preferably on a patio under the stars, at one of the restaurants for which the area is justly famous.

WINE COUNTRY ESSENTIALS

Arriving and Departing

By Bus

Greyhound-Trailways (☎ 800/231–2222) runs buses—two per day—from the Transbay Terminal at 1st and Mission streets to Sonoma and Santa Rosa.

By Car

From San Francisco, cross the Golden Gate Bridge and follow U.S. 101 to Santa Rosa and head north. Or cross the Golden Gate, go north on U.S. 101, east on Highway 37, and north on Highway 121 into Sonoma. Yet another route runs over the San Francisco–Oakland Bay Bridge and along I–80 to Vallejo, where Highway 29 leads north to Napa.

From the east, take I–80 and then turn northwest on Highway 12 for a 10-minute drive through a hilly pass to Highway 29. From the north, take U.S. 101 south to Geyserville, and follow Highway 128 southeast into the Napa Valley.

By Plane

The closest airports are in San Francisco and Oakland.

Getting Around

By Bus

Sonoma County Area Transit (☎ 707/585–7516) and **Napa Valley Transit** (☎ 707/255–7631) provide local transportation between towns in the Wine Country.

By Car

Although traffic on the two-lane country roads can be heavy, the best way to get around the Wine Country is by private car. Rentals are available at the airports and in San Francisco, Oakland, Santa Rosa, and Napa. The **Rider's Guide** (484 Lake Park Ave., Suite 255, Oakland 94610, ☎ 510/653–2553) produces tapes about the history, landmarks, and wineries of the Sonoma and Napa valleys that you can play in your car (maps also provided). The tapes are available at some local bookstores including Rand McNally Map & Travel at 595 Market, or can be ordered directly from Rider's Guide for $12.95 (Napa tape) and $11.95 (Sonoma tape), plus $2 postage.

Guided Tours

Full-day guided tours of the Wine Country usually include lunch and cost about $50. The guides, some of whom are winery owners themselves, know the area well and may show you some lesser-known cellars. Reservations are usually required.

Wine Country Wagons (Box 1069, Kenwood 95452, ☎ 707/833–2724, FAX 707/833–1041) offers four-hour horse-drawn wagon tours that include three wineries and end at a private ranch, where a lavish buffet lunch is served. Tours depart daily at 10 AM, May through October; advance reservations are required.

Gray Line (350 8th St., San Francisco 94103, ☎ 415/558–9400) has bright-red double-decker buses that tour the Wine Country.

Great Pacific Tour Co. (518 Octavia St., San Francisco 94102, ☎ 415/626–4499) offers full-day tours of Napa and Sonoma, including a summer picnic lunch and a winter restaurant lunch, in passenger vans that seat 14.

HMS Tours (707 4th St., Santa Rosa 95404, ☎ 707/526–2922 or 800/367–5348) offers customized tours of the Wine Country, for four or more people, by appointment only.

California Wine Adventures (1258 Arroyo Sarco, Napa 94558, ☎ 707/257–0353), a family-owned operation, has been custom-designing private tours for groups since 1974. Cost includes a gourmet picnic lunch or dinner.

Napa Valley Wine Train (1275 McKinstry St., Napa 94559, ☎ 707/253–2111 or 800/427–4124) allows you to enjoy lunch, dinner, or a weekend brunch on one of several restored 1915 Pullman railroad cars that now run between Napa and St. Helena on tracks that were formerly owned by the Southern Pacific Railroad. Round-trip fare costs $24 during dinner and $30 during brunch and lunch; meals of three to five courses cost between $26 and $47.50. During the winter, service is limited to Thursday–Sunday. There is a special car for families with children on weekend brunch trips and weekday lunch trips.

Important Addresses and Numbers

Emergencies

Dial **911** for fire, police, ambulance, and paramedics.

Visitor Information

Calistoga Chamber of Commerce (1458 Lincoln Ave., Calistoga 94515, ☎ 707/942–6333). **Healdsburg Chamber of Commerce** (217 Healdsburg Ave., Healdsburg 95448, ☎ 707/433–6935 or 800/648–9922 in CA).

Napa Valley Conference and Visitors Bureau (1310 Napa Town Center, Napa 94559, ☎ 707/226–7459).

Redwood Empire Association (in the Cannery, 2801 Leavenworth St., 2nd Floor, San Francisco 94133, ☎ 415/543–8334, FAX 415/543–8337) distributes the Redwood Empire Visitors' Guide free to those who stop by, or for $3 by mail.

St. Helena Chamber of Commerce (1080 Main St., Box 124, St. Helena 94574, ☎ 707/963–4456 or 800/767–8528, FAX 707/963–5396).

Sonoma County Convention and Visitors Bureau (5000 Roberts Lake Rd., Rohnert Park 94928, ☎ 707/586–8100 or 800/326–7666, FAX 707/586–8111).

Sonoma Valley Visitors Bureau (453 1st St. E, Sonoma 95476, ☎ 707/996–1090).

10 Portrait of San Francisco

LIVING WITH THE CERTAINTY OF A SHAKY FUTURE

THERE'S NEVER been any question whether or not there will be another earthquake in San Francisco. The question is how soon. Even the kids here grow up understanding that it's just a matter of time, and from grade school on, earthquake safety drills become routine. At the first rumble, duck under your desk or table or stand in a doorway, they are instructed. Get away from windows to avoid broken glass. When the shaking stops, walk—don't run—outdoors, as far away from buildings as possible.

Sure as there are hurricanes along the Gulf of Mexico and blizzards in Maine, San Francisco's earthquakes are inevitable. Nobody here is surprised when the rolling and tumbling begins—it happens all the time. Just in the six months following the jarring 1989 earthquake, for instance, seismologists reported hundreds of aftershocks, ranging from the scarcely perceptible to those strong enough to bring down buildings weakened by October's jolt.

The Bay Area itself was created in upheaval such as this. Eons ago, a restless geology of shifting plates deep in the earth gave birth to the Sierra Mountains and the Pacific Coast Range. Every spring when the snows melted, the runoff rushed down from the mile-high Sierra peaks westward across what would eventually be known as California. Here, the runoff ran up against the coastal range, and a vast inland lake was formed.

The rampaging waters from the yearly thaw eventually crashed through the quake-shattered Coast Range to meet the Pacific Ocean, creating the gap now spanned by the Golden Gate Bridge. This breakthrough created San Francisco Bay, one of the world's great natural harbors, its fertile delta larger than that of the Mississippi River. What a fabulous setting for the city-to-be—surrounded on three sides by water, set off by dramatic mountainscapes to the north and south, and blessed by cool ocean breezes.

All this and gold, too. The twisting and rolling of so-called terra firma exposed rich veins of gold at and near ground level that otherwise would have remained hidden deep underground. The great upheaval pushed the Mother Lode to the surface and set the scene for the gold rush. But before the '49 miners came the Europeans. In the late 15th century, the Spanish writer Garci Ordonez de Montalvo penned a fictional description of a place he called California, a faraway land ruled by Queen Califia, where gold and precious stones were so plentiful the streets were lined with them. Montalvo's vision of wealth without limit helped fuel the voyages of the great 15th- and 16th-century European explorers in the new world. They never did hit pay dirt here, but the name California stuck nevertheless.

Northern California was eventually settled, and in 1848, the population of San Francisco was 832. The discovery of gold in the California hills brought sudden and unprecedented wealth to this coastal trading outpost and her population exploded; by the turn of the century San Francisco was home to 343,000 people.

EN ROUTE TO ITS DESTINY as a premier city of the West, San Francisco was visited by innumerable quakes. Yet while the city's very foundations shook, residents found that each new rattler helped to strengthen San Francisco's self-image of adaptability. Robert Louis Stevenson wrote of the quakes' alarming frequency: "The fear of them grows yearly in a resident; he begins with indifference and ends in sheer panic." The big shaker of 1865 inspired humorist Mark Twain to look at the quakes in a different light by writing an earthquake "almanac" for the following year, which advised:

Oct. 23—Mild, balmy earthquakes.

Oct. 26—About this time expect more earthquakes; but do not look for them . . .

Oct. 27—Universal despondency, indicative of approaching disaster. Abstain from smiling or indulgence in humorous conversation . . .
Oct. 29—Beware!
Oct. 31—Go slow!
Nov. 1—Terrific earthquake. This is the great earthquake month. More stars fall and more worlds are slathered around carelessly and destroyed in November than in any month of the twelve.
Nov. 2—Spasmodic but exhilarating earthquakes, accompanied by occasional showers of rain and churches and things.
Nov. 3—Make your will.
Nov. 4—Sell out.

ON THE WHOLE, those who settled in San Francisco were more inclined toward Twain's devil-may-care attitude—those who succumbed to Stevenson's panic didn't stick around for long. Certainly the multitude of vices that saturated the metropolis were sufficient to distract many men from their fears; throughout Chinatown and the infamous Barbary Coast, opium dens, gin mills, and bordellos operated day and night.

Money flowed. Money tempted. Money corrupted. The city was built on graft, and city hall became synonymous with corruption under the influence of political crooks like Blind Chris Buckley and Boss Ruef. The very building itself was a scandal. Planned for completion in six months at a cost of half a million dollars, the city hall ultimately took 29 years to build at a graft-inflated cost of $8 million, an astronomical sum at the dawning of the 20th century. When the San Andreas Fault set loose the 1906 earthquake, the most devastating ever to hit an American city, city hall was one of the first buildings to come crashing down. Its ruins exposed the shoddiest of building materials, an ironic symbol of the city's crime-ridden past.

The 1906 earthquake and fire has come to define San Francisco both for itself and the outside world. In the immediate aftermath of the catastrophe, San Franciscans wondered whether they ought to believe the preachers and reformers who declared that this terrible devastation had been wrought upon their wicked city by the avenging hand of God. San Franciscans asked themselves whether, somehow, they had earned it.

But the city was quick to prove its character. Fifty years earlier, six separate fires had destroyed most of San Francisco—yet each time it was rebuilt by a citizenry not ready to give up on either the gold or the city that gold had built. Now, in 1906, heroic firefighters dynamited one of the city's main thoroughfares to prevent the inferno from spreading all the way to the Pacific. The mood of San Franciscans was almost eerily calm, their neighborliness both heartwarming and jaunty. "Eat, drink, and be merry," proclaimed signs about town, "for tomorrow we may have to go to Oakland." No sooner had the flames died than rebuilding began—true to San Francisco tradition. Forty thousand construction workers poured into town to assist the proud, amazingly resilient residents.

The 1906 earthquake provided a chance to rethink the hodgepodge, get-rich-quick cityscape that had risen in the heat of gold-rush frenzy. City fathers imported the revered urban planner Daniel Burnham, architect of the magnificent 1893 Chicago World's Fair, to reinvent San Francisco. "Make no little plans," Burnham intoned. "They have no power to stir men's souls."

The city's new Civic Center, built under Burnham's direction, was raised to celebrate the city's comeback and is regarded as one of America's most stately works of civic architecture. Its city hall stands as a monument to the city's will to prevail—from its colonnaded granite exterior to its exuberant interior, once described by Tom Wolfe as resembling "some Central American opera house. Marble arches, domes, acanthus leaves . . . quirks and galleries and gilt filigrees . . . a veritable angels' choir of gold." The inscription found over the mayor's office seems to sum it all up: "San Francisco, O glorious city of our hearts that has been tried and not found wanting, go thou with like spirit to make the future thine."

In 1915 San Francisco dazzled the world with its Panama–Pacific International Exposition, designed to prove not only that it was back, but that it was back bigger and better and badder than ever before. An architectural wonderland, the Expo was built on 70 acres of marshy landfill, which later became the residential neighborhood called the Marina District. When the October 1989 earthquake struck, this neighborhood was badly damaged, and became a focus as the entire nation tuned in to see how San Francisco and her people would fare this time around.

Like the gold that surfaced in the Mother Lode, the 1989 quake once again brought out the best in this region's people. Out at Candlestick Park, 62,000 fans were waiting for the start of the World Series between the San Francisco Giants and the Oakland A's when everything started shaking. They cut loose with a big cheer after the temblor subsided. One San Francisco fan quickly hand-lettered a sign and held it aloft: "That was Nothing—Wait Til the Giants Bat." When it became apparent that there would be no ball played that night, the fans departed from the ballpark, just like in a grade school earthquake safety drill, quietly and in good order.

This was what millions of TV viewers across the nation first saw of the local response to this major (7.1) earthquake and, by and large, the combination of good humor and relative calm they observed was an accurate reflection of the prevailing mood around the city. San Franciscans were not about to panic. Minutes after the quake struck, a San Francisco couple spread a lace tablecloth over the hood of their BMW and, sitting in the driveway of their splintered home, toasted passersby with champagne. Simultaneously, across San Francisco Bay, courageous volunteers and rescue workers set to work digging through the pancaked rubble of an Oakland freeway in the search for survivors, heedless that they, too, could easily be crushed in an aftershock. Throughout the Bay Area, hundreds volunteered to fight the fires, clear away the mess, assist survivors, and donate food, money, and clothing.

San Francisco's city seal features the image of a phoenix rising from the flames of catastrophe, celebrating the city's fiery past and promising courage in the face of certain future calamity. The 1989 shake possessed only about one-fortieth the force of the legendary 1906 quake, and all projections point to the inevitability of another Big One, someday, on at least the scale of '06. Often people from other, more stable, parts of the world have trouble understanding how it is possible to live with such a certainty.

The *San Francisco Bay Guardian,* shortly after the 1989 quake, spoke for many Bay Area residents: "We live in earthquake country. Everybody knows that. It's a choice we've all made, a risk we're all more or less willing to accept as part of our lives. We're gambling against fate, and last week our luck ran out. It was inevitable—as the infamous bumper sticker says, 'Mother Nature bats last.' "

Former San Francisco Mayor Dianne Feinstein explained it this way: "Californians seem undaunted. We will never be a match for Mother Nature. But the principal thing that seems to arise from the ash and rubble of a quake is the strong resolve to rebuild and get on with life."

MORE PORTRAITS

Books

While there are many novels with a San Francisco setting, they don't come any better than *The Maltese Falcon* by Dashiell Hammett, the founder of the hard-boiled school of detective fiction. First published in 1930, Hammett's books continue to be readily available in new editions, and the details about the fog, the hills, and the once-seedy offices south of Market continue to be accurate.

Another standout is Vikram Seth's *Golden Gate,* a novel in verse about life in San Francisco and Marin County in the early '80s. Others are John Gregory Dunne's recent *The Red White and Blue,* Stephen Longstreet's *All or Nothing* and *Our Father's House,* and Alice Adams's *Rich Rewards.* Many of the short stories in Adams's collection, *To See You Again,* have Bay Area settings.

Two books that are filled with interesting background information on the city are Richard H. Dillon's *San Francisco: Adventurers and Visionaries* and *San Francisco: As It Is, As It Was,* by Paul C. Johnson and Richard Reinhardt.

Armistead Maupin's soap-opera-style *Tales of the City* stories are set in San Francisco; they were recently made into a PBS series, much to the delight of Maupin's devoted fans.

For anecdotes, gossip, and the kind of detail that will make you feel almost like a native San Franciscan, get hold of any of the books by the longtime San Francisco *Chronicle* columnist Herb Caen: *Baghdad-by-the- Bay, Only in San Francisco, One Man's San Francisco,* and *San Francisco: City on Golden Hills.*

Fodor's has a wide range of other guides that cover San Francisco and California. Fodor's *California* covers San Francisco as well as the rest of the state. Useful companions to Fodor's standard guides include Compass *San Francisco* and Compass *California,* which team literate writing with color photos and archival material to create a celebration of the destinations, and *Exploring San Francisco* and *Exploring California,* filled with color photos with many zingy captions and short takes on special topics. Fodor's *California's Best Bed & Breakfasts* is made up of detailed critical reviews. The sassy Berkeley Guides, *California, On the Loose* and *San Francisco, On the Loose,* are budget guides with attitude, written by college students.

Videos

San Francisco, starring Clark Gable and Spencer Tracy, re-creates the 1906 earthquake with outstanding special effects.

In *Escape from Alcatraz,* Clint Eastwood plays the prisoner who allegedly escaped from the famous jail on a rock in the San Francisco Bay.

The Times of Harvey Milk, about San Francisco's first openly gay elected official, won the Academy Award for best documentary feature in 1984.

Alfred Hitchcock immortalized Mission Dolores and the Golden Gate Bridge in *Vertigo,* the eerie story of a detective with a fear of heights, starring Jimmy Stewart and Kim Novak.

A few other noteworthy films shot in San Francisco are *Dark Passage,* with Humphrey Bogart; *Foul Play,* with Chevy Chase and Goldie Hawn; and the 1978 remake of *Invasion of the Body Snatchers.*

By John Burks

INDEX

✕ = *restaurant,* 🏨 = *hotel*

D

E

F

G

Q

R

S

T

Y

Z

Fodor's Travel Publications

Available at bookstores everywhere, or call 1–800–533–6478, 24 hours a day.

Gold Guides

U.S.

Alaska
Arizona
Boston
California
Cape Cod, Martha's Vineyard, Nantucket
The Carolinas & the Georgia Coast
Chicago
Colorado
Florida
Hawaii
Las Vegas, Reno, Tahoe
Los Angeles
Maine, Vermont, New Hampshire
Maui
Miami & the Keys
New England
New Orleans
New York City
Pacific North Coast
Philadelphia & the Pennsylvania Dutch Country
The Rockies
San Diego
San Francisco
Santa Fe, Taos, Albuquerque
Seattle & Vancouver
The South
U.S. & British Virgin Islands
USA
Virginia & Maryland
Waikiki
Washington, D.C.

Foreign

Australia & New Zealand
Austria
The Bahamas
Bermuda
Budapest
Canada
Cancún, Cozumel, Yucatán Peninsula
Caribbean
China
Costa Rica, Belize, Guatemala
Cuba
The Czech Republic & Slovakia
Eastern Europe
Egypt
Europe
Florence, Tuscany & Umbria
France
Germany
Great Britain
Greece
Hong Kong
India
Ireland
Israel
Italy
Japan
Kenya & Tanzania
Korea
London
Madrid & Barcelona
Mexico
Montréal & Québec City
Moscow, St. Petersburg, Kiev
The Netherlands, Belgium & Luxembourg
New Zealand
Norway
Nova Scotia, New Brunswick, Prince Edward Island
Paris
Portugal
Provence & the Riviera
Scandinavia
Scotland
Singapore
South America
South Pacific
Southeast Asia
Spain
Sweden
Switzerland
Thailand
Tokyo
Toronto
Turkey
Vienna & the Danube

Fodor's Special-Interest Guides

Branson
Caribbean Ports of Call
The Complete Guide to America's National Parks
Condé Nast Traveler Caribbean Resort and Cruise Ship Finder
Cruises and Ports of Call
Fodor's London Companion
France by Train
Halliday's New England Food Explorer
Healthy Escapes
Italy by Train
Kodak Guide to Shooting Great Travel Pictures
Shadow Traffic's New York Shortcuts and Traffic Tips
Sunday in New York
Sunday in San Francisco
Walt Disney World, Universal Studios and Orlando
Walt Disney World for Adults
Where Should We Take the Kids? California
Where Should We Take the Kids? Northeast

Special Series

Affordables

Caribbean

Europe

Florida

France

Germany

Great Britain

Italy

London

Paris

Fodor's Bed & Breakfasts and Country Inns

America's Best B&Bs

California's Best B&Bs

Canada's Great Country Inns

Cottages, B&Bs and Country Inns of England and Wales

The Mid-Atlantic's Best B&Bs

New England's Best B&Bs

The Pacific Northwest's Best B&Bs

The South's Best B&Bs

The Southwest's Best B&Bs

The Upper Great Lakes' Best B&Bs

The Berkeley Guides

California

Central America

Eastern Europe

Europe

France

Germany & Austria

Great Britain & Ireland

Italy

London

Mexico

Pacific Northwest & Alaska

Paris

San Francisco

Compass American Guides

Arizona

Chicago

Colorado

Hawaii

Hollywood

Las Vegas

Maine

Manhattan

Montana

New Mexico

New Orleans

Oregon

San Francisco

Santa Fe

South Carolina

South Dakota

Southwest

Texas

Utah

Virginia

Washington

Wine Country

Wisconsin

Wyoming

Fodor's Español

California

Caribe Occidental

Caribe Oriental

Gran Bretaña

Londres

Mexico

Nueva York

Paris

Fodor's Exploring Guides

Australia

Boston & New England

Britain

California

Caribbean

China

Egypt

Florence & Tuscany

Florida

France

Germany

Ireland

Israel

Italy

Japan

London

Mexico

Moscow & St. Petersburg

New York City

Paris

Prague

Provence

Rome

San Francisco

Scotland

Singapore & Malaysia

Spain

Thailand

Turkey

Venice

Fodor's Flashmaps

Boston

New York

San Francisco

Washington, D.C.

Fodor's Pocket Guides

Acapulco

Atlanta

Barbados

Jamaica

London

New York City

Paris

Prague

Puerto Rico

Rome

San Francisco

Washington, D.C.

Rivages Guides

Bed and Breakfasts of Character and Charm in France

Hotels and Country Inns of Character and Charm in France

Hotels and Country Inns of Character and Charm in Italy

Short Escapes

Country Getaways in Britain

Country Getaways in France

Country Getaways Near New York City

Fodor's Sports

Golf Digest's Best Places to Play

Skiing USA

USA Today The Complete Four Sport Stadium Guide

Fodor's Vacation Planners

Great American Learning Vacations

Great American Sports & Adventure Vacations

Great American Vacations

National Parks and Seashores of the East

National Parks of the West

Before Catching Your Flight, Catch Up With Your World.

Fueled by the global resources of CNN and available in major airports across America, CNN Airport Network provides a live source of current domestic and international news, sports, business, weather and lifestyle programming. Plus two daily Fodor's features for the facts you need: "Travel Fact," a useful and creative mix of travel trivia; and "What's Happening," a comprehensive round-up of upcoming events in major cities around the world.

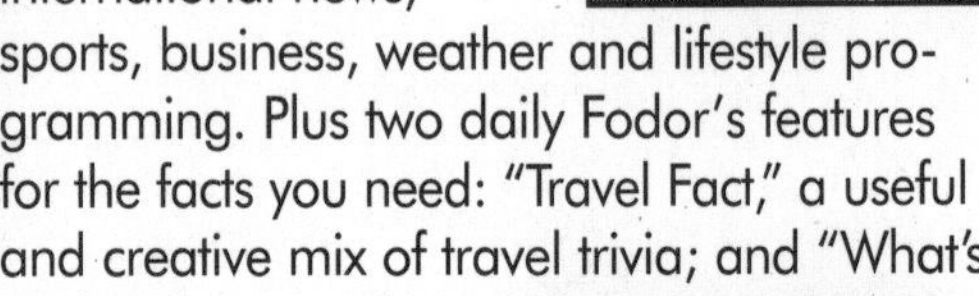

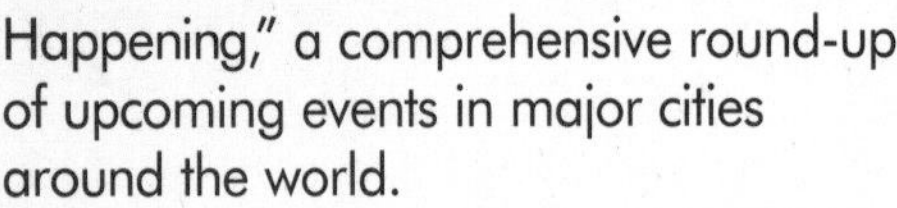

With CNN Airport Network, you'll never be out of the loop.

HERE'S YOUR OWN PERSONAL VIEW OF THE WORLD.

Here's the easiest way to get up-to-the-minute, objective, personalized information about what's going on in the city you'll be visiting—before you leave on your trip! Unique information you could get only if you knew someone personally in each of 160 destinations around the world. Everything from special places to dine to local events only a local would know about.

Fodor's WORLDVIEW TRAVEL UPDATE

It's all yours—in your Travel Update from Worldview, the leading provider of time-sensitive destination information.

Review the following order form and fill it out by indicating your destination(s) and travel dates and by checking off up to eight interest categories. Then mail or fax your order form to us, or call your order in. (We're here to help you 24 hours a day.)

Within 48 hours of receiving your order, we'll mail your convenient, pocket-sized custom guide to you, packed with information to make your travel more fun and interesting. And if you're in a hurry, we can even fax it.

Have a great trip with your Fodor's Worldview Travel Update!

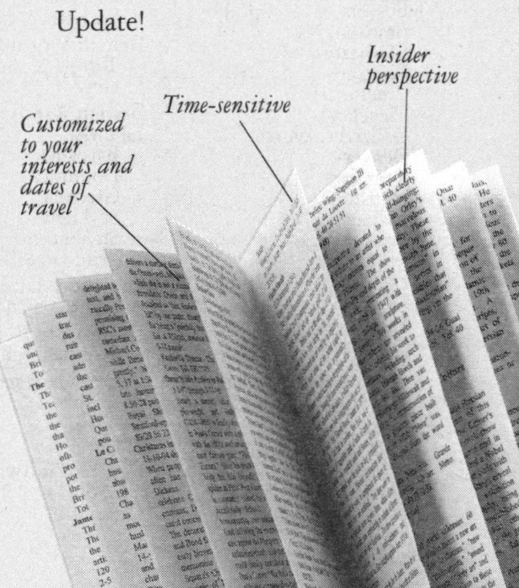

DESTINATIONS

Worldview covers more than 160 destinations worldwide. Choose the destination(s) that match your itinerary from the list below:

Europe
- Amsterdam
- Athens
- Barcelona
- Berlin
- Brussels
- Budapest
- Copenhagen
- Dublin
- Edinburgh
- Florence
- Frankfurt
- French Riviera
- Geneva
- Glasgow
- Lausanne
- Lisbon
- London
- Madrid
- Milan
- Moscow
- Munich
- Oslo
- Paris
- Prague
- Provence
- Rome
- Salzburg
- Seville
- St. Petersburg
- Stockholm
- Venice
- Vienna
- Zurich

United States (Mainland)
- Albuquerque
- Atlanta
- Atlantic City
- Baltimore
- Boston
- Branson, MO
- Charleston, SC
- Chicago
- Cincinnati
- Cleveland
- Dallas/Ft. Worth
- Denver
- Detroit
- Houston
- Indianapolis
- Kansas City
- Las Vegas
- Los Angeles
- Memphis
- Miami
- Milwaukee
- Minneapolis/St. Paul
- Nashville
- New Orleans
- New York City
- Orlando
- Palm Springs
- Philadelphia
- Phoenix
- Pittsburgh
- Portland
- Reno/Lake Tahoe
- St. Louis
- Salt Lake City
- San Antonio
- San Diego
- San Francisco
- Santa Fe
- Seattle
- Tampa
- Washington, DC

Alaska
- Alaskan Destinations

Hawaii
- Honolulu
- Island of Hawaii
- Kauai
- Maui

Canada
- Quebec City
- Montreal
- Ottawa
- Toronto
- Vancouver

Bahamas
- Abaco
- Eleuthera/ Harbour Island
- Exuma
- Freeport
- Nassau & Paradise Island

Bermuda
- Bermuda Countryside
- Hamilton

British Leeward Islands
- Anguilla
- Antigua & Barbuda
- St. Kitts & Nevis

British Virgin Islands
- Tortola & Virgin Gorda

British Windward Islands
- Barbados
- Dominica
- Grenada
- St. Lucia
- St. Vincent
- Trinidad & Tobago

Cayman Islands
- The Caymans

Dominican Republic
- Santo Domingo

Dutch Leeward Islands
- Aruba
- Bonaire
- Curacao

Dutch Windward Island
- St. Maarten/St. Martin

French West Indies
- Guadeloupe
- Martinique
- St. Barthelemy

Jamaica
- Kingston
- Montego Bay
- Negril
- Ocho Rios

Puerto Rico
- Ponce
- San Juan

Turks & Caicos
- Grand Turk/ Providenciales

U.S. Virgin Islands
- St. Croix
- St. John
- St. Thomas

Mexico
- Acapulco
- Cancun & Isla Mujeres
- Cozumel
- Guadalajara
- Ixtapa & Zihuatanejo
- Los Cabos
- Mazatlan
- Mexico City
- Monterrey
- Oaxaca
- Puerto Vallarta

South/Central America
- Buenos Aires
- Caracas
- Rio de Janeiro
- San Jose, Costa Rica
- Sao Paulo

Middle East
- Istanbul
- Jerusalem

Australia & New Zealand
- Auckland
- Melbourne
- South Island
- Sydney

China
- Beijing
- Guangzhou
- Shanghai

Japan
- Kyoto
- Nagoya
- Osaka
- Tokyo
- Yokohama

Pacific Rim/Other
- Bali
- Bangkok
- Hong Kong & Macau
- Manila
- Seoul
- Singapore
- Taipei

For your personalized Travel Update, choose the eight (8) categories you're most interested in from the following list:

1.	**Business Services**	Fax & Overnight Mail, Computer Rentals, Protocol, Secretarial, Messenger, Translation Services
	Dining	
2.	**All-Day Dining**	Breakfast & Brunch, Cafes & Tea Rooms, Late-Night Dining
3.	**Local Cuisine**	Every Price Range—from Budget Restaurants to the Special Splurge
4.	**European Cuisine**	Continental, French, Italian
5.	**Asian Cuisine**	Chinese, Far Eastern, Japanese, Other
6.	**Americas Cuisine**	American, Mexican & Latin
7.	**Nightlife**	Bars, Dance Clubs, Casinos, Comedy Clubs, Ethnic, Pubs & Beer Halls
8.	**Entertainment**	Theater – Comedy, Drama, Musicals, Dance, Ticket Agencies
9.	**Music**	Classical, Opera, Traditional & Ethnic, Jazz & Blues, Pop, Rock
10.	**Children's Activites**	Events, Attractions
11.	**Tours**	Local Tours, Day Trips, Overnight Excursions
12.	**Exhibitions, Festivals & Shows**	Antiques & Flower, History & Cultural, Art Exhibitions, Fairs & Craft Shows, Music & Art Festivals
13.	**Shopping**	Districts & Malls, Markets, Regional Specialties
14.	**Fitness**	Bicycling, Health Clubs, Hiking, Jogging
15.	**Recreational Sports**	Boating/Sailing, Fishing, Golf, Skiing, Snorkeling/Scuba, Tennis/Racket
16.	**Spectator Sports**	Auto Racing, Baseball, Basketball, Golf, Football, Horse Racing, Ice Hockey, Soccer
17.	**Event Highlights**	The best of what's happening during the dates of your trip.
18.	**Sightseeing**	Sights, Buildings, Monuments
19.	**Museums**	Art, Cultural
20.	**Transportation**	Taxis, Car Rentals, Airports, Public Transportation
21.	**General Info**	Overview, Holidays, Currency, Tourist Info

Please note that content will vary by season, destination, and length of stay.

Name
Address
City **State** **Country** **ZIP**
Tel # ( ) - **Fax #** ( ) -
Title of this Fodor's guide:
Store and location where guide was purchased:

INDICATE YOUR DESTINATIONS/DATES: You can order up to three (3) destinations from the previous page. Fill in your arrival and departure dates for each destination. **Your Travel Update itinerary (all destinations selected) cannot exceed 30 days from beginning to end.**

		Month	Day		Month	Day
(Sample) **LONDON**	From:	**6**	/ **21**	To:	**6**	/ **30**
1	From:		/	To:		/
2	From:		/	To:		/
3	From:		/	To:		/

CHOOSE YOUR INTERESTS: Select up to eight (8) categories from the list of interest categories shown on the previous page and circle the numbers below:
1 2 3 4 5 6 7 8 9 10 11 12 13 14 15 16 17 18 19 20 21

CHOOSE WHEN YOU WANT YOUR TRAVEL UPDATE DELIVERED (Check one):
❑ Please send my Travel Update immediately.
❑ Please hold my order until a few weeks before my trip to include the most up-to-date information.
Completed orders will be sent within 48 hours. Allow 7–10 days for U.S. mail delivery.

ADD UP YOUR ORDER HERE. SPECIAL OFFER FOR FODOR'S PURCHASERS ONLY!

	Suggested Retail Price	Your Price	This Order
First destination ordered	~~$ 9.95~~	$ 7.95	$ 7.95
Second destination (if applicable)	~~$ 6.95~~	$ 4.95	+
Third destination (if applicable)	~~$ 6.95~~	$ 4.95	+

DELIVERY CHARGE (Check one and enter amount below)

	Within U.S. & Canada	Outside U.S. & Canada
First Class Mail	❑ $2.50	❑ $5.00
FAX	❑ $5.00	❑ $10.00
Priority Delivery	❑ $15.00	❑ $27.00

ENTER DELIVERY CHARGE FROM ABOVE: +

TOTAL: $

METHOD OF PAYMENT IN U.S. FUNDS ONLY (Check one):
❑ AmEx ❑ MC ❑ Visa ❑ Discover ❑ Personal Check (U. S. & Canada only)
❑ Money Order/International Money Order

Make check or money order payable to: Fodor's Worldview Travel Update
Credit Card _/_/_/_/_/_/_/_/_/_/_/_/_/_/_/_/ **Expiration Date:** _/_

Authorized Signature

SEND THIS COMPLETED FORM WITH PAYMENT TO:
Fodor's Worldview Travel Update, 114 Sansome Street, Suite 700, San Francisco, CA 94104

OR CALL OR FAX US 24-HOURS A DAY
Telephone **1-800-799-9609** • Fax **1-800-799-9619** (From within the U.S. & Canada)
(Outside the U.S. & Canada: Telephone 415-616-9988 • Fax 415-616-9989)

(Please have this guide in front of you when you call so we can verify purchase.)
Code: FTG Offer valid until 12/31/97